Colt
Owners
Workshop
Manual

J H Haynes Member of the Guild of Motoring Writers
and Alec J Jones

Models covered

All Colt Galant & Celeste models;
Saloon, Hardtop, Estate & Coupe, 1597 cc & 1995 cc

Does not cover revised Galant range introduced October 1980

ISBN 0 85696 796 3

© Haynes Publishing Group 1978, 1982, 1988

Printed in England *(236-10N2)*

ABCDE

D0504191

Haynes Publishing Group
Sparkford Nr Yeovil
Somerset BA22 7JJ England

Haynes Publications, Inc
861 Lawrence Drive
Newbury Park
California 91320 USA

British Library Cataloguing in Publication Data
Jones, Alec
Colt Galant & Celeste owners work manual.
1. Cars. Maintenance & repair – Amateurs' manuals
I. Title
629.28'722
ISBN 0-85696-796-3

Acknowledgements

Thanks are due to the Chrysler Corporation of the USA for the supply of technical information and certain illustrations; to Castrol Ltd for the lubrication data and the Champion Sparking Plug Company who suppled the illustrations showing the various spark plug conditions. Thanks are also due to all those people at Sparkford who helped in the production of this manual.

About this manual

Its aims

The aim of this book is to help you get the best value from your car. It can do so in two ways. First, it can help you decide what work must be done (even should you choose to get it done by a garage) on the routine maintenance of your vehicle and the diagnosis and course of action when random faults occur. But it is hoped that you will also use the second and fuller purpose by tackling the work yourself. This can give you the satisfaction of doing the job yourself. On the simpler jobs it may even be quicker than booking the vehicle into a garage and going there twice, to leave and collect it. Perhaps most important, much money can be saved by avoiding the costs a garage must charge to cover its labour and overheads.

The book has drawings and descriptions to show the function of the various components so that their layout can be understood. Then the tasks are described and photographed in a step-by-step sequence so that even a novice can cope with complicated work.

The jobs are described assuming only normal tools are available, and not special tools unless absolutely necessary. However, a reasonable outfit of tools will be a worthwhile investment, (see 'Tools and working facilities'). Many special workshop tools produced by the makers merely speed the work, and in these cases guidance is given as to how to do the job without them. On a very few occasions, if the manu-facturer's special tool is essential to prevent damage to components, then its use is described. Though it might be possible to borrow the tool, such work may have to be entrusted to the official agent.

To avoid labour costs a garage will often give a cheaper repair by fitting a reconditioned assembly. The home mechanic can be helped by this book to diagnose the fault and make a repair using only a minor spare part.

The manufacturer's official workshop manuals are written for their trained staff, and so assume special knowledge; therefore detail is left out. This book is written for the owner, and so goes into detail.

Using the manual

The manual is divided into thirteen Chapters. Each Chapter is divided into numbered Sections which are headed in **bold type** between horizontal lines. Each Section consists of serially numbered paragraphs.

There are two types of illustration: (1) Figures which are numbered according to Chapter and sequence of occurrence in that Chapter. (2) photographs which have a reference number on their caption. All photographs apply to the Chapter in which they occur so that the reference figure pinpoints the pertinent Section and paragraph number.

Procedures, once described in the text, are not normally repeated.

If it is considered necessary to refer to a particular paragraph in another Chapter the reference is given as Chapter, Section and para-graph numbers. Cross references given without use of the word 'Chapter' apply to Section and/or paragraphs in the same Chapter (eg; 'See Section 8' means also 'in this Chapter').

When the left or right side of the car is mentioned it is as if one is seated in the driver's seat looking forward.

Whilst every care is taken to ensure that the information in this manual is correct, no liability can be accepted by the authors or publishers for loss, damage or injury caused by any errors in, or omissions from, the information given.

Contents

Colt Celeste Coupe - UK Specification

Dodge Colt Wagon - USA Specification

Introduction to the
Dodge Colt, Colt Galant and Colt Celeste

These models are manufactured in Japan by the Mitsubishi Motor Corporation and are sold in North America by the Chrysler Corporation and in the UK by the Colt Car Company. In North America the sedan and its variants are named the Dodge Colt while in the UK the same car is sold as the Colt Galant. Also covered by this manual is the UK Colt Celeste model - a striking sports coupe based on the major mechanical components of the Colt Galant.

Introduced to the North American Market in 1970 and the UK in 1974 the 'Colt' has undergone many changes during its life. The most important of these being the introduction of the unique 'balancer' engine in some models. This engine incorporates two balancing shafts which cancel the inherent vibration of a four-cylinder engine and result in uncanny smoothness. The Celeste model, introduced to the UK in 1976, is also fitted with the balanced engine.

These cars are universally recognised as being of sound design and construction and have an enviable reputation for reliability.

Buying spare parts
and vehicle identification numbers

Buying spare parts

Spare parts are available from many sources, for example: official garages, other garages and accessory shops, and motor factors. Our advice regarding spare parts is as follows:

Officially appointed garages - This is the best source of parts which are peculiar to your car and otherwise not generally available (eg: complete cylinder heads, internal gearbox components, badges, interior trim etc). It is also the only place at which you should buy parts if your car is still under warranty; other makes of component may invalidate the warranty. To be sure of obtaining the correct parts it will always be necessary to give the storeman your car's engine and chassis number, and if possible to take the old part along for positive identification. Remember that many parts are available on a factory exchange scheme - any parts returned should always be clean! It obviously makes good sense to go to the specialists on your car for this type of part for they are best equipped to supply you.

Other garages and accessory shops - These are often very good places to buy material and components needed for the maintenance of your car (eg; oil filters, spark plugs, bulbs, fan belts, oils and grease, touch-up paint, filler paste etc). They also sell general accessories, usually have convenient opening hours, charge lower prices and can often be found not far from home.

Motor factors - Good factors will stock all of the more important components which wear out relatively quickly (eg; clutch components, pistons, valves, exhaust systems, brake cylinders/pipes/hoses/seals/shoes and pads etc). Motor factors will often provide new or reconditioned components on a part exchange basis - this can save a considerable amount of money.

Vehicle identification numbers (US models)

All vehicle identification numbers contain 13 digits to a code shown in the illustration A. The number is located on a plate attached to the top left side of the instrument panel and visible through the windscreen (illustration B).

Body number location
The body number is stamped on the bulkhead inside the engine compartment (photo).

Engine type and number
The engine type 4G32 or 4G52 etc is cast on the left-hand side of the cylinder block, towards the bottom. The engine serial number is stamped onto the top face of the cylinder block on the right-hand side at the front (photo).

Gearbox serial number
The gearbox serial number is stamped on the left-hand side or top of the gearbox case (illustration C).

Automatic transmission serial number
On the Borg Warner transmission the serial number is on a plate on the side of the transmission (illustration D). The torqueflite serial number is stamped onto the oil pan mounting flange at the left-hand side (illustration E).

6 H 2 3 K 4 5 1 0 0 0 1 1

1st digit	2nd Digit	3rd & 4th Digit	5th Digit	6th Digit	7th Digit	8th Digit	9th to 13th Digit
Car line	Price class	Body type	Engine Displacement	Model year	Transmission code	Trim code	Sequence number
6-Dodge Colt	H - High	21 - 2 door coupe	K - 97.5 cu in	4 - 1974	5 - manual	Colt	
5-Plymouth Cricket	L - Low	41 - 4 door sedan	U - 121.7 cu in		9 - Automatic	0 - Super Deluxe	00011
	P - Premium	23 - 2 door hardtop				1 - Custom	00011
		45 - Station wagon				3 - Standard	000 11
						Cricket	
						2 - Super Deluxe	00011
						4 - Custom	00011
						6 - Standard	00011

Body number

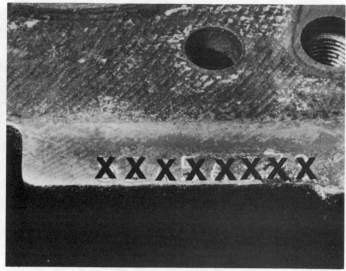

Engine number

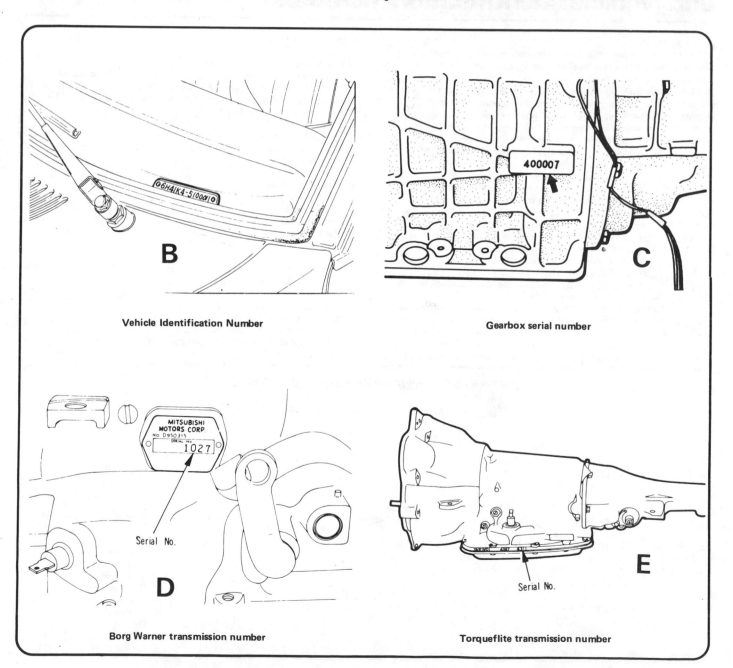

Vehicle Identification Number B

Gearbox serial number C

Serial No.

Borg Warner transmission number D

Serial No.

Torqueflite transmission number E

Jacking and towing

Safety is paramount before venturing under a car to carry out any sort of maintenance or overhaul work. Placing the jack in the wrong place or using the jack on the wrong surface (too soft) or even using a worn out jack, contribute to many unnecessary accidents a year.

The jack supplied with the car is adequate for changing a wheel and that is about all. Never get under the car using just this means to support it. It is worth the effort to install stands for every task no matter how small, that demands attention underneath the car and the illustrations A and B show the points at which a trolley jack should be situated to raise the front or rear of the car in order to install stands. If you do not own a trolley jack or cannot borrow one use the ordinary car jack to raise the car one corner at a time and then install a stand, at the positions shown in illustrations C, D or E. However, be very careful when using this method and do it gradually, so that the car is raised evenly. Jack up one corner and install the stand with the pin in the first hole (from the top). Let the car down onto the stand and remove the jack. Move to the opposite side of the car and repeat the operation. Then, returning to the side first raised jack up the car until the pin of the stand can be inserted into the second hole. Repeat this operation until the car is at the height required. This method may sound a little tedious and take some time but if the car was raised at one corner as high as required and the stand then installed, the angle of the car to the stand may be enough to topple it once the opposite side commences to be jacked.

So slowly and carefully are the key words to this operation, and do not forget to chock the wheels still left on the ground.

Towing

When towing another vehicle or being towed always use the attachment points depicted in illustrations F and G. Attaching a tow rope to other parts of the vehicle may cause damage to that component or even an accident if it were to break off.

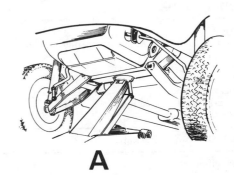

A

Jacking Point (Front)

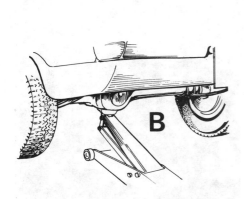

B

Jacking Point (Rear)

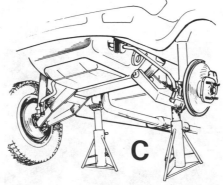

C

Stand position (Front)

D

Stand Position (Rear 1)

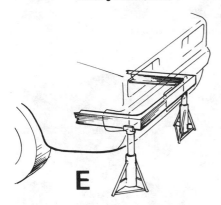

E

Stand Position (Rear 2)

F

Attachment point when being towed

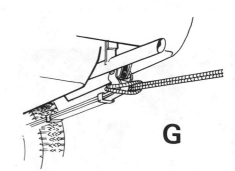

G

Attachment point when towing

Routine maintenance

For modifications, and information applicable to later models, see Supplement at end of manual

Maintenance is essential for ensuring safety and reliability as well as for obtaining maximum performance and economy. Over the years the need for periodical lubrication has been reduced considerably, but for those items which are not lubricated for life it is still essential, even though the intervals may be infrequent.

Every 250 miles (400 km) or weekly

Check tyre pressure and inflate if necessary.
Check engine oil level and top-up if necessary (photo).
Check battery electrolyte level and top-up if necessary.
Check windscreen washer fluid level and top-up if necessary.
Check coolant level and top-up if necessary.
Check brake fluid level and top-up if necessary (photo).
Check operation of all lights, instruments and controls.

Every 5,000 miles (8,000 km)

Change engine oil.
Check gearbox oil or automatic transmission fluid.
Check rear axle oil.
Check steering gear oil.
Check brake fluid.
Oil locks and hinges.
Check brake and coolant hoses.
Inspect brake disc pads.

Every 10,000 miles (16,000 km)

Renew oil filter.

Lubricate handbrake.
Lubricate transmission linkage.
Lubricate clutch cable.
Check exhaust system for leaks.
Check brake master cylinder operation.
Change tyres round.
Check rear brakes.
Check clutch pedal movement.

Every 15,000 miles (24,000 km) or annually

Lubricate distributor.
Grease front wheel bearings.
Check thermal reaction bolts (if fitted).
Check exhaust manifold bolts.
Check and adjust carburetter linkage.
Renew fuel filter.
Renew air cleaner.
Check heated air intake operation (if fitted).
Renew distributor points and condenser.
Renew spark plugs.
Check ignition wiring.
Check distributor cap and rotor.
Clean crankcase ventilation ports.
Check evaporation control system (if fitted).
Check secondary air system (if fitted).
Check exhaust gas recirculation system (if fitted).
Check anti-freeze and renew if necessary.
Check all rubber and plastic components in the engine compartment.

Replenishing the engine oil

Sump drain plug

Topping up the gearbox

Gearbox drain plug

Refitting the oil filter

Brake fluid reservoirs

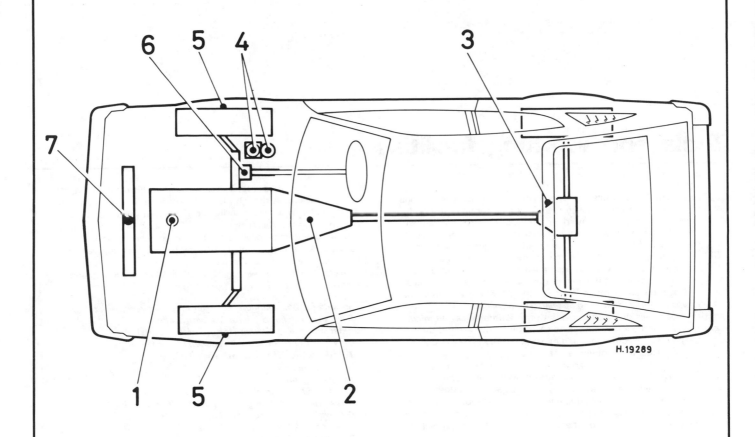

H.19289

Recommended lubricants and Fluids

Component	Lubricant type or specification
Engine (1)	SAE 20W40 multigrade engine oil
Transmission (2)	
Manual	SAE 80 oil
Automatic	ATF Dexron
Rear axle (3)	SAE 80 (below 10ºC/50ºF). SAE 90 (above 10ºC/50ºF)
Brake system (4)	Universal Brake and Clutch Fluid
Wheel bearings (5)	General purpose grease
Steering gear (6)	SAE 80 oil
Cooling system (7)	Ethylene glycol antifreeze
Door and bonnet locks, hinges	Engine oil
Clutch cable and linkages	Engine oil

Note: *The above are general recommendations only. Lubrication requirements vary between different operating requirements. If in doubt, consult the vehicle handbook or nearest dealer.*

Tools and working facilities

Introduction

A selection of good tools is a fundamental requirement for anyone contemplating the maintenance and repair of a motor vehicle. For the owner who does not possess any, their purchase will prove a considerable expense, offsetting some of the savings made by doing-it-yourself. However, provided that the tools purchased are of good quality, they will last for many years and prove an extremely worthwhile investment.

To help the average owner to decide which tools are needed to carry out the various tasks detailed in this manual, we have compiled three lists of tools under the following heads: *Maintenance and minor repair, Repair and overhaul,* and *Special.* The newcomer to practical mechanics should start off with the *Maintenance and minor repair tool kit* and confine himself to the simpler jobs around the vehicle. Then, as his confidence and experience grows, he can undertake more difficult tasks; buying extra tools as, and when they are needed. In this way, a *Maintenance and minor repair tool kit* can be built-up into a *Repair and overhaul tool kit* over a considerable period of time without any major cash outlays. The experienced do-it-yourselfer will have a tool kit good enough for most repairs and overhaul procedures and will add tools from the *Special* category when he feels the expense is justified by the amount of use these tools will be put to.

It is obviously not possible to cover the subject of tools fully here. For those who wish to learn more about tools and their use there is a book entitled *How to Choose and Use Car Tools* available from the publishers of this manual.

Maintenance and minor repair tool kit

The tools given in this list should be considered as a minimum requirement if routine maintenance, servicing and minor repair operations are to be undertaken. We recommend the purchase of combination spanners (ring one end, open-ended the other); although more expensive than open-ended ones, they do give the advantages of both types of spanner.

> Combination spanners - 6, 7, 8, 9, 10, 11, and 12 mm
> Adjustable spanner - 9 inch
> Engine sump/gearbox/rear axle drain plug key (where applicable)
> Spark plug spanner (with rubber insert)
> Spark plug gap adjustment tool
> Set of feeler gauges
> Brake adjuster spanner (where applicable)
> Brake bleed nipple spanner
> Screwdriver - 4 in. long x ¼ in. dia. (flat blade)
> Screwdriver - 4 in. long x ¼ in. dia. (cross blade)
> Combination pliers - 6 inch
> Hacksaw, junior
> Tyre pump
> Tyre pressure gauge
> Grease gun (where applicable)
> Oil can
> Fine emery cloth (1 sheet)
> Wire brush (small)
> Funnel (medium size)

Repair and overhaul tool kit

These tools are virtually essential for anyone undertaking any major repairs to a motor vehicle, and are additional to those given in the *Maintenance and minor repair* list. Included in this list is a comprehensive set of sockets. Although these are expensive they will be found invaluable as they are so versatile - particularly if various drives are included in the set. We recommend the ½ in square-drive type, as this can be used with most proprietary torque wrenches. If you cannot afford a socket set, even bought piecemeal, then inexpensive tubular box spanners are a useful alternative.

The tools in this list will occasionally need to be supplemented by tools from the *Special* list.

> Sockets (or box spanners) to cover range in previous list
> Reversible ratchet drive for use with sockets
> Extension piece, 10 inch (for use with sockets)
> Universal joint (for use with sockets)
> Torque wrench (for use with sockets)
> 'Mole' wrench - 8 inch
> Ball pein hammer
> Soft-faced hammer, plastic or rubber
> Screwdriver - 6 in. long x 5/16 in. dia. (flat blade)
> Screwdriver 2 in. long x 5/16 in. square (flat blade)
> Screwdriver - 1½ in. long x ¼ in. dia. (cross blade)
> Screwdriver - 3 in. long x 1/8 in. dia. (electricians)
> Pliers - electricians side cutters
> Pliers - needle nosed
> Pliers - circlip (internal and external)
> Cold chisel - ½ inch
> Scriber (this can be made by grinding the end of a broken hacksaw blade)
> Scraper (this can be made by flattening and sharpening one end of a piece of copper pipe)
> Centre punch
> Pin punch
> Hacksaw
> Valve grinding tool
> Steel/rule/straight edge
> Allen keys
> Selection of files
> Wire brush (large)
> Axle stands
> Jack (strong scissor or hydraulic type)

Special tools

The tools in this list are those which are not used regularly, are expensive to buy, or which need to be used in accordance with their manufacturers instructions. Unless relatively difficult mechanical jobs are undertaken frequently, it will not be economic to buy many of these tools. Where this is the case, you could consider clubbing together with friends (or a motorists club) to make a joint purchase, or borrowing the tools against a deposit from a local garage or tool hire specialist.

The following list contains only those tools and instruments freely available to the public, and not those special tools produced by the vehicle manufacturer specifically for its dealer network. You will find occasional references to these manufacturers special tools in the text of this manual. Generally, an alternative method of doing the job without the vehicle manufacturers special tool is given. However, sometimes, there is no alternative to using them. Where this is the case and the relevant tool cannot be bought or borrowed you will have to entrust the work to a franchised garage.

Valve spring compressor
Piston ring compressor
Balljoint separator
Universal hub/bearing puller
Impact screwdriver
Micrometer and/or vernier gauge
Carburetter flow balancing device (where applicable)
Dial gauge
Stroboscopic timing light
Dwell angle meter/tachometer
Universal electrical multi-meter
Cylinder compression gauge
Lifting tackle
Trolley jack
Light with extension lead

Last, but not least, always keep a supply of old newspapers and clean, lint-free rags available, and try to keep any working areas as clean as possible.

Buying tools

For practically all tools, a tool factor is the best source since he will have a very comprehensive range compared with the average garage or accessory shop. Having said that, accessory shops often offer excellent quality tools at discount prices, so it pays to shop around.

Remember, you don't have to buy the most expensive items on the shelf, but it is always advisable to steer clear of the very cheap tools. There are plenty of good tools around, at reasonable prices, so ask the proprietor or manager of the shop for advice before making a purchase.

Care and maintenance of tools

Having purchased a reasonable tool kit, it is necessary to keep the tools in a clean and serviceable condition. After use, always wipe off any dirt, grease and metal particles using a clean, dry cloth before putting the tools away. Never leave them lying around after they have been used. A simple tool rack on the garage or workshop wall, for items such as screwdrivers and pliers, is a good idea. Store all normal spanners and sockets in a metal box. Any measuring instruments, gauges, meters, etc., must be carefully stored where they cannot be damaged or become rusty.

Take a little care when the tools are used. Hammer heads inevitably become marked and screwdrivers lose the keen edge on their blades from time-to-time. A little timely attention with emery cloth or a file will soon restore items like this to a good serviceable finish.

Use of tools

Throughout this book various phrases describing techniques are used, such as:
'Drive out the bearing'.
'Undo the flange bolts evenly and diagonally'.
When two parts are held together by a number of bolts round their edge, these must be tightened to draw the parts down together flat. They must be slackened evenly to prevent the component warping. Initially the bolts should be put in finger-tight only. Then they should be tightened gradually, at first only a turn each; and diagonally, doing the one opposite that tightened first, then one to a side, followed by another opposite that, and so on. The second time each bolt is tightened only half a turn should be given. The third time round, only a quarter of a turn is given to each, and this is kept up till tight. The reverse sequence is used to slacken them.

If any part has to be driven, such as a ball bearing out of its housing, without a proper press, it can be done with a hammer provided a few rules for use of a hammer are remembered. Always keep the component being driven straight so it will not jam. Shield whatever is being hit from damage by the hammer. Soft headed hammers are available. A drift can be used, or if the item being hit is soft, use wood. Aluminium is very easily damaged. Steel is a bit better. Hard steel, such as a bearing race, is very strong. Something threaded at the end must be protected by fitting a nut. But do not hammer the nut: the threads will tear.

If levering items with a makeshift arrangement, such as a screwdriver, irretrievable damage can be done. Be sure the lever rests either on something that does not matter, or put in padding. Burrs can be filed off afterwards. But indentations are there for good, and can cause leaks.

When holding something in a vice, the jaws must go on a part that is strong. If the indentation from the jaw teeth will matter, then lead or fibre jaw protectors must be used. Hollow sections are liable to be crushed.

Nuts that will not undo will sometimes move if the spanner handle is extended with another. But only extend a ring spanner, not an open jaw one. A hammer blow either to the spanner, or the bolt, may jump it out of its contact: the bolt locally welds itself in place. In extreme cases the nut will undo if driven off with drift and hammer. When reassembling such bolts, tighten them normally, not by the method needed to undo them.

For pressing things, such as a sleeve bearing into its housing, a vice or an electric drill stand, make good presses. Pressing tools to hold each component can be arranged by using such things as socket spanners, or short lengths of steel water pipe. Long bolts with washers can be used to draw things into place rather than pressing them.

There are often several ways of doing something. If stuck, stop and think. Special tools can readily be made out of odd bits of scrap. Accordingly, at the same time as building up a tool kit, collect useful bits of steel.

Normally all nuts or bolts have some locking arrangement. The most common is a spring washer. There are tab washers that are bent up. Castellated nuts have split pins. Self-locking nuts have special crowns that resist shaking loose. Self-locking nuts should not be re-used, as the self-locking action is weakened as soon as they have been loosened at all. Tab washers should only be re-used when they can be bent over in a new place. If you find a nut without any locking arrangement, check what it is meant to have.

Working facilities

Not to be forgotten when discussing tools, is the workshop itself. If anything more than routine maintenance is to be carried out, some form of suitable working area becomes essential.

It is appreciated that many an owner mechanic is forced by circumstances to remove an engine or similar item, without the benefit of a garage or workshop. Having done this, any repairs should always be done under the cover of a roof.

Wherever possible, any dismantling should be done on a clean flat workbench, or table at a suitable working height.

Any workbench needs a vice: one with a jaw opening of 4 in (100 mm) is suitable for most jobs. As mentioned previously, some clean dry storage space is also required for tools, as well as the lubricants, cleaning fluids, touch-up paints and so on which soon become necessary.

Another item which may be required, and which has a much more general usage, is an electric drill with a chuck capacity of at least 5/16 in (8 mm). This, together with a good range of twist drills, is virtually essential for fitting accessories such as wing mirrors and reversing lights.

Spanner jaw gap comparison table

Jaw gap (in.)	Spanner size
0.250	¼ in. AF
0.275	7 mm AF
0.312	5/16 in. AF
0.315	8 mm AF
0.340	11/32 in. AF; 1/8 in. Whitworth
0.354	9 mm AF
0.375	3/8 in. AF
0.393	10 mm AF
0.433	11 mm AF
0.437	7/16 in. AF
0.445	3/16 in. Whitworth; ¼ in. BSF
0.472	12 mm AF
0.500	½ in. AF
0.512	13 mm AF
0.525	¼ in. Whitworth; 5/16 in. BSF
0.551	14 mm AF
0.562	9/16 in. AF
0.590	15 mm AF
0.600	5/16 in. Whitworth; 3/8 in. BSF
0.625	5/8 in. AF

0.629	16 mm AF	1.259	32 mm AF
0.669	17 mm AF	1.300	¾ in. Whitworth; 7/8 in. BSF
0.687	11/16 in. AF	1.312	1 5/16 in. AF
0.708	18 mm AF	1.390	13/16 in. Whitworth; 15/16 in. BSF
0.710	3/8 in. Whitworth; 7/16 in. BSF	1.417	36 mm AF
0.748	19 mm AF	1.437	1 7/16 in. AF
0.750	¾ in. AF	1.480	7/8 in. Whitworth; 1 in. BSF
0.812	13/16 in. AF	1.500	1 ½ in. AF
0.820	7/16 in. Whitworth; ½ in. BSF	1.574	40 mm AF; 15/16 in. Whitworth
0.866	22 mm AF	1.614	41 mm AF
0.875	7/8 in. AF	1.625	1 5/8 in. AF
0.920	½ in. Whitworth; 9/16 in. BSF	1.670	1 in. Whitworth; 1 1/8 in. BSF
0.937	15/15 in. AF	1.687	1 11/16 in. AF
0.944	24 mm AF	1.811	46 mm AF
1.000	1 in. AF	1.812	1 13/16 in. AF
1.010	9/16 in. Whitworth; 5/8 in. BSF	1.860	1 1/8 in. Whitworth; 1 ¾ in. BSF
1.023	26 mm AF	1.875	1 7/8 in. AF
1.062	1 1/16 in. AF; 27 mm AF	1.968	50 mm AF
1.100	5/8 in Whitworth; 11/16 in. BSF	2.000	2 in. AF
1.125	1 1/8 in. AF	2.050	1 ¼ in. Whitworth; 1 3/8 in. BSF
1.181	30 mm AF	2.165	55 mm AF
1.200	11/16 in. Whitworth; ¾ in. BSF	2.362	60 mm AF
1.250	1 ¼ in. AF		

Safety first!

Professional motor mechanics are trained in safe working procedures. However enthusiastic you may be about getting on with the job in hand, do take the time to ensure that your safety is not put at risk. A moment's lack of attention can result in an accident, as can failure to observe certain elementary precautions.

There will always be new ways of having accidents, and the following points do not pretend to be a comprehensive list of all dangers; they are intended rather to make you aware of the risks and to encourage a safety-conscious approach to all work you carry out on your vehicle.

Essential DOs and DON'Ts

DON'T rely on a single jack when working underneath the vehicle. Always use reliable additional means of support, such as axle stands, securely placed under a part of the vehicle that you know will not give way.

DON'T attempt to loosen or tighten high-torque nuts (e.g. wheel hub nuts) while the vehicle is on a jack; it may be pulled off.

DON'T start the engine without first ascertaining that the transmission is in neutral (or 'Park' where applicable) and the parking brake applied.

DON'T suddenly remove the filler cap from a hot cooling system – cover it with a cloth and release the pressure gradually first, or you may get scalded by escaping coolant.

DON'T attempt to drain oil until you are sure it has cooled sufficiently to avoid scalding you.

DON'T grasp any part of the engine, exhaust or catalytic converter without first ascertaining that it is sufficiently cool to avoid burning you.

DON'T allow brake fluid or antifreeze to contact vehicle paintwork.

DON'T syphon toxic liquids such as fuel, brake fluid or antifreeze by mouth, or allow them to remain on your skin.

DON'T inhale dust – it may be injurious to health (see *Asbestos* below).

DON'T allow any spilt oil or grease to remain on the floor – wipe it up straight away, before someone slips on it.

DON'T use ill-fitting spanners or other tools which may slip and cause injury.

DON'T attempt to lift a heavy component which may be beyond your capability – get assistance.

DON'T rush to finish a job, or take unverified short cuts.

DON'T allow children or animals in or around an unattended vehicle.

DO wear eye protection when using power tools such as drill, sander, bench grinder etc, and when working under the vehicle.

DO use a barrier cream on your hands prior to undertaking dirty jobs – it will protect your skin from infection as well as making the dirt easier to remove afterwards; but make sure your hands aren't left slippery. Note that long-term contact with used engine oil can be a health hazard.

DO keep loose clothing (cuffs, tie etc) and long hair well out of the way of moving mechanical parts.

DO remove rings, wristwatch etc, before working on the vehicle – especially the electrical system.

DO ensure that any lifting tackle used has a safe working load rating adequate for the job.

DO keep your work area tidy – it is only too easy to fall over articles left lying around.

DO get someone to check periodically that all is well, when working alone on the vehicle.

DO carry out work in a logical sequence and check that everything is correctly assembled and tightened afterwards.

DO remember that your vehicle's safety affects that of yourself and others. If in doubt on any point, get specialist advice.

IF, in spite of following these precautions, you are unfortunate enough to injure yourself, seek medical attention as soon as possible.

Asbestos

Certain friction, insulating, sealing, and other products – such as brake linings, brake bands, clutch linings, torque converters, gaskets, etc – contain asbestos. *Extreme care must be taken to avoid inhalation of dust from such products since it is hazardous to health.* If in doubt, assume that they *do* contain asbestos.

Fire

Remember at all times that petrol (gasoline) is highly flammable. Never smoke, or have any kind of naked flame around, when working on the vehicle. But the risk does not end there – a spark caused by an electrical short-circuit, by two metal surfaces contacting each other, by careless use of tools, or even by static electricity built up in your body under certain conditions, can ignite petrol vapour, which in a confined space is highly explosive.

Always disconnect the battery earth (ground) terminal before working on any part of the fuel or electrical system, and never risk spilling fuel on to a hot engine or exhaust.

It is recommended that a fire extinguisher of a type suitable for fuel and electrical fires is kept handy in the garage or workplace at all times. Never try to extinguish a fuel or electrical fire with water.

Fumes

Certain fumes are highly toxic and can quickly cause unconsciousness and even death if inhaled to any extent. Petrol (gasoline) vapour comes into this category, as do the vapours from certain solvents such as trichloroethylene. Any draining or pouring of such volatile fluids should be done in a well ventilated area.

When using cleaning fluids and solvents, read the instructions carefully. Never use materials from unmarked containers – they may give off poisonous vapours.

Never run the engine of a motor vehicle in an enclosed space such as a garage. Exhaust fumes contain carbon monoxide which is extremely poisonous; if you need to run the engine, always do so in the open air or at least have the rear of the vehicle outside the workplace.

If you are fortunate enough to have the use of an inspection pit, never drain or pour petrol, and never run the engine, while the vehicle is standing over it; the fumes, being heavier than air, will concentrate in the pit with possibly lethal results.

The battery

Never cause a spark, or allow a naked light, near the vehicle's battery. It will normally be giving off a certain amount of hydrogen gas, which is highly explosive.

Always disconnect the battery earth (ground) terminal before working on the fuel or electrical systems.

If possible, loosen the filler plugs or cover when charging the battery from an external source. Do not charge at an excessive rate or the battery may burst.

Take care when topping up and when carrying the battery. The acid electrolyte, even when diluted, is very corrosive and should not be allowed to contact the eyes or skin.

If you ever need to prepare electrolyte yourself, always add the acid slowly to the water, and never the other way round. Protect against splashes by wearing rubber gloves and goggles.

When jump starting a car using a booster battery, for negative earth (ground) vehicles, connect the jump leads in the following sequence: First connect one jump lead between the positive (+) terminals of the two batteries. Then connect the other jump lead first to the negative (–) terminal of the booster battery, and then to a good earthing (ground) point on the vehicle to be started, at least 18 in (45 cm) from the battery if possible. Ensure that hands and jump leads are clear of any moving parts, and that the two vehicles do not touch. Disconnect the leads in the reverse order.

Mains electricity

When using an electric power tool, inspection light etc, which works from the mains, always ensure that the appliance is correctly connected to its plug and that, where necessary, it is properly earthed (grounded). Do not use such appliances in damp conditions and, again, beware of creating a spark or applying excessive heat in the vicinity of fuel or fuel vapour.

Ignition HT voltage

A severe electric shock can result from touching certain parts of the ignition system, such as the HT leads, when the engine is running or being cranked, particularly if components are damp or the insulation is defective. Where an electronic ignition system is fitted, the HT voltage is much higher and could prove fatal.

Chapter 1 Engine

For modifications, and information applicable to later models, see Supplement at end of manual

Contents

Specifications

4G3 Series

General

	4G32	4G33
Type	4 stroke, ohc, petrol	
Number and arrangement of cylinders	4 in line, vertical	
Cooling method	Water cooled	
Bore x stroke	3.028 x 3.386 in (76.9 x 86 mm)	2.874 x 3.386 in (73 x 86 mm)
Capacity	1597 cc	1439 cc
Compression ratio	8.5 : 1	9 : 1
Idling speed	650 to 750 rpm	
Valve clearances (hot)		
Inlet	0.006 in (0.15 mm)	
Exhaust	0.010 in (0.25 mm)	
Firing order	1 - 3 - 4 - 2 (No 1 at front)	
Ignition timing at 700 rpm	5° BTDC	
Valve timing		
Inlet opens	20° BTDC	
Inlet closes	48° ABDC	
Exhaust opens	51° BBDC	
Exhaust closes	17° ATDC	
Cylinder bore	3.0276 in (76.9 mm)	2.8740 in (73 mm)
Permissible bore wear	0.047 in (1.2 mm)	

Pistons and piston rings

	4G32	4G33
Type	Solid	
Oversize piston sizes	3.0374 in (77.15 mm)	2.8839 in (73.25 mm)
	3.0472 in (77.40 mm)	2.8937 in (73.50 mm)
	3.0571 in (77.65 mm)	2.9035 in (78.75 mm)
	3.0669 in (77.90 mm)	2.9134 in (74.00 mm)
Piston to cylinder clearance	0.0008 to 0.0016 in (0.02 to 0.04 mm)	

Number of rings ... ...   3 (2 compression 1 oil control)
Clearance between ring and groove wall
    No. 1 ... ...   0.0012 to 0.0028 in
                          (0.03 to 0.07 mm)
    No. 2 ... ...   0.0008 to 0.0024 in
                          (0.02 to 0.06 mm)
    Oil ring ... ...   0.001 to 0.004 in
                          (0.025 to 0.075 mm)
Maximum clearance, all rings ... ...   0.006 in (0.15 mm)
Gap when fitted, all rings ... ...   0.006 to 0.014 in
                          (0.15 to 0.35 mm)
Maximum gap ... ...   0.039 in (1 mm)

Connecting rods
Permissible bend ... ...   0.0012 in (0.003 mm)
Side clearance ... ...   0.004 to 0.01 in
                          (0.1 to 0.25 mm)
 Maximum side clearance ... ...   0.02 in (0.5 mm)

Crankshaft
Journal diameter ... ...   2.2441 in (57 mm)
Maximum permissible wear ... ...   0.0256 in   0.0354 in
                          (0.65 mm)   (0.9 mm)
Crankpin diameter ... ...   1.7717 in (45 mm)
Maximum permissible wear ... ...   0.0256 in   0.0364 in
Minimum regrind diameter   (0.65 mm)   (0.9 mm)
    Journal ... ...   2.2238 to 2.2244 in
                          (56.485 to 56.50 mm)
    Crankpin ... ...   1.7514 to 1.7520 in
                          (44.485 to 44.50 mm)
Fillet radius, journals and crankpins ... ...   0.098 in (2.5 mm)
Crankshaft end play ... ...   0.002 to 0.007 in
                          (0.05 to 0.175 mm)
Maximum end play ... ...   0.01 in (0.25 mm)

Main bearings
Diameter clearance ... ...   0.0006 to 0.0031 in   0.0006 to 0.0028 in
                          (0.016 to 0.078 mm)   (0.016 to 0.07 mm)
Maximum permissible clearance ... ...   0.005 in (0.12 mm)

Big end bearings
Diametral clearance ... ...   0.0004 to 0.0028 in   0.0004 to 0.0025 in
                          (0.01 to 0.072 mm)   (0.01 to 0.064 mm)
Maximum permissible clearance ... ...   0.004 in (0.10 mm)

Valve seats
Seat angle, inlet and exhaust ... ...   45°
Contact width, inlet and exhaust ... ...   0.035 to 0.051 in
                          (0.9 to 1.3 mm)

Valves
Stem OD inlet and exhaust ... ...   0.315 in (8 mm)
Wear limit
    Inlet ... ...   0.004 in (0.1 mm)
    Exhaust ... ...   0.006 in (0.15 mm)
Stem to guide clearance, inlet ... ...   0.0010 to 0.0022 in
                          (0.025 to 0.055 mm)
Maximum permissible clearance ... ...   0.004 in (0.10 mm)
Stem to guide clearance, exhaust ... ...   0.0022 to 0.0033 in
                          (0.050 to 0.085 mm)
Maximum permissible clearance ... ...   0.006 in (0.15 mm)

Valve springs
Free length ... ...   1.805 to 1.766 in
                          (45.85 to 44.85 mm)
Fitted length (standard) ... ...   1.469 in (37.3 mm)
Fitted length (maximum) ... ...   1.508 in (38.3 mm)

Timing chain tensioner
Free length ... ...   2.181 in (55.4 mm)
Minimum permissible length ... ...   1.850 in (47 mm)

Oil pump
Shaft to case clearance ... ...   0.0008 to 0.0022 in
                          (0.021 to 0.057 mm)
Maximum permissible clearance ... ...   0.005 in (0.12 mm)

Inner to outer rotor clearance less than		0.0047 in (0.119 mm)	
Maximum permissible clearance		0.01 in (0.25 mm)	
Rotor to cover end play		0.0008 to 0.0039 in (0.02 to 0.1 mm)	
Maximum permissible end play		0.08 in (0.2 mm)	

4G5 Series

	4G51	4G52	4G52GS
General			
Type		4 stroke, ohc, petrol	
Number and arrangement of cylinders		4 in line, vertical	
Cooling method		Water cooled	
Bore x stroke	3.189 x 3.543 in (81 x 90 mm)	3.307 x 3.543 in (84 x 90 mm)	
Capacity	1855 cc	1995 cc	
Compression ratio	8.5 : 1		9.5 : 1
Idling speed	650 to 750 rpm		750 to 850 rpm
Valve clearances (hot)			
Inlet		0.006 in (0.15 mm)	
Exhaust		0.010 in (0.25 mm)	
Firing order		1 - 3 - 4 - 2 (No 1 at front)	
Ignition timing	5° BTDC at 700 rpm		13° BTDC at 800 rpm
Valve timing			
Inlet opens	25° BTDC		29° BTDC
Inlet closes	55° BBDC		59° BTDC
Exhaust opens	62° BBDC		64° BTDC
Exhaust closes	14° BTDC		20° BTDC
Cylinder bore	3.1890 in (81 mm)	3.3071 in (84 mm)	
Permissible bore wear		0.047 in (1.2 mm)	
Pistons and piston rings			
Type		Solid	
Oversize piston sizes	3.1988 in (81.25 mm) 3.2087 in (81.50 mm) 3.2185 in (81.75 mm) 3.2283 in (82.00 mm)	3.3169 in (84.25 mm) 3.3268 in (84.50 mm) 3.3366 in (84.75 mm) 3.3465 in (85.00 mm)	
Piston to cylinder clearance	0.0008 to 0.0016 in (0.02 to 0.04 mm)		0.0012 to 0.0020 in (0.03 to 0.05 mm)
Number of rings		3 (2 compression 1 oil control)	
Clearance ring and groove wall			
No. 1		0.0024 to 0.0039 in (0.06 to 0.1 mm)	
No. 2		0.0008 to 0.0024 in (0.02 to 0.06 mm)	
Maximum clearance			
No. 1		0.006 in (0.15 mm)	
No. 2		0.005 in (0.12 mm)	
Gap when fitted			
No. 1		0.0098 to 0.0157 in (0.25 to 0.40 mm)	
No. 2		0.0098 to 0.0177 in (0.25 to 0.45 mm)	
Oil ring	0.0118 to 0.0236 in (0.3 to 0.6 mm)		0.0079 to 0.0354 in (0.2 to 0.9 mm)
Maximum gap, all rings		0.039 in (1.0 mm)	
Connecting rods			
Permissible bend		0.0012 in (0.03 mm)	
Side clearance		0.0039 to 0.0098 in (0.15 to 0.25 mm)	
Maximum side clearance		0.02 in (0.5 mm)	
Crankshaft			
Journal diameter		2.5984 in (66 mm)	
Maximum permissible wear	0.035 in (0.889 mm)		0.026 in (0.64 mm)
Crankpin diameter		2.0866 in (53 mm)	
Maximum permissible wear	0.035 in (0.889 mm)		0.026 in (0.65 mm)

Minimum regrind diameter

| Journal | 2.5683 to 2.5689 in
(65.235 to 65.25 mm) | 2.5781 to 2.5787 in
(65.485 to 65.50 mm) |

Crankpin ... ...   2.0565 to 2.0571 in   2.0663 to 2.0669 in
(52.235 to 52.25 mm)   (52.485 to 52.50 mm)

Fillet radius, journals and crankpins ... ...   0.0020 to 0.0069 in
(0.05 to 0.175 mm)

Crankshaft end play ... ...   0.010 in (0.25 mm)
Maximum end play ... ...   0.010 in (0.25 mm)

Main bearings
Main bearings
Diametral clearance ... ...   0.0008 to 0.0028 in
(0.02 to 0.072 mm)

Maximum permissible clearance ... ...   0.005 in (0.12 mm)

Big end bearings
Diametral clearance ... ...   0.0006 to 0.0025 in
(0.015 to 0.064 mm)

Maximum permissible clearance ... ...   0.004 in (0.10 mm)

Valve seats
Seat angle, inlet and exhaust ... ... 45°
Contact width, inlet and exhaust ... ...   0.035 to 0.051 in
(0.9 to 1.3 mm)

Valves
Stem OD Inlet and exhaust ... ...   0.315 in (8 mm)
Wear limit
    Inlet ... ...   0.004 in (0.1 mm)
    Exhaust ... ...   0.006 in (0.15 mm)
Stem to guide clearance, inlet ... ...   0.001 to 0.003 in
(0.025 to 0.058 mm)

Maximum permissible clearance ... ...   0.004 in (0.1 mm)
Stem to guide clearance, exhaust ... ...   0.002 to 0.0035 in
(0.05 to 0.088 mm)

Maximum permissible clearance ... ...   0.006 in (0.15 mm)

Valve springs

| Free length ... ... | 1.8685 in
(47.45 mm) | 1.891 in
(48.03 mm) |

Fitted length (standard) ... ...   1.5905 in (40.4 mm)
Fitted length (maximum) ... ...   1.6295 in (41.4 mm)

Timing chain tensioner
Free length ... ...   2.587 in (65.7 mm)
Minimum permissible length ... ...   2.20 in (56 mm)

Oil pump (trochoid type)
Shaft to case clearance ... ...   0.008 to 0.0022 in
(0.21 to 0.57 mm)

Maximum permissible clearance ... ...   0.005 in (0.12 mm)
Inner to outer rotor clearance - less than ... ...   0.0047 in (0.119 mm)
Maximum permissible clearance ... ...   0.010 in (0.25 mm)
Rotor to cover end play ... ...   0.0008 to 0.0039 in
(0.02 to 0.1 mm)

Maximum permissible end play ... ...   0.008 in (0.21 mm)

Torque wrench settings

	1600 cc		2000 cc	
	lb f ft	kg f m	lb f ft	kg f m
Front insulator to sub-frame ...	22 to 29	3.1 to 4.1	22 to 29	3.1 to 4.1
Front insulator to engine bracket	10 to 14	1.4 to 2.0	10 to 14	1.4 to 2.0
Cylinder block to engine bracket	29 to 36	4.0 to 5.0	29 to 36	4.0 to 5.0
Rear insulator to engine support bracket	10 to 12	1.4 to 1.7	10 to 14	1.4 to 2.0
Rear insulator to transmission:				
Manual	15 to 17	2.1 to 2.4	15 to 17	2.1 to 2.4
Automatic	9.5 to 11.5	1.3 to 1.6	9.5 to 11.5	1.3 to 1.6
Engine support bracket to body	7.2	1.0	7.2	1.0
Cylinder head attachment bolt:				
Cold engine	51 to 54	7.1 to 7.6	65 to 72	9.0 to 10.0
Hot engine	58 to 61	8.1 to 8.5	72 to 79	10.0 to 11.0
Camshaft bearing cap	13 to 14	1.8 to 2.0	13 to 14	1.8 to 2.0
Camshaft sprocket	36 to 43	5.0 to 6.0	36 to 43	5.0 to 6.0
Spark plug	15 to 21	2.1 to 3.0	18 to 21	2.5 to 2.9

Rocker cover	4 to 5	0.55 to 0.7	4 to 5	0.55 to 0.7
Heater joint	15 to 28	2.1 to 3.9		
Main bearing cap	36 to 39	5.0 to 5.5	54 to 61	7.1 to 8.5
Connecting rod cap	23 to 25	3.2 to 3.5	33 to 34	4.6 to 4.7
Flywheel or drive plate	83 to 90	11.6 to 12.6	94 to 101	13.2 to 14.2
Crank pulley	43 to 50	6.0 to 7.0	80 to 94	11.2 to 13.2
Tensioner holder	36 to 43	5.0 to 6.0		
Oil pan	4.3 to 5.8	0.6 to 0.8	4.3 to 5.8	0.6 to 0.8
Oil pan drain plug	43 to 57	6.0 to 8.0	43 to 57	6.0 to 8.0
Oil filter	8 to 9	1.1 to 1.3	8 to 9	1.1 to 1.3
Oil pump cover	11 to 14	1.5 to 2.0	11 to 14	1.5
Intake/exhaust manifold or thermal reactor	11 to 14	1.5 to 2.0	11 to 14	1.5 to 2.0
Oil temperature gauge unit	22 to 28	3.0 to 4.0	22 to 28	3.0 to 4.0
Counterbalance chamber cover			3 to 4	0.42 to 0.56
Counterbalance shaft bolts			22 to 28	3.1 to 3.9

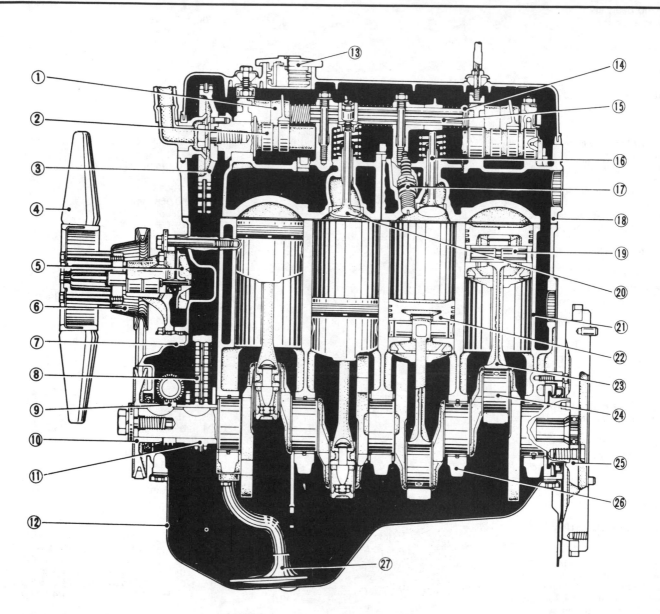

Fig. 1.1. Engine longitudinal section (4G32)

1	Rocker arm	8	Chain	15	Rocker arm shaft	22	Piston
2	Camshaft	9	Crankshaft gear	16	Exhaust valve	23	Connecting rod
3	Camshaft sprocket	10	Crankshaft pulley	17	Spark plug	24	Crankshaft
4	Cooling fan	11	Crankshaft sprocket	18	Cylinder head	25	Flywheel
5	Water pump	12	Sump	19	Piston pin	26	Crankshaft bearing cap
6	Water pump pulley	13	Oil filler cap	20	Intake valve	27	Oil screen
7	Chain case	14	Rocker arm shaft spring	21	Cylinder block		

1 General description

Two basic engines are used which, with minor differences, give five engines of different capacities and powers. They are all of the overhead camshaft type, with four vertical cylinders. The crankshafts have five main bearings which are of the renewable shell type, as are the big end bearings. The camshaft has five bearings which are **not** renewable.

The engine lubrication is force fed from a trochoid or conventional spur gear pump, which is mounted in the bottom of the chaincase on the smaller engines and inside the sump on the larger ones. Some 2000 cc engines are fitted with two chain driven balancing shafts which rotate at twice the crankshaft speed. These shafts cancel the secondary vibrations which are produced by the reciprocating forces and transverse moments in the engine. Engine cooling is by water

circulation in a conventional system, with a belt driven pump mounted on the front of the engine.

2 Removal of engine and gearbox

The following sequence of operations does not necessarily need to be performed in the order given, but is a check list of everything which needs to be disconnected or removed before the engine and gearbox can be lifted out. In a few instances, items are removed to give additional clearance and so make it easier to lift out the power unit.
1 Remove the bonnet cover, air cleaner and breather hose.
2 Drain the coolant by removing the plug from the bottom of the radiator and the plug behind the exhaust manifold, for which a socket spanner is required.

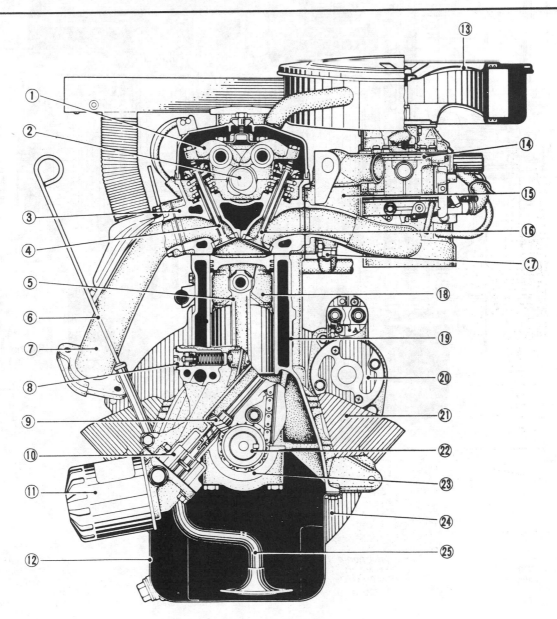

Fig. 1.2. Engine cross section (4G32)

1 Rocker arm	8 Tensioner	14 Carburetter	20 Starting motor
2 Camshaft	9 Distributor drive gear	15 Intake manifold	21 Engine support
3 Cylinder head	10 Oil pump	16 Intake valve	22 Crankshaft
4 Exhaust valve	11 Oil filter	17 Water temperature gauge unit	23 Bearing cap
5 Connecting rod	12 Sump	18 Piston	24 Bellhousing cover
6 Oil level gauge	13 Air cleaner	19 Cylinder block	25 Oil screen
7 Exhaust manifold			

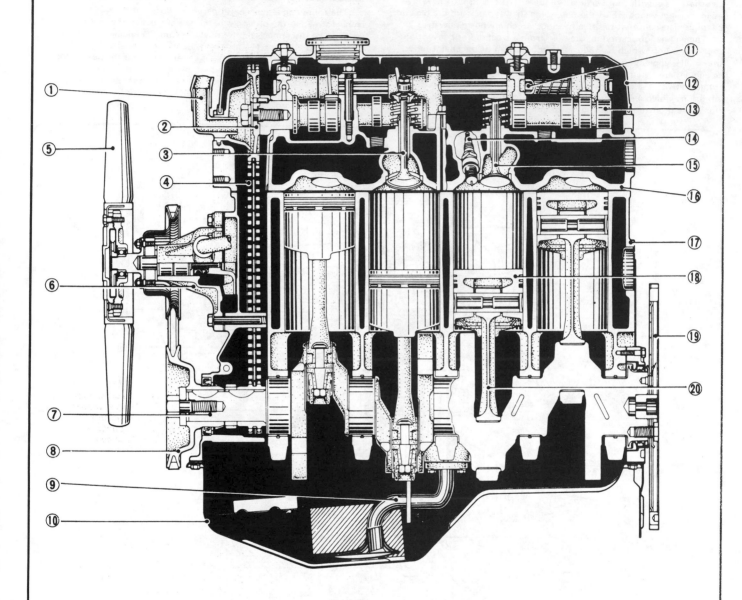

Fig. 1.3. Engine longitudinal section (4G52)

1	Breather	6	Water pump	11	Rocker shaft
2	Camshaft sprocket	7	Crankshaft	12	Rocker cover
3	Intake valve	8	Crankshaft pulley	13	Camshaft
4	Chain	9	Oil screen	14	Spark plug
5	Cooling fan	10	Sump	15	Exhaust valve

16	Cylinder head
17	Cylinder block
18	Piston
19	Flywheel
20	Connecting rod

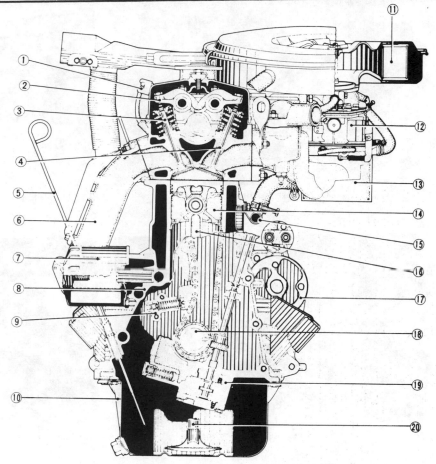

Fig. 1.4. Engine cross section (4G52)

1	Spark plug cable	6	Exhaust manifold	11	Air cleaner	16	Connecting rod
2	Rocker arm	7	Oil filter	12	Carburetter	17	Starting motor
3	Exhaust valve	8	Cylinder block	13	Intake manifold	18	Crankshaft
4	Intake valve	9	Tensioner	14	Piston	19	Oil pump
5	Oil level gauge	10	Sump	15	Heater pipe	20	Oil screen

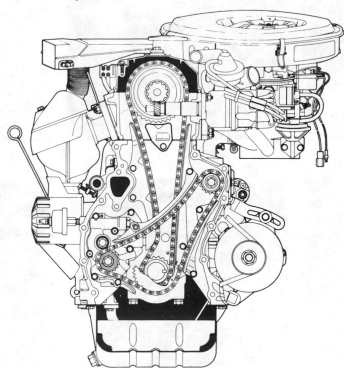

Fig. 1.5. Engine cross section (4G52 with balance shafts)

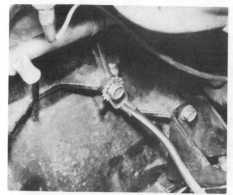
2.7 Engine earth bonding wire

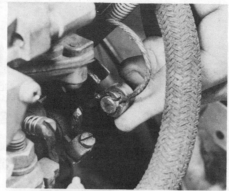
2.8 Remove the throttle cable

2.11 Heater hoses

2.13 Removing the clutch cable bracket

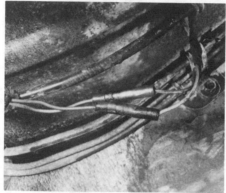
2.15 Reversing light connections

2.16 Speedometer drive connection

2.18 Removing the gaiter clamping plate

2.19 Removing the gear lever

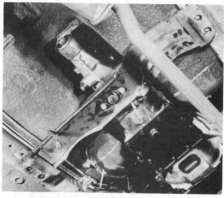
2.20 Gearbox support member

2.21 Engine front mounting

2.22 Removing the engine and gearbox

3.2 Removing the starter motor

3 Remove the front grille, radiator cowl (when fitted), radiator hoses and radiator. On automatic transmission models also remove oil pipes to the oil cooler.
4 Remove the fan, fan pulley and fan belt.
5 Drain the oil from the engine sump and gearbox.
6 For safety, remove both leads from the battery. Remove the ignition harness and contact breaker connection. Take care to avoid damaging your hands when pulling off the spark plug caps.
7 Disconnect the battery earth bonding strap below the intake manifold (photo), the alternator plug and field connection, and the oil pressure switch.
8 Remove the nipple from the throttle lever (photo) and secure the throttle cable out of the way.
9 Remove the servo pipe bracket from the rocker box cover, pull off the servo pipe from the inlet manifold and secure the pipe out of the way.
10 Disconnect the bonding wire between the inlet manifold and the bulkhead. Disconnect and remove the starter motor cable.
11 Remove the heater hoses (photo) and the feed and return pipes to the carburettor.
12 From underneath the car undo the exhaust pipe flange and remove the exhaust pipe support bracket.
13 Remove the split pin from the clutch operating lever, remove two bolts from the clutch cable bracket (photo) and disengage the clutch cable from the operating lever.
14 Remove the four nuts and bolts from the propellor shaft/rear axle joint flange and remove the propellor shaft. On cars fitted with dynamic dampers, remove the dampers and the locking bolts attaching the flange yoke at the rear of the propellor shaft (see Chapter 7, Fig. 7.1). On 1975 models fitted with Torqueflite automatic transmission, remove the tie rod.
15 Undo the bullet connectors to the reversing light (photo) and remove the bonding wire, cable clamps and the cable strap. Secure the reversing light wires out of the way.
16 Unscrew and remove the speedometer drive from the gearbox (photo).
17 From inside the car, remove the four screws from the console, then loosen the locknut. Unscrew and remove the gear lever knob.
18 Push back the carpet from around the gaiter and remove the three screws. Lift off the gaiter clamping plate (photo) and the console fixing bracket.
19 Remove the bolts from the turret and lift off the turret and gear lever (photo), taking care not to damage the joint gasket.
20 From underneath the car, support the tail of the gearbox. Bend back the locking tabs of the four bolts on the gearbox support member and then unscrew and remove the support member bolts. Remove the bonding strap from the gearbox rear end.
21 In the engine compartment, remove the two bolts securing each of the engine front mountings to the chassis (photo).
22 Sling the engine from the lifting lugs on each side of the rocker box cover, with the rear sling longer than the front one so that the engine will lift out at an angle of about 30°. Place a rag over the tail of the gearbox to prevent any remaining oil from draining out when the power unit is lifted and then hoist the engine clear of the engine

compartment. Watch for the bellhousing fouling the steering rod in the early stages of lifting.
23 Transfer the power unit to a suitable area and thoroughly clean the outside, using a degreasing agent which can subsequently be washed off with water.
24 If the power unit is to be dismantled, transfer it to a suitably strong workbench.

3 Separating the engine from the gearbox

1 Support both the engine and gearbox with the engine resting on its sump.
2 Remove the starter motor (photo), which is held by two bolts.
3 Remove the remaining nuts and bolts from around the periphery of the bellhousing and ease the gearbox away from the engine. Be careful to keep the gearbox in line until it is clear of the engine, so that the input shaft is not damaged.

4 Cylinder head - removal (engine out of car)

1 Remove the two bolts securing the rocker box cover and lift it off.
2 Turn the crankshaft until No. 1 piston is at the top of its compression stroke. This is when the crankshaft pulley notch is aligned with the timing mark on the front of the timing chaincase and the dowel pin of the camshaft sprocket is in the position shown in Fig. 1.6.
3 Paint a mating mark on the timing chain in line with the mating mark on the camshaft sprocket unless the timing chain has a plated link in this position. On the 4G3 series engines the chain should be locked to the sprocket with a piece of wire as shown in Fig. 1.7.
4 Lock the flywheel pulley so that it cannot rotate. Unscrew and remove the sprocket fixing bolt and pull the sprocket off the camshaft.
5 Remove the cylinder head bolts in the sequence shown in Fig. 1.8. Each bolt should be released in about three stages, to prevent distortion of the cylinder head.
6 The cylinder head is located on two dowels and when all the bolts have been removed, the cylinder head should be lifted vertically, to avoid damaging the dowels.

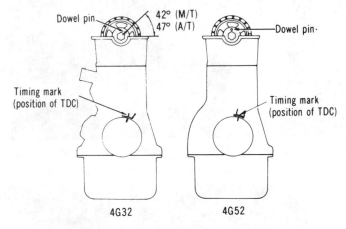

Fig. 1.6. Removing the camshaft sprocket

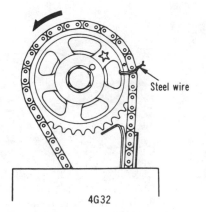

Fig. 1.7. Locking the camshaft sprocket

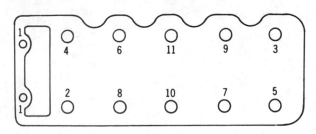

Fig. 1.8. Head bolt removal sequence

5 Camshaft and rocker arms - removal and dismantling

1   Remove the spark plugs to avoid the risk of accidental damage to them.

2   Remove the ten camshaft bearing cap nuts and the two fixings for the rocker box cover (photo).

3   Holding the front and rear bearing caps and applying pressure along the axis of the camshaft, remove the rocker arm assembly.

4   Separate the assembly into the caps, rocker arms, springs and waved washer, being careful to keep all the parts in the same relative positions as fitted on the shaft. Note that the bearing caps have locating dowels between them and the cylinder head. Take care not to lose any of the dowels.

6 Crankshaft pulley, clutch and flywheel - removal

1   If a major dismantling operation of the bottom end of the engine is being undertaken, it is convenient to remove the crankshaft pulley at this stage. If only the clutch and flywheel are to be removed, the pulley need not be taken off.

2   Mark the position of the distributor body on the cylinder block and the position of the rotor when No. 1 piston is at top dead centre on its firing stroke. Temporarily lock the flywheel with a suitably shaped piece of metal (Chapter 5, photo 2.15b), and remove the crankshaft pulley bolt. Draw off the pulley, taking care not to lose the key (photo).

3   Unlock the flywheel locking tabs, mark the position of the flywheel on the crankshaft, undo the bolts from the tab washer and remove the six bolts securing the flywheel (photo).

4   Remove the bolts securing the engine adaptor plate and remove it (photo).

7 Cylinder head - dismantling

1   Remove the spark plugs and then the camshaft (Section 5).

2   Using a valve spring compressor, compress the valve springs and remove the valve collets. Carefully release the spring compressor and remove together with spring retainer, spring, spring seat and valve. The parts of each valve assembly should be kept together in the correct position for each cylinder.

3   Using a screwdriver, prise off the stem seals and discard them.

4   The valve guides are a shrink fit in the cylinder head and if they need to be removed, the cylinder head should be heated to about 480°F and the guides hammered out using a suitable drift.

8 Cylinder block - dismantling

1   Remove the oil pressure switch, then turn the engine upside down and support it firmly with blocks.

2   Remove the sump retaining bolts, tap the sump to break the gasket seal and remove the sump.

3   Remove the oil screen (photo).

4   Remove the timing chaincase, the chain guides and the sprocket locking bolts. If the engine is fitted with counterbalance shafts, remove the counterbalance sprockets.

5   Remove the crankshaft sprocket, camshaft sprocket and timing chain. It is necessary to depress the chain tensioner in order to remove the chain.

6   Remove the camshaft sprocket holder and the right and left-hand timing chain guides.

7   Remove the bolt locking the oil pump driven gear to the right-hand counterbalance shaft when fitted, then remove the oil pump mounting bolts and take off the oil pump.

8   Take the counterbalance shaft out of the cylinder block. If the bolt locking the oil pump gear to the counterbalance shaft is difficult to undo, remove the oil pump and counterbalance shaft as an assembly and separate them afterwards.

9   Remove the thrust plate supporting the front of the left-hand counterbalance shaft and take the shaft out of the cylinder block. Use two bolts in the threaded holes of the flange as jacking screws to remove the thrust plate.

5.2. Rocker box cover fixing

6.2 Crankshaft pulley with key in position

6.3 Flywheel mounting bolts and tab washer

6.4 Engine adaptor plate

8.3 Removing the oil screen

10 Remove the crankshaft rear oil seal housing and take out the seal and spacer.

11 Turn the cylinder block on its side, remove the connecting rod caps and push each piston out through the top of the cylinder block. Use a piece of soft wood to push them upwards, so as not to damage them. If the big end bearings are removed and the same ones are being used again, take care to keep them in order, so that they can be refitted in exactly the same position from which they were removed.

9 Crankshaft - removal

1 Unscrew and remove the five crankshaft bearing caps.
2 Lift out the crankshaft.
3 Remove the bearings from the crankcase webs and the crankshaft bearing caps, being careful to keep them in pairs and associated with their correct journal. Also, take care not to mix up the upper and lower bearings.

10 Pistons - dismantling

1 Carefully remove the piston rings to avoid damaging the piston or the piston rings, taking care to place them the same way up as fitted to the piston, in order and associated with the piston from which they were removed.

2 The gudgeon pins are a press fit into the connecting rods and should not be removed unless it is absolutely necessary. To remove them without the special tool, support the piston on a piece of soft wood having a hole in it through which the gudgeon pin can pass and, using a soft metal drift, drive out the gudgeon pin from the side of the connecting rod which faces the front of the engine (Fig. 1.9).

11 Oil pump - dismantling and reassembly

Gear type (Fig. 1.10)
1 Remove the two screws securing the cover and take it off.
2 Remove the plug and withdraw the relief spring and plunger.
3 Examine the pump body to see that there are no cracks, then check the gear teeth for wear. Make sure that all holes and ports in the body are clear and if necessary blow them through with compressed air. Check the cover for signs of wear from the ends of the gear and fit a new cover if the existing one is worn excessively. Check the bearings for wear and if excessive, fit a new pump body assembly.

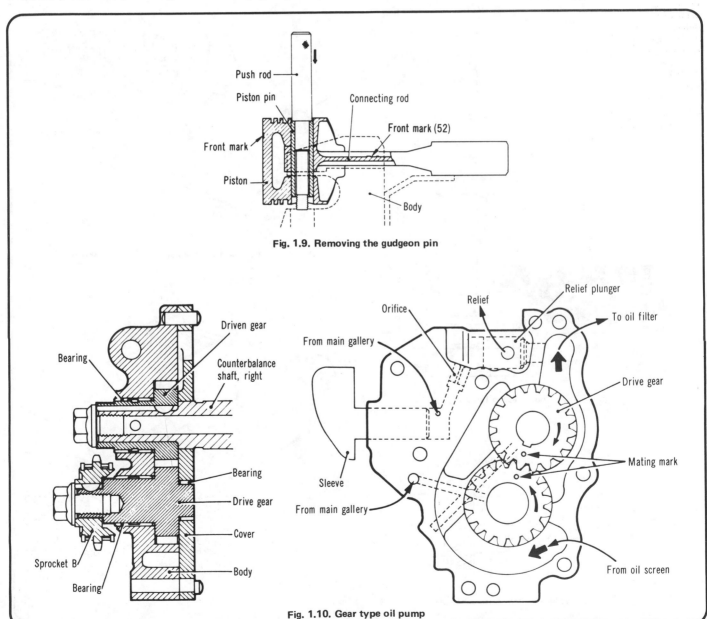

Fig. 1.9. Removing the gudgeon pin

Fig. 1.10. Gear type oil pump

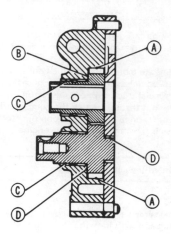

Fig. 1.11. Oil pump clearances

Clearance between gear addendum and body (A)	*0,0041 to 0.0059 in*
Gear end play (B)	*0.0024 to 0.0047 in*
Clearance between gear and bearing (C)	*0.0008 to 0.0047 in*
Clearance between gear and bearing (Drive gear rear end) (D)	*0.0017 to 0.0026 in*

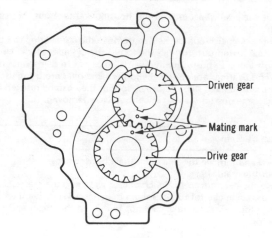

Fig. 1.12. Gear mating marks

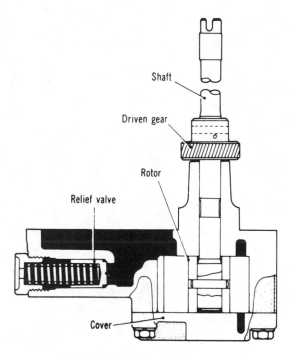

Fig. 1.13. Trochoid type oil pump

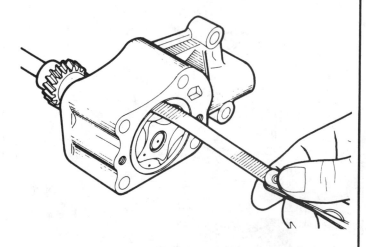

Fig. 1.14. Checking the rotor to cover clearance

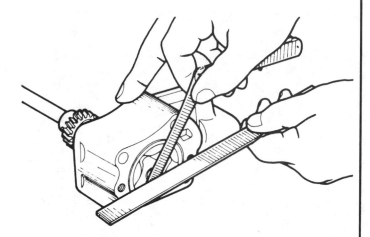

Fig. 1.15. Checking the outer rotor clearance

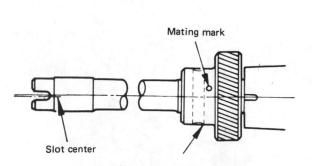

Fig. 1.16. Installing the gear onto the shaft

4 Check the clearances (Fig. 1.11) after assembling the gears into the pump, then lubricate the gears.
5 Fit the relief plunger and ensure that it moves smoothly. Insert the spring, checking that it is not bent or broken. Oil the plunger and refit the plug.
6 Check that the gear mating marks are aligned (Fig. 1.12) then refit the cover.

Trochoid type (Fig. 1.13)
7 Remove the cover fixing bolts, take off the cover and then remove and discard the gasket.
8 If it is necessary to renew the rotor assembly, or the gear, drill away the peened section of the gear fixing pin and drive the pin out.
9 Check that the rotor to cover clearance does not exceed 0.008 in (Fig. 1.14), that the outer rotor to body clearance is not more than 0.012 in (Fig. 1.15), and that the inner rotor clearance (photo) is not more than 0.010 in. Check that the relief plunger slides freely and that the oil passage and plunger bore are undamaged. Examine the spring (photo) to see that it is not bent or broken.
10 Reassemble the pump, using a new gasket. If the gear has been removed, refit it with the mating marks as shown in Fig. 1.16. Fit the gear locking pin and peen it at both ends.

12 Valves - removal

1 Remove the spark plugs and then turn the cylinder head onto its side.
2 Carefully position a valve spring compressor over a valve and compress the spring until the collets can be removed.
3 Slowly release the spring pressure, remove the valve spring compressor and lift off the spring retainer, valve spring and spring seat.
4 Remove the valve and if the stem seals are not being removed in order to fit new ones, valve removal needs great care in order to avoid damaging the seals. If new stem seals are being fitted, prise off the old ones with a screwdriver (Fig. 1.17).
5 Store each valve with its spring and associated parts in such a way that they can be refitted exactly as they were removed.

13 Engine components - cleaning, examination; general note

When the engine has been dismantled, thoroughly clean all components with petrol or a proprietary solvent. Remove any traces of gasket material which is still adhering, using a blunt scraper, but take care not to score any of the sealing faces.
Once the components have been cleaned, both before and after inspection, keep them wrapped or covered so that they stay clean. Renew all badly worn components.

14 Crankshaft - examination and renovation

1 Examine the crankpins and journals for signs of scoring or other damage. Using a micrometer, check the ovality of the crankpins at different points around their periphery. The crankshaft should be reground to one of the dimensions given in the Specifications if there is serious scoring, or if the ovality is greater than 0.001 in (0.025 mm). The main bearing journals should also be inspected to the same standard as the crankpins.
2 A crankshaft regrinding specialist will recondition the crankshaft and supply a set of suitable bearing shells.

15 Big end and main bearing shells - examination

1 Big end bearing failure produces a characteristic knocking and a drop in oil pressure. Main bearing failure is often accompanied by vibration and a pronounced drop in oil pressure.
2 Examine the bearings for signs of scoring and pitting. The bearings should be a uniform matt grey colour and with lead indium bearings the presence of a copper colour indicates that the bearing material has worn away and the underlay is exposed, necessitating new bearings.
3 If the bearings have deteriorated, but the crankshaft is serviceable, fit new bearings of standard size. If the crankshaft is reground, new bearings of the appropriate size must be fitted.

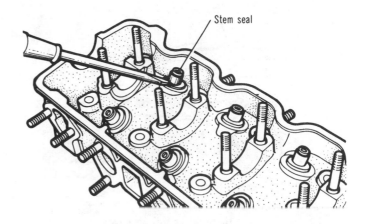

Fig. 1.17. Removing the valve stem seals

11.9a Checking the inner rotor clearance

11.9b Relief plunger and spring

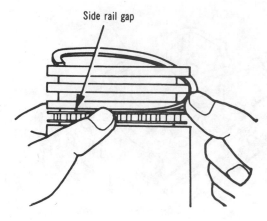

Fig. 1.18. Installing the side rails

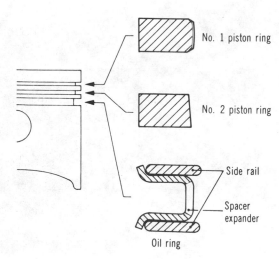

No. 1 piston ring

No. 2 piston ring

Side rail

Spacer expander

Oil ring

Fig. 1.19. Position of piston rings

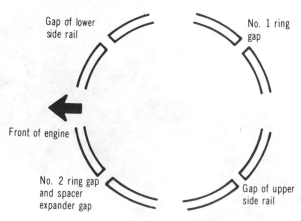

Gap of lower side rail

No. 1 ring gap

Front of engine

No. 2 ring gap and spacer expander gap

Gap of upper side rail

Fig. 1.20. Piston ring gap position

16 Cylinder bores - examination and renovation

1   Worn cylinder bores and piston rings are indicated by high oil consumption and blue smoke from the exhaust, particularly when accelerating.
2   Examine the bores for signs of scoring and for the presence of a step at the top of the bore. Bore wear may be overcome by fitting new standard size piston rings, special oil control rings, or by reboring the cylinders. The method decided upon depends upon the condition of the bores and the additional mileage which is hoped for and it is best to obtain specialist advice.

17 Camshaft bearings - inspection

With the camshaft fitted and the bearing caps tightened to the correct torque wrench setting, measure the clearance between the camshaft and the bearing cap. If the clearance exceeds 0.0035 in (0.0889 mm) the bearings are worn excessively and a new cylinder head is required.

18 Valves - examination and renovation

1   Examine the heads of the valves for pitting and burning; especially the heads of the exhaust valves. The valve seating should be examined at the same time. If the pitting on the valves and seats is very light the marks can be removed by grinding the seats and the valves together with coarse and then fine, valve grinding paste. Where bad pitting has occurred to the valve seats it will be necessary to recut them to fit new valves. If the valve seats are so worn that they cannot be recut, then it will be necessary to fit new valve seat inserts. These latter two jobs should be entrusted to the local official agent or automobile engineering works. In practice it is very seldom that the seats are so badly worn that they require renewal. Normally, it is the valve that is too badly worn for refitment, and the owner can easily purchase a new set of valves and match them to the seats by valve grinding.
2   Valve grinding is carried out as follows: Place the cylinder head upside down on a bench, with a block of wood at each end to give clearance for the valve stems.
3   Smear a trace of coarse carborundum paste on the seat face and apply a suction grinder tool to the valve head. With a semi-rotary action, grind the valve head to its seat, lifting the valve occasionally to redistribute the grinding paste. When a dull matt even surface finish is produced on both the valve seat and the valve, wipe off the paste and repeat the process with fine carborundum paste, lifting and turning the valve to redistribute the paste as before. A light spring placed under the valve head will greatly ease this operation. When a smooth unbroken ring of a light grey matt finish is produced, on both valve and the valve seat faces, the grinding operation is complete.

19 Timing chain, sprockets and chain tensioner - examination and renovation

1   Examine the teeth of the sprockets and ensure that none of them are damaged or broken. If this is the case, a new sprocket must be fitted.
2   Examine the teeth for wear and if it is obvious that the teeth are no longer symmetrical because of wear on one side, the sprocket should not be refitted but renewed.
3   Because a worn timing chain causes a lot of engine noise, it is worth fitting a new timing chain when the engine is stripped down. Likewise it is worth fitting a new head to the tensioner.

20 Engine components - examination

Sump
1   Thoroughly wash out the sump to remove all sludge. Dry it with a lint-free cloth.
2   Inspect the casing for cracking or distortion. Cracks and splits may be repaired by specialist welding, but if the damage cannot be repaired satisfactorily, fit a new sump.

3   Check that the seating face is clean, has no old gasket adhering and is not distorted.

Clutch pilot bearing (spigot bush)

4   Fit the clutch shaft into the crankshaft end to see whether it is a good fit. A sloppy pilot bush will cause unnecessary wear to the gearbox front bearing, and should be renewed.

Studs, nuts and bolts

5   Examine all studs, nuts and bolts for damage and wear. For slight thread damage clean the threads up with the appropriate tap or die, otherwise fit a new fastening. Where self-locking nuts are used, any which have been removed should be renewed.

21 Decarbonising

1   Remove the cylinder head as described in Section 4 and, using a blunt screwdriver, or a rotary wire brush, remove all the carbon from the cylinder head while all the valves are still in place.
2   Remove the valves, taking the precautions given in Section 12 and remove the carbon from the valves and from the valve ports. Grind the valves in (see Section 18) and then refit them.
3   Turn the crankshaft so that two of the pistons are at the top of their bores. Put clean rag in the bores of the other two cylinders and cover up the waterways, then carefully scrape all the carbon from the crowns of the two exposed pistons. Use a flat, blunt scraper, taking care not to scratch the piston crowns. Ensure that no carbon gets down the side of the pistons. Carefully clean away all of the loose carbon.
4   Rotate the crankshaft, so that the two clean pistons descend into their bores, insert clean rag into the bores and remove the carbon ring from the top of the cylinder. Carefully remove the rag from the bores, so that the carbon which has fallen onto it is removed with the rag.
5   Turn the crankshaft, so that the two pistons left to be decarbonised are at the top of their bores and proceed as in paragraphs 3 and 4.

22 Piston rings - refitting

1   Fit the piston rings onto the piston using the following method. First fit the three piece oil ring, which is fitted by installing the spacer expander, then the upper side rail, then the lower side rail. Do not attempt to open the gaps in the side rails, but fit them as shown in Fig. 1.18, by inserting one end and holding it firmly then gradually pressing the adjacent part into the groove until the entire ring has been fitted. Fit the side rails so that the size and maker's identification stamped on their side, is uppermost. Check that the upper and lower side rails can be turned smoothly and that the gaps in the spacer expander and side rails are staggered by 45°.
2   When fitting the No. 2 piston ring, be careful to have the surface marked 'Top' uppermost because the ring section is not symmetrical (Fig. 1.19). Fit No. 1 piston ring and then space all the ring gaps as shown in Fig. 1.20.

23 Engine reassembly - general note

1   To ensure maximum life and minimum trouble from a rebuilt engine, everything must be assembled correctly and must be spotlessly clean.
2   All oilways and ports must be clear, mating surfaces must be clean and all rotating and sliding surfaces must be oiled on assembly.
3   Make sure that all nuts, bolts and washers are in good condition and are fitted exactly as they were before dismantling.
4   Check that all core plugs are in good condition and show no sign of weeping. Renew any which are suspect.
5   Have ready a supply of clean cotton rags, an oil can filled with engine oil and all the required gaskets and seals, as well as all the necessary tools.

24 Crankshaft - refitting

1   Ensure that the crankcase is scrupulously clean and that all oilways are clear. If possible, blow them out with compressed air. Treat the

crankshaft in the same way and then inject engine oil into the crankshaft oilways.
2   Fit the upper halves of the main bearings into the webs of the crankcase, after wiping their locations clean. Note that each half bearing has a tab which locates in a groove in the crankcase and ensure that it is fitted correctly and that its ends are flush. The centre bearing has thrust washers on the side (photo). If new bearings are being fitted, carefully wipe away their protective grease coating.
3   Taking the same precautions, fit the lower bearing shells to their caps.
4   Fit the crankshaft to the crankcase (photo) and fit the bearing caps, noting that each one has a number to indicate its position and an arrow to show the side which must face the front of the engine (photo). Fit the main bearing bolts and tighten them to a torque wrench setting of 36 to 39 lbf ft (5.0 to 5.5 kgf m) for the 4G32 engine and 54 to 61 lbf ft (7.5 to 8.5 kgf m) for the 4G52 engine. The cap bolts should be tightened successively, in several stages.
5   Ensure that the crankshaft rotates freely and has a thrust clearance at the centre bearing of between 0.002 and 0.007 in (photo).
0   Lay the cylinder block on its side, fit a piston ring compressor to a piston and insert the piston/con-rod assembly into the top of the bore

24.2 Fitting the upper main bearing shells

24.4a Installing the crankshaft

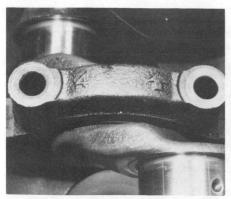
24.4b Main bearing cap identification marks

24.5 Measuring crankshaft end play

24.6a Inserting a piston

24.6b Piston identification marks

24.6c Cylinder number stamped on connecting rod

24.9a Oil hole in oil seal separator

24.9b Fitted crankshaft oil seal assembly

24.12a Crankshaft sprocket mating mark and plated link

24.12b Camshaft sprocket mating mark and plated link

24.12c Timing chain in chain guide ...

24.12d ... and against the tensioner

24.12e Crankshaft gear and oil slinger

(photo). Note that the piston is marked with the engine type number (Fig. 1.21) and an arrow to indicate which side of the piston should be towards the front of the engine (photo). The identification of the correct cylinder for each piston is stamped on the connecting rod (photo).

7   As each piston is inserted, fit the appropriate big end bearing cap and fit the cap bolts finger tight.

8   When all four pistons have been fitted, tighten the big end bearing cap bolts progressively to a torque wrench setting of 23 to 25 lbf ft (3.2 to 3.5 kgf m) for the 4G32 engine and 33 to 35 lbf ft (4.6 to 4.9 kgf m) for the 4G52 engine, then check that the crankshaft can still be turned by hand.

9   Fit the oil seal to the crankshaft oil seal housing. Fit the separator with the oil hole at the bottom (photo) and then bolt on the oil seal assembly (photo). Smear the oil seal with engine oil when it is fitted.

10 Rotate the crankshaft so that No. 1 piston is at top dead centre.

11 With the cylinder block upside down, fit the timing chain guide, sprocket holder (4G52 only) and the tensioner. On the 4G32 engine, the chain guide must be fitted so that the jet is directed towards the chain and sprocket meshing point.

12 With the mating marks of the crankshaft sprocket and the camshaft sprocket aligned with the chrome plated links in the timing chain (photo), fit the sprocket to the crankshaft, with the chain fitted in the guide (photo) and against the tensioner (photo). Fit the key, the crankshaft gear and oil slinger, 'F' mark (4G32), the 'C' or 'A' mark (4G52) towards the front of the engine and the slinger as shown in the photos.

13 Fit the gasket and then bolt on the timing chaincase to the cylinder block (photo).

14 On the 4G32 engine, insert the tensioner lever plunger and spring through the hole in the right-hand side of the chaincase and tighten the holder, using a 5/16 in hexagon socket wrench, to a torque wrench setting of 29 to 36 lbf ft (4.0 to 5.0 kgf m).

15 On the 4G52 engine, fit the oil pump assembly beneath the timing chaincase (photo) with its mating marks lined up (photo).

16 Fit the oil screen then coat the sump joint face, the timing case to block and rear oil seal to block joints with sealer (Fig. 1.22).

17 Fit the gasket to the sump, then place the sump on the cylinder block, insert the bolts and tighten them in diagonal sequence, starting with the ones furthest from the centre. Final tightening should be to a torque wrench setting of 4.3 to 5.8 lbf ft (0.52 to 0.7 kgf m).

18 Fit and temporarily tighten the crankshaft pulley, taking care not to move the position of the crankshaft. Fit the oil pressure switch, then set the engine upright, again being careful not to move the crankshaft until the camshaft assembly and camshaft sprocket have been fitted.

19 Cover the top of the chaincase with rag to prevent anything from falling into it.

20 Fit the flywheel with the mating marks made at the time of dismantling aligned and then lock it while the mounting bolts are tightened. Fit a new tab washer and tighten the bolts to a torque wrench setting of 83 to 90 lbf ft (11.6 to 12.6 kgf m) and bend over the tabs to lock the bolts.

21 Again prevent the crankshaft from turning by locking the flywheel and finally tighten the crankshaft pulley to a torque of 43 to 50 lbf ft (6.0 to 7.0 kgf m) for the 4G32 engine and 80 to 93 lbf ft (11.2 to 13.0 kgf m) for the 4G52 engine.

22 Fit the engine support bracket.

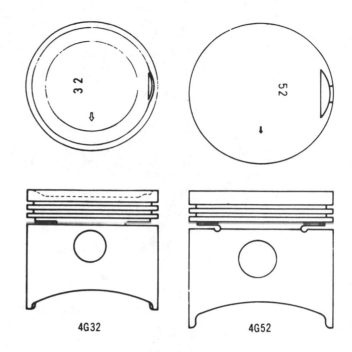

Fig. 1.21. Piston identification

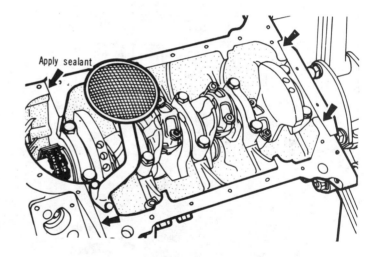

Fig. 1.22. Sealer application points

24.13 Timing chain case installed

24.15a Fitting the oil pump (4G52)

24.15b Oil pump mating marks

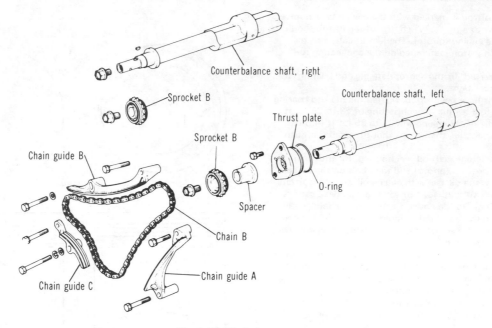

Fig. 1.23. The balancer system

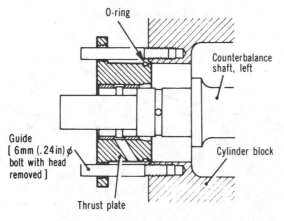

Fig. 1.24. Fitting the thrust plate

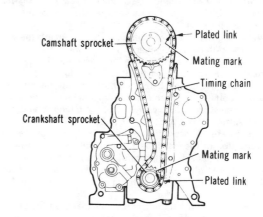

Fig. 1.25. Installing the timing chain

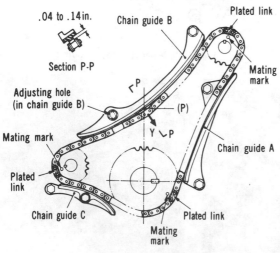

Fig. 1.26. Balancer system drive

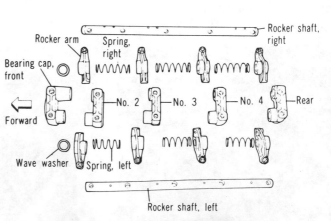

Fig. 1.27. Assembling the rocker arm shafts

25 Crankshaft refitting (balancer shaft engines)

1   Proceed as for the engine without the balancer shafts fitted (Section 24) until the end of paragraph 9.

2   Fit the engine rear plate, then the flywheel and tighten its mounting bolts (see Section 24, paragraph 20). In the case of an engine with automatic transmission, fit the drive plate and adaptor plate.

3   Fit the right-hand counterbalance shaft to the cylinder block, inserting it gently, so that it does not damage the rear bearing.

4   Fit the oil pump assembly, making sure that the keyway of the oil pump driven gear fits the Woodruff key at the end of the counterbalance shaft and that the key is not moved or displaced. After the oil pump assembly has been fitted, tighten its mounting bolts.

5   Tighten the counterbalance shaft and driven gear mounting bolt. If the fit of the Woodruff key and the driven gear is too tight, first insert the counterbalance shaft into the oil pump, temporarily tighten the bolt. Insert the counterbalance shaft and oil pump as an assembly into the cylinder block.

6   Fill the oil pump with oil and tighten the counterbalance shaft bolt to a torque wrench setting of 22 to 28 lbf ft (3 to 4 kgf m).

7   Insert the left counterbalance shaft into the cylinder block, taking care not to damage the rear bearing.

8   Fit a new O-ring to the outer peripheral groove of the thrust plate (Fig. 1.24) taking care not to twist the ring. Smear the O-ring with oil and fit the thrust plate to the cylinder block. Use a bolt without a head as a guide when fitting the thrust plate, so that the plate does not have to be turned to align the holes and so possibly distort the O-ring.

9   After bolting on the thrust plate, fit the spacer.

10 Fit the sprocket holder and the right and left-hand chain guides.

11 Turn the crankshaft until the piston of No. 1 cylinder is at the top of its stroke.

12 Fit the tensioner spring and sleeve to the oil pump body.

13 Fit the camshaft sprocket, crankshaft sprocket and chain as in Section 24, paragraph 12.

14 With the parts assembled as above and being held with both hands, align the key of the crankshaft with the keyway on the crankshaft sprocket and fit the sprocket (Fig. 1.25).

15 Fit crankshaft sprocket 'B' (Fig. 1.23) (for driving the counterbalance shaft) onto the crankshaft.

16 Fit the two counterbalance drive sprockets 'B' onto chain 'B' (for driving the counterbalance shaft), taking care to align the mating marks (Fig. 1.26) and fit the sprockets to the shafts.

17 Tighten the locking bolts of sprockets 'B' and temporarily install chain guides 'A', 'B' and 'C'.

18 Adjust the tension of chain 'B' in the following sequence.

a)   Firmly tighten chain guide 'A' mounting bolt.

b)   Firmly tighten chain guide 'C' mounting bolt.

c)   Move sprockets 'B' to collect the slack chain at point 'P', then adjust the position of chain guide 'C' so that when the chain is pulled in the direction of arrow 'Y' with the finger tips, the clearance between chain guide 'B' and the links of chain 'B' will be 0.04 to 0.14 in (1.02 to 3.56 mm), then tighten the bolts.

19 Fit the timing chaincase and gasket and after refitting remove any gasket which protrudes from the top and bottom of the case.

20 Complete the assembly as in Section 24, paragraphs 16 to 22, except that the flywheel has already been fitted.

26 Cylinder head - reassembly

Valves

1   Fit the valve spring seats (photo), then press on the stem oil seals (photo). Apply engine oil to each valve stem, insert the valves (photo) carefully to avoid damaging the seals and then check to see that each valve moves smoothly.

2   Fit the valve springs with the enamel identification mark towards the rocker arm and fit the spring retainers (photo).

3   Compress the spring with a valve spring compressor, check to see that the stem seal is not being compressed by the lower side of the spring retainer, then fit the collets (photo). Release the valve spring compressor and tap the valve head with a soft hammer to make sure

26.1a Fitting the valve spring seat ...

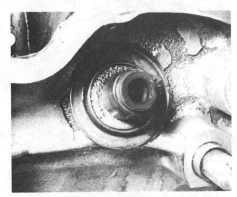

26.1b ... stem seal ...

26.1c ... and valve

26.2 Fitting a valve spring and spring retainer

26.3 Fitting the split collet

26.6 Fitting the rocker shaft assembly

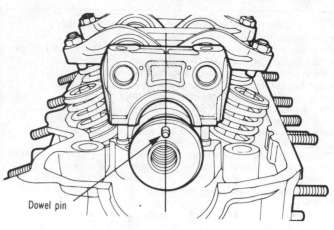

Fig. 1.28. Camshaft dowel position

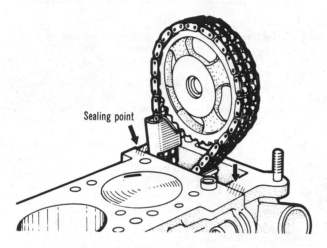

Fig. 1.29. Sealing point

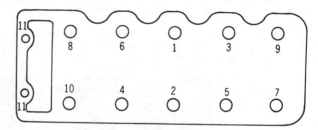

Fig. 1.30. Head bolt tightening sequence

that the collets have seated correctly.

Camshaft
4   Fit the camshaft and check that it has an end play of between 0.004 and 0.008 in (0.102 to 0.204 mm). Tighten the bearing caps to a torque wrench setting of 13 to 14 lbf ft (1.8 to 2.0 kgf m).
5   Assemble the rocker arm shafts (Fig. 1.27) and temporarily insert a bolt through the front and rear bearing caps to keep the assembly together. The front bearing cap has a mating mark embossed on its front and the rocker arm shafts have a mark near the front end. When assembling the front rocker shaft to the bearing cap, do so with the shaft oil hole facing downwards and the mating marks aligned. Bearing caps are marked Front, Rear, No. 2, 3 and 4 and should be fitted in the correct order and with the arrow on them pointing towards the front of the engine. Although all the rocker arms are the same, they should be refitted to their original positions. Note that the right rocker arm shaft has eight oil holes and the left one only four and that the springs on the right shaft are longer than those of the left. Fit the wave washer with its convex side towards the front of the engine.
6   Fit the assembled rocker arm shaft assembly to the camshaft (photo) and ensure that the dowel pin on the front end is as shown in Fig. 1.28. When all the bearing caps have been seated without using undue force, fit the two rocker box cover attachments, on the front and No. 4 caps, then fit the nuts and tighten progressively to a torque of 13 to 14 lbf ft (1.82 to 1.96 kgf m).
7   Fit the spark plugs and tighten to a torque of 18 to 21 lbf ft (2.5 to 3.0 kgf m).

27 Cylinder head - fitting to cylinder block

1   Remove the covering from the top of the chaincase and apply sealant to the two points indicated in Fig. 1.29.
2   Fit the head gasket over the dowel on the top of the cylinder block after ensuring that the joint between the top of the chaincase and the cylinder block is smooth, then carefully lower the cylinder head onto the block, after ensuring that No. 1 piston is still at the top of its cylinder and the dowel hole in the camshaft sprocket is in the position shown in Fig. 1.29. Because the cylinder head fits on the cylinder block dowels, it must be positioned carefully before lowering, so that it mates with the dowels.
3   Fit the cylinder head fixing bolts finger tight, then tighten them progressively in the order shown in Fig. 1.30 to a final torque wrench setting of 51 to 54 lbf ft (7.1 to 7.6 kgf m) for the 4G3 series engines and 65 to 72 lbf ft (9.0 to 10.0 kgf m) for the 4G5 series. (After the engine has been run for a short time the cylinder head bolts should be re-tightened to 58 to 61 lbf ft (8.1 to 8.5 kgf m) for the 4G3 series and 72 to 79 lbf ft (10.0 to 12.8 kgf m) for the 4G5 series).
4   Fit the camshaft sprocket over the dowel on the end of the camshaft (photo), insert the fixing bolt and washers (photo) and tighten to a torque wrench setting of 36 to 43 lbf ft (5.0 to 6.0 kgf m).

28 Valves - adjustment

1   When assembling the engine adjust the valves as follows: With each

27.4a Fitting the camshaft sprocket

27.4b Inserting the sprocket locking bolt

28.1 Adjusting the valve clearances

29.3 The intake manifold correctly fitted

piston in turn at top dead centre, loosen the rocker arm nuts and temporarily adjust the valve clearance to 0.003 in (0.076 mm) on the intake side and 0.007 in (0.178 mm) on the exhaust. Insert a feeler gauge to check the gap and while holding the adjusting screw so that it does not move, secure it with the locknut (photo).

2   After completion of engine assembly run the engine until normal operating temperature is reached and when the cylinder head is re-torqued, the valve clearances of the hot engine should be readjusted to 0.006 in (0.152 mm) for the intake valves and 0.010 in (0.254 mm) for the exhaust.

29 Engine assembly - completion

1   After applying sealant to the mating surfaces, fit the breather and semi-circular packing at the front of the cylinder head.

2   Fit the rocker cover and gasket and tighten the fixing bolts to a torque wrench setting of 4 to 5 lbf ft (0.55 to 0.7 kgf m).

3   Fit the intake manifold and the lifting lug on its front stud and bonding wire on the rear stud (photo).

4   Fit the fuel pump and the water pump.

5   Fit the distributor, after lining up its mating marks and ensuring that the rotor is in the position for No. 1 cylinder to fire. Tighten the fixing nut and reconnect the vacuum pipe.

6   Fit the exhaust manifold (photo) and heatshield (photo), remember-

29.6a Fitting the exhaust manifold ...

29.6b ... and heat shield

31.2 Engine front mounting and rolling stopper

31.4 Engine rear mounting

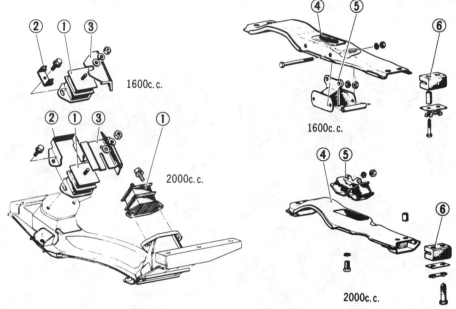

Fig. 1.31. Exploded view of engine mountings

1 Front insulator	3 Heat deflection plate	4 Engine support bracket,	5 Rear insulator
2 Rolling stopper	(right side only)	rear	6 Pad

ing to fit the lifting lug to the rear upper stud.

7 Ensure that the cylinder block and sump drain plugs are fitted and tightened.

30 Engine - refitting

1 If the clutch and gearbox were removed, refit them taking care when fitting the gearbox that the input shaft is not strained.

2 Fit all the bellhousing bolts and put the nuts on finger tight, then tighten the bolts progressively in a diagonal sequence.

3 Sling the engine at an angle of about 30° (the gearbox lower than the engine) and lower it into the engine compartment, allowing it to rest on its mountings. As with engine removal, it will be necessary to support the gearbox on a jack until the crossmember has been fitted.

4 The remainder of the operation is the reverse of engine removal.

31 Engine mountings and stabilizers - removal and refitting

Front mountings

1 Remove the leads from the battery, then support the weight of the engine on a jack.

2 Remove the bolts from the crossmember to insulator mounting and

remove the rolling stopper (photo).

3 Remove the two bolts fixing the engine mounting to the engine, withdraw the assembly and separate the insulator from the engine mounting bracket.

4 Refitting is a reversal of the removal sequence.

Rear mountings

5 Support the weight of the gearbox, remove the four fixings (photo) from the engine rear support, lift the gearbox on the jack to enable the mounting to be separated from the gearbox and remove the insulator assembly.

6 Refitting is a reversal of the removal sequence.

32 Fault diagnosis - engine

Symptom	Reason/s
Engine fails to turn over when starter switch is operated	Discharged or defective battery. Dirty or loose battery leads. Defective solenoid or starter switch. Loose or broken starter motor leads. Defective starter motor.
Engine spins, but does not start	Ignition components wet or damp. Spark plug insulators dirty. Distributor cap 'tracking'. Disconnected low tension lead. Dirty contact breaker. Faulty condenser. Faulty coil. No petrol, or petrol not reaching carburetter. Faulty fuel pump. Too much choke, leading to wet spark plugs.
Engine stops and will not re-start	Ignition failure. Fuel pump failure. No petrol in tank. Water in fuel system.
Engine lacks power	Burnt out exhaust valve. Sticking valve. Incorrect timing. Blown cylinder head gasket. Leaking carburetter gasket. Incorrect mixture. Blocked air intake, or dirty air filter. Ignition automatic advance faulty.
Excessive oil consumption	Defective valve stem oil seals. Worn pistons and bores. Blocked engine breather.
Engine noisy	Incorrect valve clearances. Worn timing chain. Worn distributor drive. Worn bearings.

Chapter 2 Cooling system

For modifications, and information applicable to later models, see Supplement at end of manual

Contents

Specifications

System type ... ... Pressurized water with thermostatic control; pump and variable speed fan assisted

Pump ... ... Engine driven centrifugal

Thermostat

Type	Wax
Thermostat opening temperature	180°F (82°C) Type number 82
	190°F (88°C) Type number 88
Fully open temperature	203°F (95°C) Type number 82
	212°F (100°C) Type number 88
Maximum opening	More than 0.315 in (8 mm)

Pressure cap setting

High pressure side	11.4 to 14.2 lb/in^2 (0.8 to 1.0 kg/cm^2)
Vacuum side	−0.7 to −1.4 lb/in^2 (−0.05 to −0.10 kg/cm^2)

Antifreeze type ... ... Ethylene glycol with inhibitors for mixed metal engines. (Specifications SAE J1034, BS 3151 or BS3152)

Cooling system capacity

	Model A73	Model A112
1600 cc engine	12.8 Imp. pints (7.3 litres)	10.6 Imp. pints (6.0 litres)
	Model A78	**Model A115**
2000 cc engine	15.8 Imp. pints (9.0 litres)	13.6 Imp. pints (7.7 litres)

Torque wrench settings

	lbf ft	kgf m
Fan blades	10	1.4
Water pump bolts	15	2.1
Thermostat housing bolts	20	2.8
Alternator mounting and adjusting bolts	20	2.8

1 General description

The engine coolant is circulated by a pump assisted thermo-system and the whole system is pressurised so that the boiling point of the coolant is increased considerably. The pressure is controlled by the radiator filler cap which vents the system to the overflow pipe when the correct pressure is exceeded. It is therefore important to ensure that the cap is fitted properly and that the sealing washer and its spring are in good condition.

The cooling system consists of a radiator, water pump on which the radiator cooling fan is mounted, thermostat and interconnecting hoses. Some of the heat from the system is used for interior heating and for heating the inlet manifold and automatic choke.

The system functions by the pump drawing water from the bottom of the radiator and circulating it around the passages in the cylinder block to take away the heat of combustion and keep the cylinder bores and pistons cool. The water then passes to the cylinder head and circulates around the combustion areas and valve seats to the thermostat. When the engine has reached its correct operating temperature, the thermostat opens and coolant flows into the radiator header tank. Coolant from the header tank passes through the

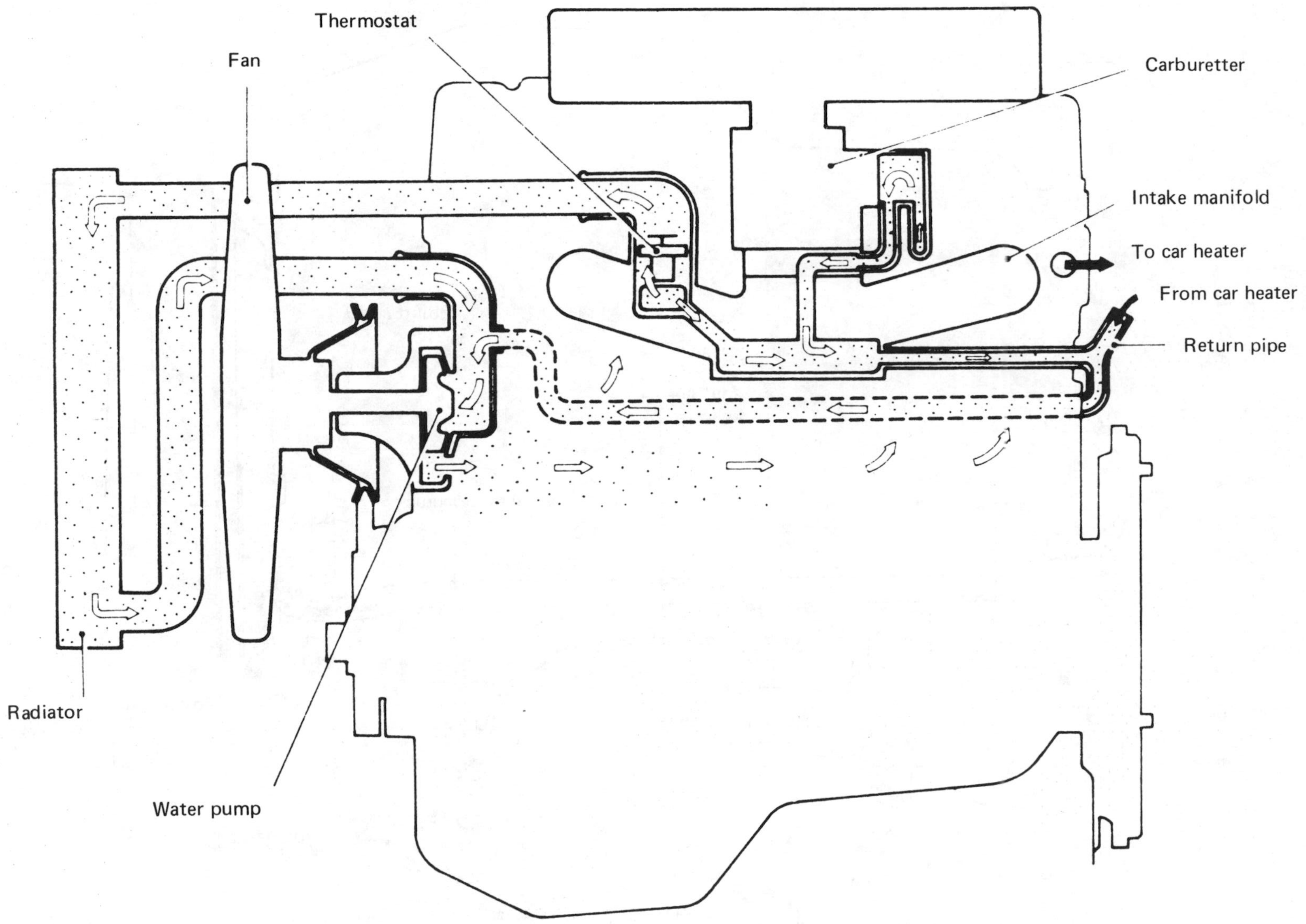

Carburetter

Intake manifold

To car heater

From car heater

Return pipe

Thermostat

Fan

Water pump

Radiator

Fig. 2.1. Cooling system (4G32)

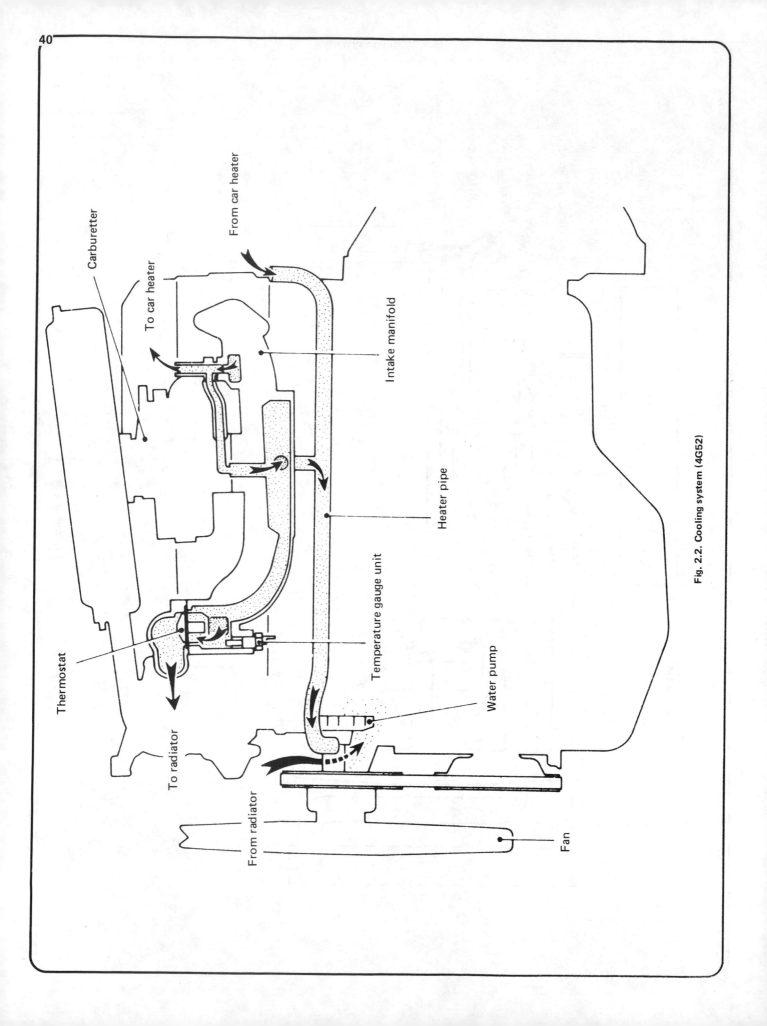

Fig. 2.2. Cooling system (4G52)

radiator core where it is cooled rapidly by the airflow resulting from the fan and the forward motion of the vehicle. On reaching the bottom of the radiator, the cooled liquid is recirculated. When the engine is cold, the thermostat is closed and maintains the recirculation of the same coolant in the engine. Only when the correct minimum operating temperature has been reached, as shown in the Specification, does the thermostat begin to open and allow coolant to return to the radiator.

There are some variations in the system and the position of components on different models. Some have a fan fitted with a torque type clutch, which covers the fan speed when pulley speed increases beyond a certain value. This speed reduction is independent of ambient temperature and is to reduce the loss of engine power in the fan drive at high speeds.

On models fitted with automatic transmission, the base of the radiator is fitted with a cooler, through which the automatic transmission oil is circulated.

2 Cooling system - draining

1   Unscrew and remove the radiator cap (Fig. 2.3). If the engine is hot, this operation should be done slowly and carefully because the cooling system will be under pressure.
2   If the engine contains anti-freeze which is less than two years old and is therefore reusable, place a clean container below the radiator drain plug (photo). Otherwise allow the coolant to run to waste. Remove the radiator drain plug.
3   Place a container below the cylinder block drain plug and remove the plug.

3 Cooling system - flushing

1   With the passing of time, the cooling system will gradually lose its efficiency as the radiator becomes choked with rust, scale deposits from water and other sediment. To clear the system out, initially drain the system as described previously, then allow water from a hose to run through from the top hose connection and out of the bottom hose connection for several minutes. Install the cylinder block drain plug while this is being done.
2   Refit the hoses and fill the system with fresh, 'soft' water (use rain water if possible) and a proprietary flushing compound, following the manufacturer's instructions carefully. (Refer to the next Section).
3   If the cooling system is very dirty, reverse flush it, by forcing water from a hose up through the bottom hose connection for about five to ten minutes, then complete the operation as described in paragraph 2, of this Section.

4 Cooling system - filling

1   Ensure that the radiator drain plug and the cylinder block drain plug are screwed in firmly and that all hoses are in place and their clips tightened.
2   Pour water (preferably soft water or rain water) through the radiator filler until the system is full.

3   Fit the radiator filler cap and run the engine for about three minutes then remove the filler cap and top up the system if necessary.

5 Anti-freeze solution

1   Prior to the onset of cold winter weather, it is essential that anti-freeze is added to the engine coolant if it has not been previously used.
2   Any anti-freeze which conforms with specification 'SAE J1034', 'BS 3151' or 'BS 3152' can be used. Never use an anti-freeze with an alcohol base.
3   Anti-freeze can be left in the cooling system for up to two years, but after six months it is advisable to have the specific gravity of the coolant checked at your local garage, and thereafter, every three months.
4   Listed below are the amounts of anti-freeze which should be added to ensure adequate protection down to the temperature given:

Percentage of anti-freeze by volume	Protection provided down to:
25%	-13°C ($+9^{\circ}$F)
33%	-19°C (-2°F)
50%	-36°C (-33°F)
55%	-45°C (-49°F)

6 Fan - removal

Fixed hub fan
1   Unscrew and remove the four bolts securing the fan blades and pulley hub to the water pump flange, then lift the blades clear of the pulley hub (photo).
2   Loosen the alternator fixing bolts to slacken the fan belt and then remove the pulley hub from the water pump flange.

Torque hub fan
3   Remove the six bolts securing the fan to the torque hub and lift the fan off.
4   Undo the four nuts securing the torque hub to the studs of the water pump flange and remove the torque hub (Fig. 2.4).

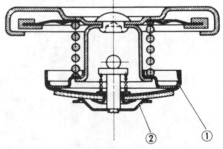

Fig. 2.3. Radiator cap

1 *High-pressure valve*	2 *Vacuum valve*

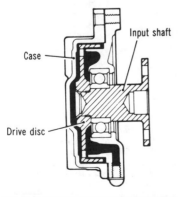

Fig. 2.4. Sectional view of torque hub

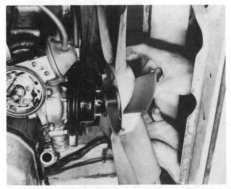

2.1 Radiator drain plug

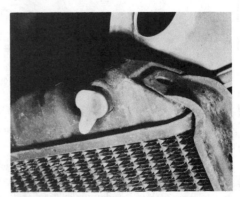

6.1 Removing the radiator fan

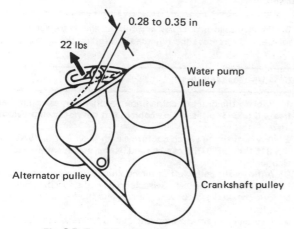

Fig. 2.5. Fan belt adjustment 1600 cc engine

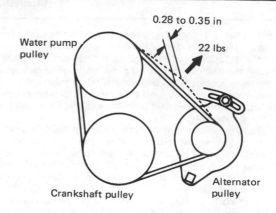

Fig. 2.6. Fan belt adjustment 2000 cc engine

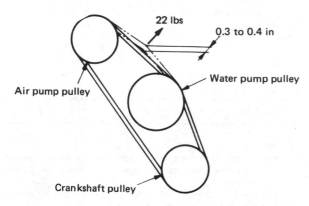

Fig. 2.7. Fan belt adjustment for vehicles with air pump

8.1 Correct fitting of radiator top hose

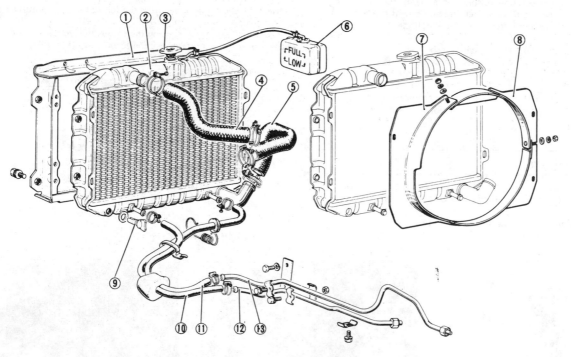

Fig. 2.8. Exploded view of radiator

1	Radiator cowl (1600 cc model only)	6	Reserve tank	9	Drain plug
2	Radiator	7	Radiator shroud, left (2000 cc model only)	10	* Oil return hose
3	Radiator cap			11	* Oil feed hose
4	Radiator hose, upper	8	Radiator shroud, right (2000 cc model only)	12	* Oil return tube
5	Radiator hose, lower			13	* Oil feed tube

NOTE: * Mark indicates parts for cars with automatic transmission

7 Fan belt - removal and adjustment

1   Loosen the alternator fixing bolts and lift the alternator in towards the engine to release the tension on the fan belt.
2   Remove the fan belt from the alternator pulley and then lift it clear of the crankshaft and fan pulleys. If the belt shows any sign of cracking, damage or excessive wear, fit a new belt.
3   After fitting the belt over the fan and crankshaft pulleys and then over the alternator pulley, tension the belt by lowering the alternator. Correct belt tensioning is when a load of 22 lbs (9.98 kg) applied at right angles to the mid point of the span between the fan pulley and alternator pulley, will deflect the belt between 0.28 and 0.35 in (7.1 and 8.89 mm) (Figs. 2.5 and 2.6). The adjustment for vehicles fitted with an air pump is shown in Fig. 2.7.
4   Having checked that the belt tension is correct, fully tighten the alternator fixing bolts.

8 Radiator - removal and refitting

1   Remove the radiator filler cap and radiator drain plug and drain the radiator, saving the coolant if appropriate.
2   Remove the hoses from the top and bottom of the radiator. On models fitted with automatic transmission, remove the oil feed and return pipes from the bottom of the radiator and plug the ends to prevent loss of oil and the entry of dirt.
3   Remove the radiator shroud if fitted (Fig. 2.9), then remove the four radiator fixing bolts (photo), and lift the radiator out (photo).
4   Having removed the radiator, examine it for leaks and damage. Flush the radiator thoroughly while it is off the vehicle and fit new radiator hoses if the existing ones are damaged, cracked or are no longer supple.
5   Refit the radiator, check that the drain plug and all the hose connections are fitted (photo) and fully tightened, then refill the cooling system.
6   Examine the radiator cap for deterioration of the washer and spring and fit a new cap if either the spring or sealing washer are damaged.

9 Thermostat - removal, testing, and refitting

A wax type thermostat is fitted and when this type fails, they do so in the closed position, which will lead to the system boiling and losing coolant. The removal procedure is as follows:
1   Drain the coolant until it is below the level of the thermostat.
2   Remove the water outlet hose from the thermostat housing.
3   Remove the nuts of the thermostat housing, pull the housing off

and carefully pull the thermostat out.
4   Examine the thermostat for damage. If at room temperature the valve is not closed tightly, the thermostat is defective and a new one should be fitted.
5   To test the thermostat, place it in a pan of water with a thermometer capable of indicating at least 212°F (100°C). Raise the temperature of the water and note the temperature at which the thermostat begins to open and at which it is fully open. Fit a new thermostat if any of the values is seriously outside the specified limits.
6   Refit the thermostat, taking care that it is properly seated. Refit the thermostat housing using a new gasket and apply sealant to both sides of the gasket. All traces of the old gasket and sealant must be removed from the thermostat housing and its mating face before the new gasket is fitted.

10 Water pump - removal and refitting

To dismantle the water pump requires a special puller and also a press. If these are not available it is preferable to fit a new or factory reconditioned water pump

8.3a Radiator fixing bolt

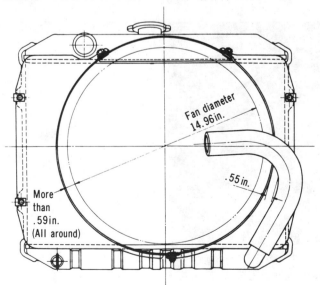

Fig. 2.9. Shroud-to-fan clearance and shroud-to-lower hose clearance

Fan diameter 14.96 in.

.55 in.

More than .59 in. (All around)

Fig. 8.3b Removing the radiator

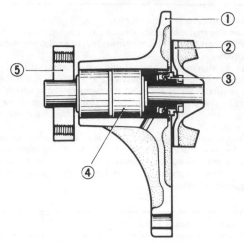

Fig. 2.10. Water pump construction (4G32)

1	Pump body	4	Shaft assembly
2	Impeller	5	Bracket
3	Seal unit		

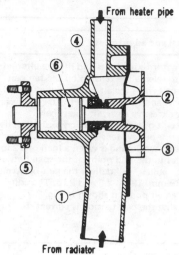

Fig. 2.11. Water pump construction (4G52)

1	Water pump body	4	Seal unit
2	Impeller	5	Pulley bracket
3	Water pump plate	6	Shaft assembly

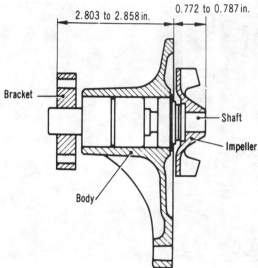

Fig. 2.12. Impeller press-in position (4G32)

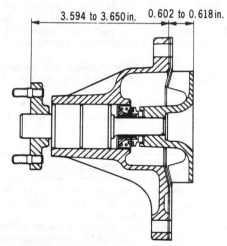

Fig. 2.13. Impeller press-in position (4G52)

10.9 Fitting the water pump

1   Drain the cooling system, unclamp and remove the pump hose. On the 2000 cc engine the heater hose must also be removed.

2   Remove the fixing nuts and washers and carefully prise off the pump. On the 2000 cc engine where the water pump is integral with the timing chain cover, there is a water pump plate between the pump body and the timing chain cover (Fig. 2.11). Care must be taken to remove the pump so that this plate is not damaged and its gasket remains intact. If the gasket is damaged, it can only be renewed if the impeller is removed

3   To dismantle the pump, pull off the impeller using a suitable puller.

4   Remove the seal assembly by prising it out with a screwdriver.

5   Heat the pump body in boiling water and push out the shaft assembly, using a press. If the pump is cold, a force of at least a ton is required to press out the shaft assembly.

6   Check the parts for damage or excessive wear and renew where necessary. The bearings are grease packed and sealed for life and do not require any other lubrication. If the bearings are worn, or the pump shaft does not rotate freely and smoothly, renew the shaft assembly.

7   To reassemble, heat the pump body in boiling water and press in the pump shaft assembly until the end face of the bearing is flush with the pump body (Fig. 2.12 and 2.13).

8   Fit new seals to both the body and impeller sides then press the impeller on until the shaft is flush with the end of the impeller bore. Check that the distances between the body end face and the shaft end face are correct (Figs. 2.12 and 2.13). On the 4G52 engine, the water pump plate and gasket must be fitted before the impeller is pressed on.

9   Using new gaskets, coated on both sides with a jointing compound, refit the pump (photo) and tighten the fixing bolts to a torque wrench setting of 15 lbf ft (2.1 kgf m).

11 Fault diagnosis - cooling system

Symptom	Reason/s
Coolant loss	Faulty or incorrect radiator pressure cap.
	Split hose or leaking hose joint.
	Leaking water pump to engine joint.
	Leaking core plug.
	Blown cylinder head gasket.
Overheating	Low coolant level.
	Faulty radiator pressure cap.
	Thermostat failed and stuck shut.
	Drive belt loose, or slipping.
	Ignition timing incorrect.
	Blocked radiator.
	Corroded system.
Cool running	Defective thermostat.
	Outside temperature excessively low.

Chapter 3 Carburation; fuel, exhaust and emission control systems

For modifications, and information applicable to later models, see Supplement at end of manual

Contents

Specifications

	Engine model		
	4G32 4G33	4G51 4G52	4G52 G3
Air cleaner	Renewal filter cloth type		
Carburetter			
Type	Stromberg downdraught		Stromberg downdraught
Size	0.83 in, 1.06 in (21 mm, 27 mm)	0.866 in, 1.102 in (22 mm, 28 mm)	0.83 in, 1.06in (21 mm, 27 mm)
Primary main jet	97.5	103.8	97.5
Secondary main jet	185	190	185
Primary pilot jet	60	57.5	60
Secondary pilot jet	60	60	60
Enrichment jet	40 (2 off)	40	40 (2 off)
Choke type	Automatic 4G32 Manual 4G33	Automatic Automatic	Manual Manual
Fuel pump			
Type	Diaphragm (mechanical or electrical)		
Pump pressure (mechanical)	3.7 to 5.1 lb/in^2		
Pump discharge (electrical)	12 cu in (200 cc) in 15 secs		
Fuel tank capacity			
Celeste	9.9 Imp. Gall (11.9 US gal, 45 litres)		
Galant 1600	Sedan, Hardtop 11.2 Imp. gall (13.5 US gall, 51 litres) Estate 9.2 Imp. gall (11.1 US gall, 42 litres)		

Torque wrench settings	lbf ft	kgf m
Fuel pump cap screw	0.5 to 1.6	0.07 to 0.22
Fuel pump body screw	1.4 to 3.6	0.2 to 0.5
Accelerator rod to lever bolt	7 to 11	0.97 to 1.52
Thermal reactor or exhaust manifold	10 to 14	1.4 to 1.9
Vapour check valve	25 to 28	3.5 to 3.9

Fuel check valve ...	...	...	...	...	...	...	...	...	2 to 3	0.27 to 0.52
Front pipe to manifold ...	...	...	...	...	...	...	...	...	11 to 18	1.5 to 2.5
Front pipe bellhousing clamp ...	...	...	...	...	...	...	...	...	14.5 to 21.7	2.2 to 3.4
Main silencer to front pipe ...	...	...	...	...	...	...	..	...	14.5 to 21.7	2.2 to 3.4
Main silencer to tail pipe clamp	...	...	...	...	...	...	..		7.2 to 10.9	1.0 to 1.5

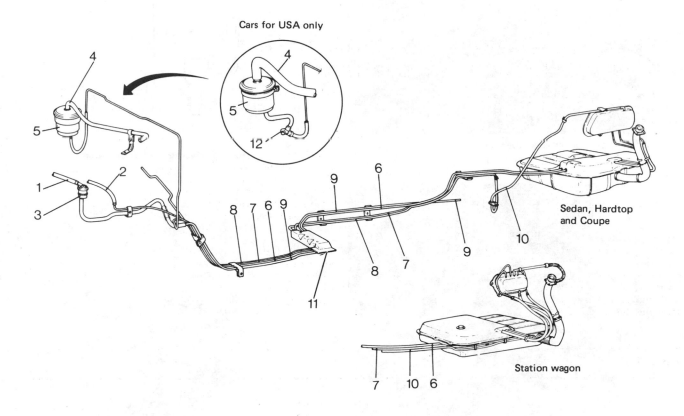

Fig. 3.1. Details of fuel system

1 Fuel hose	4 Purge hose	7 Fuel return pipe	10 Fuel vapour tube
2 Fuel hose	5 Canister	8 Fuel vapour pipe	11 Protector
3 Fuel strainer	6 Fuel main pipe	9 Brake pipe	12 Fuel check valve (USA only)

1 General description

The fuel system consists of a rear mounted fuel tank, a fuel pump, which may be either electrically operated, or driven mechanically from the engine camshaft, a carburetter and all the necessary fuel lines, filters and a fuel gauge.

Cars operating in North America are equipped with emission control systems of varying sorts, dependent on operating territory and production date. These systems are described later in the Chapter.

2 Air cleaner - dismantling, cleaning and reassembly

The air cleaner uses a filter cloth element having a high filtration efficiency and low suction resistance. To the air cleaner body is connected a breather hose, through which blow-back from the engine is sent with the intake air into the combustion chambers. The air cleaner has an adjustable spout, so that during cold weather it can be turned to take in warm air from the exhaust manifold.

1   To remove the filter, undo the clips securing the lid of the cleaner and take the lid off (photo).
2   Remove the element, clean the inside of the casing and at the same time check the casing and sealing washers for signs of damage.
3   If the existing element is reusable, clean it by tapping the element lightly on a flat surface and then blowing compressed air from the inside.

2.1 Removing the air cleaner

2.5 Correct position of air cleaner cover

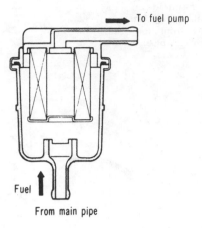

Fig. 3.2. Fuel strainer construction

2.6 Air intake pipe in winter position

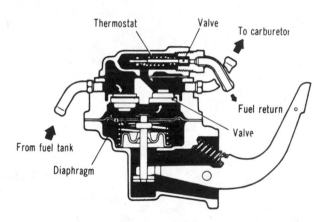

Fig. 3.3. Fuel pump construction (4G32)

3.1 Fuel strainer

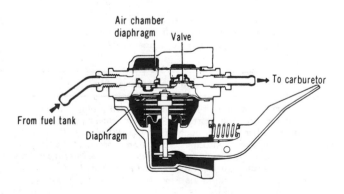

Fig. 3.4. Fuel pump construction (4G52)

4   Fit the element into the cleaner body, making sure that it is properly seated and sealed. If you are reusing an element, ensure that the oil stained part is placed by the engine breather inlet, so that the oil stained area will not spread.

5   Refit the cover, lining up the mating marks on it and refasten the clips (photo).

6   Check that the position of the air intake pipe is drawing in hot air or or cold air as appropriate to the time of year (photo).

3   Fuel strainer - cleaning and refitting

The cartridge type fuel strainer is held by a spring clip (photo) on the side of the engine compartment.

1   Check the fuel strainer for damage and an excessive accumulation of dirt and water. Renew it if it is defective.

2   When there is only a small quantity of water inside, remove the strainer from its clip and with the outlet direction downwards blow compressed air through the fuel inlet pipe (Fig. 3.2).

3   Refit the filter in its clip, or if it has been in service for 12,000 miles fit a new one, then refit the inlet and outlet hoses and tighten their clips.

4   Mechanical fuel pump - description

The mechanical fuel pump is mounted on the left-hand side of the engine (photo) and is driven from the camshaft. The pump is of the diaphragm type, incorporating inlet and outlet valves and as the diaphragm is moved up and down by a rocker arm that is operated by an eccentric on the camshaft, fuel is alternately sucked in and discharged. There are two different models of pump (Figs. 3.3 and 3.4) and the one on the 4G32 engine has an additional valve for fuel return. If the fuel temperature rises above $122^\circ F$, a bimetal operated valve opens and passes excess fuel back to the fuel tank after cooling the accelerator pump area of the carburetter. This reduces the risk of vapour locking.

5   Mechanical pump - removal and refitting

1   Loosen the hose clamps and remove the fuel pump inlet and outlet pipes.

2   Remove the two fixing bolts then lift the pump upwards to disengage the rocker arm from the camshaft lobe and so allow the pump to be withdrawn.

3   Remove the spacer and gasket from the cylinder head.

4   When refitting the pump, fit a new gasket to both sides of the spacer and apply jointing compound to both sides of each gasket.

5   Insert the rocker arm under the camshaft lobe (photo) and then position the pump so that the bolts can be inserted through the pump flange and spacer into the cylinder head. Tighten the bolts to a torque of 20 lbf ft (2.8 kgf m).

6   Fit the fuel hoses to the appropriate nipple, pushing the hoses on as far as possible, then clamp them firmly with a hose clip.

7   Start the engine and check for fuel leaks.

6   Mechanical pump - dismantling and reassembly

1   Remove the cap and the diaphragm from the upper body and then separate the upper body from the lower body. The two valves are sealed into the body and no attempt should be made to remove them. On pumps with a fuel return line, no attempt should be made to remove the bimetal valve.

2   Pull out the rocker arm pivot pin and dismantle the pump into the diaphragm assembly, seal, rocker arm, diaphragm spring and rocker arm spring.

3   Examine the diaphragm carefully and look for cracks, tears or porosity. Check the valves for full movement and correct seating. Examine the end of the rocker arm which bears against the camshaft lobe and check that it is not damaged, or worn excessively. Check the pivot pin hole and pivot pin for wear. Look for signs of cracking in the pump body.

4   Reassemble the pump in the reverse order, pushing the centre of the diaphragm down when inserting it and making sure that it is not

creased or folded.

5   After refitting the cap, screw on the cap nut to a torque of 6 to 9 lbf inches (7 to 22 kgf cms). It is important that the cap is not overtightened.

6   After reassembly, move the rocker arm up and down to ensure that it moves freely and smoothly with a full range of movement.

7   Mechanical pump - testing

1   Remove the outlet hose from the pump and connect the pump outlet to a pressure gauge having a range of 0 to 10 lb/in^2. Spin the engine with the starter motor and check pump pressure which should be between 3.7 and 5.1 lb/in^2.

2   After checking the pressure, carefully inspect the pump to make sure that there are no fuel leaks.

8   Electric fuel pump - description

The electric fuel pump (Fig. 3.5) is either mounted in the

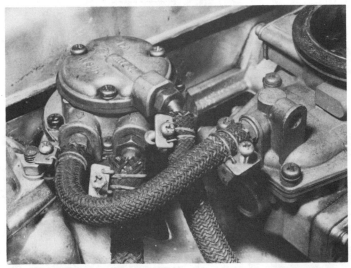

4.1. Fuel pump and pipes

5.5 Refitting the fuel pump

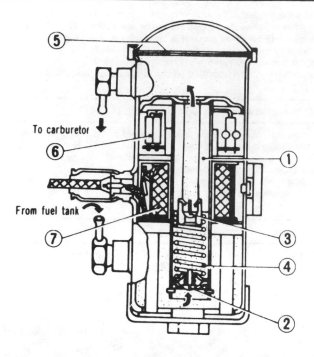

Fig. 3.5. Electric fuel pump

1	Plunger	5	Diaphragm
2	Suction valve	6	Oscillator
3	Delivery valve	7	Electromagnetic coil
4	Spring		

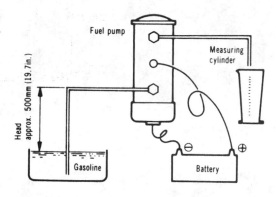

Fig. 3.6. Testing the fuel pump

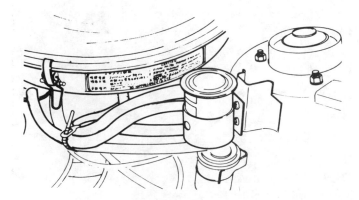

Fig. 3.7. Vapour separator position

luggage compartment or under the left-hand side rear wing. It is a sealed unit and cannot be dismantled. The pump is of the diaphragm type, incorporating inlet and outlet valves and as the diaphragm moves up and down, fuel is alternately sucked in and discharged. Movement of the diaphragm is produced by a solenoid which is energised in pulses by a transistor oscillator. When the solenoid is energised, the plunger pulls the diaphragm down against the action of a spring. When current is switched off, the spring pushes the plunger and diaphragm upwards. A fuel control relay is fitted on the left-hand side of the engine compartment (beside the ignition coil), so that the fuel supply stops if the engine stalls, even though the ignition switch is in the ON position.

9 Electric fuel pump - removal and refitting

1 Disconnect the electrical connections, unclamp the two hoses and pull the fuel hoses off.
2 Remove the two fixing screws securing the pump mounting bracket to the vehicle and remove the pump.
3 When refitting the pump, fit the fuel hoses on the appropriate nipples, pushing the hoses on as far as possible, then clamp them firmly with a hose clip.
4 Reconnect the two electric supply wires, making sure that the connections are tight and that the positive and earth leads are connected to the correct terminals.

10 Electric fuel pump - testing

1 Check that when the ignition is switched ON, the pump produces a clicking noise. If this is so, the pump mechanism is functioning.
2 If no sound is heard, connect a 12V battery directly to the fuel pump, taking care to connect the positive terminal of the pump to the correct terminal on the battery. If the pump produces a clicking noise, its mechanism is operating, so check for faulty wiring or a blown fuse.
3 If the normal operating sound is heard, but there is no delivery, or low delivery, remove the pump and test it as shown in Fig. 3.6. If the pump delivers more than 12 cu in (200 cc) in 15 seconds the pump is in a good operating condition. If the pump is functioning correctly, check for blocked fuel hoses or clogged fuel strainer.
4 If the pump output is not satisfactory, fit a new pump.

11 Electric fuel pump - precautions

1 Handle the pump carefully and do not drop it.
2 Never connect the electrical supply the wrong way round.
3 Make sure that the electrical connections are clean and firm.
4 Do not operate the pump without a good fuel supply to the inlet hose.
5 Do not apply a voltage higher than the rated operating voltage.
6 Make sure that the pump is not fitted in a place which it will overheat. The pump temperature must not exceed 100°C (212°F).

12 Vapour separator - fitting and inspection

The vapour separator (Fig. 3.7) is only fitted on cars for the USA market. Fuel from the fuel pump passes into the vapour separator through a nipple roughly in the middle of it and flows out to the carburetter through a nipple at the bottom. Vapour separated from the fuel passes to the upper part of the separator and out through the top nipple. After being passed to the accelerator pump to cool it, the vapour is returned to the fuel tank.
1 Always fit the vapour separator with the red mark uppermost. (Fig. 3.8).
2 To eliminate the possibility of error, the nipples are colour coded and the two different systems of marking used are down in Fig. 3.8. The correct connections are as follows:

Top (Red) nipple on separator to   *nipple at the bottom of the accelerator pump on carburetter (with red mark)*

Middle (Green) nipple on separator to   *nipple at outlet of fuel pump (with green mark)*

Bottom (Yellow) nipple on separator to   *nipple at inlet of carburetter (with yellow or no colour mark)*

3 Push the hoses as far as possible on to the nipples and then clamp firmly with a hose clip. Check each hose for signs of cracking and damage and renew if necessary.

4 Start the engine and make a careful check that there is no leakage from any joint.

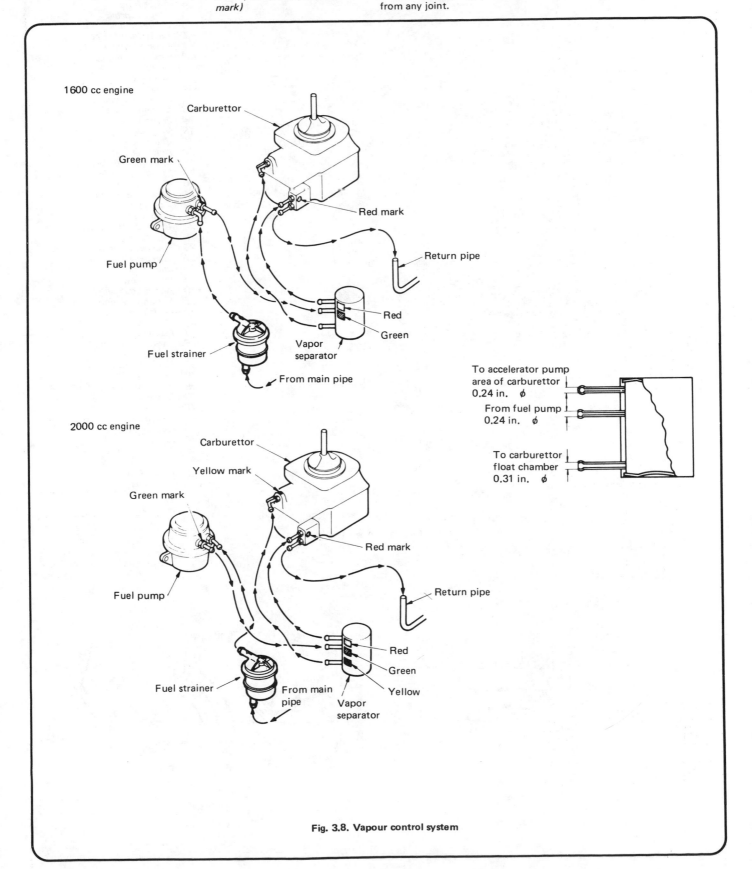

Fig. 3.8. Vapour control system

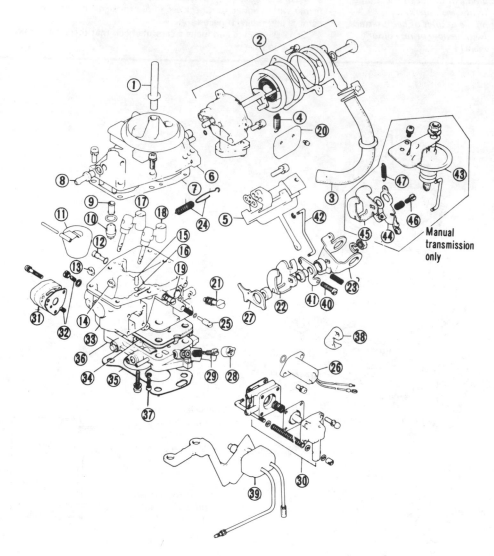

1 Stud
2 Auto-choke
3 Water hose
4 Return spring
5 Depression chamber
6 Float chamber cover
7 Float chamber packing
8 Fuel inlet nipple
9 Filter
10 Needle valve
11 Float
12 Secondary pilot jet
13 Secondary main jet
14 Primary main jet
15 Valve weight
16 Check valve
17 Inner secondary venturi
18 Inner primary venturi
19 Primary pilot jet
20 Choke valve
21 Throttle stop screw
22 Abatement plate
23 Throttle lever
24 Throttle return spring
25 Bypass screw
26 Fuel cut solenoid
27 Intermediate lever
28 Idle limiter
29 Pilot screw
30 Accelerator pump
31 Enrichment body assy
32 Enrichment jet
33 Main body
34 Insulator
35 Carburetter gasket
36 Throttle body
37 Throttle stop screw
38 Lever (A/T)
39 Kickdown switch (A/T)
40 Screw
41 Lever
42 Choke rod
43 Dash pot
44 Lever
45 Abatement plate
46 Adjusting screw
47 Lever spring

Manual
transmission
only

Fig. 3.9. Exploded view of carburetter

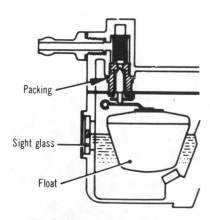

Packing

Sight glass

Float

Fig. 3.10. Float level adjustment

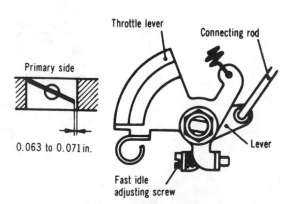

Throttle lever

Connecting rod

Primary side

0.063 to 0.071 in.

Fast idle
adjusting screw

Lever

Fig. 3.11. Fast-idle adjustment

13 Carburettor - general description

The carburetter is of the dual barrel downdraft type and has four basic fuel metering systems. The slow running system provides a mixture for idling and low speed operation; the main system gives optimum mixture for economical cruising conditions; the accelerator pump provides additional fuel during acceleration and the enrichment system provides a richer mixture when high power output is required.

In addition to these four basic systems, there is a fuel inlet system which provides a constant supply of fuel to the metering systems and a choke to enrich the mixture to make starting and cold running easier. The choke may be manual or automatic, depending upon the model of the vehicle. Engines with manual transmission are equipped with a dashpot to retard the return of the throttle to the idling position.

14 Carburetter - inlet system adjustment

There is a sight glass (Fig. 3.10) in the float chamber and the level of fuel should be within the limits of the level mark. If it is necessary to adjust the level:
1   Remove the air cleaner.
2   Disconnect the fuel inlet pipe and remove the screws securing the float chamber cover. Remove the float chamber cover and gasket.
3   Pull out the float pivot pin and remove the float and jet needle.
4   Unscrew and remove the needle valve and adjust the number of packing washers to achieve the correct level. A sheet of needle valve packing washers are 0.039 in (0.99 mm) thick. Adding or removing a sheet of packing washers will change the float level by 0.118 in (2.997 mm).

15 Carburetter - fast-idle adjustment

1   Start the engine and close the choke valve fully.
2   Check the engine speed and if it is in excess of 2000 rpm, turn the fast idle screw (Fig. 3.11) until the engine speed falls to 2000 rpm or less.

16 Carburetter - idle speed and mixture adjustments

For twin carburetter models see Chapter 13, Section 6.
1   Bring the engine to operating temperature. The ignition timing and valve clearances must be correct. Automatic transmission models must be in 'N'.
2   When so equipped, disconnect the reed valve air hose and plug the valve (Fig. 3.12 or 3.13).
3   Turn the idle speed adjusting screw to achieve the specified idle speed (Chapter 1 Specifications).
4   Connect an exhaust gas analyser (if available) and turn the mixture adjusting screw to achieve a CO level of $2.5 \pm 1\%$. If no analyser is available, turn the screw to obtain the highest possible idle speed, then turn the screw clockwise from this point until the speed just starts to drop. The mixture adjusting screw may be protected by a limiter cap (Fig. 3.15) or other tamperproof device which will have to be removed for adjustment - see Chapter 13, Section 6, paragraphs 50 and 51.
5   Readjust the idle speed if necessary.
6   Run the engine at around 2500 rpm for half a minute, then allow it to idle again and recheck the speed and mixture adjustments.
7   Stop the engine, disconnect any test gear and fit new tamperproof caps if required. Reconnect the reed valve air hose, if applicable.

17 Carburetter - dashpot adjustment

This adjustment is only applicable on US models with manual transmission.
1   After completing the idling adjustments push up the lower end of the dashpot rod until it comes up against its stop and then check the engine speed to see if it is between 1500 and 2000 rpm.
2   Release the pushrod quickly and check the time which elapses before the engine speed drops to 900 rpm. This should be within the

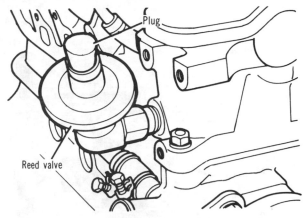

Fig. 3.12. Removing the air hose - 1600 cc engine

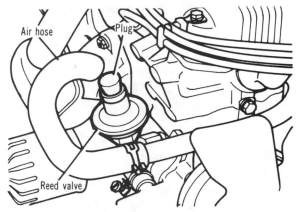

Fig. 3.13. Removing the air hose - 2000 cc engine

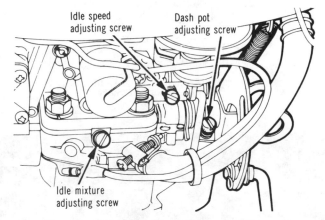

Fig. 3.14. Carburetter adjusting screws

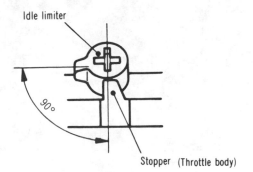

Fig. 3.15. Adjusting the idle limiter

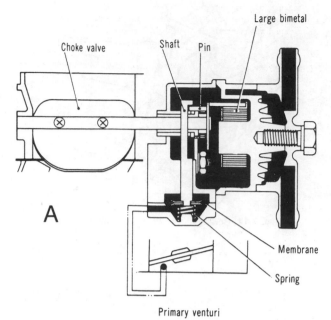

Choke valve   Shaft   Pin   Large bimetal

Membrane

Spring

A

Primary venturi

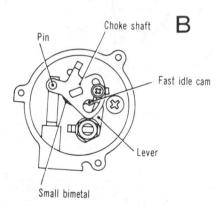

B

Pin   Choke shaft

Fast idle cam

Lever

Small bimetal

Fig. 3.16. Automatic choke

19.7 Accelerator pump cover

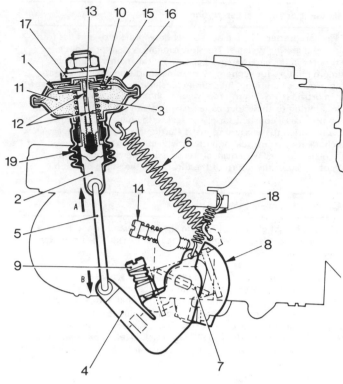

Fig. 3.17. Dash pot construction

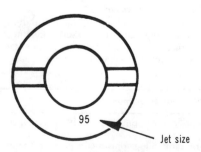

1   Diaphragm
2   Rod
3   Diaphragm spring
4   Lever
5   Link
6   Throttle return spring
7   Throttle valve
8   Abatement plate
9   Adjusting screw
10   Diaphragm chamber
11   Diaphragm chamber
12   Jet
13   Needle screw
14   Speed adjusting screw
15   Check valve
16   Dash pot body
17   Bracket
18   Lever spring
19   Cover

95

Jet size

Fig. 3.18. Jet identification marking

range 1.5 to 3.5 seconds.

If necessary, adjust the dashpot adjusting screw to achieve the correct timing (Fig. 3.17).

18 Carburetter - removal and refitting

1 Remove the air cleaner breather hose and undo the clips, or ring nuts, of the air cleaner cover. Remove the cover and the element. Remove the fixing bolts of the air cleaner case and remove the case.
2 Disconnect the accelerator cable, the choke cable (manual choke models) at the carburetter, then remove the vacuum and fuel pipes.
3 Place a clean container underneath the cylinder block drain plug (Chapter 2, Section 2), remove the plug and drain the coolant. Remove the hose between the carburetter and the cylinder head.
4 Remove the nuts from the carburetter mounting flange and remove the carburetter.
5 Refit the carburetter in the reverse order, using a new gasket between the carburetter flange and the intake manifold. Apply jointing compound to both faces of the gasket before fitting it

19 Carburetter - dismantling, cleaning and reassembly

The dismantling and reassembly of a carburetter requires clean conditions and systematic methods of working. Make sure that all spanners and screwdrivers are a good fit, so that they do not damage the components and use only lint-free cleaning cloths. As each unit of the carburetter is dismantled, keep all its parts together, preferably in an individual container and lay all the parts out in the exact position and order in which they were removed. The following procedure relates specifically to a carburetter with automatic choke, but the method for a manual choke carburetter does not differ significantly.
1 Wash the outside of the carburetter with petrol and dry it with a clean lint-free cloth.
2 Remove the throttle return spring and the intermediate return spring, disconnect the choke rod and the depression chamber rod end and disconnect the coolant hose.
3 Remove the float chamber cover and gasket, then the accelerator pump valve ball and weight. Extract the float pin and remove the float, clip and needle valve. Remove the valve seat, packing washers and filter.
4 Remove the depression chamber and dismantle it into the body, cover, diaphragm and spring.
5 Remove the idling cam assembly of the automatic choke (Fig. 3.16) then the water case and gasket, the bimetal case and plate, then remove the choke valve and shaft, the membrane cover, spring and membrane. Remove the recessed screws and withdraw the automatic choke body. It is not necessary to dismantle the automatic choke assembly.
6 Disconnect the accelerator pump lever rod at the throttle shaft, remove the screws from the throttle body and separate the main body from the throttle body. Remove the gasket and spacer. The pump lever rod nut is factory adjusted and should not be removed.
7 Remove the accelerator pump cover (photo) and remove the spring and the membrane.
8 Remove the enrichment cover, the spring and the valve body. It is not necessary to dismantle the valve body.
9 Remove the main and pilot jets, but do not attempt to remove the inner venturi and do not remove the bypass screw, which is sealed with white paint.
10 Remove the throttle lever nut, throttle lever, collar abutment plate and intermediate lever. When fitted, remove the dashpot fixing screws and dashpot assembly. Do not attempt to dismantle the throttle shaft and valve.
11 Clean all components in clean petrol and blow them dry.
12 Check the carburetter body and the water passages for cracks, sealing or blockage. Check the needle valve seat for wear, the filter for damage and blockage and the jets for damage and blockage. Do not attempt to clean out any jet or air passage with wire. If the dirt cannot be dislodged by blowing, use a nylon bristle or a piece of nylon line.
13 Check each membrane for damage, examine the pilot screw seat for wear of the contact surface, the throttle valve shaft for wear and distortion and the linkage for smoothness of operation.
14 Check the float for damage and leaks, the lip for damage, the float

lever pin locations for wear and the float lever bracket for deformation.
15 Using new packings and gaskets and making sure that they are fitted properly, reassemble, by first fitting the intermediate lever of the throttle body then fitting the thin collar, abutment plate, thick collar and throttle lever onto the primary throttle shaft. Secure them with a nut and spring washer. When a dashpot assembly is fitted it should be refitted at this stage (Fig. 3.17).
16 Adjust the secondary throttle valve stop screw with the throttle in the fully closed position, rotate it a quarter of a turn and secure it with the locknut.
17 Fit the main jets and pilot jets, noting that each jet has an identification mark on its end (Fig. 3.18). The correct jet sizes are given in the Specifications.
18 Fit the enrichment valve, checking that the free length of the spring is nominally 1 in (25 mm) and then fit the accelerator pump and pump cover. The length of the accelerator pump spring is nominally 0.5 in (13 mm).
19 Fit the throttle body and the main body, connect the pump rod end to the throttle shaft, then fit the idle compensator within the float chamber cover. Fit the case of the automatic choke, then the membrane and spring. The free length of the spring should be 1.3 in (33 mm). Fit the choke shaft and valve, taking care to ensure that the valve is the right way round.
20 Ensure that the diaphragm ring fits snugly in the groove in the body then assemble the depression chamber (Fig. 3.19) so that the float chamber joint face and the shaft onto which the nylon bearing is fitted, are parallel and the small diameter end of the bushing is facing outward.
21 Fit the depression chamber to the float chamber cover, then fit the filter and valve seat. Do not overtighten the valve seat because this can cause damage to the filter.
22 Fit the needle valve and retaining clip, then fit the float and its support pin. Fit the accelerator pump ball and weight, then fit the float chamber cover.
23 Connect the bent section of the choke connecting rod and with the fast idle cam engaged in the third stage turn the fast idle adjusting screw so that the clearance between the throttle valve and bore is 0.063 to 0.071 in (1.6 to 1.8 mm)
24 Insert the choke ring in the bimetal and tighten with the red line on the case aligned with the highest part of the automatic choke case (Fig. 3.20). Set the choke valve to a fully closed position at an ambient temperature of about 73°F.

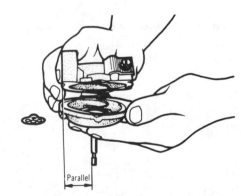

Fig. 3.19. Reassembling the depression chamber

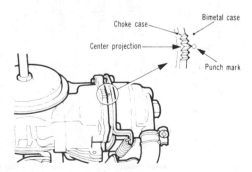

Fig. 3.20. Mating mark of automatic choke

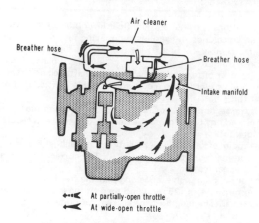

Fig. 3.21. Crankcase ventilation system

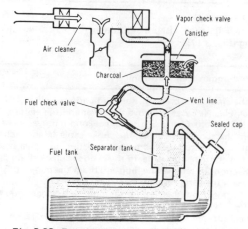

Fig. 3.22. Evaporation control system schematic

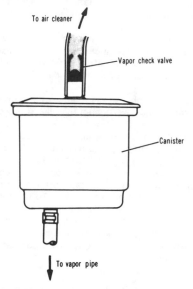

Fig. 3.23. Construction of the filter canister

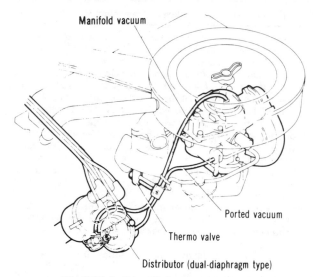

Fig. 3.24. Ignition timing control system

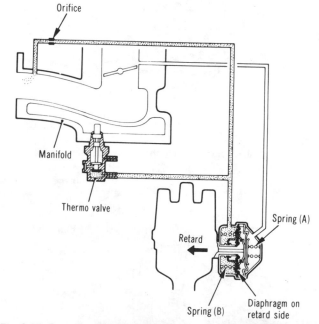

Fig. 3.25. Operation of ignition timing control system (during normal idling)

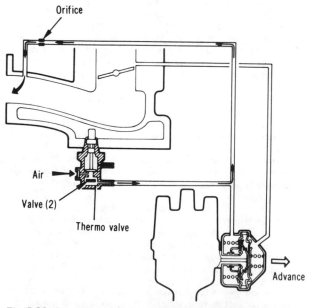

Fig. 3.26. Operation of ignition timing control system (at high temperature)

20 Emission control systems - description and application

All cars are fitted with a positive crankcase ventilation system (Fig. 3.21) and a variety of other systems may be fitted to cars which operate in countries whose anti-pollution laws require them. These systems are:

a) *Evaporation control,* in which a canister of activated charcoal is fitted between the fuel tank and the air cleaner (Fig. 3.22). Petrol vapours are directed to the canister (Fig. 3.23) for temporary storage and while the engine is running, air is drawn through the canister to purge it and the air vapour mixture is then routed to the combustion chambers through the air cleaner. In cars for the USA, a fuel check valve is fitted, which is closed when the engine is idling, to prevent vapourised fuel entering the air cleaner and giving excessive carbon monoxide emission during idling.

b) *Temperature controlled ignition,* (Figs. 3.25 and 3.26) is fitted to offset the low exhaust gas temperature and consequent incomplete combustion which occurs when the engine is idling, operating at low speeds, is lightly loaded, or decelerating. Under these conditions, ignition timing is retarded. To prevent the engine coolant from over-heating after prolonged periods of idling with retarded ignition and also from periods of overload, or high ambient temperatures, a thermo-valve is fitted. The thermo-valve removes the vacuum from the retard side of the distributor diaphragm, so that spring 'B' (Fig. 3.25) causes the ignition to advance with a consequent increase in engine speed and fan speed until the coolant temperature drops, the thermo-valve restores the vacuum on the retard side of the diaphragm and the ignition is retarded again. On cars fitted with automatic transmission the increase in idling speed produced by temperature controlled ignition is prevented by an idle speed control system (Fig. 3.27). This is done to prevent creep during idling and to reduce shift shock. A vacuum motor is fitted to the throttle lever and is controlled by the pressure output of the thermo-valve. When the thermo valve is in the normal position, ie. closed, manifold vacuum is applied to the vacuum motor, and the vacuum motor pulls the throttle in opposition to the throttle spring against the stop screw 'C'. When the thermo-valve opens and vents to the atmosphere, the vacuum motor spring pushes the rod downwards and this and the throttle spring allow the throttle to close slightly until limited by the stop screw 'B'.

c) *Heated air intake,* is fitted (Fig. 3.28) to prevent the lean mixture and lowered engine output which results from the incomplete vaporisation of fuel and cold air. A cowl is fitted over the thermal reactor and is joined by a duct to the air intake. A flap valve, controlled by a bimetallic element, ensures that all intake air is sucked over the thermal reactor if the under bonnet temperature is less than 41°F. When the underbonnet air temperature exceeds 100°F, the valve prevents any further air from being drawn over the thermal reactor and air flows directly to the air cleaner.

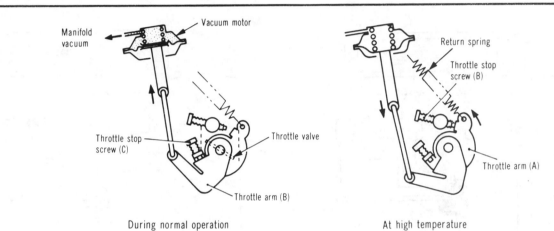

During normal operation   At high temperature

Fig. 3.27. Operation of throttle adjuster

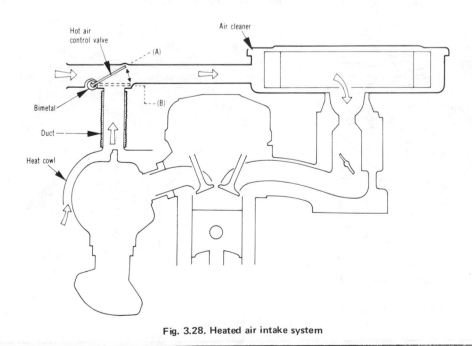

Fig. 3.28. Heated air intake system

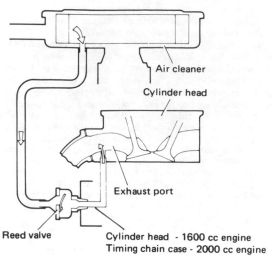

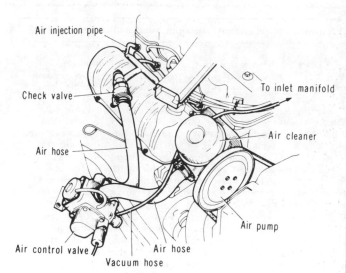

Fig. 3.29. Secondary air supply system

Fig. 3.30. Air injection system

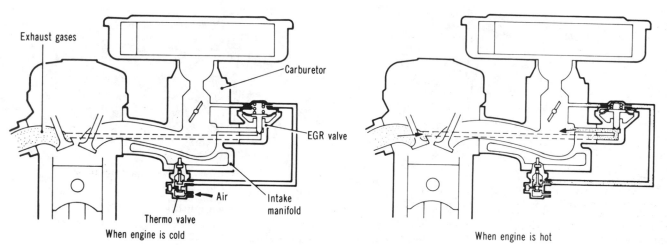

Fig. 3.31. Exhaust Gas Recirculation System

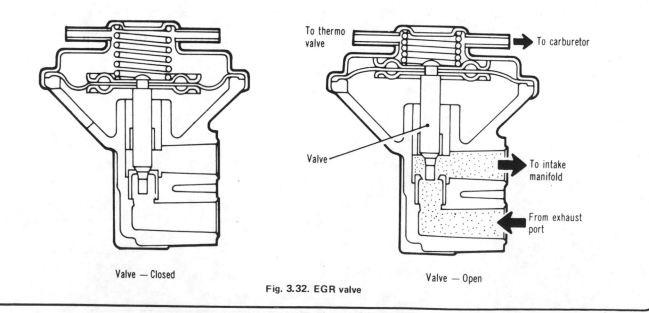

Fig. 3.32. EGR valve

d) *Secondary air supply,* is required for cars for California, which have a thermal reactor. Air for the further combustion of the exhaust gases is drawn from the air intake, via a reed valve and delivered to the exhaust ports (Fig. 3.29). The reed valve is operated by the pulsation of the exhaust port pressure.

Models from 1975 are fitted with an air pump driven from the crankshaft pulley (Fig. 3.30). Air from the pump is fed to the reactor through a solenoid valve which has electrical control circuits to control the quantity of secondary air under different operating conditions.

e) *Exhaust gas recirculation,* dilutes the air fuel mixture in the engine cylinders in order to reduce the oxides of nitrogen in the exhaust gases. The quantity of exhaust gas being used is controlled by a valve which operates according to engine temperature. When the engine is cold, the level of oxides of nitrogen in the exhaust is low and there is no recirculation. When engine temperature rises above 131ºF, the thermo-valve connects manifold suction to the EGR (Fig. 3.32) valve which opens and allows recirculation. During engine idling, manifold vacuum is too low to keep the EGR valve open, even though the thermo-valve is above its operating temperature.

f) *Thermal reactor,* applicable only to cars for California. This consists of an insulated core which always remains hot because of the insulation and the passage of the exhaust gases. Secondary air (paragraph d) is fed into the core to produce further oxidation of carbon monoxide and hydrocarbons in the exhaust gas.

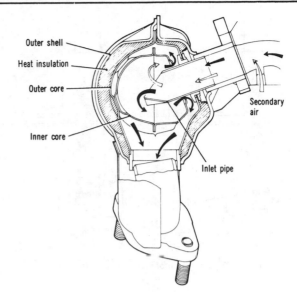

Fig. 3.33. Thermal reactor

---

21 Emission control systems - maintenance and testing

Positive crankcase ventilation

1 Check the crankcase ventilation breather hoses and jet to make sure that they are not blocked and clean if necessary. An indication of poor crankcase breathing is a build up of deposits inside the rocker box cover.

Evaporation control

2 Remove the clamp on the canister side of the hose leading to the air cleaner, remove the clamp coupling on the canister side of the vapour hose from the separator tank, then remove the canister band tightening bolt.
3 Check that the lines and canister ports are free of obstruction. Clean the canister (Fig. 3.34) every 15000 miles and renew the filter every 30000 miles. When renewing the filter, also renew the hoses to it.
4 Inspect the vapour check valve for blockage and if necessary wash it in petrol so that it moves freely.

Temperature controlled ignition

5 The construction, operation and checking of the distributor is given in Chapter 4.
6 To check the thermo-valve on 1974 models, pull off the vacuum hoses and connect two short pieces of plastic hose to the ports. Test the valve operation by applying mouth pressure to the ends of the tubes.

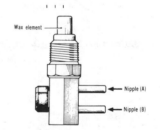

Fig. 3.34. Cleaning the canister cover

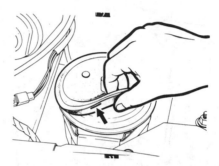

Fig. 3.35. Checking the thermo valve

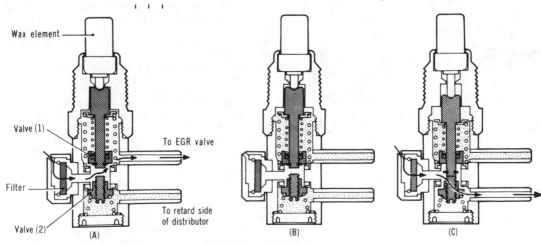

Fig. 3.36. Operation of thermo valve (USA)

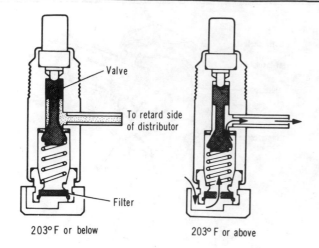

Fig. 3.37. Operation of thermo valve (Canada)

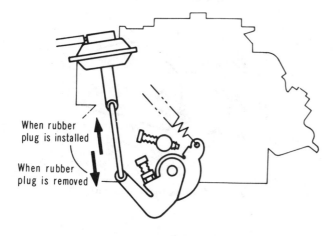

Fig. 3.38. Checking the throttle adjuster

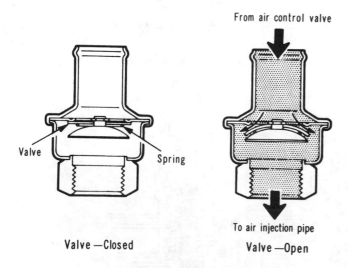

Fig. 3.39. Exhaust check valve

7   With the valve in place on the engine, check that the valve is closed when the engine is cold (below 140°F). Run the engine and check that the valve opens when the engine temperature exceeds 140°F.

8   On post 1974 models, drain the engine coolant (Chapter 2, Section 2) and then pull off the vacuum hoses and remove the valve.

9   On USA models, allow the valve to cool to room temperature. Fit a piece of plastic tubing to each port and check that by blowing into the tubes, nipple 'A' allows air to pass without resistance and nipple 'B' does not allow air to pass. Immerse the heat sensing element in water at 140°F for at least 60 seconds and check that neither nipple 'A' or 'B' allow air to pass. Finally, immerse the valve in boiling water for at least 60 seconds and check that nipple 'A' does not allow air to pass and 'B' allows unrestricted passage.

10 On Canadian models, remove the valve from the engine and allow it to cool. Blow air into the nipple and check that the valve is closed. Immerse the heat sensing element in boiling water at least 60 seconds and check that the nipple allows an unrestricted passage of air.

11 In all cases, check when refitting the valve that the vacuum hoses are free from blockage and are in good condition.

Throttle control

12 On cars fitted with automatic transmission which have a throttle adjuster, check the vacuum motor diaphragm for damage and the linkage for smooth operation, oiling the linkage if necessary.

13 With the engine idling, remove the rubber plug on the retard side of the distributor vacuum unit and check that the vacuum motor rod lowers and the throttle closes (Fig. 3.38). Refit the plug and check that the vacuum motor rod rises and the throttle opens.

Heated air intake

14 When the engine is cool, check that the hot air control valve has closed the cold air intake. Run the engine until the under bonnet temperature exceeds 108°F and check that the heated air intake is fully closed. Check the air cleaner cover and case for damage and distortion and renew if necessary. The air control valve is integral with the air cleaner case and the case must be renewed if the valve is faulty. Check that the air cleaner element is not excessively dirty and that the gaskets and sealing washers are in good condition.

Secondary air supply - reed valve system

15 Check the reed valve by starting the engine and leaving it to run at idling speed. Disconnect the air hose from the reed valve and place a hand tightly over the intake port of the reed valve. If suction can be felt the reed valve is satisfactory.

Secondary air supply - air pump system

16 Disconnect the air hose on the discharge side of the air pump and with the engine idling, ensure that the pump is discharging air. Renew the pump if it is defective. Inspect all hoses for signs of deterioration and damage, renew if necessary and ensure that all hose clips are tight. It is important not to allow dirt or oil to get into the air pump.

17 Check the air valve by disconnecting the air hose and running the engine at idling speed to see that air is being discharged from the outlet pipe, but not from the relief outlet.

18 Check the operation of the solenoid valve by ensuring that the solenoid is energised when the engine is switched ON. Remove the air hose on the discharge side and with the engine running at 3000 rpm, disconnect the solenoid cable coupling. If air is discharged only from the relief outlet when the solenoid is disconnected, the valve is satisfactory. Reconnect the cable coupling and confirm that the air discharge from the relief outlet ceases.

19 The exhaust check valve (Fig. 3.39) prevents exhaust gases from flowing back into the air control and air pump. Remove the air hose from the check valve and race the engine to see if there are any signs of exhaust blow back. If there are none, the valve is satisfactory. Check the condition of the air hose and then reconnect it.

Exhaust gas recirculation

20 Checking the thermo-valve is described in paragraphs 7 to 10 of this Section. To check the EGR valve, warm the engine up until the coolant temperature is 176°F, then set the engine speed to 3000 to 3200 rpm. Disconnect the vacuum hose to the valve (Fig. 3.32) and check that the diaphragm lowers and closes the valve. Reconnect the vacuum hose and check that the diaphragm rises and allows exhaust gas to recirculate. If these conditions are confirmed, the valve is satisfactory. After completing the checks, re-set the EGR warning

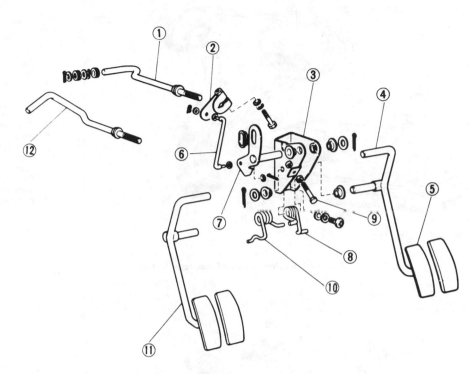

Fig. 3.40. Accelerator pedal components

1	Accelerator rod, front	4	Accelerator arm	7	Lever (B)	10	* Spring
2	Lever (A)	5	Accelerator pedal	8	Spring	11	* Accelerator arm
3	Accelerator arm support	6	Rod	9	Adjusting bolt	12	** Accelerator rod, front

Parts for a vehicle with automatic transmission
**Parts for 2000 cc engine*

light (Chapter 10, Section 35).

Thermal reactor
21 The thermal reactor cannot be dismantled and the only checks which can be made are to look for damage and listen for any abnormal noise. Check the flanges for distortion and gas leakage and renew the reactor if it is in any way suspect.

22 Accelerator pedal - removal and refitting

1 Loosen the locking bolt of lever 'A' (Fig. 3.40) and pull the lever from the accelerator rod.
2 Remove the two fixing bolts of the accelerator arm support and withdraw the assembly.
3 Remove the accelerator arm split pin and withdraw the arm.
4 When refitting the pedal support to the body, apply a sealant to the threaded holes. Reconnect rod 'A' and tighten the accelerator rod to lever bolt to a torque wrench setting of 11 - 14 lbf ft (1.5 to 1.9 kgf m).

23 Accelerator pedal - adjustment

1 With the carburetter throttle valve fully closed, slide the front end of lever 'A' over the accelerator rod until the rod end is 3/8 in (9.53 mm) clear of the lever as shown (Fig. 3.41).
2 When the engine is warm, turn lever 'A' until the prescribed clearance exists between it and its stop, then tighten the accelerator rod to lever bolt to a torque wrench setting of 11 to 14 lbf ft (1.5 to 1.9 kgf m).

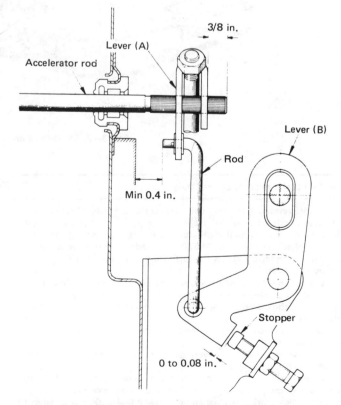

Fig. 3.41. Adjusting the accelerator rod

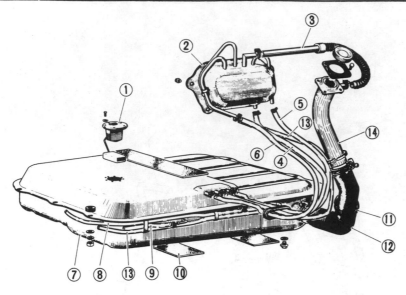

1	Fuel gauge unit
2	Separator tank
3	Breather tube
4	Fuel tube
5	Fuel tube
6	Fuel tube
7	Fuel tank
8	Fuel tube
9	Fuel return tube
10	Pad
11	Grommet
12	Fuel tank hose
13	Vapour tube
14	Filler neck

Fig. 3.42. Exploded view of fuel tank (estate)

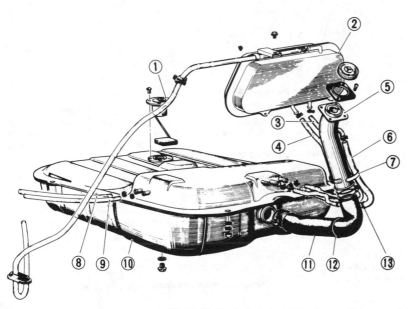

1	Fuel gauge unit
2	Separator tank
3	Fuel tube
4	Fuel tube
5	Filler neck
6	Breather tube
7	Clip band
8	Fuel main hose
9	Fuel return hose
10	Fuel tank
11	Fuel tank hose
12	Grommet
13	Grommet

Fig. 3.43. Exploded view of fuel tank (Saloon and Coupe)

24 Fuel tank - removal and refitting

Before removing the fuel tank reduce the quantity of fuel in it as much as possible by normal usage.

1 With the car in a well ventilated place, free from naked lights or sources of sparking, remove the battery leads, then remove the drain plug from the tank and run the fuel into a metal container with a vapour-tight cap.

2 Loosen the clamps of the main and return fuel hoses (Figs. 3.42 and 3.43) then disconnect the hoses from the fuel tank.

3 Loosen the clamps at the side of the separator tank and remove the vents lines.

4 Loosen the hose clamp on the side of the tank and pull off the filler hose.

5 Remove the rear floor covering and disconnect the fuel tank gauge from the wiring harness.

6 Remove the fuel tank mounting bolts, lower the tank sufficiently to unclamp and pull off the vent lines and then remove the tank.

Caution: Never bring any naked light near a fuel tank, nor attempt to solder or weld it unless it has been steamed out for at least two hours.

7 When fitting the tank, check that the fuel pipes are free from cracks, damage and corrosion.

8 Ensure that the main and return hoses and the vent lines are connected to their outlets and that they will not be trapped, kinked or strained. Make sure that all hose clamps are fitted and tightened adequately.

9 Where pipes pass through places in the body, ensure that there is a grommet correctly and securely fitted to the hole.

25 Exhaust system - removal and refitting

The exhaust system should not be removed unless it requires repair, or renewal of part of the system, or the sealing of gas leaks. It is usually easier to remove the entire system, rather than try to take out only part of it and when renewal is required it is often cheaper to have the job done by an exhaust fitting specialist. There are several versions of the exhaust system (Figs. 3.44 and 3.45) which may require variations in the following procedure.

1 With the car over a pit, or with the rear axle supported as high as possible on firmly placed axle stands, loosen the exhaust pipe and

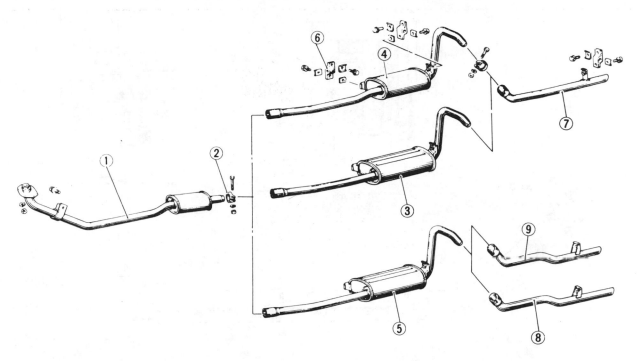

Fig. 3.44. Details of exhaust system (except USA)

1	Front exhaust pipe	4 Main muffler assembly	6 Hanger	8 Tail pipe
2	Clamp	5 Main muffler assembly	7 Tail pipe	9 Tail pipe
3	Main muffler assembly	(station wagon)		

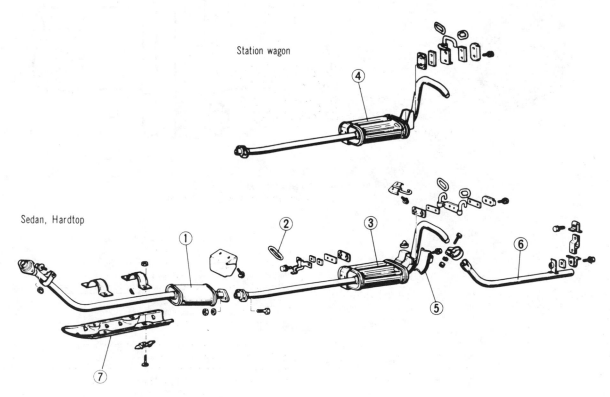

Station wagon

Sedan, Hardtop

Fig. 3.45. Details of exhaust system

1 Front exhaust pipe	4 Main muffler assembly (station wagon)	6 Tail pipe
2 O-ring	5 Heat deflection plate	7 Protector
3 Main muffler assembly (Sedan, hardtop)		

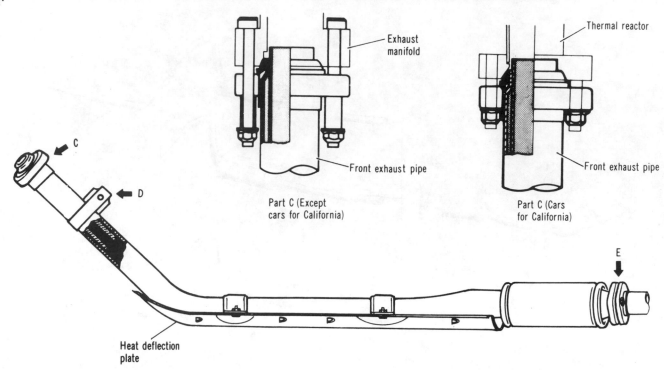

Fig. 3.46. Front exhaust pipe installation

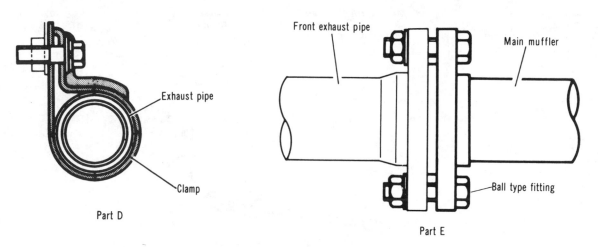

Fig. 3.47. Exhaust system to car body gap

Rear engine support bracket-to-exhaust pipe clearance (a)	0.75 in
Floor-to-main muffler clearance (b)	0.95 in
Floor-to-main muffler pipe clearance (c)	1.3 in
Floor-to-main muffler pipe clearance (d)	1.0 in
Rear skirt panel-to-tail pipe clearance (e)	1.3 in
Floor-to-premuffler clearance (f)	0.8 in
Fuel tank flange-to-tail pipe clearance	1.2 in

main silencer clamps. Exhaust system fixings are usually corroded severely and should be saturated with an anti-corrosion fluid before any attempt to undo them is made.

2 Remove the nuts connecting the exhaust manifold to the exhaust pipe (photo), then remove the bellhousing exhaust pipe clamp bolt.

3 Remove the main silencer to tail pipe clamp bolt and the tail pipe hanger bolt.

4 Remove the exhaust pipe to main silencer clamp bolt (photo).

5 Remove the main silencer hanger bolt and lower the silencer.

6 If the joints in the system can be pulled apart, separate the front pipe, main silencer and tail pipe and remove separately. Otherwise remove the assembly, saturate the joints with an anti-corrosion fluid and separate the system when this has taken effect.

7 When refitting the system, apply a sealer such as Three Bond TBX-383M to the inside and outside surfaces of the connecting ends of each exhaust system section and insert the pipes as deep as the

punch mark (Fig. 3.48).

8 Fit the system with all clamp bolts loose and temporarily secure it on the main silencer hanger, tail pipe hanger and bellhousing clamp.

9 Align the front pipe at right angles to the manifold, hold it in this position by tightening the bellhousing clamp, then tighten the nuts of the front pipe to manifold joint. The nuts should be tightened evenly and alternately.

10 Temporarily tighten the clamp bolts and after making sure that the specified clearance exists between the various parts of the exhaust system and the car body (Fig. 3.47) and that none of the hangers are twisted, tighten the bolts, starting with those at the front of the vehicle and working rearwards.

11 Tighten the clamp bolts and then check that no part of the system is under any strain.

12 After refitting an exhaust system do not race the engine until the sealer is dry, otherwise leaks may occur.

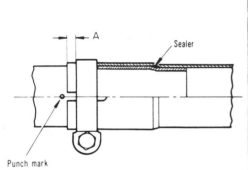

Fig. 3.48. Pipe clamping position

Pipe-to-clamp end clearance (A).   0.24 in

25.2 Exhaust pipe to manifold nuts and bolts

25.4 Main silencer mountings

26 Fault diagnosis - fuel system

Unsatisfactory engine performance and excessive fuel consumption are not necessarily the fault of the fuel system or carburetter. In fact they more commonly occur as a result of ignition faults. Before acting on the fuel system it is necessary to check the ignition system first. Even though a fault may lie in the fuel system it will be difficult to trace unless the ignition is correct.
The table below therefore, assumes that the ignition system is in order.

Symptom	Reason/s
Smell of petrol when engine is stopped	Leaking fuel lines or unions. Leaking fuel tank.
Smell of petrol when engine is idling	Leaking fuel line unions between pump and carburetter. Overflow of fuel from float chamber due to wrong level setting. Ineffective needle valve or punctured float.
Excessive fuel consumption for reasons not covered by leaks or float chamber faults	Worn needle. Sticking needle.
Difficult starting, uneven running, lack of power, cutting out	Incorrectly adjusted carburetter. Float chamber fuel level too low or needle sticking. Fuel pump not delivering sufficient fuel. Intake manifold gaskets leaking, or manifold fractured.

27 Fault diagnosis - emission control system

Symptom	Reason/s
Low CO content of exhaust gases (weak or lean mixture)	Fuel level incorrect in carburetter. Incorrectly adjusted carburetter.
High CO content of exhaust gases (rich mixture)	Incorrectly adjusted carburetter. Choke sticking.

Absorption canister blocked.
Fuel level incorrect in carburetter.
Air injection system fault.

Noisy air injection pump

Belt tension incorrect.
Relief valve faulty.
Diverter faulty,
Check valve faulty.

Chapter 4 Ignition system

For modifications, and information applicable to later models, see Supplement at end of manual

Contents

Specifications

Distributor
Contact breaker gap	0.018 to 0.021 in (0.457 to 0.533 mm)
Dwell angle	49 to 55°
Condenser capacity	0.22 mf

Ignition timing
Static or at idle:	
1597 cc (except GS)	5° BTDC
1995 cc (except GS)	5° BTDC
1597 and 1995 cc (GS)	13° BTDC

Ignition coil
Primary coil resistance	1.26 to 1.59 ohms
Secondary coil resistance	8.670 to 11.730 ohms
External resistor resistance	1.26 to 1.49 ohms
Insulation resistance at 500V	Over 60 megohms

Spark plug types	BPR - 6ES (NGK)
	RN9YC (Champion)
Spark plug gap	0.028 to 0.031 in (0.711 to 0.787 mm)
Firing order	1 - 3 - 4 - 2

Torque wrench setting
	lbf ft	kgf m
Spark plug	14 to 21	1.9 to 3.0

1 General description

In order that the engine may run correctly, the fuel/air charge in the cylinder needs to be ignited at exactly the right moment and the optimum time depends upon engine load and speed.

The ignition system ignites the charge by producing a high voltage electrical discharge between the electrodes of the spark plug. The moment of discharge is automatically varied to suit the engine load and speed.

The system has two main components, the ignition coil (photo), which consists of a low voltage and a high voltage winding which are coupled electromagnetically, and the distributor, (photo) which is a mechanically operated switch, which produces a spark at the required moment and routes it to the appropriate cylinder. During engine starting, the high current required by the starter motor produces a drop in the output voltage of the battery, and the ignition coil is designed to give its optimum output at this voltage and so ensure easy starting. When the engine is running and the battery output voltage rises, a resistor is switched into the ignition coil circuit so that the coil will not be overloaded.

Ignition timing is controlled automatically by a mechanical governor which produces the timing variations required at different engine speeds. A vacuum control (Fig. 4.4), which is operated by the suction of the induction manifold, varies the ignition timing according to engine load. On some engines there is a dual diaphragm

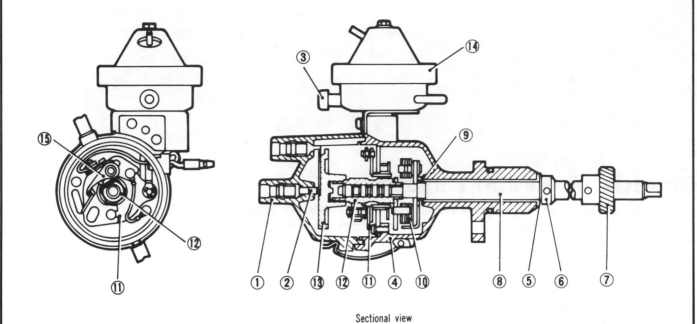

Sectional view

Fig. 4.1. Distributor - for 1600 cc engine

1	Cap	5	Washer	9	Spacer	13	Rotor
2	Contactor	6	Space collar	10	Governor	14	Vacuum controller
3	Rubber cap	7	Gear	11	Breaker assembly	15	Arm support
4	Housing	8	Shaft	12	Cam		

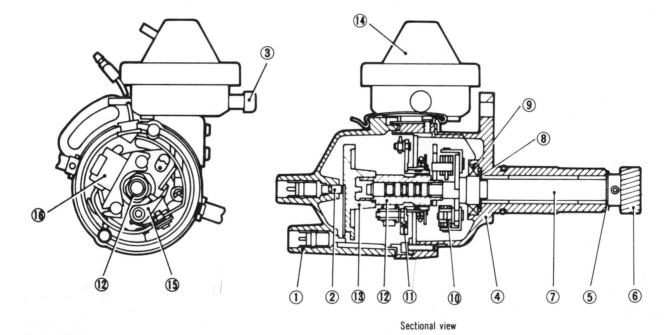

Sectional view

Fig. 4.2. Distributor - for 2000 cc engine

1	Cap	5	Washer	9	Oil seal	13	Rotor
2	Contactor	6	Gear	10	Governor	14	Vacuum controller
3	Rubber cap	7	Shaft	11	Breaker assembly	15	Arm support
4	Housing	8	Washer	12	Cam	16	Condensor

vacuum control to provide the additional facility of retarding the ignition during idling to comply with anti-pollution legislation (Chapter 3, Section 20b).

2 Distributor - removal

1   Using a spanner on the crankshaft pulley nut, rotate the pulley until the notch in its rim is in line with the 'T' mark on the indicator plate (photo), and No1 piston is at TDC on its compression stroke.
2   Disconnect the battery leads, pull the ignition leads off the spark plugs and the high tension lead from the coil, remove the low tension lead from the contact breaker, then unclip and remove the distributor cap.
3   Disconnect the vacuum hose(s) from the vacuum unit(s) taking care to label them if there is more than one.
4   Mark the position of the distributor mounting flange in relation to the cylinder block and note the position of the rotor arm.
5   Remove the distributor fixing screw and pull out the distributor.

3 Distributor - refitting

1600 cc engine

1   Turn the crankshaft until number 1 piston is at top dead centre on its compression stroke and the notch in the rim of the crankshaft pulley is opposite the 'T' mark on the timing plate.

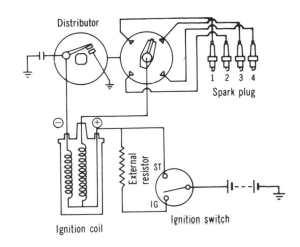

Fig. 4.3. Ignition system circuit

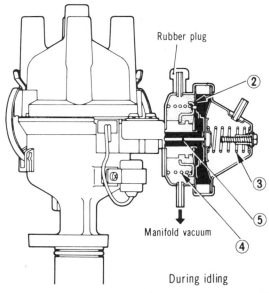

During idling

During ordinary driving

Fig. 4.4. Distributor operation

1   Diaphragm on advance side   2   Diaphragm on retard side   3   Spring (A)   4   Spring (B)
5   Control rod

1.1a Ignition coil and ballast resistor

1.1b Distributor

2.1 Crankshaft pulley timing mark

2   Turn the oil pump drive shaft until the groove is in the position shown in Fig. 4.5. The shaft can be turned easily by a long screwdriver.

3   Align the mating mark on the lower end of the distributor body with that on the spacer as shown in Fig. 4.5 and insert the distributor until it fits snugly into the oil pump groove. If the distributor shaft and oil pump drive do not engage each other, turn the distributor spindle slightly until they are felt to engage.

4   Adjust the contact breaker gap (see Section 6).

5   Fit the distributor cap, reconnect the low tension lead, the spark plug leads and the high tension lead to the ignition coil.

6   Connect the vacuum hose(s) making sure that the hose is on the correct nipple and is pushed on securely.

7   Check the ignition timing as described in Section 7.

2000 cc engine

8   The procedure is identical with that given for the 1600 cc engine, but the distributor mating marks are as shown in Fig. 4.6.

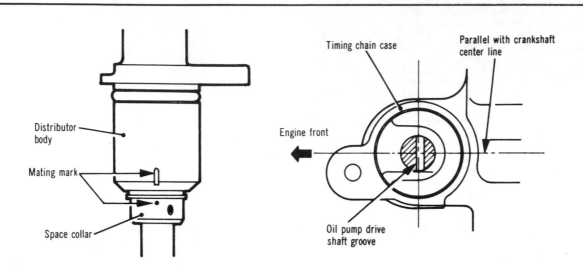

Fig. 4.5. Oil pump shaft groove position

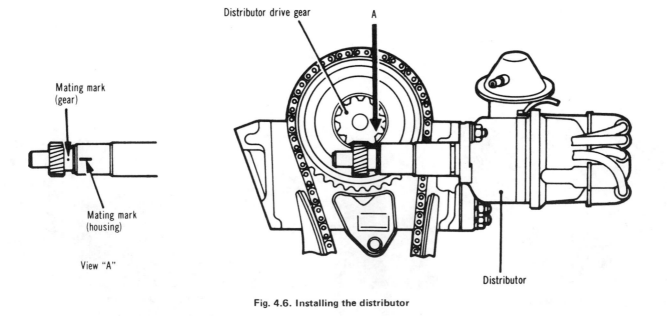

Fig. 4.6. Installing the distributor

4 Distributor - dismantling and reassembly

1 Remove the distributor from the car as described previously and then remove the rotor arm.
2 Remove the circlip from the vacuum control post on the contact breaker baseplate and lift the vacuum control rod off the post.
3 Remove its two fixing screws then take off the vacuum control unit.
4 Remove the low tension lead to the contact breaker and the contact breaker assembly.
5 Remove the contact breaker baseplate assembly.
6 Put mating marks on the gear and shaft, then, using a pin punch, drive out the pin, and remove the gear, collar and washer.
7 From the top of the distributor, pull out the governor and shaft assembly.
8 With the exception of the contact breaker assembly, wash all the parts in petrol and allow to dry.
9 Examine the gear for signs of wear and fit a new gear if the wear is excessive.
10 Check the shaft for excessive play, in its bearing, and endfloat and renew if necessary.
11 Examine the contact breaker for signs of roughness and damage of the contact points. Unless the contacts are almost free of any signs of wear, fit a new contact breaker assembly.
12 Reassemble the distributor after lightly lubricating the spindle, pivots of the centrifugal weights and the bore of the cam. Smear a small quantity of multipurpose grease onto the cam surface.
13 Before refitting the distributor cap, suck the vacuum connection and check that the diaphragm is not punctured and that the rod moves and turns the contact breaker plate.

5 Distributor lubrication

1 It is important that the distributor is lubricated every six months or 6,000 miles whichever comes sooner.
2 Remove the distributor cap and rotor arm. Apply a single drop of engine oil to the contact breaker pivot and the vacuum rod eye.
3 Smear oil onto the surface of the cam and apply as many drops of oil as it will absorb to the cam felt.
4 Apply two drops of oil to the recess in the top of the cam spindle and refit the rotor arm and distributor cap.

6 Contact breaker - adjustment

1 Turn the engine over until the contact breaker points are as wide apart as possible. Check the gap. If it is incorrect proceed as follows:
2 Loosen the two contact breaker assembly clamping screws (Fig. 4.8) and insert a screwdriver into hole 'A'. Fit the screwdriver to the edge of the visible part of the contact breaker base, so that as the screwdriver is turned, the top plate moves and alters the separation of the contacts.
3 Adjust the gap between the contacts to 0.018 to 0.021 in (0.457 to 0.533 mm) and tighten the clamping screws. When checking the gap, take care to wipe the feeler gauge to free it of any oil or dirt before inserting it between the contacts.

7 Ignition timing - setting and adjustment

Procedures are given for static setting and for dynamic setting. Although the static setting is generally satisfactory, dynamic setting is preferable because it is easier to compensate for backlash and wear in the distributor drive.

Static setting
1 Check the contact breaker gap as described in Section 6.
2 Take a 12V bulb of low wattage, such as a panel lamp or sidelamp and if no lamp holder is available, solder a wire to each of its contacts.
3 Turn the engine until the contact on the rotor arm points in the direction of where the number 1 cylinder plug lead segment in the distributor cap should be and the notch in the crankshaft pulley rim is opposite the 'T' mark on the timing plate, then turn the crankshaft pulley until the notch is opposite the basic ignition timing position

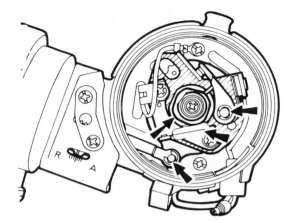

Fig. 4.7. Distributor lubrication

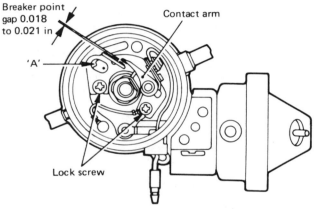

Fig. 4.8. Adjusting the breaker point gap

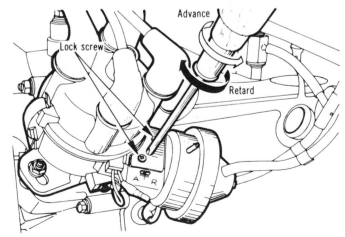

Fig. 4.9. Adjusting the ignition timing (1600 cc engine)

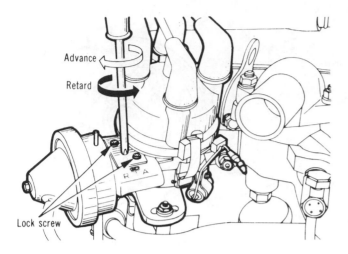

Fig. 4.10. Adjusting the ignition timing (2000 cc engine)

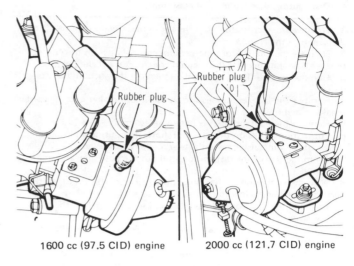

1600 cc (97.5 CID) engine   2000 cc (121.7 CID) engine

Fig. 4.11. Distributor rubber plug

given in the Specifications.

4   Loosen the distributor fixings so that the distributor can be rotated between its end stops. Unlock the adjustment plate and set the ignition adjuster to its middle position (Fig. 4.9).

5   Disconnect the low tension lead to the contact breaker and connect the contact breaker terminal to one of the test lamp wires. Connect the other test lamp wire to the positive terminal of the battery.

6   Switch on the ignition and if the contact breaker points are closed the test lamp will light and if they are open the lamp will not be lit. Turn the distributor head until a position is found where the lamp just goes from **on** to **off** ie. the contacts start to separate.

7   Tighten the distributor fixings, taking care not to move the distributor from this position.

8   Rotate the crankshaft until the crankshaft pulley notch again approaches the basic timing mark, then, turning the crankshaft as slowly as possible, check that the lamp goes out as the motor passes the basic timing mark.

9   Switch off the ignition, remove the test lamp, reconnect the lead to the distributor contact breaker and refit the distributor cap.

Dynamic setting

10 Connect a timing light in accordance with its manufacturer's instructions.

11 Start the engine and, if possible, using an external tachometer, set it to the timing speed given in the Specification and check whether the timing is correct.

12 To alter the timing, switch the engine off, undo the two locking screws of the ignition timing adjuster (Fig. 4.9 and 4.10), insert a Phillips type screwdriver and turn the adjuster in the required direction. Turning the adjuster alters the timing about 4° of crank angle for every division on the scale.

13 Start the engine again and recheck that the adjustment is correct. If so, stop the engine, lock the distributor adjuster and remove the timing light.

8   Distributor - advance and retard check

1   Connect a timing light in accordance with its manufacturer's instructions.

2   With the engine idling, check the timing as in the previous Section.

3   Remove the rubber plug from the distributor (Fig. 4.11) and see if the timing advances - and retards again when the plug is refitted.

4   Increase the engine speed to see if the timing advances as speed increases and retards as speed falls. If the timing does not alter, renew the vacuum control.

9   Distributor - condenser check

A faulty condenser will give bad starting and cause excessive burning of the contact breaker points.

1   Connect a 500V Megger between the positive condenser terminal and the case. The condenser is satisfactory if a reading of 5 Megohms or more is obtained.

2   While the Megger is still turning, disconnect it from the condenser and immediately bring the condenser positive wire close to the case. If the condenser is satisfactory, a spark will jump from the wire to the case.

3   If no condenser testing equipment is available, the condenser can be checked by separating the points by hand with the ignition switched on. If this is accompanied by a flash it is indicative that the condenser has failed. If the condenser is suspect the quickest method of testing is to renew the condenser and to note if there is any improvement.

10 Spark plugs and HT leads

See illustrations on page 73

1   The correct functioning of the spark plugs is vital for the smooth running and efficiency of the engine.

2   At intervals of 5,000 miles (8,000 km), the plugs should be removed, examined, and cleaned. The condition of the spark plugs will also tell much about the overall condition of the engine. The plugs should be renewed at intervals of 15,000 miles (24,000 km).

3   If the insulator nose of the spark plug is clean and white, with no deposits, this is indicative of a weak mixture, or too hot a plug (a hot plug transfers heat away from the electrode slowly - a cold plug transfers it away quickly).

4   The plugs fitted as standard are as listed in Specifications at the head of this Chapter. If the tip and insulator nose are covered with hard black looking deposits, then this is indicative that the mixture is too rich. Should the plug be black and oily, then it is likely that the engine is fairly worn, as well as the mixture being too rich.

5   If the insulator nose is covered with light tan or greyish brown deposits, then the mixture is correct and it is likely that the engine is in good condition.

6   If there are any traces of long brown tapering stains on the outside of the white portion of the plug it will have to be renewed, as this shows that there is a faulty joint between the plug body and the insulator, and compression is being allowed to leak away.

7   Plugs should be cleaned by a sand blasting machine which will free

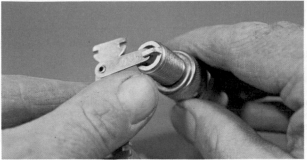

Measuring plug gap. A feeler gauge of the correct size (see ignition system specifications) should have a slight 'drag' when slid between the electrodes. Adjust gap if necessary

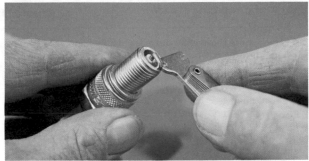

Adjusting plug gap. The plug gap is adjusted by bending the earth electrode inwards, or outwards, as necessary until the correct clearance is obtained. Note the use of the correct tool

Normal. Grey-brown deposits, lightly coated core nose. Gap increasing by around 0.001 in (0.025 mm) per 1000 miles (1600 km). Plugs ideally suited to engine, and engine in good condition

Carbon fouling. Dry, black, sooty deposits. Will cause weak spark and eventually misfire. Fault: over-rich fuel mixture. Check: carburettor mixture settings, float level and jet sizes; choke operation and cleanliness of air filter. Plugs can be re-used after cleaning

Oil fouling. Wet, oily deposits. Will cause weak spark and eventually misfire. Fault: worn bores/piston rings or valve guides; sometimes occurs (temporarily) during running-in period. Plugs can be re-used after thorough cleaning

Overheating. Electrodes have glazed appearance, core nose very white – few deposits. Fault: plug overheating. Check: plug value, ignition timing, fuel octane rating (too low) and fuel mixture (too weak). Discard plugs and cure fault immediately

Electrode damage. Electrodes burned away; core nose has burned, glazed appearance. Fault: pre-ignition. Check: as for 'Overheating' but may be more severe. Discard plugs and remedy fault before piston or valve damage occurs

Split core nose (may appear initially as a crack). Damage is self-evident, but cracks will only show after cleaning. Fault: pre-ignition or wrong gap-setting technique. Check: ignition timing, cooling system, fuel octane rating (too low) and fuel mixture (too weak). Discard plugs, rectify fault immediately

them from carbon more thoroughly than cleaning by hand. The machine will also test the condition of the plugs under compression. Any plug that fails to spark at the recommended pressure should be renewed.

8   The spark plug gap is of considerable importance, as, if it is too large or too small, the size of the spark and its efficiency will be seriously impaired. The spark plug gap should be set to the figure given in Specifications at the beginning of this Chapter.

9   To set it, measure the gap with a feeler gauge, and then bend open, or close, the outer plug electrode until the correct gap is achieved. The centre electrode should never be bent as this may crack the insulation and cause plug failure if nothing worse.

10 When refitting the plugs, remember to use new plug washers, and refit the leads from the distributor in the correct firing order, which is 1, 3, 4, 2, No. 1 cylinder being the one nearest the radiator.

11 The plug leads require no routine attention other than being kept clean and wiped over regularly.

12 At intervals of 5,000 miles (8,000 km) or 3 months, however, pull the leads off the plugs and distributor one at a time and make sure no water has found its way onto the connections. Remove any corrosion from the brass ends, wipe the collars on top of the distributor, and refit the leads.

11 Ignition system - fault diagnosis

There are two main symptoms indicating faults. Either the engine will not start or fire, or the engine is difficult to start and misfires. If it is a regular misfire, ie; the engine is only running on two or three cylinders, the fault is almost sure to be in the secondary, or high tension circuit. If the misfiring is intermittent, the fault could be in either the high or low tension circuits. If the car stops suddenly or will not start at all, it is likely that the fault is in the low tension circuit. Loss of power and overheating (apart from carburation or emission control system faults - see Chapter 3), are normally due to faults in the distributor or incorrect ignition timing.

Engine fails to start

1   If the engine fails to start and the car was running normally when it was last used, first check there is fuel in the petrol tank. If it turns over normally on the starter motor and the battery is evidently well charged, then the fault may be in either the high or low tension circuits. First check the HT circuit. **Note:** If the battery is known to be fully charged, the ignition light comes on, and the starter motor fails to turn the engine **check the tightness of the leads on the battery terminals** and the secureness of the earth lead at its **connection to the body.** It is quite common for the leads to have worked loose, even if they look and feel secure. If one of the battery terminal posts gets very hot when trying to work the starter motor, this is a sure indication of a faulty connection to that terminal.

2   One of the commonest reasons for bad starting is wet or damp spark plug leads and distributor. Remove the distributor cap. If condensation is visible internally dry the cap with a rag and also wipe over the leads. Refit the cap.

3   If the engine still fails to start, check that current is reaching the plugs, by disconnecting each plug lead in turn at the spark plug end, and holding the end of the cable about 3/16 in (5 mm) away from the cylinder block. Spin the engine on the starter motor.

4   Sparking between the end of the cable and the block should be fairly strong with a strong regular blue spark. (Hold the lead with rubber to avoid electric shock). If current is reaching the plugs, then remove them and clean and regap them to 0.030 in (0.76 mm).

5   If there is no spark at the plug leads take off the HT lead from the centre of the distributor cap and hold it to the block as before. Spin the engine on the starter once more. A rapid succession of blue sparks between the end of the lead and the block indicate that the coil is in order and that the distributor cap is cracked, the rotor arm faulty, or the carbon brush in the top of the distributor cap is not making good contact with the spring on the rotor arm. Possibly, the points are in bad condition.

6   If there are no sparks from the end of the lead from the coil, check the connections at the coil end of the lead. If it is in order start checking the low tension circuit.

Engine misfires

7   If the engine misfires regularly run it at a fast idling speed. Pull off each of the plug caps in turn and listen to the note of the engine. Hold the plug cap in a dry cloth or with a rubber glove as additional protection against a shock from the HT supply.

8   No difference in engine running will be noticed when the lead from the defective circuit is removed. Removing the lead from one of the good cylinders will accentuate the misfire.

9   Remove the plug lead from the end of the defective plug and hold it about 3/16 in (5 mm) away from the block. Re-start the engine. If the sparking is fairly strong and regular the fault must lie in the spark plug.

10 The plug may be loose, the insulation may be cracked, or the points may have burnt away giving too wide a gap for the spark to jump. Worse still, one of the points may have broken off. Either renew the plug, or clean it, reset the gap, and then test it.

11 If there is no spark at the end of the plug lead, or if it is weak and intermittent, check the ignition lead from the distributor to the plug. If the insulation is cracked or perished, renew the lead. Check the connections at the distributor cap.

12 If there is still no spark, examine the distributor cap carefully for tracking. This can be recognised by a very thin black line running between an electrode and some other part of the distributor. These lines are paths which now conduct electricity across the cap thus letting it run to earth. The only answer is a new distributor cap.

13 Apart from the ignition being incorrect, other causes of misfiring have already been dealt with under the section dealing with the failure of the engine to start. These are:

a)   *The coil may be faulty giving an intermittent misfire.*
b)   *There may be a damaged lead or loose connection in the low tension circuit.*
c)   *The condenser may be short circuiting; or*
d)   *There may be a mechanical fault in the distributor.*

Chapter 5 Clutch

For modifications, and information applicable to later models, see Supplement at end of manual

Contents

Specifications

	4G32	4G33	4G52
Type		Cable operated	
Clutch plate dimensions (OD x ID x thickness)	7.874 x 5.512 x 0.138 in (200 x 140 x 3.5 mm)	7.252 x 5.000 x 0.126 in (184.2 x 127 x 3.2 mm)	8.465 x 5.906 x 0.126 in (215 x 150 x 3.2 mm)
Facing area	24.8 in^2 (160 cm^2)	21.7 in^2 (140 cm^2)	28.8 in^2 (190 cm^2)
Facing material		Semimold	Special woven
Pressure plate:			
Type		Spring diaphragm	
Setting load	793.7 lbs (360 kg)	727.5 lbs (330 kg)	882 lbs (400 kg)

Torque wrench settings	lb f ft	kg f m
Pressure plate mounting bolts	11 - 15	1.5 - 2.2

1 General description

The clutch is fitted so that the engine may be separated from the gearbox during the car's motion to enable a smooth and progressive gearchange. It also enables the engine torque to be applied progressively to the gearbox for starting from rest smoothly and isolates engine torque while changing gear. The pressure plate is of the single dry plate type, with a diaphragm spring. A cable transfers the force applied to the pedal and operates the clutch lever and shaft assembly.

The clutch plate is riveted together and should not be dismantled. No adjustment is required during the life of the clutch facing and when necessary, the complete plate assembly is renewed.

2 Clutch - removal, inspection and refitting

1 Remove the gearbox from the engine as described in Chapter 6.
2 Mark the clutch cover and flywheel so that the clutch may be refitted in its original position, unless it is to be renewed. The clutch cover, pressure plate and diaphragm spring assembly must be renewed as a unit if it is found to be faulty. Only the clutch plate is able to be renewed as a separate entity.
3 Insert a clutch centralising tool, or a suitable piece of round material into the clutch plate, so that it does not fall out when the

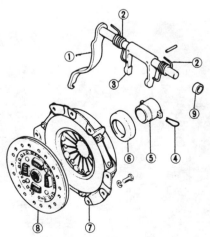

Fig. 5.1. Clutch components

1 Clutch shaft	*6 Release bearing*
2 Return spring	*7 Pressure plate assembly*
3 Shift fork	*8 Clutch plate*
4 Clip	*9 Felt*
5 Bearing carrier	

2.10 Removing the clutch bearing retainer

2.14 Gearbox shaft used as clutch centralising tool

2.15a Fitting the clutch and pressure plates

2.15b Locking the flywheel

pressure plate is removed. Progressively slacken the six pressure plate to flywheel bolts, a turn at a time, so releasing them evenly. As they are being released, check that the pressure plate flange is not binding on the dowels, otherwise it could fly off causing an accident.

4   Lift away the six bolts and spring washers, followed by the pressure plate assembly and clutch plate. **Note which way round the clutch plate is fitted.** The longer boss is facing towards the gearbox.

5   Using a stiff brush or clean rags, clean the face of the flywheel, the pressure plate assembly and the clutch plate. Note that the dust is harmful to the lungs as it contains asbestos, so do not inhale it.

6   It is important that neither oil nor grease comes into contact with the clutch facings, and that absolute cleanliness is observed at all times.

7   Inspect the friction surfaces of the clutch plate and, if worn, a complete new assembly must be fitted. The linings are completely worn out when the faces of the rivets are flush with the lining face. There should be at least 0.012 in (0.3 mm) of lining material left clear of the rivet faces, or the clutch plate is not worth refitting. Check that the friction linings show no signs of heavy glazing or oil impregnation. If evident, a new assembly must be fitted. If a small quantity of lubricant has found its way onto the facing, due to heat generated by the resultant slipping, it will be burnt off. This will be indicated by darkening of the facings. This is not too serious provided that the grain of the facing material can be clearly identified. Fit a new assembly if there is any doubt at all. It is important that if oil impregnation is present, the cause of the oil leak is found and rectified to prevent recurrence.

8   Carefully inspect the pressure plate and flywheel contact faces for signs of overheating, distortion, cracking and scoring; if any serious evidence of scoring exists, then it will probably be necessary to have the flywheel skimmed; if you simply renew the clutch plate, you could very soon be faced with the same faulty condition. Renew the pressure plate assembly if necessary.

9   Mount the clutch plate onto the input shaft and check for looseness or wear on the hub splines. Also check the clutch plate damper springs for damage or looseness.

10   Remove the spring clip retaining the bearing carrier (photo), then remove the bearing carrier and bearing.

11   Drive out the two lock pins from the shift arm and remove the shift arm, springs and felts.

12   Clean the clutch bearing, but do not use any solvent because the bearing is grease packed. If the bearing shows any signs of burning, roughness, sloppiness or abnormal wear of the contact face against the diaphragm claws, fit a new bearing. Also clean the components of the release mechanism, examine them for wear and renew as required.

13   Check the condition of the clutch pilot bearing (spigot bush). Further reference to this is made in Chapter 1, Section 20.

14   Using a clutch centralising tool, or a makeshift means of keeping the clutch plate concentric with the spigot bush, fit the clutch plate.

If the clutch plate is not centralised accurately, it will be very difficult to insert the gearbox first motion shaft into the clutch when refitting the gearbox. Ensure that the clutch plate is fitted so that the larger boss is towards the gearbox.

15 Offer up the pressure plate assembly (photo), align the scribed marks if refitting the original assembly, refit the fixing bolts and washers then tighten the bolts progressively a turn at a time until the recommended torque wrench setting is achieved.

It will be necessary to prevent the flywheel from rotating while tightening the pressure plate bolts. This can be done by engaging a suitable piece of metal in the flywheel teeth (photo), or by jamming a spanner on the crankshaft pulley.

16 Smear a little thin grease or engine oil onto the splines of the gearbox shaft and refit the gearbox.

---

3 Clutch bearing - removal, inspection and refitting

When it is required to remove the bearing, without dismantling the clutch assembly, it is only necessary to carry out the operations described in paragraphs 1, 10, 11, 12 and 16 of the previous Section.

---

4 Clutch cable - removal and refitting

1 Loosen the cable adjusting wheel inside the engine compartment (Fig. 5.3).
2 Loosen the locknut of the clutch pedal adjuster bolt and partially

unscrew the bolt.
3 Disconnect the cable from the clutch pedal and from the clutch operating lever.
4 Inspect the cable for breakage and damage, renewing it if necessary.
5 Lubricate the cable with engine oil, refit and adjust. After fitting the cable, use pads at the following points to prevent the cable from touching the adjacent parts.

Right-hand drive cars - Side of alternator and inside of engine front mounting (photo).

Left-hand drive cars - Intake manifold side of engine and rear of engine front mounting (car with single carburetter).

Inside of master cylinder connector and inside of engine front mounting (cars with twin carburetters).

---

5 Clutch pedal and clutch cable - adjustment

1 By means of the adjusting bolt, adjust the clutch pedal until the top face of the pedal is approximately 6.8 in (173 mm) from the toe-board.
2 Pull the clutch outer cable from the cable holder of the toeboard just enough to turn the adjusting wheel and adjust the free play to 0.2 to 0.24 in (5 to 6 mm).
3 Check that the stroke of the pedal is 5.9 in (150 mm) (Fig. 5.4). Insufficient pedal stroke results in insufficient clutch movement for complete disengagement. If necessary, readjust the clutch pedal stop to achieve this dimension and then tighten the locknut.

4.5 Clutch cable buffer pad

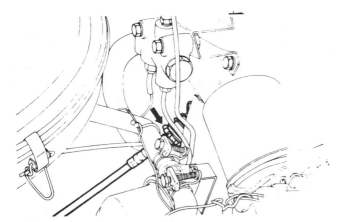

Fig. 5.2. Exploded view of clutch control system

1 Clutch cable	3 Clutch pedal
2 Spring	4 Pedal support

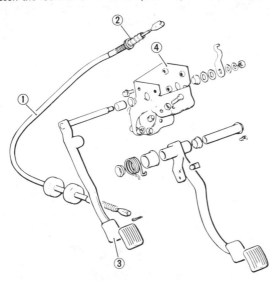

Fig. 5.3. Clutch adjusting wheel

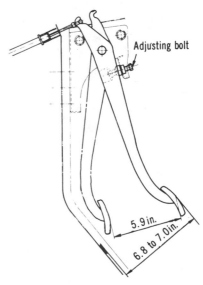

Adjusting bolt

5.9 in.

6.8 to 7.0 in.

Fig. 5.4. Clutch pedal adjustment

6   Fault diagnosis - clutch

Symptom	Reason/s
Judder when taking up drive	Loose engine mountings. Worn or oil contaminated clutch plate friction linings. Worn splines on clutch plate hub or first input shaft. Worn crankshaft spigot bush (pilot bearing).
Clutch slip	Damaged or distorted pressure plate assembly. Clutch plate linings worn or oil contaminated.
Noise on depressing clutch pedal	Dry-worn or damaged clutch release bearing. Excessive play in input shaft splines.
Noise as clutch pedal is released	Distorted clutch plate. Broken or weak clutch plate hub cushion coil springs. Distorted or worn input shaft. Release bearing loose.
Difficulty in disengaging clutch for gearchange	Clutch operating cable incorrectly adjusted or damaged. Gearbox drive shaft splines worn or damaged. Gearbox drive shaft splines need lubricating.

Chapter 6 Manual gearbox and automatic transmission

For modifications, and information applicable to later models, see Supplement at end of manual

Contents

Specifications

Three-speed gearbox

Number of gears	3 forward, 1 reverse
Synchromesh	All forward gears

Ratios

First	3.198 : 1
Second	1.635 : 1
Third	1.000 : 1
Reverse	4.012 : 1

Control system	Column shift
Oil capacity	2.6 Imp pints (1.6 US qts, 1.5 litres)

Four-speed gearbox

Number of gears	4 forward, 1 reverse
Synchromesh	All forward gears

Ratios

First	3.525 : 1
Second	2.193 : 1
Third	1.442 : 1
Fourth	1.000 : 1
Reverse	3.867 : 1

Control system	Floor shift

| Oil capacity | 3.0 Imp pints (1.8 US qts, 1.7 litres) |

Five-speed gearbox

Number of gears ... ...   5 forward, 1 reverse

Synchromesh ... ...   All forward gears

Ratios
First	3.369
Second	2.035
Third	1.360
Fourth	1.000
Fifth	0.856
Reverse	3.635

Control system ... ...   Floor shift

Oil capacity ... ...   4.0 Imp pints (2.4 US qts, 2.3 litres)

Borg Warner automatic transmission

Stalling torque ratio ... ...   2.5 : 1

Torque converter
Nominal diameter ... ...   9½ in

Ratios
First	2.393 : 1
Second	1.450 : 1
Third	1.000 : 1
Reverse	2.094 : 1

Fluid ... ...   Dexron type

Refill capacity ... ...   1.2 Imp gal (1.4 US gal, 5.3 litre) (excluding oil cooler)

Weight ... ...   127.4 lbs (57.8 kg) (including oil)

Torqueflite automatic transmission

Stalling torque ratio ... ...   2.5 : 1

Torque converter
Nominal diameter ... ...   9½ in

Ratios
First	2.45 : 1
Second	1.45 : 1
Third	1.00 : 1
Reverse	2.2 : 1

Fluid ... ...   Dexron type

Refill capacity ... ...   1.4 Imp gal (1.7 US gal, 6.4 litres)

Torque wrench settings

	lbf ft	kgf m
Manual gearbox		
Transmission mounting bolts	22 to 30	3 to 4.2
Starter mounting bolts	15 to 21	2 to 3
Mainshaft locknut	36 to 72	5 to 10
Front bearing retainer	7 to 9	1 to 1.3
Extension housing bolts	11 to 16	1.5 to 2.2
Bottom cover bolts	5.8 to 7.2	0.8 to 1
Borg Warner		
Mounting attachment through bolts	8	1.12
Mounting to transmission nuts	10	1.4
Front brake-band screw	0.83	0.116
Rear brake-band screw	10	1.4
Brake-band locknuts	20 to 25	2.8 to 3.5
Oil pan to transmission case	8 to 13	1.12 to 1.82
Oil pan drain plug	8 to 10	1.2 to 1.4

Transmission mounting bolts	...	...	...	...	...	...	...	21 to 25	2.9 to 3.5
Bottom cover attachment bolts		...	...	...	...	...	...	6 to 7	0.8 to 1.0

Torqueflite

Converter drive plate to crankshaft	...	...	...	...	...	...	...	83 to 90	11.5 to 12.4
Converter housing	...	...	...	...	...	...	...	22 to 30	3. to 4.1
Kickdown band adjusting screw	...	...	...	...	...	...	...	6	0.8
Kickdown band locknut	...	...	...	...	...	...	...	35	4.8
Low and reverse band adjuster	...	...	...	...	...	...	...	3.4	0.47
Low and reverse band locknut	...	...	...	...	...	...	...	30	4.1
Oil pan	...	...	...	...	...	...	...	12.5	1.75
Cooler line nuts	..	...	...	...	...	...	...	7	0.98
Transmission mounting bolts	...	...	...	...	...	...	...	21 to 25	2.9 to 3.5
Bottom cover attachment bolts	...	...	...	...	...	...	...	6 to 7	0.8 to 1.0

PART A: MANUAL GEARBOX

1 General description

The manual gearbox fitted to models covered by this manual will be one of three types, depending upon the engine fitted. The number of forward gears may be 3, 4 or 5 and all have synchromesh on the forward gears. A reverse gear of the sliding spur type is fitted to all models. Gear operation for the 4 and 5 speed gearboxes is by floor shift, while the 3-speed box has a steering column shift. Automatic transmission is available on some models and information on this is given in Part B of this Chapter.

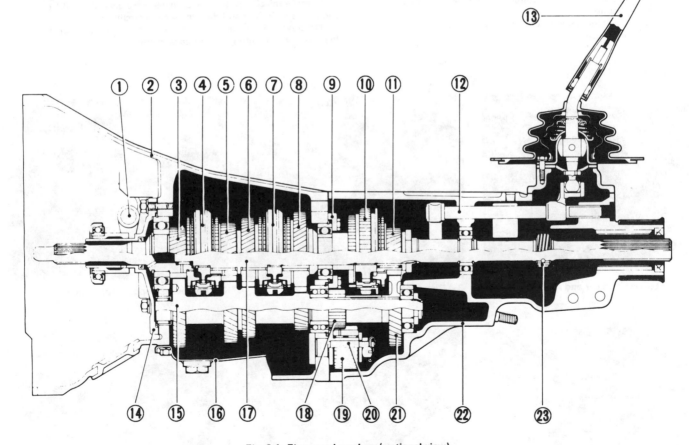

Fig. 6.1. Five-speed gearbox (sectional view)

1	Clutch control shaft	7	Synchronizer (1-2 speed)	12	Control shaft	18 Counter reverse gear
2	Transmission case	8	1st speed gear	13	Control lever	19 Reverse idler gear
3	Main drive gear	9	Rear bearing retainer	14	Front bearing retainer	20 Reverse idler gear shaft
4	Synchronizer (3-4 speed)	10	Synchronizer (reverse and	15	Countershaft gear	21 Counter overtop gear
5	3rd speed gear		overdrive)	16	Under cover	22 Extension housing
6	2nd speed gear	11	Overdrive gear	17	Mainshaft	23 Speedometer drive gear

2 Manual gearbox - removal and refitting

At the time of publication there was no information available on removal and refitting of the 3-speed gearbox. The procedure is basically the same as for the 4 and 5-speed gearbox but the column change linkage must be carefully removed from the gearbox side before removal.

1 Remove the air cleaner and battery leads.
2 Remove the starter motor.
3 Remove the two bolts from the top of the gearbox.
4 From inside the car remove the console base. For cars not fitted with the console base, remove the back bone carpet upwards.
5 Remove the dust cover retaining plate upwards by removing the lock screws.
6 Remove the four attaching bolts at the lower part of the extension housing. For the four or five speed gearbox, remove the gear shift lever assembly. **Note:** On cars fitted with the 4-speed gearbox, remove the gearshift lever while it is in the second gear position. On cars fitted with the 5-speed gearbox, remove the gear shift lever while it is in the first speed position.
7 With the car supported on stands, drain the transmission fluid.
8 Remove the speedometer cable and the reversing light switch wiring from the gearbox.
9 Remove the bolts from the propeller shaft and draw the propeller shaft out of the gearbox.
10 Disconnect the exhaust pipe from its bracket.
11 Disconnect the clutch cables.
12 With the gearbox supported on a trolley jack, remove the insulator from the members by removing the attaching bolts.
13 Detach each member from the frame and pull them off sideways.
14 Remove the bellhousing cover.
15 Remove the remaining bolts from the gearbox and carefully draw it rearwards from the engine.

16 Refitting is a reversal of the removal procedure but note the following:

a) *Check that the bellhousing cover is not bent.*
b) *When refitting the gear shift assembly, place the shift lever in the second gear position for the 4-speed gearbox and in the first speed position for the 5-speed gearbox. Carefully refit the linkage on the 3-speed gearbox.*
c) *Adjust the clutch if it is out of adjustment.*
d) *Refill the gearbox with the correct grade of oil.*
e) *Tighten all bolts to the correct torque wrench settings.*

3 Five-speed gearbox - dismantling

1 Before starting to dismantle the gearbox, clean the exterior with a water-soluble degreasing agent. This will make the gearbox easier to handle and will lessen the chance of the interior being contaminated with dirt.
2 Ensure that the gearbox oil has been drained out and that the plug is refitted securely.
3 Remove the clutch release bearing and operating levers as described in Chapter 5, then remove the front bearing retainer and its spacer (photo).
4 Remove the bolts attaching the extension housing, then remove the reversing light switch, taking care not to lose the ball (photo). Unscrew the plug of the neutral return plunger on the right of the turret mounting until about one complete thread is still screwed in and then turn the gear shifter anticlockwise (Fig. 6.2). With the gear shifter held as far as it will go in this direction, pull back the extension housing until it is free.
5 Remove the circlip, the speedometer drive gear, the ball from the end of the mainshaft and then the second circlip.
6 Unscrew and remove the three poppet spring plugs, then remove the three poppet springs and three balls (photo).

3.3 Front bearing retainer and spacer

3.4 Reversing light switch and ball

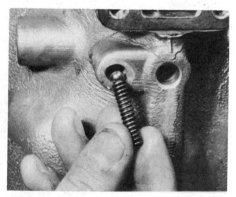

3.6 Removing a poppet spring and ball

3.9 Countershaft gear and bearing

3.16 Removing the main drive pinion

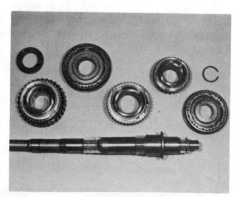

3.17 Mainshaft assembly dismantled

7   Drive out the spring pins from the 3rd/4th and 1st/2nd speed shift forks inside the gearbox (Fig. 6.3) and the pin from the overdrive and the reverse gear outside the gearbox.

8   Engage with reverse and second gears to lock the gear train, unpeen the locknuts of the mainshaft and countershaft, unscrew and remove the two nuts.

9   Using a claw extractor, pull off the countershaft gear and bearing (photo) which will then make it possible to withdraw the 1st/2nd gear selector rod. Withdraw the 3rd/4th gear and overdrive reverse selector rods, then remove the selector forks from the synchronizers. Shake out the two interlock plungers which engage in the shift rods and place these, the poppet valves and balls and the selector fork spring pins in a suitable container.

10 Remove the spacer, the counter reverse gear and the second spacer from the countershaft.

11 Remove the overdrive gear and sleeve from the mainshaft and then remove the overdrive synchronizer and spacer.

12 Pull out the split pin, loosen the nut and then remove the reverse idler gear.

13 Remove the three bolts and lift off the retainer of the mainshaft rear bearing, then remove the four bolts from the reverse idler gear shaft mounting. The shaft is spigot mounted into the end of the gearbox and should be driven out from inside the gearbox (Fig. 6.4).

14 Press the countershaft gear to the rear and remove the circlip from the rear bearing. Using a drift from inside the gearbox, drive out the countershaft rear bearing.

15 Remove the circlip from the countershaft front bearing. Insert a nut between the largest gear and the front bearing and tap the gear assembly forward so that the bearing is pushed out of the front of the box. Remove the bearing with a puller and then lift the countershaft from inside the box.

16 Pull the main drive pinion assembly from the front of the box (photo). Push the mainshaft assembly as far as possible to the rear, remove the bearing circlip and carefully tap the bearing off the mainshaft. Lift the mainshaft assembly from inside the gearbox.

17 Dismantle the mainshaft in the following order and place all the components on the bench in the same relative position as when they were assembled.

   a) *Pull off the 1st speed gear, the 1st/2nd speed synchronizer and the 2nd speed gear.*

   b) *Remove the circlip from the forward end of the mainshaft, then remove the 3rd/4th speed synchronizer and the 3rd speed gear (photo).*

18 Dismantle the extension housing by removing the locking plate and pulling out the speedometer drive (photo). Remove the three plugs and remove three springs, two neutral return plungers and one ball.

---

4   Five-speed gearbox - inspection

1   Support the mainshaft between centres and check that the maximum bend in it is less than 0.0008 in (0.02 mm).

2   Check the synchronizer taper surfaces for wear and damage.

3   Check all gear teeth for wear and damage. The faces of the teeth should be highly polished and free from defects.

4   Check the clutch disc splines for wear and damage, ensure that the disc slides freely and smoothly along it without excessive play.

5   Examine all bearings for damage and wear. Because dismantling the gearbox is a major operation and undertaken infrequently, it is worth fitting new bearings unless the existing ones have only had a little service.

6   With each synchronizer hub and sleeve assembled, check for excessive clearance and see that they slide smoothly. Check the hubs and sleeves for wear, ensure that the springs are not distorted or broken and examine the fork grooves for wear and damage.

7   Examine the shift rods for signs of damage and excessive wear.

---

5   Five-speed gearbox - reassembly

Renew all gaskets and oil seals. Apply jointing compound to all gaskets before fitting them. Ensure that all parts are clean before reassembly and apply oil to all sliding and rotating parts as they are assembled. Do not re-use any spring pins which are removed and

3.18 Removing the speedometer drive

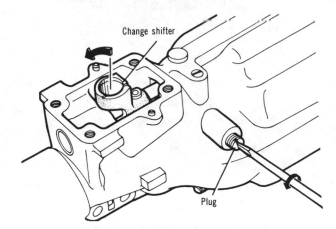

Fig. 6.2. Removing the extension housing

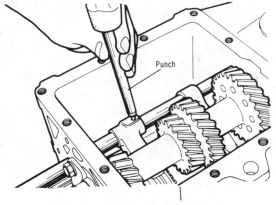

Fig. 6.3. Removing the shift fork pin

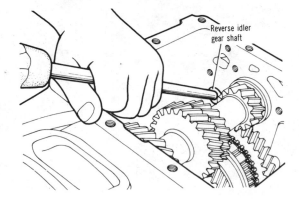

Fig. 6.4. Removing the reverse idler gear shaft

5.2a Fitting second speed bearing and gear ...

5.2b ... the 1-2 synchronizer ...

5.2c ... and the first speed gear

5.2d Mainshaft bearing spacer

5.3 Inserting the mainshaft

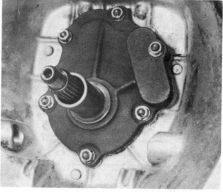
5.5a Inserting the countershaft

5.5b Inserted main drive pinion assembly and countershaft front bearing

5.5c Countershaft rear bearing and circlip

5.6 Front bearing retainer installed

5.7 Fit the rear bearing retainer

5.8 Lining up the reverse idler shaft

5.9a Reverse idler gear and bearing

only re-use circlips if they are not bent. Apply grease to the lips of all oil seals after they have been inserted.

1   Fit the bearing to the main drive pinion with the groove in the outer track away from the pinion and secure it with a circlip. Check the clearance between the circlip and the bearing, which should not exceed 0.0024 in (0.06 mm) (Fig. 6.5). Different thickness circlips are available to give the correct clearance. Fit a circlip in the outer track groove.

2   Assemble the mainshaft in the following order: First fit the needle cage, then the 3rd speed gear, the 3rd/4th synchronizer and the front circlip. Note that the large chamfer on the synchronizer is towards the rear of the gearbox. Check that the end play between the circlip and synchronizer does not exceed 0.0031 in (0.08 mm) and if necessary fit a selective circlip to achieve this clearance. Fit the 2nd speed gear bearing, followed by the 2nd speed gear (photo) the 1st/2nd synchronizer and 1st speed gear. Fit the bearing spacer and with the spacer pushed forward check that the 1st and 2nd speed gears end play does not exceed 0.0016 to 0.0079 in (0.004 to 0.2 mm). Identification of the 1st/2nd speed and 3rd/4th speed synchronizers and the correct fitting of the synchronizer springs is shown in Fig. 6.6.

3   Insert the assembled mainshaft into the case (photo) and drive in the rear bearing with its outer circlip fitted while holding the end of the mainshaft at the front of the case.

4   Fit the needle bearing and the synchronizer ring to the main drive pinion assembly and insert the assembly through the front of the case, tapping it until the bearing circlip is against the casing. Using a brush, rub clutch grease MC2 on to the splines on which the clutch plate slides.

5   Fit the countershaft gear into the casing (photo) and after fitting the circlip to the countershaft front needle bearing (photo) drive the bearing into the case by tapping the outer race with a soft faced mallet. Fit the circlip to the countershaft rear bearing and tap it fully home.

6   Fit a new oil seal to the front bearing retainer, fit the front bearing spacer, smear the oil seal lip with gear oil. Apply jointing compound to both faces of the gasket, then fit the gasket and bearing retainer. Tighten the retaining nuts (photo).

7   Fit the rear bearing retainer.

8   Fit the reverse idler gear shaft, line up the bolt holes by inserting one bolt (photo) and then insert the remaining bolts and tighten progressively.

9   Fit the needle bearing, the reverse idler gear (photo) and thrust washer, the ground face of the washer being towards the gear. Screw on and fully tighten the nut, then fit a split pin to prevent it from unscrewing (photo).

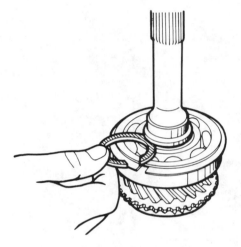

Fig. 6.5. Main drive pinion assembly

5.9b Washer and nut installed on gear

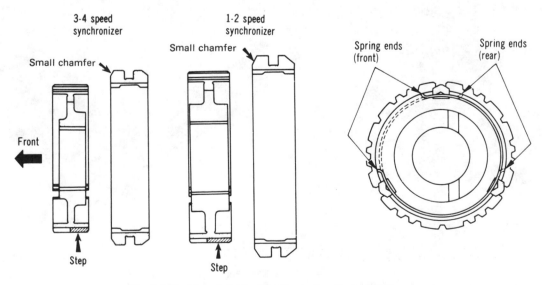

Fig. 6.6. Synchronizer identification and spring installation

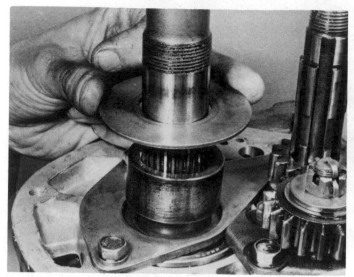
5.10a Mainshaft spacer and stop ring

5.10b Fitting the overdrive synchronizer

5.10c Fitting the overdrive gear and bearing

5.11a Spacer, reverse counter gear ...

5.11b ... and second spacer

5.11c Flat on 3rd-4th gear shift rod

5.11d Fitting the shift rod and overdrive counter gear

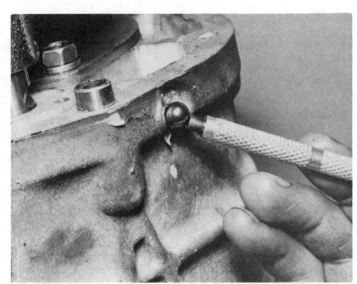

5.11e Countershaft ball bearing and nut

5.13 Inserting spring pins in shift forks

5.14a Poppet ball

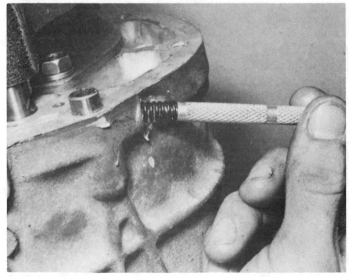

5.14b ... poppet spring

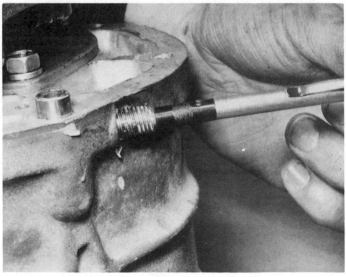

5.14c ... and plug

5.15 Ballrace at end of mainshaft

5.16 Circlip, speedometer gear and ball

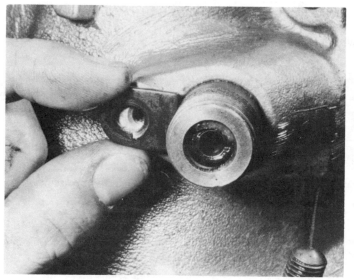

5.19 Speedometer drive locking plate

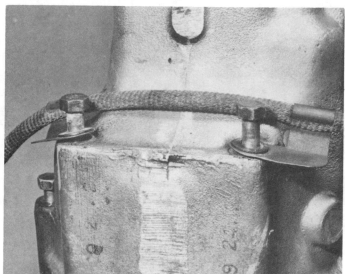

5.20 Fitting the reversing light cable

5.22a Fitting spring pin to installed clutch arm

5.22b Locating upper end of clutch rod spring

10 Assemble the overdrive synchronizer hub and sleeve as shown in Fig. 6.7. Fit the spacer and stop plate to the mainshaft (photo) and then fit the synchronizer assembly (photo) followed by the overdrive gear bearing sleeve, needle bearing and synchronizer ring. Fit the overdrive gear (photo) followed by the locknut which should be screwed on lightly.

11 The overdrive countergear has to be fitted at the same time as the 3rd/4th gear shift rod. Fit the spacer, reverse countergear (photo) and second spacer (photo) to the countershaft end, then insert the two interlock plungers between the shift rods, the three shift forks and the 1st/2nd gear and overdrive/reverse shift rods. Fit the 3rd/4th gear shift rod and while holding the overdrive countergear against the flat on the rod (photo) fit the gear to the countershaft (photo). Fit the ball bearing on top of the gear and then the countershaft nut (photo).

12 Engage reverse and 2nd gears to lock the shafts then fully tighten the nuts on the mainshaft and countershaft. When tight, peen the nuts into the slots in their shafts.

13 Line up the holes in the shift forks and those in the selector rods, fit the new spring pins (photo) with their slots in line with the axis of the shift rod and drive the pins in fully.

14 Fit a ball (photo) and poppet spring (photo) into each shift rail, the smaller diameter end of the spring being against the ball. Screw in the plugs (photo) until their top faces are about 0.23 in (6 mm) below the surface and seal the plug heads with sealer KE41, or a similar non-hardening sealer.

15 Fit the ballrace to the rear end of the mainshaft (photo).

16 Fit the front circlip of the speedometer drive, insert the ball into the shaft, slide the gear over it (photo) and then fit the rear circlip.

17 Apply jointing compound to both sides of the gearbox extension gasket and to the threads of the attachment bolts. Line up the slots in the lugs of the three shift levers, then, while holding the gear shifter of the extension housing as far over to the left as it will go, fit the

extension housing to the gearbox casing. Make sure that the forward end of the control finger is fitted snugly into the slots of the shift lugs. Fit the fixing bolts, except the two bottom ones, and tighten, ensuring that the washers have their convex side towards the bolt head.

18 Fit the neutral return plungers and springs (Fig. 6.8) then the ball and spring. The spring for the ball is shorter than the return plunger springs. Insert and tighten the screw plugs until their heads are flush with the casting boss and seal with KE41 or a similar non-hardening sealer.

19 Apply jointing compound to the outside surface of the sleeve of the speedometer drive and fit it into its pocket in the extension housing. Check that the gear is properly meshed then insert the locking plate (photo) into the locking plate groove and insert and tighten the bolt.

20 Apply sealer to the threads of the reversing light switch, drop the ball into the reversing light pocket in the extension housing, then insert the switch and tighten it. Fit the two remaining housing extension bolts after threading them through the reversing light cable clips and tighten the bolts (photo).

21 Fit the gearbox cover and gasket, then insert and tighten the retaining bolts to a torque wrench setting of 5.9 to 7.2 lbf ft (0.8 to 1 kgf m). Do not overtighten the bolts, because this will cause the gasket to be squeezed out and may result in oil leakage.

22 Grease the shaft of the clutch arm. Enter the clutch arm into the bellhousing and thread onto it a felt packing, spring, clutch shift arm, spring and felt packing in that order. Insert the two spring pins with their slots in line with the axis in the shaft and drive them in fully (photo). Locate the upper ends of the springs in the grooves in the housing casting (photo) and the lower ends against the front faces of the clutch shift arms. Fit the clutch thrust bearing and its two retaining spring clips (photo).

Synchronizer hub   Synchronizer sleeve

Front

Fig. 6.7. Overdrive synchronizer identification

5.22c Inserting clutch bearing retainer

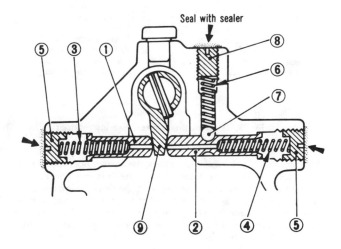

Seal with sealer

Fig. 6.8. Installing the neutral return plungers

1 Neutral return plunger (A)	6 Resistance spring
2 Neutral return plunger (B)	7 Ball
3 Spring (A)	8 Plug
4 Spring (B)	9 Neutral return finger
5 Plug	

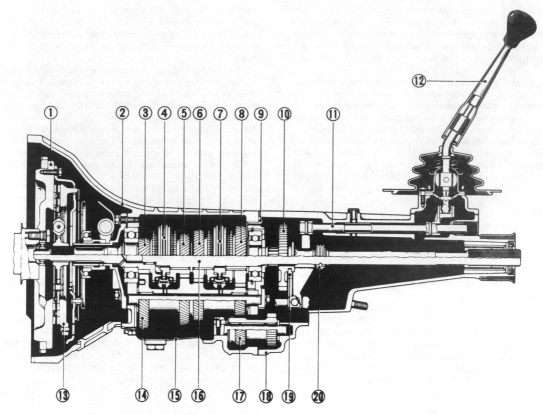

Fig. 6.9. Four-speed gearbox (sectional view)

1	Flywheel	10	Reverse gear
2	Transmission case	11	Control shaft
3	Main drive gear	12	Gearshift lever assembly
4	Synchronizer sleeve (for	13	Pressure plate assembly
	third-fourth speed)	14	Counter gear
5	Third-speed gear	15	Under cover
6	Second-speed gear	16	Mainshaft
7	Synchronizer sleeve (for	17	Reverse idler gear
	first-second speeds)	18	Extension housing
8	First-speed gear	19	Shift fork (reverse)
9	Rear bearing retainer	20	Speedometer drive gear

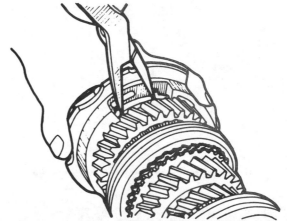

Fig. 6.10. Removing the rear bearing retainer

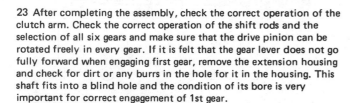

23 After completing the assembly, check the correct operation of the clutch arm. Check the correct operation of the shift rods and the selection of all six gears and make sure that the drive pinion can be rotated freely in every gear. If it is felt that the gear lever does not go fully forward when engaging first gear, remove the extension housing and check for dirt or any burrs in the hole for it in the housing. This shaft fits into a blind hole and the condition of its bore is very important for correct engagement of 1st gear.

6 Four-speed gearbox - dismantling

1 Remove the clutch operating lever, extension housing and speedometer gear as described in detail in Section 3, paragraphs 1 to 5.
2 Remove the bearing retainer of the main drive gear (Fig. 6.10). If it is stuck hard, tap it lightly with a soft hammer.
3 Remove the countershaft retaining plate and pull the countershaft towards the rear of the case. Remove the countergear, a total of 42 needle rollers from the front and rear ends and also a spacer and a thrust washer from both the front and the rear end.
4 Remove the rear thrust washer, rear idler gear, needle bearing and spacer from the reverse idler gear shaft.

5 Remove the gear shaft locking bolt and pull the shaft out towards the rear of the case. Remove the other needle bearing, front thrust washer and front idler.
6 Remove the three plugs from the right-hand side of the case and extract the three poppet springs and three balls.
7 Unscrew the locking bolt on the reverse gear shift fork and remove the shift fork and distance piece.
8 Drive out the spring pins from the two remaining shift forks and pull out the shift rods with their selectors. Do not remove the selectors from the shift rods. Remove the two shift forks from the box then shake out tne two interlock plungers which are fitted between the shift rods.
9 Remove the reverse gear and then pull the mainshaft assembly to the rear until the bearing retainer is free and the assembly can then be removed. Take the assembly out and also remove the synchronizer ring from the main drive gear.
10 Dismantle the mainshaft assembly by expanding the circlip with a pair of pliers and pulling the rear bearing retainer off the bearing. Remove the locking nut, lever and tap off the bearing if a special bearing puller is not available and then proceed as follows:

a) Remove the spacer, first gear, needle bearing, spacer

bushing, synchronizer ring. 1st/2nd speed synchronizer assembly, synchronizer ring, second speed gear and needle bearing. Lay all the parts out in the exact order and facing in the same relative directions as when fitted (Fig. 6.11).

b) Remove the circlip from the front end of the mainshaft and pull off the 3rd/4th speed synchronizer assembly, synchronizer ring, third speed gear and needle bearing.

c) Dismantle each synchronizer assembly into the synchronizer

sleeve, synchronizer hub, two springs and three fingers. All parts other than the hubs are identical on the three synchronizers, but it is good practice to refit all parts in the same position as that from which they were removed.

11 Remove the main drive gear assembly from the front of the box, remove the circlips from the shaft and from the outer track of the bearing and pull the bearing off.

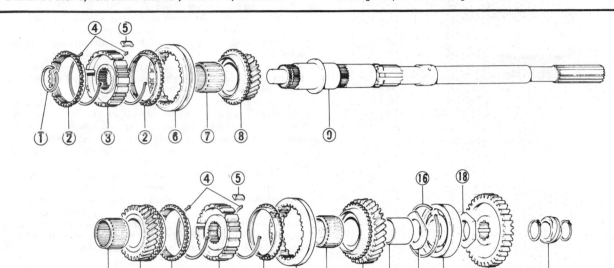

Fig. 6.11. Mainshaft components

1 Snap-ring	6 Synchronizer sleeve (3rd-4th speeds)	11 Synchronizer hub (1st-2nd speeds)	15 Spacer
2 Synchronizer ring	7 Needle bearing	12 Synchronizer sleeve (1st-2nd speeds)	16 Snap-ring
3 Synchronizer hub (3rd-4th speeds)	8 3rd-speed gear	13 1st speed gear	17 Ball bearing
4 Synchronizer spring	9 Mainshaft	14 Spacer bushing	18 Lock nut
5 Synchronizer piece	10 2nd-speed gear		19 Reverse gear
			20 Speedometer drive gear

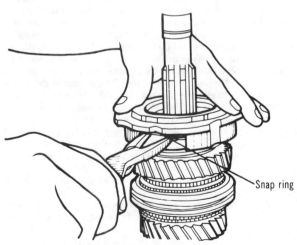

Fig. 6.12. Fitting the rear bearing retainer

Snap ring

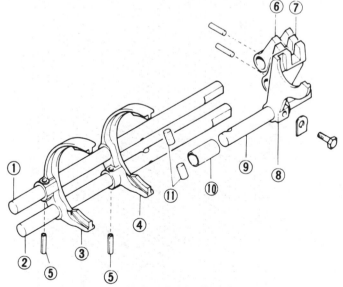

Fig. 6.13. Details of shift rod assembly

1 Shift rail (3rd-4th speed)	7 Selector (1st-2nd speed)
2 Shift rail (1st-2nd speed)	8 Shift fork (reverse)
3 Shift fork (3rd-4th speed)	9 Shift rail (reverse)
4 Shift fork (1st-2nd speed)	10 Distance piece
5 Spring pin	11 Interlock plunger
6 Selector (3rd-4th speed)	

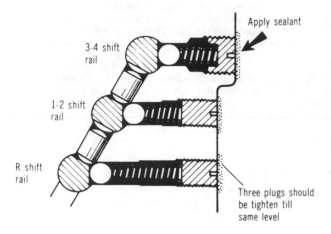

Fig. 6.14. Fitting the poppet balls, springs and plugs

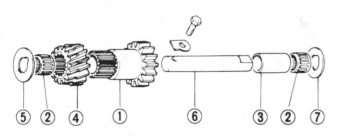

Fig. 6.15. Exploded view of reverse idler gear

1	Reverse idler gear, rear	5	Thrust washer, front
2	Needle bearing	6	Idler shaft
3	Distance piece	7	Thrust washer, rear
4	Reverse idler gear, front		

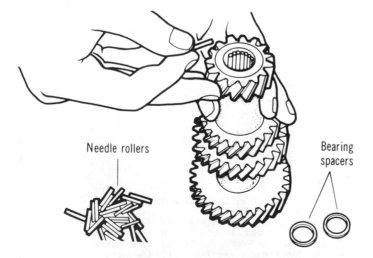

Fig. 6.16. Installing the needle rollers

7 Four-speed gearbox - inspection

The points to be checked are essentially the same as those detailed in the inspection of the five-speed gearbox in Section 4. However, the maximum bend in the mainshaft is different and should not exceed 0.001 in (0.03 mm).

8 Four-speed gearbox - reassembly

Renew all gaskets and oil seals and apply jointing compound to all the gaskets before fitting them. Ensure that all parts are clean before reassembly and apply oil to all sliding and rotating parts as they are assembled. Do not re-use any spring pins which are removed and only re-use circlips if they are not bent. Apply grease to the lips of all oil seals after they have been inserted.

1 Fit the bearing to the main drive pinion with the groove in its outer track away from the pinion and secure it with a circlip. Check the clearance between the circlip and the bearing, which should not exceed 0.0024 in (0.061 mm). Different thickness circlips are available to give the correct clearance. Fit a circlip in the outer track groove.

2 Assemble the synchronizers with the sleeve and hub in the correct directions and the spring fitted as shown in Fig. 6.6.

3 Fit the needle bearing and third speed gear to the front end of the mainshaft, followed by a synchronizer ring, the 3rd/4th speed synchronizer and then a circlip. The width of the circlip should be selected to give a third speed gear end play of 0.001 to 0.007 in (0.03 to 0.19 mm) and a synchronizer hub end play of 0 to 0.003 in (0. to 0.08 mm).

4 Fit the needle bearing and the 2nd gear to the rear end of the mainshaft, followed by the synchronizer ring and 1st/2nd synchronizer ring, first speed gear and spacer. The spacer must be fitted so that the identification mark 'I' is towards the rear. Press or tap the bearing on, screw on the locking nut and tighten it fully before peening the collar of the nut into the keyway of the mainshaft.

5 Fit the circlip in the rear bearing retainer and with the ring expanded by pliers (Fig. 6.12), fit the retainer over the bearing. Fit the main drive gear assembly into the casing, grease the front end needle bearing and fit it into the front end of the main drive gear, then fit the synchronizer ring.

6 Insert the mainshaft assembly through the rear end of the case and mesh it with the main drive gear.

7 Fit the reverse gear to the mainshaft and then by reference to Fig. 6.13 insert the shift forks into the grooves of the appropriate synchronizer sleeves. Holding the forks with one hand inside the case, insert the 3rd/4th speed shift rod assembly into the case through the lower hole and push the end through each fork. Fit an interlock plunger and push it down until it engages the 3rd/4th speed shift rod.

8 Fit the 1st/2nd speed shift rod into the case through the middle hole and push it through the shift rods. Set the rods in their correct position relative to the case and then align the holes in the shift forks with those in the shift rods. Insert spring pins with the slot in the pin in line with the axis of the shift rods and tap the pins in fully.

9 Fit the other interlock plunger to engage the 1st/2nd speed shift rod. Fit the reverse gear shift rod end into the groove of the reverse gear and then push the reverse shift rod through the hole in the fork. Fit the distance piece over the end of the fork and then push the rod through its hole in the end of the case. When the rod is in its correct position tighten the locking bolt.

10 Install the three poppet balls and then insert the springs with the smaller diameter end against the ball. Note that the reverse shift fork spring is longer than the other two (Fig. 6.14). Screw in the plugs until their tops are flush with the surface of the case and then seal them with sealer KE41 or a similar non-hardening sealer.

11 Install the reverse idler gear assembly by first fitting the needle bearing, distance piece and needle bearing onto the reverse idler gear. Insert the assembled gear into the case from the rear. Assemble the front idler gear and the thrust washer onto the rear of the case, then pass the shaft through the gears and tighten the bolt to secure the shaft. Bend the tongued washer up to lock the bolt against unscrewing. The components of the reverse idler gear are shown in Fig. 6.15.

12 Fit 21 needle rollers and a spacer into each of the front and rear bores of the countergear (Fig. 6.16) packing the needles in grease so that they do not drop out. The spacer is fitted outside the needle

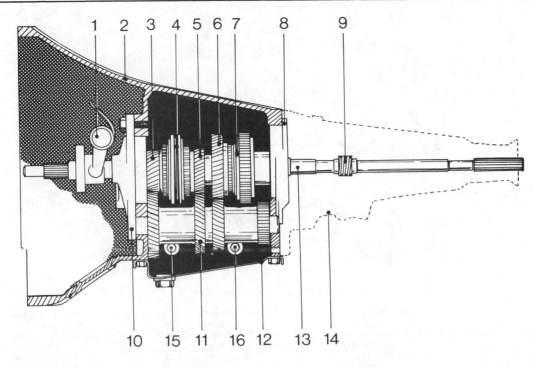

Fig. 6.17. Three-speed gearbox (sectional view)

1 Clutch control shaft	5 2nd speed gear	9 Speedometer drive gear	13 Mainshaft
2 Transmission case	6 1st speed gear	10 Front bearing retainer	14 Extension housing
3 Main drive gear	7 Synchronizer sleeve (1st-reverse)	11 Counter gear	15 Shift shaft (3rd-4th)
4 Synchronizer sleeve (2nd-3rd)	8 Rear bearing retainer	12 Under cover	16 Shift shaft (1st-2nd)

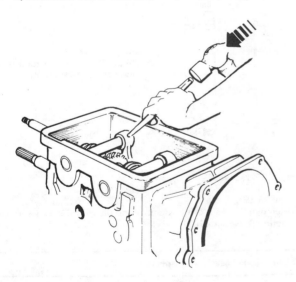

Fig. 6.18. Removing the lock pins

rollers. Grease the larger of the two thrust washers (35 mm dia) and attach it to the front of the countergear. Grease the smaller one (30 mm dia) and attach it to the rear end. Hold the assembly in its place in the case and insert the shaft, making sure that the tang of the thrust washer fits properly into the slot in the case. Secure the rear end of the countershaft by fitting the stop plate.

13 Complete the assembly by fitting the front bearing retainer, speedometer gear and extension housing etc., which is described in detail in Section 5, paragraphs 6, and 16 to 22.

9 Three-speed gearbox - dismantling

1 Clean the outside of the gearbox and drain the oil. Remove the clutch operating levers, reversing light switch, bottom cover, speedometer drive and rear bearing retainer as described in detail in Section 3.

2 Drive out the lock pins of the first/reverse and second/top speed control shafts (Fig. 6.18). Pull the shafts out of the case, pull off the spacer and remove the circlip from them.

3 Pull off the shift arm and draw its shaft out of the case, taking care not to damage the oil seal with the shaft groove.

4 Draw the countershaft out from the back, remove the counter-gear and take out the 20 needle rollers and the thrust spacer from each end of the gear.

5 Remove the two plugs from the left-hand side of the case and withdraw the poppet spring and ball from underneath each of them.

6 Drive out the spring pins securing the shift forks to the shift rods. Draw each rod out of the rear of the box and then remove the shift forks. Shake out the interlock plunger from its hole in the case and keep it with the rods and forks.

7 Pull the mainshaft assembly to the rear until it is free of the bearing retainer. Withdraw the mainshaft assembly and the synchronizer ring of the main drive gear.

8 Dismantling of the mainshaft is detailed in Section 6, paragraph

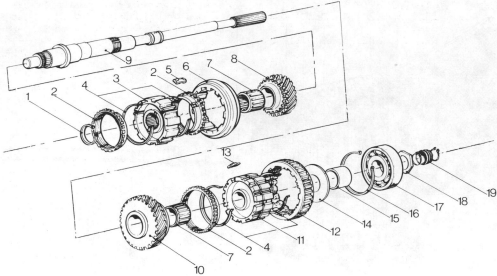

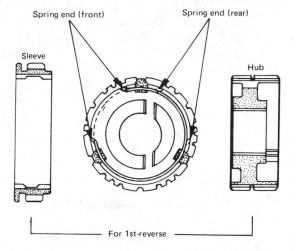

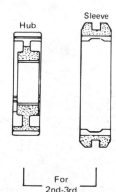

Fig. 6.19. Mainshaft components

1 Snap-ring	6 Synchronizer sleeve (2nd-3rd speeds)	11 Synchronizer hub (1st-reverse)	14 Stop plate
2 Synchronizer ring	7 Needle bearing	12 Synchronizer sleeve (1st-reverse)	15 Spacer
3 Synchronizer hub (2nd-3rd speeds)	8 2nd speed gear	13 Synchronizer piece (1st-reverse)	16 Snap ring
4 Synchronizer spring	9 Mainshaft		17 Bearing
5 Synchronizer piece	10 Low-speed gear		18 Lock nut
			19 Speedometer drive gear

Fig. 6.20. Synchronizer identification, and spring installation.

10 (Fig. 6.19).

9   Remove the main drive assembly and dismantle it as described in Section 6, paragraph 11.

10 Three-speed gearbox - inspection

1   The points to be checked are essentially the same as those detailed in the inspection of the five-speed gearbox in Section 4. The maximum permissible bend in the mainshaft must not exceed 0.001 in (0.03 mm).

11 Three-speed gearbox - reassembly

1   The assembly of the main drive assembly, mainshaft assembly and countershaft are similar to those of the four-speed gearbox, Section 8.

2   After fitting the main gear trains into the box, fit the selector rods and forks as well as the shaft arm using the reverse of the dismantling procedure in Section 9, paragraphs 2 to 6.

3   Assemble the rear extension, fit the front bearing retainer and clutch operating levers as described in Section 5, paragraphs 6 and 16 to 22.

For 'Fault diagnosis - manual gearbox see page 101.

Fig. 6.21. Poppet balls, springs and plugs

PART B: AUTOMATIC TRANSMISSION

13 General description

Either a Borg Warner, or a Torqueflite automatic transmission system may be fitted and both combine a torque converter with a fully automatic 3-speed gear system. The torque converter in both cases is a sealed unit and cannot be dismantled. The hydraulic control system and clutch systems are complex and it is not recommended that stripping of the unit is attempted. Certain auxiliary parts of the system can be changed and the procedures for doing this are given for the Borg Warner and Torqueflite transmissions separately. When the unit is faulty and the fault cannot be rectified, repair should be entrusted to a specialist.

14 General precautions

Parking

When parking, the selector lever must not be moved to the Parking position until the vehicle is stationary or transmission damage may occur.

Starting

The engine will start with the selector lever in either the 'P' (park) or 'N' (neutral) positions. When starting in the neutral position, apply the footbrake or handbrake as a safety precaution.

The automatic transmission will not permit the vehicle to be started by pushing or towing.

Long gradients and heavy loads

When ascending long gradients which require a wide throttle opening for distances of greater than half a mile, the '2' (second) or 'L' (lock up) position should be selected to reduce the possibility of overheating the transmission and converter. This also applies when towing, or carrying heavy loads which result in the vehicle needing a wide throttle opening at low speeds.

Vehicle being towed

If the vehicle has to be towed when the transmission is inoperative, it must be towed with either the rear wheels off the ground, or the propeller shaft must be removed before towing is started.

If the transmission is operating properly, the vehicle may be towed safely with its rear wheels on the ground if the transmission is in neutral and towing speed is less than 30 mph. Because the transmission is only lubricated when the engine is running, the propeller shaft should be removed if the vehicle needs to be towed more than 20 miles.

15 Transmission - removal and refitting (Borg Warner)

1 Remove the air cleaner assembly and then disconnect the downshift cable from the carburetter.
2 Disconnect the battery cable from the starter motor, bend back the two clips securing the cable to the transmission, move the cable clear of the transmission and then remove the starter motor.
3 Remove the two upper bolts attaching the transmission to the engine and remove the clips.
4 Jack up the car, support it on two firmly placed axle stands, then drain the transmission oil.
5 Disconnect and remove the speedometer cable from the transmission.
6 Remove the bolts from the flange joint of the differential and draw

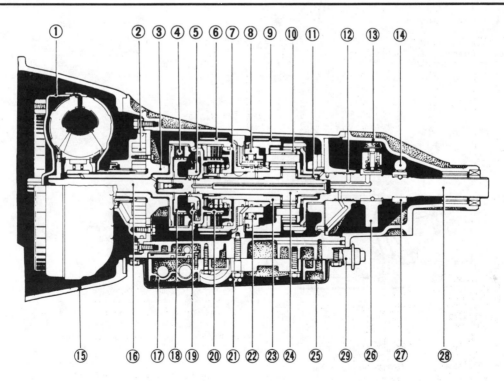

Fig. 6.22. Borg Warner automatic transmission (sectional view)

1 Torque converter	8 One-way clutch outer race	16 Input shaft	23 Reverse sun gear
2 Oil pump gear	9 Rear brake band	17 Valve body assembly	24 Forward sun gear
3 Pump adapter and converter support	10 Long pinion	18 Front clutch hub	25 Oil pan
4 Front clutch plate	11 Planet cover	19 Front clutch spring	26 Governor assembly
5 Front clutch piston	12 Rear adapter	20 Front clutch cylinder	27 Speedometer drive gear
6 Front brake band	13 Extension housing	21 Oil tube	28 Output shaft
7 Front drum	14 Speedometer driven gear	22 One-way clutch assembly	29 Vacuum diaphragm
	15 Converter housing		

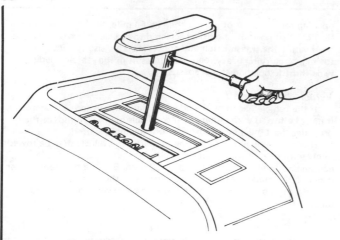

Fig. 6.23. Removing the shift handle assembly

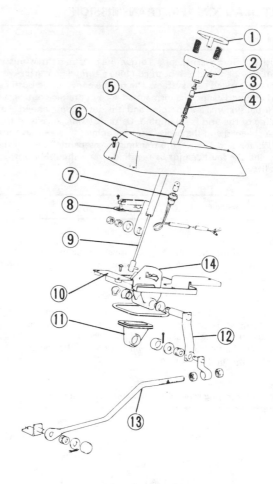

Fig. 6.24. Exploded view of transmission control

1 Push button
2 Shift handle
3 Rod adjusting nut
4 Rod return spring
5 Selector lever assembly
6 Position indicator assembly
7 Indicator lamp socket assembly   } except Plymouth
8 Inhibitor switch
9 Shift lever rod
10 Shift lever bracket assembly
11 Lever bracket cover
12 Transmission control arm
13 Transmission control rod
14 Selector lever position plate

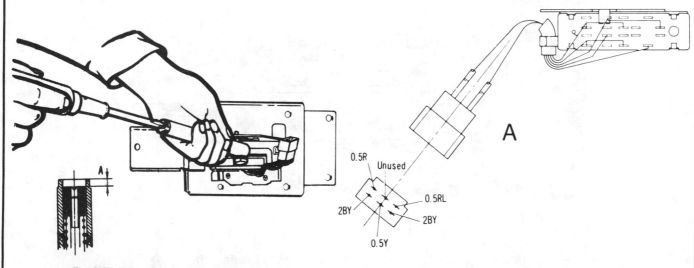

Fig. 6.25. Transmission control adjusting nut

A

0.5R
Unused
2BY
0.5RL
2BY
0.5Y

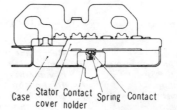

Fig. 6.26. Construction of inhibitor switch

B

Case   Stator   Contact   Spring   Contact
cover   holder

the propeller shaft out of the transmission. Remove the exhaust pipe fixing bracket.

7 Remove the front and rear transmission oil pipes and then disconnect the control rod assembly from the arm.

8 Remove the engine bellhousing cover and remove the four special bolts while rotating the torque converter.

9 With the underneath of the transmission supported on a jack and with the supporting area as large as possible so that no high stress is induced in the oil pan, remove two bolts from the vibration mounting, remove the bonding wire and distance piece and then disconnect the vibration mounting from the bracket.

10 Remove the support bracket from the crossmember and pull it off sideways.

11 Remove the converter housing to engine fixing bolts and remove the transmission.

12 Refitting is the reverse of the foregoing procedure, but the following points must be watched:

   a) Tighten the vibration mounting bolts to the following torques:
      Mounting attachment through bolts -   8 lbf ft (1.1 kgf m)
      Mounting to transmission nuts   -   10 lbf ft (1.14 kgf m)
   b) With the selector lever placed in the 'N' or 'P' position, turn the ignition switch and check that the starter motor turns. If it does not, check the electrical connections and wiring of the circuit.
   c) Refit the control lever and adjust the control (see following paragraph).

16 Transmission control - removal, refitting and adjustment (Borg Warner)

1 Remove the handle assembly from the lever by loosening the set-screw (Fig. 6.23). Remove the attaching screws of the position indicator assembly and lift it off, then remove the indicator lamp.

2 Disconnect the control rod from the arm by loosening the nut from under the floor. Loosen the screws of the lever bracket assembly and remove it.

3 When refitting the transmission control arm to the selector lever assembly, apply grease to the sliding surfaces. Tighten the locknut, making sure that the arm is not loose and that a force of about 3 lbs (1.4 kg) applied to the knob will move the lever. If this value is not obtained, select an appropriate wave washer to achieve it.

4 Before refitting the control knob, adjust the screwed plug in the top of the selector lever when in the 'N' position, so that the plug is flush with the bottom of the groove cut in the rod end (Fig. 6.25).

5 With the lever in the 'N' position and the transmission also in neutral, connect the rod and the lever and tighten the locknut.

17 Inhibitor switch - checking and adjustment (Borg Warner)

1 In cases of a malfunction of the inhibitor switch, first check that the switch is operating correctly. Using a meter or battery and lamp and the selector in the 'P', 'R', 'N', 'D' and 'L' positions in turn, the switch connections should be in accordance with the following table.

Lower position	Terminal identification				
	2BY	2BY	0.5RL	0.5R	0.5Y
P	o————o				
R			o————o	o————o	
N	o————o				
D				o————o	
L				o————o	

2 With the selector lever in the 'N' position temporarily fix the switch with a single screw so that when the pin on the rod assembly is near the crest of the pawl on the detent plate (Fig. 6.27) the detent switch is at the forward end of the 'N' connection range. Check that there is a clearance of 0.059 in between the selector lever and the switch and then tighten the fixing screws securely.

18 Kickdown - adjustment (Borg Warner)

The kickdown switch is operated by the throttle lever on the carburetter and its setting is given in Fig. 6.28. The kickdown cable requires no regular inspection or adjustment, but if a problem develops the cable should be checked and adjusted as follows:

Run the engine until it is warm, then adjust the cable by turning the outer cable adjusting screw until the clearance between the adjusting screw and the stop adjacent to the end fork is 0.004 to 0.002 in (0.1 to 0.05 mm).

19 Front brake-band - adjustment (Borg Warner)

1 Drain the transmission oil and remove the oil pan by removing the

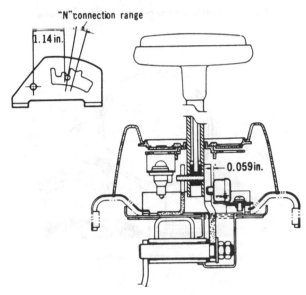

Fig. 6.27. Installation of inhibitor switch

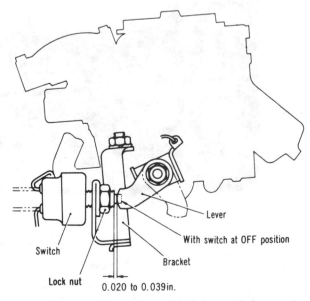

Fig. 6.28. Adjustment of kickdown switch

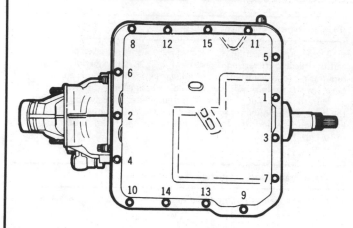

Fig. 6.29. Removing the oil pan attachment bolts

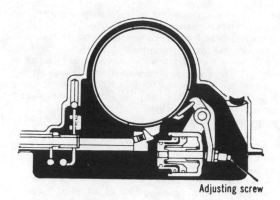

Fig. 6.30. Adjustment of front brake band

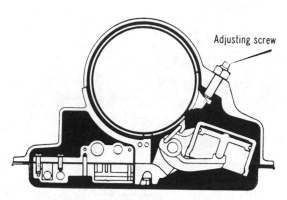

Fig. 6.31. Adjustment of rear brake band

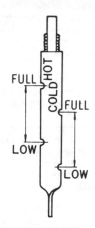

Fig. 6.32. Oil level gauge

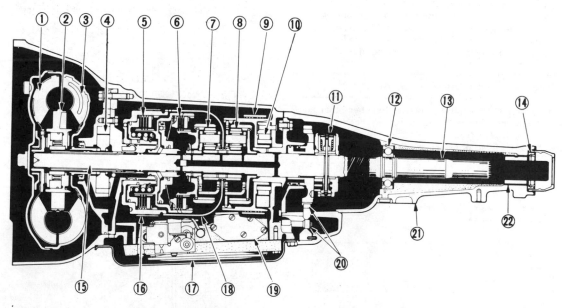

Fig. 6.33. Torqueflite automatic transmission (sectional view)

1	Turbine	7	Front planetary gear set	13	Output shaft	18	Sun gear driving shell
2	Stator	8	Rear planetary gear set	14	Seal	19	Valve body
3	Impeller	9	Low and reverse band	15	Input shaft	20	Parking lock assembly
4	Oil pump	10	Overrunning clutch	16	Kickdown band	21	Extension housing
5	Front clutch	11	Governor	17	Oil filter	22	Bushing
6	Rear clutch	12	Bearing				

15 bolts in the order shown (Fig. 6.29).
2   Press the servo lever outwards and insert a gauge 0.25 in thick
(6.3 mm) between the adjusting screw and the servo piston pin. With
the gauge in place, tighten the servo adjusting screw (Fig. 6.30) to
10 lbf ins (0.115 kgf m). (Note that it is lbf INCHES and not lbf ft).
Tighten the locknut to 20 to 25 lbsf ft (2.77 to 3.46 kgf m).

20 Rear brake-band - adjustment (Borg Warner)

The rear brake-band adjustment is by means of a screw located
outside the transmission case on its right-hand side (Fig. 6.31). To
make an adjustment, loosen the locknut, tighten the screw to a torque
of 10 lbf ft (1.383 kgf m). (Inside the front brake-band, this torque is
in lbs f FEET). Having achieved this torque, back the screw off ¾ turn
and tighten the locknut to secure it in this position.

21 Checking and refilling transmission fluid (Borg Warner)

Checking the fluid level
1   With the selector lever in the 'P' position, start the engine and turn
it at tick-over speed for two minutes, regardless of whether the engine
is hot or cold. While the engine is still running, pull out the dipstick,
which is fitted to the fluid filler cap and examine the fluid level.
2   If the engine is still hot after a run, read the scale on the left-hand
side (Fig. 6.32), otherwise take the reading on the COLD scale. The oil
level should be between the two marks on the appropriate scale.
3   If necessary add Castrol TQ-Dexron or an equivalent Dexron type
fluid. The transmission is filled at the factory with Mobile ATF 210
fluid.

22 Transmission - removal and refitting (Torqueflite)

The transmission and torque converter must be removed as an
assembly, otherwise the converter drive plate, pump bushing or oil
seal may be damaged. The drive plate is not load bearing and none of
the weight of the transmission should be allowed to rest on it during
the removal operation.
1   As a safety precaution, remove the battery leads.
2   Remove the cooler pipes at the transmission, then remove the
starter motor and the cooling pipe bracket.
3   Place a container with a large opening under the transmission.
Loosen the oil pan bolts and tap the pan at one corner to break it
loose allowing fluid to drain into the container, then remove the pan.
4   Rotate the engine by means of a spanner attached to the crankshaft pulley, to gain access to the bolts attaching the torque
converter to the drive plate, and remove them.
5   Put mating marks on the two flanges of the propeller shaft to rear
axle coupling, remove the four fixing bolts then disconnect the shaft
and carefully pull it out of the transmission.
6   Disconnect the throttle rod from the lever at the left-hand side of
the transmission and remove the bellcrank from the transmission if
fitted. Disconnect the gearshift rod and torque shaft assembly from
the transmission.
7   Remove the oil filler tube and the speedometer cable.
8   Support the rear of the engine on a jack, or blocks, and place a
jack under the transmission to support it over as large an area as
possible, so that no high stress is induced in the oil pan.
9   Raise the transmission jack slightly to relieve the load on the
supports, remove the bolts securing the transmission mounting to the
crossmember. Remove the bolts securing the crossmember to the
chassis and take away the crossmember.
10 Remove the bellhousing bolts and carefully draw the transmission
and converter assembly to the rear to separate it from the cylinder
block dowels and to disengage the converter hub from the end of the
crankshaft. When this has been done, place a small G-clamp over the
edge of the bellhousing to prevent the converter from falling out while
the transmission is being removed.
11 Lower the transmission assembly and take it out from under the
vehicle.
12 Remove the G-clamps from the bellhousing, then carefully slide
the converter out of the housing.

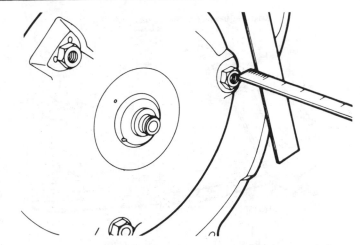
Fig. 6.34. Measuring converter for full engagement in transmission

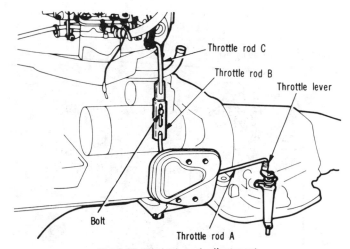
Fig. 6.35. Throttle rod adjustment

13 When refitting the transmission, first check that the converter is
fully engaged by placing a straight edge on the front of the case and
measuring the distance to a front cover lug (Fig. 6.34). This
dimension should be at least ½ in (13 mm).
14 Inspect the converter drive plate for cracks and distortion, and
renew if necessary. Ensure that the bolts securing it to the crankshaft
are tightened to a torque wrench setting of 83 to 90 lbf ft (11.5 to
12.4 kgf m).
15 Smear some multi-purpose grease into the bore of the hub hole in
the crankshaft, fit a G-clamp over the edge of the bellhousing to
hold the converter in place during the refitment of the transmission
and proceed with refitting in the reverse order of removal. The
converter housing and converter drive plate bolts should be tightened
to a torque wrench setting of 22 to 30 lbf ft (3 to 4.1 kgf m).

23 Throttle rod - adjustment (Torqueflite)

1   Run the engine until it reaches normal operating temperature.
2   With the carburetter automatic choke off the fast idle cam (see
Chapter 3, Section 19) adjust the engine idling speed to 750 rpm,
checking it with a tachometer.
3   With all linkages in place, loosen their clamp bolts so that rods 'B'
and 'C' (Fig. 6.35) are free to slide. Lightly push rod 'A' towards the
idling stop and with the carburetter choke fully released tighten the
bolt connecting rods 'B' and 'C'.
4   Check that when the carburetter throttle is wide open, the trans-

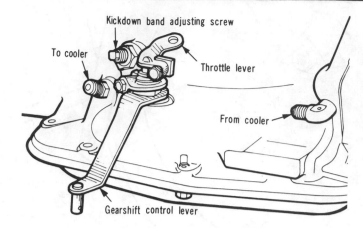

Fig. 6.36. Kickdown band adjustment

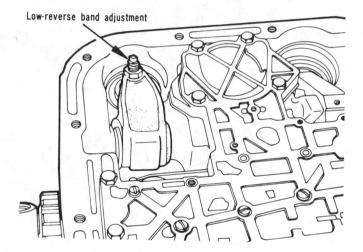

Fig. 6.37. Low and reverse band adjustment

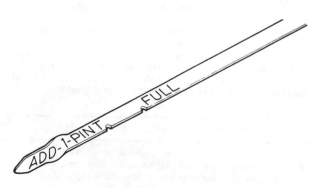

Fig. 6.38. Dipstick markings

mission throttle lever moves smoothly from the idling to the wide open position and that the lever has not moved its full stroke. The angle of operation of the transmission throttle lever is 45° to 54°.

24 Kickdown band - adjustment (Torqueflite)

The kickdown band adjusting screw is on the left-hand side of the transmission case as shown in Fig. 6.36. (**Note:** Band adjustment is not normally required for average passenger car usage).
1   Loosen the locknut and undo it about five turns then check that the adjusting screw turns freely.
2   Tighten the band adjusting screw to a torque of 6 lbf ft (0.8 kgf m). Unscrew the adjusting screw three complete turns and while holding the screw in this position, tighten the locknut to 35 lbf ft (4.8 kgf m).

25 Low and reverse band - adjustment (Torqueflite)

Note: Band adjustment is not normally required for average passenger car usage.
1   Drain the transmission fluid and remove the oil pan (see Section 22, paragraph 3).
2   Adjustment is by means of a socket head screw at the servo end of the lever (Fig. 6.37). Release the locknut and unscrew it several turns. Tighten the screw to 3.4 lbf ft (0.47 kgf m) then unscrew it 7½ turns from this torque. Lock the screw in this position with the locknut tightened to 30 lbf ft (4.1 kgf m).
3   Refit the oil pan, using a new gasket and tighten the fixing bolts to 12.5 lbf ft (1.75 kgf m).
4   Refill the transmission with Castrol TZ Dexron or an equivalent Dexron type. (See following Section).

26 Refilling the transmission (Torqueflite)

Fluid and filter changes are not required for average passenger car usage, but under the following operating conditions the fluid and filter must be changed every 24,000 miles:

a)   *More than 50% operation in heavy city traffic during hot weather (above 90°F).*
b)   *Commercial type operation and towing.*

If the transmission is dismantled for any reason, the filter should be changed and the bands adjusted.
1   After refitting and tightening the bolts of the oil pan, pour four quarts of Dexron type automatic transmission fluid through the filler tube.
2   Start the engine and allow it to idle for at least two minutes then, with the handbrake on, move the selector momentarily to each position, ending in the neutral position.
3   Hold sufficient fluid to bring the level to the *'Add 1 Pint'* mark (Fig. 6.38). Recheck the level when the engine is at its normal operating temperature, when the level should be between the *'Full'* mark and the *'Add 1 Pint'* mark.
4   **Caution:** To prevent dirt from entering the transmission, make sure that the dipstick is clean and that the dipstick cap is properly seated on the dipstick tube.

27 Inhibitor switch - checking and adjustment (Torqueflite)

The procedure is identical to that given in Section 17.

28 Transmission control - removal, refitting and adjustment (Torqueflite)

The procedure is identical to that given in Section 16.

12 Fault diagnosis - manual gearbox

Symptom	Reason/s
Weak or ineffective synchromesh	Malfunction of gear shift lever or control shaft. Synchronising cones worn, split or damaged. Synchronising spring weak or damaged. Synchromesh dogs worn or damaged.
Jumps out of gear	Shift fork worn or poppet spring broken. Gearbox coupling dogs worn. Selector fork groove worn excessively. Gear or bushing worn.
Excessive noise	Incorrect grade, or insufficient oil in gearbox. Bearings worn excessively, or damaged. Gear teeth worn excessively or damaged.
Gears difficult to engage	Selector rods not moving freely, or having restricted travel.
Difficult to engage reverse gear	Ball of reversing light switch not free in its bore.

29 Fault diagnosis - automatic transmission

The repair of an automatic transmission requires specialist knowledge and equipment and should not be attempted without these. The following faults, however, are within the capability of the non-specialist.

Symptom	Reason/s
Starter does not operate in P and N positions	Inhibitor switch faulty or not adjusted correctly.
Starter operates in all positions of selector lever	Inhibitor switch requires adjusting.
Abnormal shock when D, L or R are selected	Engine idling speed too high. Vacuum leak.
Kickdown does not operate	Switch or solenoid faulty or broken wiring.

Chapter 7 Propeller shaft

For modifications, and information applicable to later models, see Supplement at end of manual

Contents

Specifications

Type	Single piece tubular	
Universal joints	Needle bearing Hooke	

Torque wrench settings

	lbf ft	kgf m
Flange coupling bolts	11 to 14	1.5 to 2.0
Borg Warner dynamic damper		
Damper bracket to damper	9 to 12	1.3 to 1.7
Damper bracket to extension housing	0.7 to 1.1	0.1 to 0.15
(Tighten after tightening damper bracket)		
Damper bracket to damper arm	25 to 33	3.5 to 4.6
Damper arm to weight	43 to 51	6.0 to 7.1
Torqueflite dynamic damper		
Damper bracket to damper	15 to 17	2.1 to 2.4
Damper bracket to extension housing	9 to 12	1.3 to 1.7
Damper bracket to damper arm	25 to 33	3.5 to 4.6
Damper arm to weight	43 to 51	6.0 to 7.1

1 General description

Drive is transmitted from the transmission to the rear axle by a balanced tubular propeller shaft. To cater for the axial misalignment of the gearbox and rear axle, a conventional Hooke's joint is fitted at each end of the shaft, and a sliding coupling at the gearbox end permits a small amount of longitudinal movement. The propeller shaft is attached to the rear axle by a flanged coupling, and by a splined sleeve at the transmission end. The shafts for manual and automatic transmissions differ in length and have different sleeve yokes. The bearings of the universal joints are of the needle type and are sealed for life. They do not require lubrication unless dismantled. Vehicles fitted with automatic transmission have a dynamic damper fitted to the rear of the transmission to prevent resonance of the propeller shaft.

2 Propeller shaft - removal and refitting

1 Jack up the rear of the car to minimise the quantity of oil which runs out when the transmission end of the shaft is removed.
2 Mark the two flanges of the rear axle, so that the coupling will be reassembled in exactly the same way, and then remove the four bolts from the flange (photo).
3 Push the shaft forward slightly to disengage the spigot of the flange coupling, then lower the rear axle end of the shaft.
4 Place a container under the rear of the transmission to catch any oil which runs out and then pull the shaft out from the transmission (photo). When removing the sleeve yoke, take care not to damage the oil seal at the rear of the transmission.
5 Before refitting the propeller shaft clean the outside of the sleeve yoke very carefully, then smear it with gear oil.
6 Insert the sleeve yoke, taking care not to damage the oil seal, line up the mating marks on the two parts of the rear flange joint, insert the bolts and screw on the nuts to a torque of 11 to 14 lbf ft (1.5 to 2 kgf m).

3 Universal joints - dismantling, overhaul and reassembly

1 Support the driveshaft in a soft jawed vice and remove the circlips which retain the bearing yokes in the sleeve yoke and the driveshaft. If new bearings are not being fitted, it is important that each circlip and bearing is refitted to exactly the same position as the one from which it was removed.
2 Using a vice, a short piece of bar and a short piece of tube of suitable size, press the bearing out of the joint as far as possible (Fig. 7.2), then grip it with a pair of pliers and pull it off. Reverse the positions of the bar and tube to remove the opposite bearing, then remove the other three pairs of bearings in the same manner.

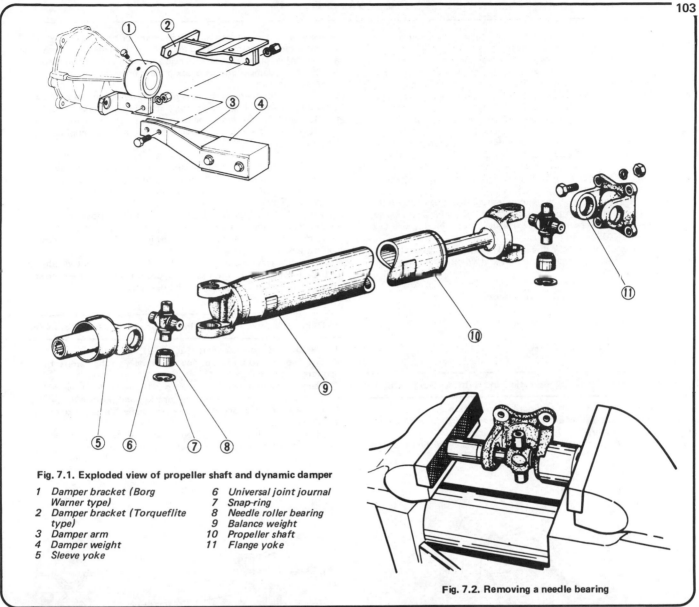

Fig. 7.1. Exploded view of propeller shaft and dynamic damper

1	Damper bracket (Borg Warner type)
2	Damper bracket (Torqueflite type)
3	Damper arm
4	Damper weight
5	Sleeve yoke
6	Universal joint journal
7	Snap-ring
8	Needle roller bearing
9	Balance weight
10	Propeller shaft
11	Flange yoke

Fig. 7.2. Removing a needle bearing

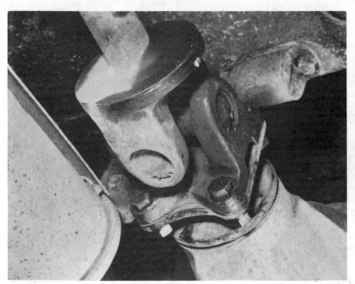

2.2 Propeller shaft rear attachment

2.4. Removing the propeller shaft front end

3   After removing all the bearings of a joint, take out the spider, marking it so that it can be refitted in the same position.

4   Thoroughly clean the bearings and all other parts of the joint and inspect them for damage and wear. If the journals of the spider show impressions of needle rollers, pitting, or rust, renew both the spider and the needle bearings. If the dust seals are damaged, renew the needle bearing assembly.

5   Check the sleeve yoke and the transmission mainshaft for wear and damage and renew any part which is defective.

6   Fill the grease grooves of the journals with multipurpose grease and apply a thin coat of grease evenly to the needle bearings and journals of the coupling halves. If too much grease is put in the grease grooves, the bearing outer track will not fit in position properly and will result in the selection of an incorrect circlip.

7   Press the bearings in, using the same method as for dismantling the joints. Fit a circlip over each bearing, selecting the circlip thickness so that the clearance between the needle bearing and the circlip does not exceed 0.001 in (0.025 mm).

8   Circlips are available in four thicknesses, coded as follows. If possible, fit the same thickness ring on each pair of yokes, to preserve the balance of the shaft.

Thickness	Colour code
0.0504 ± 0.0006 in	None
0.0516 ± 0.0006 in	Yellow
0.0528 ± 0.0006 in	Blue
0.0539 ± 0.0006 in	Purple

4   Dynamic damper - removal, inspection and refitting (Borg Warner)

1   Remove the propeller shaft as described in Section 2.

2   Remove the two bolts securing the damper to the damper bracket and remove the damper (Fig. 7.1).

3   Remove the two nuts securing the damper bracket to the extension housing and use a puller to remove the damper housing (Fig. 7.3). Do not attempt to remove the damper bracket in any other way, such as hammering, otherwise the extension housing will be damaged.

4   Check the damper and its bracket for damage and renew or repair any defective part.

5   Clean the following joint faces of the extension housing, being careful to remove all oil and grease, but do not use either petrol or trichloro-ethylene for removing oil and grease from the joint faces.

The following are points for cleaning and adhesive application (see Fig. 7.4).

a) Damper bracket and extension housing mating surfaces.
b) Damper bracket and damper arm mating surfaces.
c) Threads of damper bracket mounting bolts.

6   Apply THREE-BOND 105Q or 103KG to the above points, assemble the damper and tighten all the bolts to the recommended torque as quickly as possible and certainly within 15 minutes of adhesive application.

7   If possible leave the vehicle for three hours to allow the adhesive to harden fully. If this is not possible, avoid running the engine at speeds in excess of 3000 rpm for the first three hours.

5   Dynamic damper - removal, inspection and refitting (Torqueflite)

1   Remove the propeller shaft (Section 2).

2   Remove the two bolts securing the damper to the damper bracket and remove the damper.

3   Remove the two nuts from the front fixings and the two bolts from the rear fixings of the damper bracket and remove the bracket.

4   Check the damper and its bracket for damage and renew or repair any defective part.

5   Refit the damper bracket, then the damper and tighten the bolts to the recommended torque wrench setting.

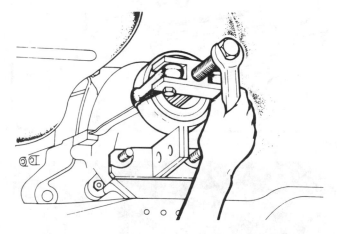

Fig. 7.3. Removing the damper bracket (Borg Warner)

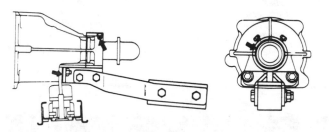

Fig. 7.4. Cleaning and adhesive application points of extension housing and damper bracket

6   Fault diagnosis

Symptom	Reason/s
Propeller shaft noisy during high speed driving	Propeller shaft bent. Propeller shaft unbalanced. Axle flange bolts loose. Excessive clearance between end of bearing and circlip. Universal joint worn.
Propeller shaft noisy, but not vibrating during medium speed and high speed driving	Dynamic damper attachment bolts loose.

Chapter 8 Rear axle

For modifications, and information applicable to later models, see Supplement at end of manual

Contents

Specifications

Type	Semi-floating live axle with hypoid bevel gears and two pinion differential
Oil capacity	1.94 Imp pints (1.1 litres/1.16 US qt)
Oil type	Multi-purpose gear oil conforming to API GL5 (MIL-L-2105B)

Ratio	**1600 cc**	**2000 cc**
	3.889*	3.545
	4.222 (5 speed M/T)	3.889* (5 speed M/T)
	These axles are not interchangeable	

Torque wrench settings	**lbf ft**	**kgf m**
Outer bearing retainer to brake backplate	25 to 29	3.5 to 4.0
Oil drain plug	51	7.1
Oil level plug	29	4.0

1 General description

The rear axle is of the hypoid, semi-floating type, supported by grease packed bearings at the end of each half shaft. All 1600 cc models use the same rear axle and the axles on 2000 cc models are basically similar to each other, although there are differences on some models having 5-speed gearboxes. The axle is attached to two asymetrical semi-elliptic leaf springs, which operate in combination with telescopic double-acting shock absorbers.

The dismantling of the rear axle and the refitment of parts requires special tools and the work should only be undertaken by an authorised dealer.

2 Rear axle - removal and refitting

1 Loosen the rear wheel nuts and then raise the rear of the car by placing a jack beneath the differential case.
2 Remove the rear wheels and place a firmly based axle stand on each side of the vehicle at a point forward of the rear spring front attachment.

3 Lower the jack under the differential until it is just supporting the rear axle.
4 Remove the propeller shaft (Chapter 7, Section 2).
5 Undo the joint between the brake hose and brake pipe and disconnect the brake hose to each rear brake.
6 Disconnect the handbrake cable from the brake extension lever of both the rear brakes (photo) and remove the brake equalizer assembly from the rear axle casing.
7 Remove the four U-bolts, the U-bolt seat plates and the shock absorbers.
8 Remove the shackle pin nuts, (Fig. 8.2), take off the shackle plate and withdraw the shackle assembly. Take care not to knock the rear axle off the jack when the U-bolts have been removed.
9 With an assistant steadying the axle, lower the jack and then take the axle from beneath the vehicle.
10 After refitting the axle using the reverse order of removal, bleed the braking system (Chapter 9, Section 14).

3 Rear axle - halfshaft removal and refitting

1 Loosen the wheel nuts, then jack up the rear axle so that the wheel

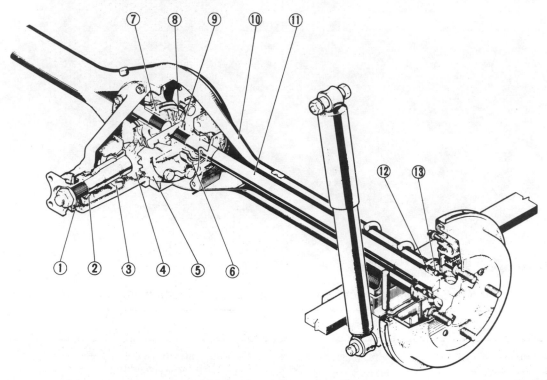

Fig. 8.1. Rear axle and differential construction

1	Drive pinion oil seal	5	Final drive gear	8	Differential pinion
2	Drive pinion front bearing	6	Differential carrier side	9	Differential side pinion
3	Drive pinion rear bearing		bearing	10	Rear axle housing
4	Drive pinion	7	Differential case		

11   Rear axle shaft
12   Rear axle shaft oil seal
13   Rear axle shaft bearing

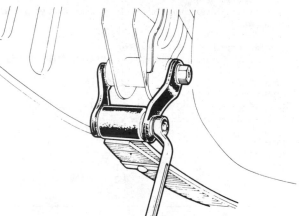

Fig. 8.2. Removing the shackle pin nuts

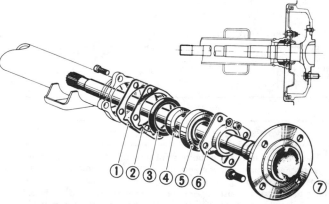

Fig. 8.3. Exploded view of rear axle shaft

1	Packing	5	Bearing
2	Shim	6	Bearing retainer, outer
3	Oil seal	7	Rear axle shaft
4	Bearing retainer, inner		

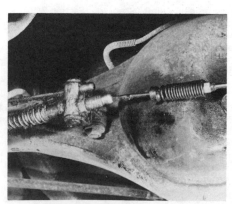

2.6. Brake equaliser and brake cable connections

is clear of the ground and support the car on axle stands and then remove the wheel.

2   Remove the four nuts securing the brake backplate, then disconnect the brake pipe from the wheel cylinder.

3   Remove the halfshaft using a suitable puller, or if one is not available the halfshaft can sometimes be prised off by using a bar on each side of the hub. Secure the brake backing plate in a suitable place, with the handbrake cable still connected. Dismantling of the halfshaft assembly should be done by an authorised dealer.

4   Halfshaft oil seal - renewal

1   The removal of the oil seal without damaging it requires a special tool, but if the oil seal is defective and a new one is required, the following method may be adopted.

2   Remove the halfshaft assembly as described in Section 3.

3   Break the flange of the oil seal with a chisel and then carefully drive a thin screwdriver between the rim of the oil seal and its housing at the point where the flange is broken and prise the rim up

4   Use a pair of cutters to cut the rim of the seal and then pull the seal out with a pair of pliers.

5   Before fitting the new seal, carefully clean the oil seal housing in the rear axle and apply a thin coat of chassis grease. Taking great care to ensure that the seal is square with the bore of the axle, press the seal in by thumb pressure as far as possible. Then, using a block of wood which is just small enough to go into the axle bore, carefully tap the seal home.

6   Smear the lip of the oil seal with a bearing grease containing at least 50% molybdenum disulphide and also smear grease over the area of the shaft which is in contact with the seal.

7   Make sure that all the packing washers which were on the halfshaft when it was removed are still in place, then thread the halfshaft through the brake backing plate.

8   Carefully refit the halfshaft assembly, taking care not to damage the oil seal and engage the splined end in the side pinion of the differential.

9   Align the oil holes in the packing washers and the outer bearing retainer, fit the spring washers and nuts and do the nuts up finger tight.

10   Tighten the outer bearing nuts in diagonal sequence to a torque wrench setting of 25 to 29 lbf ft (3.5 to 4.0 kgf m), then reconnect the brake pipe and bleed the brakes (Chapter 9, Section 13).

11   Check the level of oil in the rear axle, then refit the plugs (photo) and tighten to the specified torque wrench setting.

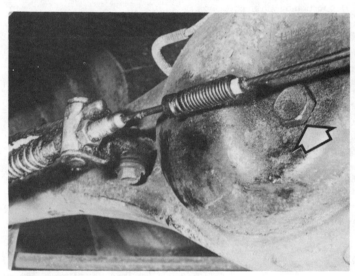

4.12a Rear axle oil filler plug ...

4.12b ... and drain plug

5   Fault diagnosis - rear axle

Symptom	Reason/s
Vibration	Worn halfshaft bearings.
	Loose drive flange bolts.
	Propeller shaft out-of-balance.
	Wheels require balancing.
Noise	Insufficient lubricant.
	Worn differential gears.
'Clunk' on acceleration or deceleration	Incorrect crownwheel and pinion mesh.
	Excessive backlash due to wear in differential gears.
	Worn halfshaft or differential side gear splines.
	Loose drive flange bolts.
	Worn drive pinion flange splines.
Oil leakage	Faulty pinion or halfshaft seals.
	Blocked axle housing breather.

Chapter 9 Brakes

For modifications, and information applicable to later models, see Supplement at end of manual

Contents

Specifications

Type of systems ... ...
Disc at front, drum at rear. Dual line, tandem master cylinder and servo assisted

Footbrake ... ...
Hydraulic on all four wheels

Handbrake ... ...
Mechanical to rear wheels only

Front brake layout ... ...
Floating caliper

Brake dimensions

Front	Celeste	1600	1600 Estate	2000
Disc diameter	7.24 in (184 mm)			
Disc thickness	0.38 in (9.7 mm)			
Cylinder diameter	2 in (51.5 mm)			
Rear				
Drum diameter - twin carb models...	9 in (228.6 mm)	9 in (228.6 mm)	9 in (228.6 mm)	9 in (228.6 mm)
- others	7 in (184 mm)	7 in (184 mm)	7 in (184 mm)	7 in (184 mm)
-		8 in (203 mm)	9 in (228.6 mm)	9 in (228.6 mm)
Lining width - twin carb models	1.57 in (40 mm)			
- others	1.37 in (35 mm)			
		1.37 in (35 mm)	1.57 in (40 mm)	1.57 in (40 mm)
Lining thickness - twin carb models	0.217 in (5.5 mm)			
- others	0.169 in (4.3 mm)			
-		0.157 in (4 mm)	0.167 in (4.3 mm)	0.167 in (4.3 mm)
Cylinder diameter	0.75 in (19.05 mm)			

Vacuum servo unit

	Celeste	1600	1600 Estate	2000
Boost ratio	1.9 : 1	2.2 : 1	2.2 : 1	2.2 : 1
Effective dia of power cylinder - twin carb models	4.5 in (114.3 mm)			
- others		6 in (152.4 mm)		
			6 in (152.4 mm)	6 in (152.4 mm)

Combination valve ... ...
(Proportioning valve and failure indicator switch)
All 2000 engine cars and 1600 engine cars for Europe

Proportioning valve	Provided	Provided	Provided

1 General description

Disc brakes are fitted to the front wheels of all models, together with drum brakes of the single leading shoe type on the rear. The mechanically operated handbrake works on the rear wheels only.

The brakes fitted to the front wheels are of the rotating disc and static caliper type, with one caliper per disc which contains two piston operated friction pads. Application of the footbrake causes the rotating disc to be pinched between the two friction pads. The front brakes are of the trailing caliper type, an arrangement which minimises the entry of water. Applying the footbrake creates a hydraulic pressure in the master cylinder and this pressure is transmitted by the fluid in the brake system to the caliper operating cylinder. Movement of the brake cylinder piston forces the friction pads into contact with the two sides of the brake disc.

The operating cylinder has two seals, an outer one prevents moisture and dirt from entering and the inner one, which fits into a groove in the cylinder bore, prevents the leakage of fluid.

As the friction pads wear, the piston moves further out of its cylinder and the level of fluid in the brake reservoir drops.

Disc pad wear is therefore taken up automatically and eliminates the need for periodic adjustments by the owner.

All models have a centrally mounted handbrake lever between the front seats and is either a 'T' or a 'Y' layout, dependent upon the model of the vehicle.

In the case of the 'T' layout, a single cable runs from the brake lever to a compensator mechanism on the rear axle, from which a separate cable runs to each brake.

The handbrake control is the pivoted lever type.

The rear brakes contain a self-adjusting mechanism of the ratchet type, to take up the wear of the friction linings.

The only adjustment required is on the handbrake compensator mechanism, where cable stretching and wear in the brake linkages may be taken up.

All models have a dual line braking system with a tandem master cylinder and separate hydraulic systems for the front and rear wheels. In the event of a failure of either a pipe, or one of the hydraulic seals, half the braking system will still operate and servo assistance in this condition is still available. On some models a dashboard indicator will light when a failure of the braking system occurs.

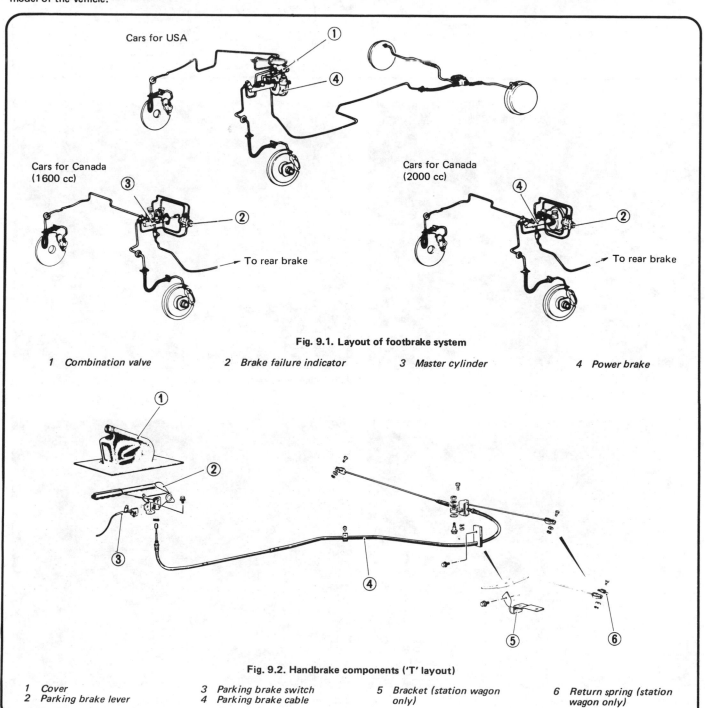

Fig. 9.1. Layout of footbrake system

| 1 Combination valve | 2 Brake failure indicator | 3 Master cylinder | 4 Power brake |

Fig. 9.2. Handbrake components ('T' layout)

| 1 Cover | 3 Parking brake switch | 5 Bracket (station wagon only) | 6 Return spring (station wagon only) |
| 2 Parking brake lever | 4 Parking brake cable | | |

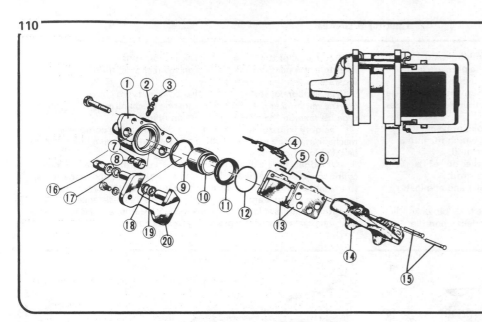

Fig. 9.3. Exploded view of brake caliper

1 Caliper, inner
2 Bleeder screw
3 Bleeder screw cap
4 Pad protector
5 K-spring
6 M-clip
7 Torque plate pin cap
8 Cap plug
9 Piston seal
10 Piston
11 Dust seal
12 Retaining ring
13 Pad assembly
14 Caliper, outer
15 Pad retaining pin
16 Torque plate pin bushing
17 Spacer
18 Wiper seal retainer
19 Wiper seal
20 Torque plate

2.2a Brake pad protector

2.2b Caliper after removal of 'M' clip

2.7a Friction pad against brake disc

2.7b Pins, 'K' spring and 'M' clip in position

2 Front disc pads - inspection and renewal

Always renew both left and right-hand sets when renewing the brake pads. Renew the pads before they are worn past 5/64 in (2 mm).

1 Apply the handbrake, loosen the front wheel nuts and then raise the front wheels and either support the car on firmly based axle stands, or on blocks. Remove the front wheels.

2 Remove the pad protector (photo) by prising up one end with a screwdriver. Remove the loop of the 'M' clip from the hole in the outer brake pad, slide the clip to disengage it from one of the pad retaining pins and then pull its other end from the other pin (photo). Pull out the two pad retaining pins and then remove the 'K' spring. In case of difficulty, the lower pin may be driven out from the back using a soft drift, but the upper pin goes into a blind hole.

3 Using a pair of locking pliers to grip the backing plate area, withdraw one of the brake pads.

4 If the level of fluid in the brake reservoir is high, syphon fluid until the reservoir is only half full, to prevent the reservoir overflowing when the caliper pistons are pushed back. Insert a piece of flat metal or hard wood between the piston and the disc and then insert a screwdriver to lever back the piston. Remove the second brake pad.

5 Clean the pads and check that the thickness of friction material is above 5/64 in (2 mm). Clean the recesses in the calipers to remove dirt and corrosion and clean the pad retaining pins to ensure easy refitting. Do not inhale the dust, as it contains asbestos.

6 Remove the two caliper fixing bolts and pull off the outer caliper. Remove the torque plate and clean it and its shaft. Because the caliper is of the floating type, this shaft must be kept clean to ensure effective operation. If the shaft is encrusted with dirt and mud, the caliper and bushing will wear prematurely. After cleaning, refit the torque plate, outer caliper and retaining bolts.

7 Insert the brake pads, ensuring that the friction pad is towards the brake disc (photo). Refit the two pad retaining pins, the 'K' spring, the 'M' clip (photo) and pad protector.

8 Refit the roadwheels and lower the car, then tighten the wheel nuts securely.

9 Top up the brake reservoir and operate the brake pedal to force the brake pads against the discs. Recheck the level of fluid in the reservoir and top up again if necessary.

10 Check that there is no excessive brake drag by rotating each wheel. A tangential force of 13 lb (6 kg) applied to a wheel nut should be sufficient to turn the wheel.

3 Front brake caliper - removal, overhaul and refitting

Removal

1 Remove the brake pads as described in Section 2.

2 Pull off the brake hose clip from the strut area and then disconnect the brake hose at the caliper.

3 Remove the torque plate and adapter mounting bolts and then remove the caliper assembly.

Dismantling and overhaul

4 Remove the caliper attachment bolts and separate the inner and outer calipers. Remove the cylinder dust seal and then apply air pressure to the brake hose fitting to blow the piston out.

5 Remove the piston seal, being careful not to damage the cylinder bore.

6 Clean all removed parts in methylated spirit, taking care that rubber parts are not in contact with the cleaning fluid for more than 30 seconds.

7 Inspect the cylinder and piston for wear, damage and corrosion and renew them if there is a significant amount of deterioration. It is preferable to renew the piston seal, dust seal and wiper seal whenever the cylinder is dismantled and in any case, to renew them every two years. The wiper seal retainer, plug cap, spacer and bushing should also be renewed whenever the unit is dismantled.

8 Service kits contain special lubricants as well as new parts. Smear a little of the rubber grease (red) onto the piston seal and carefully insert the seal into the recess in the piston bore. Smear the piston surface with the same grease and insert the piston into the bore, taking care not to dislodge or damage the seal. If it is necessary to lubricate

the piston cylinder bore, brake fluid should be used.

9 Clean the torque plate shaft and the bores of the caliper. Smear the special grease (yellow) onto the rubber bushing, wiper seal inner surface and torque plate shafts and reassemble.

10 Insert and then tighten the inner and outer caliper bridge bolts to the recommended torque. Refit the caliper to the brake backplate then reconnect the brake hose.

11 Bleed the brake system as described in Section 14. Because the wheel cylinder has a large diameter piston, even a small amount of air will reduce brake performance seriously and bleeding should be done carefully and thoroughly.

4 Brake disc - removal, inspection and refitting

1 Remove the wheel and brake caliper assembly as described in Section 3.

2 Remove the hub cap, split pin and locking nut and prise off the washer.

3 Pull the brake disc and hub assembly off the stub axle, taking care that the wheel outer bearing cone does not fall off.

4 Inspect the disc for damage or obvious distortion then measure the disc thickness at several points around its circumference. If the disc thickness is less than 0.45 in (11.4 mm) the disc should be renewed.

5 Brake disc - renewal

1 Remove the disc and hub assembly as described in Section 4.

2 Remove the four nuts and bolts securing the disc to the hub, hold the disc in a soft jawed vice or place a piece of soft metal on each side of the disc before gripping it and prise the hub away from the disc.

3 Fit the new disc, refit the four bolts and nuts and tighten them to the recommended torque wrench settings.

4 Refit the assembly onto the stub axle (see Chapter 11, Section 3) and with a dial gauge mounted on the brake backplate (Fig. 9.4) and set to zero, rotate the disc slowly and note the deflection of the dial gauge needle. If the deflection exceeds 0.006 in (0.15 mm), change the position of the disc on the hub and recheck.

6 Rear brakes - dismantling, inspection and renewal

After a high mileage, it will be necessary to fit new brake shoes, or new linings. Refitting new brake linings to shoes is not normally considered to be economic, or possible without special equipment. However, if the services of a local garage, or workshop having brake lining equipment are available, there is no reason why the original shoes cannot be relined satisfactorily. It is necessary to ensure that the new linings are of the correct specification.

1 Securely chock the front wheels, loosen the rear wheel hub nuts, jack up the rear wheel and support the axle with a firmly based axle stand, or blocks and remove the roadwheel.

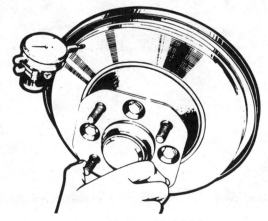

Fig. 9.4. Checking brake disc deflection

6.3 Removing the hold-down spring

2   Remove the brake drum securing screw and using a soft faced hammer on the outer circumference of the brake drum, remove the drum. Because the brakes are fitted with a wear compensating mechanism which limits the clearance between the shoes and the drum, removal may prove difficult. If this is the case, two screws should be inserted in the tapped holes in the brake drum and tightened alternately half a turn at a time.

3   Remove the shoe hold down spring and pin (photo).

4   Detach the strut-to-shoe spring and the end hook of the upper shoe return spring from the trailing brake shoe, then remove the trailing shoe with the lower shoe return spring attached to it.

5   Holding the adjusting latch down, pull the adjusting lever towards the centre of the brake (photo). Hold the parking brake strut at its pivot (photo), release the adjusting lever from the hooked end of the parking brake strut and remove the leading shoe, the upper return spring and strut-to-shoe spring.

6   Remove the upper return spring and the strut-to-shoe spring from the shoe. Pull off the retainer and separate the brake shoe and the adjusting lever. Also remove the adjusting latch.

7   Clean all the dust from the brake shoes, brake drum and other components, taking care not to inhale the dust.

8   Inspect the brake linings and fit new shoes if the lining thickness is less than 0.04 in (1 mm). Inspect the inside of the brake drum and

6.5a Brake adjusting lever and latch

6.5b Parking brake strut hooked end

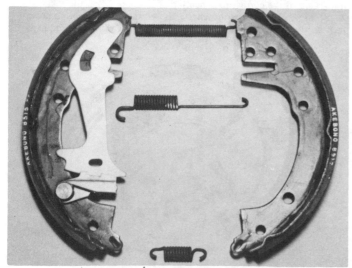

6.9 Leading shoe with adjusting lever fitted

Fig. 6.13 Strut spring and shoe to strut spring fitted

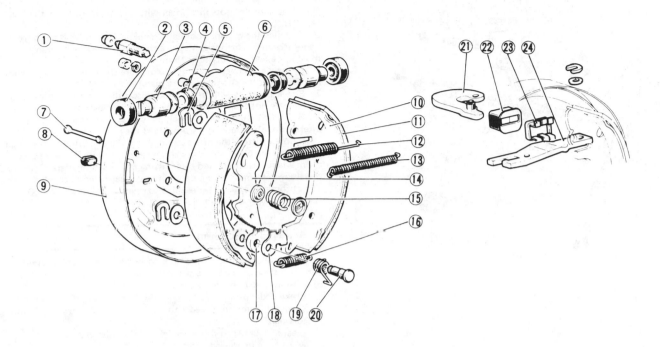

Fig. 9.5. Exploded view of rear brake

1	Bleeder screw	8	Adjusting wheel cover
2	Wheel cylinder boot	9	Backing plate
3	Wheel cylinder piston	10	Brake shoes assembly
4	Wheel cylinder cup	11	Brake lining
5	Retainer	12	Shoe return spring (upper)
6	Wheel cylinder body	13	Automatic adjusting spring
7	Shoe hold-down pin	14	Adjusting lever

15	Shoe hold-down spring	21	Parking brake extension lever
16	Shoe return spring (lower)	22	Parking brake extension
17	Adjusting latch		lever cup
18	Stopper	23	Parking brake extension
19	Return spring		lever retainer
20	Pin	24	Parking brake strut

renew it if it is excessively worn or is scored badly enough to damage the new brake linings.

An 8 in diameter brake drum has a permissible wear limit of 8.071 in (205 mm) and a 9 in drum should not exceed 9.079 in (230.6 mm).

9 Fit the adjusting lever and latch to the leading brake shoe (photo).

10 Apply brake grease (PLASTILUBE or an equivalent) to the brake shoe contact surfaces of the backplate, to the wheel cylinder, adjuster plate and parking brake strut surfaces in contact with the shoes.

11 Disengage the adjusting lever from its latch, engage it with the parking brake strut, re-engage the strut and latch and fit the shoe into the slot of the brake cylinder piston.

12 Fit the upper brake spring and strut-to-shoe spring forward ends. Join the two shoes with the lower brake spring and fit the trailing brake shoe into the other brake cylinder piston. When fitting the shoes to the pistons, take care not to damage the wheel cylinder boots.

13 Engage the rear ends of the upper shoe spring and strut-to-shoe spring in the trailing shoe (photo). There are differences in fitting the strut-to-shoe spring and upper return spring between the 8 in and 9 in brake drums (Fig. 9.6). There are also differences in the adjusting lever and latch spring of the left-hand side and right-hand side rear brakes. Correct fitting is as follows:

Description		Identification colour
Adjusting lever	Left	White
(colour of plating)	Right	Yellow
Latch spring	Left	Black
	Right	Grey

Note also that the right strut-to-shoe spring differs in colour from the left one.

Strut-to-shoe spring	Left	White
(colour of paint)	Right	—

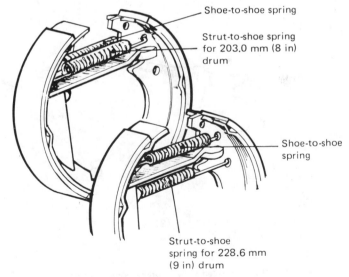

Fig. 9.6. Installing the strut-to-shoe spring

Shoe-to-shoe spring

Strut-to-shoe spring for 203.0 mm (8 in) drum

Shoe-to-shoe spring

Strut-to-shoe spring for 228.6 mm (9 in) drum

7 Rear brake cylinder - removal and overhaul

1 Remove the brake drum and shoes as described in Section 6.

2 Disconnect and remove the flexible brake pipe at the wheel cylinder. Remove the two fixing nuts and washers behind the brake back plate and remove the cylinder.

3 Remove the boots from the cylinder ends, withdraw the pistons and remove the wheel cylinder cups.

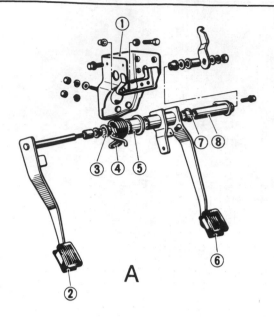

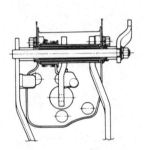

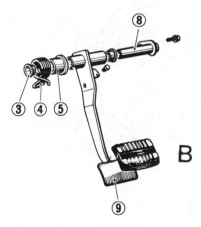

Fig. 9.7. Exploded view of brake pedal control

A   *Manual gearbox models*
1   *Pedal bracket*
2   *Clutch pedal*
3   *Bushing*
4   *Return spring*
5   *Silencer*

B   *Automatic transmission models*
6   *Brake pedal*
7   *Bushing*
8   *Pedal rod*
9   *Brake pedal (A/T)*

4   Clean all the brake cylinder parts in methylated spirit, but do not allow the cups or boots in contact with the spirit for more than 30 seconds.

5   Examine the cylinder bore and renew the cylinder if the bore is badly scored or corroded. Measure the piston-to-bore clearance, which must not exceed 0.006 in (0.15 mm).

6   Fit new cups to the piston, making sure that the flat end of the cup is against the shoulder of the piston.

7   Smear the cups with brake fluid, insert the pistons into the cylinder, taking care not to distort the cups, and refit the boots.

8   Refit the cylinder to the back plate, reconnect the brake pipe and after fitting the shoes and drum, bleed the system (see Section 14).

Before refitting the brake drum, move the adjusting lever along the latch until the brake shoes are almost in contact with the inside of the drum when it is fitted; and after fitting and bleeding, depress the brake pedal several times to take up any unnecessary clearance which remains. The automatic adjuster is designed to operate about every 0.003 in (0.08 mm) wear of the linings.

8   Brake pedal adjustment

Effective operation of the braking system is dependent upon correct setting of the brake pedal position and travel. The following dimensions must be maintained.

Brake pedal play	0.4 to 0.6 in (10 to 15 mm)
Distance from top of pedal to toeboard	6.5 to 6.7 in (165 to 170 mm)
Clearance between top of pedal when fully depressed and toeboard	1.6 in (40 mm)

Pedal operating pressure should be approximately 110 lbs (50 kg).

1   Remove the pin connecting the brake booster operating rod to the pedal. Unscrew the pedal stopper a small amount and then screw it in until the specified dimension between the top of the pedal and the toeboard is achieved. Lock the pedal stopper in this position.

2   Ensure that the booster operating rod is not pushed in at all, line up the hole in the operating rod clevis with the hole in the brake pedal, insert the hinge pin and split cotter. If, after setting the brake pedal stop, the pedal travel is excessive, check the master cylinder to brake booster push rod clearance and the brake shoe-to-drum clearance.

9   Master cylinder - removal and servicing

1   Disconnect the brake pipes from the master cylinder and then slowly depress the brake pedal to drain the fluid.

2   Remove the two nuts and washers attaching the master cylinder to the brake booster and remove the master cylinder.

3   Remove the boot and stopper ring, then withdraw the primary piston assembly, secondary piston assembly and secondary return spring in that order.

4   Unscrew the check valve cases and remove the check valves and check valve springs.

5   Inspect the pistons and if worn or damaged, renew the complete piston assembly. Inspect the cylinder bore for corrosion and wear and renew the cylinder if the piston to cylinder clearance exceeds 0.006 in.

6   Wash all parts in methylated spirit, ensuring that non-metal parts are not in contact with spirit for longer than 30 seconds. Allow to dry and reassemble.

7   Refit the master cylinder and bleed the system (Section 14).

10 Brake booster - dismantling and overhaul

Although there are variations in dimensions and different models of brake booster, the following instructions are applicable generally.

Failure in the check valve may be mistaken for a booster failure and the check valve in the vacuum line should always be tested before dismantling the brake booster. With the vacuum hose disconnected from the check valve at the booster side, spin the engine while holding a finger against the end of the check valve to see if a vacuum is produced and maintained. If there is no vacuum, renew the check valve. If a satisfactory vacuum is produced, proceed as follows.

1   Remove the master cylinder.

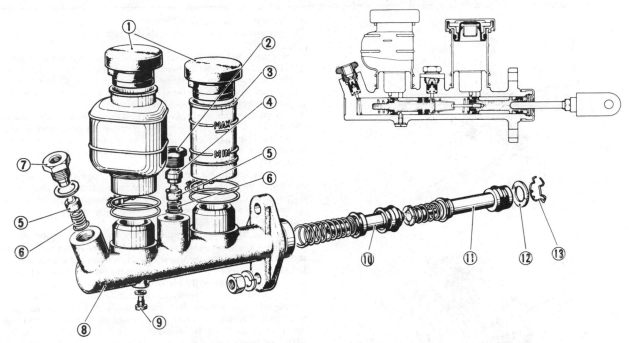

Fig. 9.8. Exploded view of master cylinder

1 Reservoir cap
2 Check valve cap
3 Fluid reservoir
4 Outer pipe seat

5 Check valve
6 Check valve spring
7 Valve case
8 Master cylinder

9 Piston stopper
10 Secondary piston
   assembly

11 Primary piston assembly
12 Piston stopper
13 Stopper ring

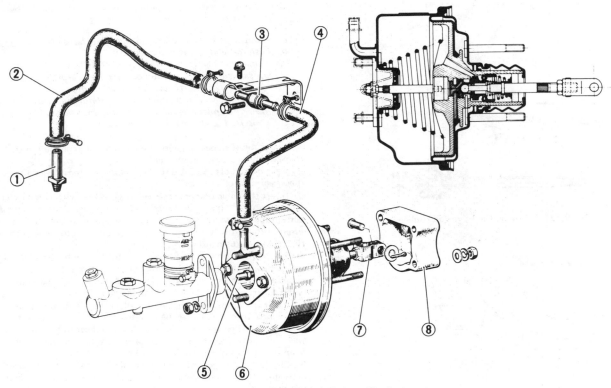

Fig. 9.9. Exploded view of brake booster

1 Fitting
2 Vacuum hose
3 Check valve

4 Vacuum hose
5 Push rod

6 Power brake (booster
   assembly)

7 Yoke
8 Booster spacer

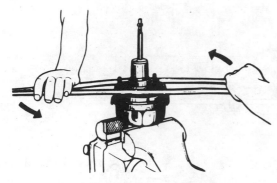

Fig. 9.10. Removing the rear shell

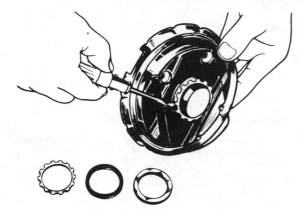

Fig. 9.11. Removing the rear shell seal

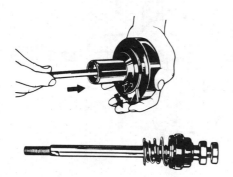

Fig. 9.12. Removing the valve rod plunger

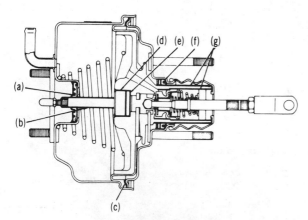

Fig. 9.13. Silicone grease lubrication points

2 Disconnect the vacuum hose from the brake booster.
3 Remove the pin connecting the brake booster operating rod to the pedal.
4 Remove the brake booster attachment nuts (which also secure the pedal support bracket) and withdraw the brake booster assembly.
5 Before starting to dismantle the booster, clean all dirt from its outside and ensure that a repair kit is to hand, so that components subject to deterioration can be renewed.
6 Ensure that the work can be carried out in a clean, dry place. Hold the front shell flange in a vice, then remove the clevis and locknut.
7 Scribe mating marks on the front and rear shells and then, holding the rear shell clamped between two bars, unscrew it anticlockwise (Fig. 9.10).
8 Remove the diaphragm spring and diaphragm plate, taking care not to damage the plate which is made of plastic and is fragile.
9 Remove the rear shell assembly and dismantle it by pulling off the retainer with a screwdriver and then removing the bearing and the valve body seal (Fig. 9.11).
10 Remove the diaphragm plate assembly, pull the diaphragm from the plate, remove the silencer retainer from the diaphragm plate with a screwdriver, then remove the silencer filter and the silencer. Remove the valve plunger stop key and gently pull off the valve rod and plunger assembly (Fig. 9.12). To remove the key, hold the valve plunger with the key downwards and while pushing on the rod, gently tap the assembly against the bench. Finally, remove the reaction disc. Some valve rod plunger assemblies cannot be dismantled and the entire assembly has to be renewed.
11 When dismantling has been completed, clean all the parts carefully then check the diaphragm plate for damage and cracks and the front and rear shells for cracks and distortion. Check that the push rod is not bent or damaged and that there is no cracking or damage around the stud mountings.

11 Brake booster - assembly

Before starting assembly, apply silicone grease to the following places (Fig. 9.13).

a) *Front shell seal and push rod sliding surfaces.*
b) *Push rod and seal contact surfaces.*
c) *Diaphragm lug, to rear shell, contact surfaces.*
d) *Outside surface of reaction disc (grease sparingly).*
e) *Reaction disc inserting part of diaphragm plate.*
f) *Rear shell seal and diaphragm plate sliding surfaces.*
g) *Interior of piston plate into which plunger assembly is inserted; and seal sliding surfaces.*

1 Insert the seal, bearing and retainer into the rear shell in that order, then lightly press in the retainer.
2 Carefully insert the valve rod and plunger assembly into the diaphragm plate.
3 Insert the valve plunger stop key (Fig. 9.14), with its chamfered face towards the piston and then pull the plunger assembly to make certain that the valve plunger is locked securely. If the valve key is inserted the wrong way round, it may be difficult to remove the next time that it is dismantled.
4 Fit the reaction disc and diaphragm to the diaphragm plate. After fitting make sure that the diaphragm has been inserted into the diaphragm plate securely. When fitting the diaphragm, care must be taken to ensure that it is not contaminated with oil.
5 Insert the urethane foam silencer filter (Fig. 9.15) and then the felt silencer into the rear of the diaphragm plate and then fit the retainer. Inserting the foam filter and felt silencer in the wrong order will adversely affect the operation of the diaphragm, due to fibres from the felt becoming stuck in the valve.
6 Fit the diaphragm plate in the rear shell and then fit the valve body guard to the rear shell, with the rear of the guard into the end of the retainer.
7 Fit the plate and seal assembly into the front shell, fit the push rod and then attach the flange to the front shell by pressing it in, as with the front shell seal.
8 Roughly align the mating marks on the front and rear shell, fit the front shell and turn it until the mating marks are in line and its notch is against the stop.
9 Measure the clearance between the brake booster push rod and

the back of the master cylinder (Fig. 9.16) and if necessary adjust the length of the push rod to obtain the recommended clearance of 0 to 0.3 in (0 to 7.6 mm).

10 Fit the yoke to the threaded end of the operating rod, with 0.512 $+0.8$ in (13 ± 2 mm) of rod inserted into the yoke.
-0.16 4

11 Apply sealing compound (Cemedine 366E) to the brake booster mounting surface and toeboard, install the booster, refit the master cylinder and tighten to the recommended torque wrench setting.

12 Connect the vacuum hose to the check valve, ensuring that the check valve is fitted the right way round (Fig. 9.17), with the arrow on its casing pointing towards the engine vacuum connection. Apply sealing compound (THREE BOND No 4) to the valve end before

fitting the pipes and then clamp the connections so that there are no air leaks.

13 Connect the brake booster operating rod to the brake pedal and check that the pedal is adjusted correctly (Section 8).

14 Bleed the brake system (Section 14). If braking performance is not satisfactory, check the brake booster and master cylinder for leaks.

12 Proportioning valve - checking

A proportioning valve (Fig. 9.18) is fitted to some models and is mounted either on the front toeboard or on the rear axle. Its function

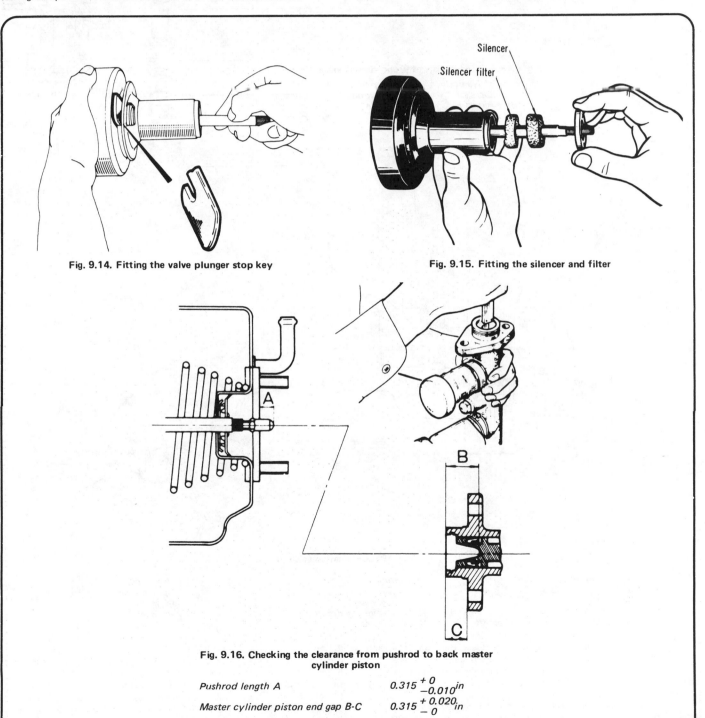

Fig. 9.14. Fitting the valve plunger stop key

Fig. 9.15. Fitting the silencer and filter

Fig. 9.16. Checking the clearance from pushrod to back master cylinder piston

Pushrod length A	$0.315 \begin{smallmatrix} +0 \\ -0.010 \end{smallmatrix}$ in
Master cylinder piston end gap B-C	$0.315 \begin{smallmatrix} +0.020 \\ -0 \end{smallmatrix}$ in
Pushrod-to-master cylinder piston end clearance (B-C)-A	0 to 0.3 in

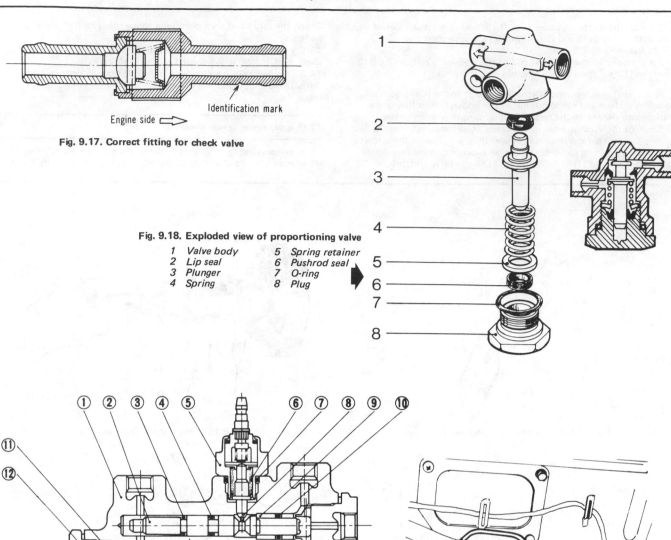

Engine side ⟹   Identification mark

Fig. 9.17. Correct fitting for check valve

Fig. 9.18. Exploded view of proportioning valve

1	*Valve body*	5	*Spring retainer*
2	*Lip seal*	6	*Pushrod seal*
3	*Plunger*	7	*O-ring*
4	*Spring*	8	*Plug*

Fig. 9.19. Combination valve

1	*Combination valve body*	6	*Spring*	11	*Cylinder cup*
2	*Differential valve piston*	7	*O-ring*	12	*Proportioning valve piston*
3	*No. 1 ring*	8	*Plunger switch*	13	*Spring*
4	*No. 2 ring*	9	*Differential valve sleeve*	14	*Valve seal*
5	*Differential valve switch assembly*	10	*No. 3 ring*		

is to make an ideal distribution of pressure between the front and rear brakes to give maximum braking efficiency and to prevent the rear wheels from locking under heavy braking conditions. The setting of the valve is done on assembly and under no circumstances should it be dismantled.

To test for correct operation of the valve it is necessary to have two oil pressure gauges with a range of 0 to 1,400 lb/in^2 (0 to 100 kg/cm^2).

1 Connect one gauge in the outlet line of the master cylinder and the second gauge in the line to a rear brake cylinder.

2 Apply pressure at the brake pedal (with the engine running if a brake booster is fitted). For a master cylinder pressure of up to 525 lb/in^2 (37 kg/cm^2) the brake cylinder pressure should be the same as the master cylinder pressure. For a master cylinder pressure of 850 lb/in^2 (60 kg/cm^2) the brake cylinder pressure should be 625 lb/in^2 (44 kg/cm^2). A tolerance of + 30 lb/in^2 to 60 lb/in^2 is permissible on the above value of the cylinder pressure and if it is not within this range a new valve must be fitted.

3 After disconnecting the pressure gauges and/or renewing the proportioning valve, bleed the hydraulic system.

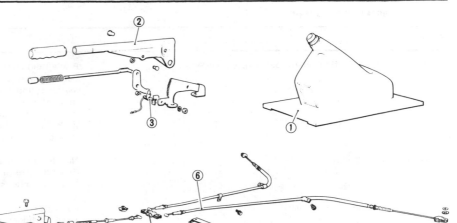

Fig. 9.20. Handbrake components ('Y' layout)

1   *Cover*
2   *Parking brake lever*
3   *Parking brake switch*
4   *Parking brake cable*
5   *Bracket*
6   *Return spring*

13 Combination valve - checking hydraulic and electrical functioning

The combination valve (Fig. 9.19) has the following three functions

1) *Pressure control of the rear brakes.*
2) *Stopping control of rear brake pressure in case of failure of the front brakes.*
3) *Providing a visual warning of brake failure.*

The valve is calibrated on assembly and under no circumstances should it be dismantled.

To test the correct operation of the valve it is necessary to have two oil pressure gauges with a range of 0 to 1,400 lb/in^2 (0 to 100 kg/cm^2).

1   Connect one gauge in the outlet line of the master cylinder and the second gauge in the line to a rear brake cylinder.
2   Apply pressure at the brake pedal (with the engine running if a brake booster is fitted). For a master cylinder pressure of up to 525 lb/in^2 (37 kg/cm^2) the brake cylinder pressure should be the same as the master cylinder pressure. For a master cylinder pressure of 850 lb/in^2 (60 kg/cm^2), the brake cylinder pressure should be 625 lb/in^2 (44 kg/cm^2). A tolerance of + 30 lb/in^2 to − 60 lb/in^2 is permissible on the above valve of the cylinder pressure and if it is not within this range, a new valve must be fitted.
3   To test the operation of the brake failure indicator, loosen the bleeder screw of a front brake and depress the brake pedal. If the lamp does not light, check the electrical circuit by shorting together the two switch connections to see if the lamp then lights. If this is so, renew the switch.
4   Having checked the switch operation on the front brakes, close the front brake bleed nipple. Unscrew one of the rear brake bleed nipples and depress the brake pedal to reset the switch. If the switch is tested by opening a rear brake bleed nipple, it must be reset by opening a front brake bleed nipple.
5   After completing the checks on the combination valve, bleed the hydraulic system.

14 Bleeding the hydraulic braking system

Have ready a tin of brake fluid conforming to SAE J1703 or SAE 70R3. The fluid should be clean and preferably fresh because brake fluid absorbs water which leads to corrosion of components. The brake system should be bled whenever any brake hose, brake pipe, master cylinder, brake valve or wheel cylinder has been disconnected. Bleeding the brakes should also be done whenever the brake pedal feels spongy when pressed. The sequence of bleeding should be: left rear wheel, right rear wheel, left front wheel, right front wheel.
1   Ensure that the brake fluid reservoir is full of fluid and make sure that the level is topped up frequently during bleeding. If the level is allowed to fall to the bottom of the reservoir, air is likely to

enter the system and nullify all previous work.
2   Remove the bleed nipple cap of a wheel cylinder, slide a piece of plastic tubing over the nipple and place the other end of the tube in a clean container containing enough brake fluid to submerge the end of the pipe.
3   With an assistant to operate the brake pedal, open the bleed screw while the assistant slowly depresses the brake pedal the full length of its travel, keeping the pedal depressed until the bleed screw has been closed. Repeat this sequence as many times as is necessary until no air bubbles can be seen in the fluid coming out of the plastic pipe. Check the level of fluid in the reservoir at frequent intervals during bleeding.
4   On completion of bleeding, tighten the bleed screw to the recommended torque wrench setting, refit the bleed screw cap and top up the fluid reservoir.
5   Repeat operations 1 to 4 on each of the brake cylinders in turn.

15 Handbrake lever assembly - removal, refitting and adjustment

Lever type

1   Remove the clevis pin and disconnect the clevis.
2   Remove the brake lever fixing bolts and withdraw the brake lever assembly.
3   After fitting check that there is a clearance of 0.04 in (1 mm) between the handbrake extension lever and its stop. Also check that the clearance between the extension lever and the stop on the rear brake assembly is 0.04 in (1 mm) and if necessary rotate the cable adjuster on the handbrake lever to obtain this dimension.
4   After making any necessary adjustments, check that the total travel of the handbrake lever is between 4 and 6 notches. If the stroke is larger than this, the rear brake automatic adjusters are malfunctioning. Dismantle and check the automatic adjusters.

16 Handbrake cables - removal, refitting and adjustment

'T' type (Fig. 9.2)

1   Remove the clevis pins from both sides of the rear brakes and disconnect the cables from the extension levers. Remove the cables by unscrewing them from the compensator on the rear axle.
2   Disconnect the handbrake lever cable from the compensator and then unscrew its other end on the handbrake lever.
3   After refitting the cables as the reverse of the above, adjust them as described in Section 15.

'Y' type (Fig. 9.20)

The removal, refitting and adjustment of the cables is similar to the 'T' type cable arrangement.

17 Fault diagnosis - braking system

Symptom	Reason/s
Pedal travels almost to floorboards before brakes operate	Brake fluid level too low. Caliper leaking. Master cylinder leaking (bubbles in master cylinder fluid). Brake flexible hose leaking. Brake line fractured. Brake system unions loose. Rear automatic adjusters seized.
Brake pedal feels springy	New linings not yet bedded in. Brake discs or drums badly worn or cracked. Master cylinder securing nuts loose.
Brake pedal feels spongy and soggy	Caliper or wheel cylinder leaking. Master cylinder leaking (bubbles in master cylinder reservoir). Brake pipe line or flexible hose leaking. Unions in brake system loose. Air in hydraulic system.
Excessive effort required to brake car	Pad or shoe linings badly worn. New pads or shoes recently fitted - not yet bedded-in. Harder linings fitted than standard causing increase in pedal pressure. Linings and brake drums contaminated with oil, grease or hydraulic fluid. Servo unit inoperative or faulty. One half of dual brake system inoperative.
Brakes uneven and pulling to one side	Linings and discs or drums contaminated with oil grease or hydraulic fluid. Tyre pressures unequal. Radial ply tyres fitted at one end of the car only. Brake caliper loose. Brake pads or shoes fitted incorrectly. Different type of linings fitted at each wheel. Anchorages for front suspension or rear suspension loose. Brake discs or drums badly worn, cracked or distorted.
Brakes tend to bind, drag or lock-on	Air in hydraulic system. Wheel cylinders seized. Handbrake cables too tight.

Chapter 10 Electrical system

For modifications, and information applicable to later models, see Supplement at end of manual

Contents

Specifications

Battery

Model	N50Z
Voltage	12V
Capacity (20 hour rate)	60Ah

Alternator

Model	AH2040K (early models), AH2045K (later models)
Output	12V 40A (AH204-OK), 12V 45A (AH2045K)
Polarity	Negative earth
Direction of rotation	Clockwise viewed from pulley end

Voltage regulator

Model	RQB2220D
Type	Tirrill type with temperature compensation
Polarity	Negative earth
Range	14.3 to 15.8V at 68°F

Bulbs

Indicator lamps	12V 3.4W
Panel and instrument lamps	12V 3.4W
Headlamps	12V 50/40W
Front side marker lamps	12V 8W
Rear side marker lamps	12V 8W
Number plate lamps	12V 8W
Roof light	12V 10W festoon

	Saloon and Coupe	Estate
Front indicator and sidelight	12V 27/8W	12V 23/8W
Stop and tail lights	12V 27/8W	12V 23/8W
Reversing lights	12V 27W	12V 23W

Torque wrench settings

	lbf ft	kgf m
Wiper arm fixing nut	8 to 12	1.1 to 1.7
Pivot shaft nut	7 to 11	1 to 1.5

1 General description

All models have a 12 volt negative earth system consisting of an alternator, the necessary voltage control equipment and a battery. Fuse protection is provided on all circuits and in addition to this there is a fusible link, which protects the entire system from excessive current. The safety systems, such as seat belt switches, door switches and ignition inhibit are controlled by an integrated circuit logic unit, the output of which operates the interlock relay and warning system. A variety of electrical testing devices are required for the complete diagnosis and adjustment of the electrical system, but much preliminary work can be done with a multimeter and a test lamp. Electrical parts can be removed and taken to an automotive electrical specialist and it is recommended that this is done unless the reader is sufficiently knowledgeable and has the necessary testing facilities.

2 Battery removal and refitting

1 Loosen the clamps and detach the battery leads from the battery terminals. Disconnect the negative (earth) lead first.
2 Remove the two nuts securing the battery clamp and lift the lamp off (photo).
3 Remove the battery from its tray.
4 Before refitting the battery, clean the tray and wash and dry the outside of the battery. Ensure that the battery terminals and cable connections are free from corrosion and smeared with vaseline.
5 Fit the battery, refit the battery clamp and tighten the nuts until they are firm, but do not overtighten or bend the clamp. Refit the battery leads (negative last) and tighten the clamps.

3 Battery maintenance

1 Make a weekly check of the level of electrolyte and make sure that the separators are covered. Using distilled water, top up the level to the full level mark, but do not overfill. If any electrolyte is spilled, wipe it up immediately to prevent corrosion.
2 After checking the electrolyte, refit the filler plugs securely.

3 Keep the top of the battery and the terminals clean and dry.
4 A long and reliable battery life depends upon the battery never being left for long in a discharged condition. During the winter when the normal load on the electrical system absorbs most of the generator output, the battery should be charged weekly.

4 Battery charging

1 When charging the battery on the car, connect the positive battery terminal first, then the negative and disconnect in the reverse order, taking care that neither the battery, nor the charger becomes short-circuited.
2 When using a booster charge to give a high rate of charge when the battery is fitted in the car, first remove with the positive and negative battery cables, otherwise the diodes in the alternator may be damaged.
3 Make sure that the charger is connected with the same polarity as the battery, ie. positive lead from the charger connected to the positive terminal of the battery, etc.
4 For normal charging, the charging current should be approximately 1/10th of the ampere hour capacity of the battery. A 60 Ah battery should not normally be charged at a current higher than 6 amps and during charging the temperature of the electrolyte should not exceed 113°F.

5 Alternator - general description

An alternator is an electrical generator which produces an alternating current which is changed into direct current by a rectifier inside the alternator. The advantage of an alternator over a direct current generator is that the output of an alternator is constant over a wide range of speeds, so that a high rate of charge can be produced at low speeds such as when driving in heavy traffic, thus reducing the drain on the battery.

6 Alternator - routine maintenance

1 The equipment has been designed for the minimum amount of

2.2 Battery and fixing clamp

8.3 Alternator adjustment arm bolt

maintenance in service, the only items subject to wear being the brushes and bearings.

2   Brushes should be examined after about 75,000 miles (120,000 km) and renewed if necessary. The bearings are prepacked with grease for life, and should not require further attention.

3   Check the fan belt every 3,000 miles (5,000 km) for correct adjustment which should be 1/3 inch (8 mm) total movement at the centre of the run between the alternator and water pump pulleys.

7   Alternator - special precautions

Whenever the electrical system of the car is being attended to, and external means of starting the engine is used, there are certain precautions that must be taken otherwise serious and expensive damage can result.

1   Always make sure that the negative terminal of the battery is earthed. If the terminal connections are accidentally reversed or if the battery has been reverse charged the alternator diodes will be damaged.

2   The output terminal on the alternator marked 'BAT' or 'B+' must never be earthed but should always be connected directly to the positive terminal of the battery.

3   Whenever the alternator is to be removed or when disconnecting the terminals of the alternator circuit, always disconnect the battery earth terminal first.

4   The alternator must never be operated without the battery to alternator cable connected.

5   If the battery is to be charged by external means always disconnect both battery cables before the external charger is connected.

6   Should it be necessary to use a booster charger or booster battery to start the engine always double check that the negative cable is connected to negative terminal and the positive cable to positive terminal.

7   When washing the car, take care not to get the alternator wet.

8   If the brushes are worn down to the wear limit line (Section 9) renew them with approved spares.

9   The bearings are sealed and lubricated for life but if there is any sign of leakage of lubricant, the bearings should be renewed with approved spares.

8   Alternator - removal and refitting

1   Disconnect the battery leads.

2   Remove the plug connections and also the wire from the screwed terminal on the alternator.

3   Undo and remove the adjustment arm bolt (photo), then slacken the mounting bolts until the alternator can be swung towards the engine and the fan belt removed.

4   Remove the nut of the mounting bolt and withdraw the bolt, being careful not to lose any shims which may be fitted. Hold the alternator while removing the bolt, so that the alternator does not fall.

5   When refitting the alternator, hold it with its mounting lugs in position and insert shims on the inside of each mounting lug until the shims are sufficiently tight to stay in on their own. Insert the mounting bolt and fit its nut loosely.

6   Refit the fan belt.

7   Insert the clamp bolt into the adjuster arm and tension the fan belt (Chapter 2, Section 7) then tighten the nut of the support bolt to a torque of 15 to 18 lbf ft (2 to 2.5 kgf m) and the adjuster bolt to 11 to 14 lbf ft (1.5 to 2.0 kgf m).

8   Reconnect the alternator leads and then the battery leads.

9   Alternator - renewing brushes

1   Remove the alternator from the engine.

2   Remove the three through bolts between the front and rear housing.

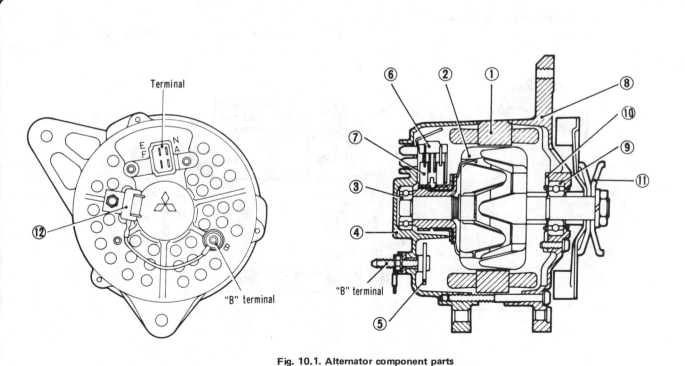

Fig. 10.1. Alternator component parts

1 Stator	4 Rear bracket	7 Brush	10 Bearing retainer
2 Rotor	5 Rectifier assembly	8 Front bracket	11 Pulley
3 Ball bearing	6 Brush holder assembly	9 Ball bearing	12 Condenser

3   Insert a screwdriver in the hole between the front housing and the stator assembly (Fig. 6.2) and prise off the front bracket and rotor assembly. Do not insert a screwdriver in the vent holes because this might damage the stator windings.

4   Unsolder the three stator leads from the diodes and the set of three neutral leads, noting carefully the terminals to which they are connected and remove the stator assembly. Unsolder the leads to the diodes as quickly as possible, because the heat of a soldering iron on the diodes for more than about three seconds will damage them.

5   Unsolder the brush leads and remove the brushes.

6   If the brushes are worn down to the wear limit line (Fig. 10.3) fit new ones, soldering the brush leads onto the terminals and cutting off any surplus wire.

7   Refit the stator and solder the wires back onto the same terminals as the ones from which they were removed.

8   Push the brushes up into their holders and temporarily keep them in place with a piece of wire (Fig. 10.4).

9   Refit the rotor and front housing, then release the brushes.

10 Reconnect and refit the alternator.

10 Starter motor - general description

The starter motor incorporates a solenoid mounted on top of the starter body, the solenoid operating switch contacts and also a mechanical clutch.

When the starter switch is operated, the voltage coil of the solenoid is energised which operates the clutch and starts to engage the starter pinion in the flywheel ring gear, (or the torque converter on automatic transmission). After the pinion has engaged, the solenoid closes the contacts which connect the battery to the starter motor and this also energises the solenoid hold on coil, so that the starter motor continues to spin until the engine starts, even if the starter switch is released. When the engine starts, the starter motor is no longer exerting a driving torque and the free running clutch of the starter motor comes into operation to break the starter motor circuit and disengage the pinion. Pre-engagement of the starter pinion reduces wear on the starter pinion and starter ring and it is unlikely that they will need to be renewed.

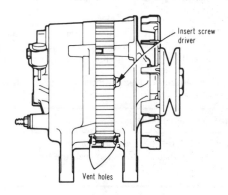

Fig. 10.2. Prising off the front bracket

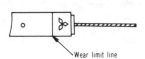

Fig. 10.3. Brush wear check

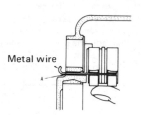

Fig. 10.4. Supporting the brushes clear of the rotor

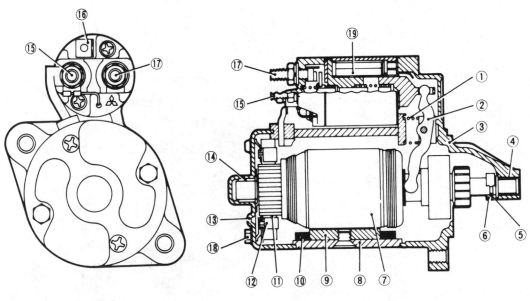

Sectional view

Fig. 10.5. Starting motor for 1600 cc engine with manual transmission

1	Spring	6	Stopper	11	Brush
2	Lever	7	Armature	12	Brush holder
3	Front bracket	8	Yoke	13	Rear bracket
4	Bearing	9	Pole	14	Bearing
5	Ring	10	Field coil	15	'M' terminal

16	'S' terminal
17	'B' terminal
18	Through bolt
19	Magnetic switch

11 Starter motor - removal and refitting

1   Remove the battery leads.
2   Disconnect the cables from the three terminals of the starter motor.
3   Remove the starter mounting bolts, pull the starter motor back slightly to disengage the starter motor spigot and then remove the starter motor. If the vehicle is equipped with an air conditioner, or with a large steering box, disconnect the drop arm from the starter motor attachment bolts and then remove the motor from beneath the vehicle.
4   When refitting the motor, make sure that there is no misalignment between the motor and its mounting on the engine. Clean the mating surfaces between the motor and engine to ensure a good electrical contact and tighten the fixing bolts to a torque of 14 to 21 lbf ft (2 to 3 kgf m).

12 Starter motor - dismantling, overhaul and reassembly

1   Remove the connection from the 'M' terminal, take out the solenoid switch fixing screw and remove the solenoid switch.
2   Remove the two through bolts and separate the motor into the armature and yoke.
3   Remove the armature and the lever from the front housing, being careful to note which way round the lever is fitted and also the positions of the spring and spring holder.
4   Remove the small washer which is fitted to the pinion end of the armature. This may be adhering to the inside of the pinion housing.
5   Remove the two screws and pull off the rear housing, then pull out the brushes and remove the brush holder assembly.
6   To remove the clutch, tap the stop ring towards the pinion until the circlip is exposed, then remove the circlip and the pinion and clutch assembly off the shaft.
7   Thoroughly clean all parts, examine the brushes and fit new ones if the existing ones are down to the wear limit line (Fig. 10.8).
8   Reassemble by inserting the brushes, then screwing the brush holder in its position in the rear housing.
9   Smear silicone or white grease on the armature shaft then slide the pinion/clutch assembly onto the shaft. Fit the stop ring and circlip, then use a puller to pull the stop ring tight up to the circlip.
10 Grease the faces of the small washer and fit it over the shaft.

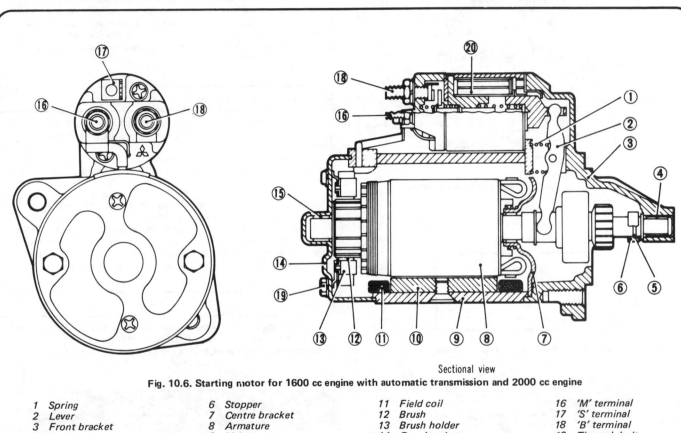

Sectional view

Fig. 10.6. Starting motor for 1600 cc engine with automatic transmission and 2000 cc engine

1	Spring	6	Stopper	11	Field coil	16	'M' terminal
2	Lever	7	Centre bracket	12	Brush	17	'S' terminal
3	Front bracket	8	Armature	13	Brush holder	18	'B' terminal
4	Bearing	9	Yoke	14	Rear bracket	19	Through bolt
5	Ring	10	Pole	15	Bearing	20	Magnetic switch

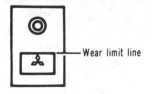

Fig. 10.7. Starting motor circuit

Fig. 10.8. Brush wear check

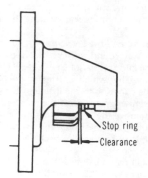

Fig. 10.9. Starter pinion to stop clearance

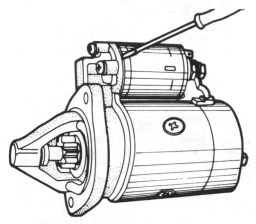

Fig. 10.10. Adjustment of pinion to stop clearance

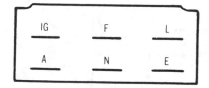

Fig. 10.11. Voltage regulator connections (viewed from front of coupler)

11 Fit the solenoid lever, spring and spring welder into the pinion housing, being careful to refit them in the same positions as they were when removed, then fit the armature into the pinion housing.
12 Fit the yoke and starter housing to the armature and pinion housing and fit and tighten the through bolts.
13 Fit the solenoid, tighten the three mounting screws and reconnect the wire on the rear solenoid terminal.
14 With the drive pinion at its outer limit of travel, measure the clearance (Fig. 10.9) between the pinion and the stop. If this is outside the limits 0.02 to 0.08 in (0.5 to 2.1 mm) correct the clearance by adding or removing packing washers between the solenoid assembly and the pinion housing (Fig. 10.10).

13 Voltage regulator - general description

The voltage regulator is mounted in the engine compartment on the right-hand side of the car (photo). It consists of two elements, a constant voltage relay and a pilot lamp relay, each relay comprising an·electromagnet, armature, frame and contacts. The regulator has a temperature compensation which automatically adjusts the setting of the constant voltage relay to give a higher voltage and therefore a higher battery charging rate in cold weather and a lower voltage and lower charging rate in hot weather. The regulator is a sealed unit and should not be tampered with, but its setting can be checked as described in the following Section.

14 Voltage regulator - testing

1 Separate the two halves of the regulator connector just enough to be able to insert meter test probes, but do not disconnect the connector.
2 Connect a voltmeter with a range of 0 to 20 volts between terminals 'A' and 'E', the voltmeter positive lead being connected to 'A' (Fig. 10.11).
3 With the engine running at idling speed, disconnect one of the battery leads, then increase the engine speed to 2,000 rpm. Do not exceed this speed, or the alternator diodes may be damaged.
4 The voltage indicated by the voltmeter should be between 14.3 and 15.8 volts for an ambient temperature of 68°F. If there is a serious deviation from this value, a new regulator should be fitted, or the existing one adjusted by an automotive electrical workshop.

15 Fuses

1 Fuses are mounted in a multi-way fuse block mounted below the instrument panel at the side of the driver (photo).
2 When a fuse has blown, locate the fault and correct it before

13.1 Voltage regulator

15.1 Fuse block

Circuit No.	Fuse Capacity (A)	Rated Load (A)	Intermittent Load (A)	Maximum Load (A)	Remarks
1	10	4.5		4.5	Head upper (R.H.) 50W x 1=4.23A, Upper beam indicator 3.4Wx1=0.25A
2	10	4.3		4.3	Head upper (L.H.) 50Wx1=4.23A
3	10	5.5 *6.7		5.5 *6.7	Tail 8Wx2=1.26A (*8Wx4=2.52A), Rear side marker 8Wx2=1.26A, Radio 1Wx1=.16A, Lisense 8Wx2=1.26A, Comb. meter all 3.4Wx4=1.0A, Ash tray, panel lamp 3.4Wx2=0.5A
4	10	2.6		2.6	Front side marker 8Wx2=1.26A, Parking 8Wx2=1.26A
5	10	3.7	2.9	6.6 (Lock 16.9)	Wiper=3.7A (Lock 14A), Washer=2.8A
6	10	5.9		5.9	Regulator=2A, Heater=3.4A, Defogger relay=0.3A, Air shut-off solenoid=0.2A (cars for U.S.A.)
7	15	6.1 *5.2	3.8 (75%) *4.7	11.1 *11.4	Turn 27Wx2+3.4W=5.0A (*23Wx3+3.4W=6.2A), Back 27Wx2=4.8A (*23Wx2=3.9A), Gauge=0.1A, Shift indicator=0.13A, Indicator 3.4Wx4=1.0A, Warning=0.45A (cars for Canada)
8	10	3.4		3.4	Head lower (R.H.) 40Wx1=3.4A
9	10	3.4		3.4	Head lower (L.H.) 40Wx1=3.4A
10	5	1.3 *2.2		1.3 *2.2	Dome lamp 10Wx1=0.85A (*10Wx2=1.7A), Warning buzzer=0.2A, Safety belt indicator 3.4Wx1=0.25A (cars for U.S.A.)
11	15	—	7.5 *1.5 (75%)	10*12.6 (100%)	Hazard 27Wx4=9.45A (*23Wx6=12.1A), Indicator 3.4Wx2=0.5A
12	15	—	7.0 *10.3	7.0 *10.3	Horn=2.25A Stop 27Wx2=4.72A (*23Wx4=8A)
13	15	9.3		9.3	Defogger=9A, Warning=0.25A
14	15	1.7	8.0	9.7	Radio 10W=0.7A, Cigarette=8A, Air-conditioner=1A

Note: Asterisked are the values for station wagon.

Fig. 10.12. Fuse capacity table

tting a new fuse.

3   Always use the correct fuse rating and never use heavier fuses than fitted originally, unless additional equipment has been connected to a circuit (see Table Fig. 10.12).

4   If a fuse holder becomes loose, it may become sufficiently hot to burn out the fuse and damage the holder. To prevent this, check the fuse holders for tightness of contact.

5   If a fuse holder becomes defective, it is necessary to renew the entire fuse block assembly.

16 Fusible link

1   A fusible link is fitted in the battery positive lead to give electrical protection to the electrical system which is not protected by the distribution fuses (Fig. 10.13).

2   A melted fusible link can be detected by a swelling or discolouration of the harness covering and should be renewed by one of the same rating, after the cause of failure has been found and corrected.

3   Because the melting of a fusible link means that a current of 100 or 150 amps has flowed, it is very important to locate and correct the fault.

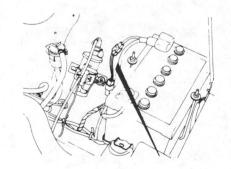

Fig. 10.13. Fusible link

17.1 Ignition switch and steering lock

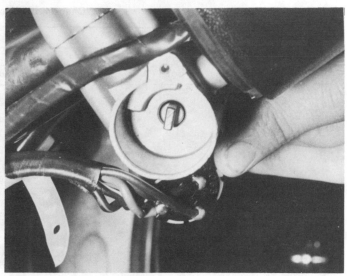

17.4 Ignition switch separated from steering lock

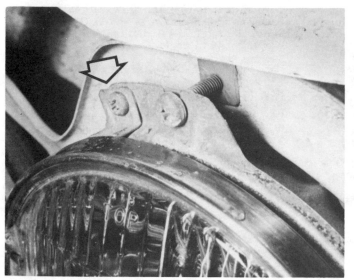

18.2. Headlamp bezel screw (arrowed) and headlamp adjusting screw

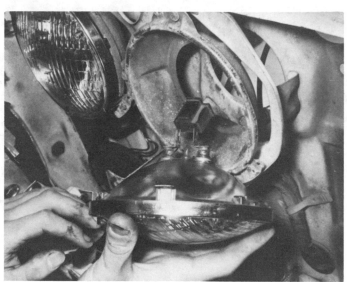

18.3. Headlamp plug connector

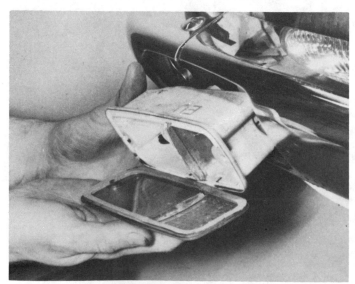

20.3 Sidelight and flasher bulb refitting

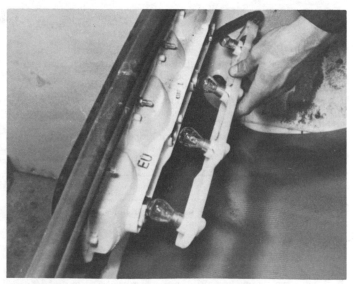

21.2. Refitting the rear lights

4   The ratings and identifications of fusible links is as follows:

	Lighting circuit (green)	Other circuits (red)
Fusible link size	$0.00078 \ in^2$ $(0.5 \ mm^2)$	$0.00132 \ in^2$ $(0.85 \ mm^2)$
Continuous rating	27 amps	34 amps
Fusing current	100 amps	150 amps

17 Ignition switch - removal and refitting

1   The ignition switch is combined with the steering wheel lock (photo), so that when the switch is turned to the LOCK position and the key is withdrawn, the lock pin automatically enters the steering wheel shaft.
2   The switch incorporates a warning circuit which is activated when the key is inserted, as well as circuits to control the ignition and starter motor.
3   The switch assembly is fixed by shear bolts, the heads of which break off when tightened to the correct torque and the assembly cannot easily be removed unless the bolts are sawn through.
4   The switch mechanism can be renewed if faulty, by removing the fixing screw (Fig. 10.14) and pulling out the switch (photo).
5   Refitting is a reversal of the removal procedure.

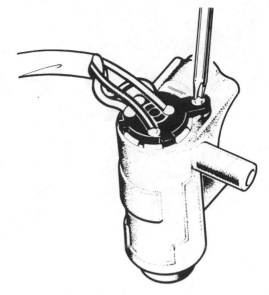

Fig. 10.14. Removing the ignition switch

18 Headlamp sealed beam unit - renewal

1   Remove the front badge then take out the three retaining screws from the top of the grille, the three from the bottom and remove the grille.
2   Remove the three screws securing the lamp bezel, taking care not to disturb the headlamp adjusting screws (photo). Remove the bezel while supporting the front of the lamp unit.
3   Allow the lamp to tip downwards to give access to the plug connector (photo) and pull off the plug.
4   Fit the plug to the new units, refit the bezel and the front grille.

19 Headlamp - beam alignment

Headlamp setting is achieved by a vertical adjustment screw which is above the headlamp and a horizontal adjustment screw on the horizontal centre line of the lamp, both screws being accessible without removing the grille (Fig. 10.15). Approximate alignment may be carried out with the car standing on level ground with the lamps shining on a vertical surface about ten feet in front, but it is recommended that the headlamps are aligned by a service station using optical beam setting equipment.

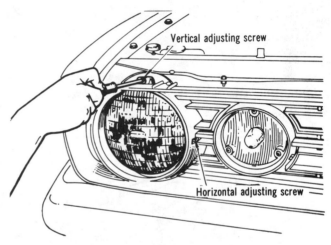

Vertical adjusting screw

Horizontal adjusting screw

Fig. 10.15. Headlamp adjusting screws

20 Sidelight/flasher bulb renewal

1   Remove the two screws from the lens and pull out the lamp assembly.
2   To change the complete combination lamp assembly, disconnect the plug and socket connector and fit a new unit.
3   To renew a bulb, carefully prise off the lens, taking care not to damage the gasket. (photo). Renew the defective bulb, refit the lens against the gasket and screw the unit back onto the car.

21 Rear lights, bulb renewal

1   The tail light, stop light, reversing light and rear flashers are in a common fitting. To renew a bulb, remove the three screws from the rear of the fitting, access to which is obtained from inside the boot.
2   Pull off the back of the fitting (photo) and renew the bulbs as necessary.

22 Number plate lamp - bulb renewal

1   Remove the two screws from the lamp housing which is beneath the rear bumper and take off the housing (photo).

22.1 Removing the number plate lamp housing

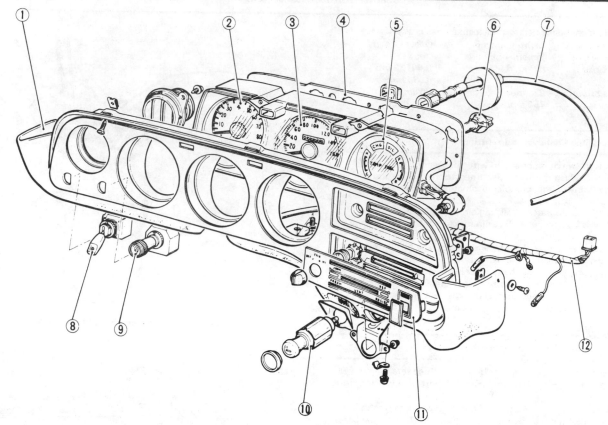

Fig. 10.16. Instrument cluster arrangement (Left-hand drive)

1 Instrument cluster panel	4 Printed board	7 Speedometer cable	10 Cigarette lighter
2 Tachometer	5 Combination gauge	8 Lighting switch	11 Heater control panel
3 Speedometer	6 Indicator bulb socket	9 Rheostat	12 Instrument cluster harness

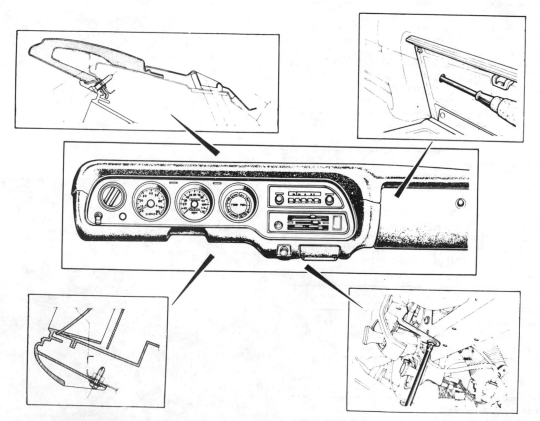

Fig. 10.17. Instrument cluster attachments

2 Renew the bulb and refit the housing, checking that the sealing gasket is in place and in good condition.
3 Fit a new gasket if the existing one shows any signs of allowing the ingress of water.

23 Interior light - bulb renewal

1 Pull down the switch end of the diffuser and then unhook the diffuser at its front end to expose the lamp (photo).
2 Renew the festoon bulb, making sure that it fits tightly by bending the contacts inwards before inserting the bulb.

24 Instrument panel - removal and refitting

1 Disconnect the battery leads.
2 Remove three screws from the top and two from the bottom of the instrument panel.
0 Remove the screws securing the heater control knob, ash tray and cigarette lighter to their respective brackets.

4 Remove the blind cover on the side of the glove box and remove the screws from the side of the instrument panel (Fig. 10.17).
5 Take off the control knobs of the radio and remove the hexagon nuts underneath them.
6 Pull the instrument panel forward and disconnect the speedometer drive, and electrical connections, then remove the panel assembly (photo).
7 Remove the clock knob, loosen the instrument case attachment screws from the meter assembly and remove the glass and bezel (photo).
8 Remove the fixing screws and remove the speedometer (photo) fuel gauge, temperature gauge, tachometer and clock.
9 When reassembling the instrument cluster, do not tighten the screws too much, otherwise the cluster may be damaged and take care to lay and clip the wiring harness so that it is not strained.
10 During the refitting procedure, check that all the parts of the harness are plugged in and that the necessary electrical connections of flanges are made. Insert the instrument cluster back into the car carefully, so that no part of the wiring harness is trapped and after refitment, ensure that there is no loose wire behind the instrument panel by lightly pulling the wires from inside the engine compartment

23.1 Roof light with cover removed

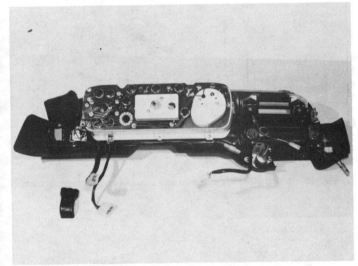

24.6 Rear view of instrument panel after removal

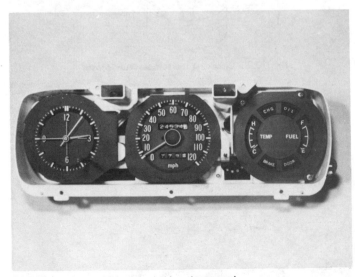

24.7 Meter cluster with glass and bezel removed

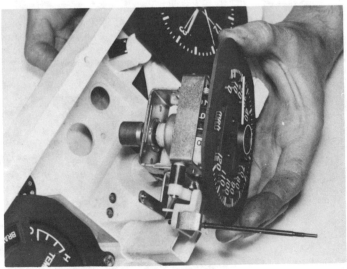

24.8 Removing the speedometer

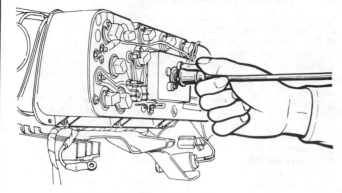

Fig. 10.18 Fitting the speedometer cable

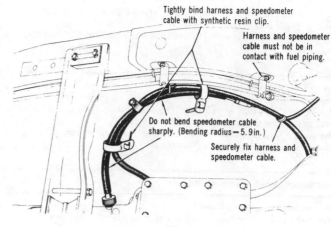

Tightly bind harness and speedometer cable with synthetic resin clip.

Harness and speedometer cable must not be in contact with fuel piping.

Do not bend speedometer cable sharply. (Bending radius—5.9 in.)

Securely fix harness and speedometer cable.

Fig. 10.19. Under floor fitting of speedometer cable

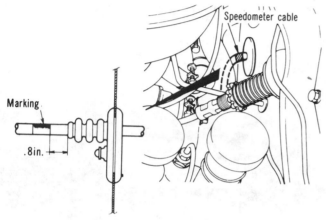

Speedometer cable

Marking

.8 in.

Fig. 10.20. Installing the speedometer cable in engine compartment

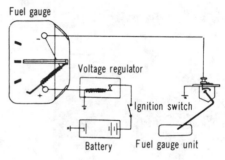

Fuel gauge

Voltage regulator

Ignition switch

Battery

Fuel gauge unit

Fig. 10.21. Fuel gauge circuit

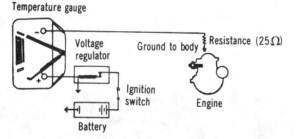

Temperature gauge

Voltage regulator

Ground to body

Resistance (25Ω)

Ignition switch

Battery

Engine

Fig. 10.22. Checking the temperature gauge

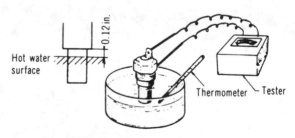

0.12 in.

Hot water surface

Thermometer

Tester

Fig. 10.23. Checking the temperature sensor

29.1 Removing an instrument panel lamp

32.1 Stop lamp switch (arrowed)

25 Speedometer drive - refitting

1 When a speedometer drive needs renewing, it should be renewed as an assembly and the correct one must be fitted as follows:

	4 speed manual Transmission	5 speed manual Transmission	Automatic Transmission
Overall cable length	53 in	57 in	57 in
Marking tape colour	Green	White	Red

2 When connecting the cable to the speedometer, push it on until its retainer engages the groove in the speedometer and then pull it to make sure that it is firmly engaged in the groove (Fig. 10.18).
3 If a cable is being renewed without removing the instrument cluster, remove the choke bracket to gain access to the back of the speedometer.
4 If the speedometer drive is not fitted carefully, it can give rise to a fluctuating pointer, noise and damage to the wiring harness of the instrument panel. Make sure that the cable is fitted securely at both ends, that it is not strained and that a bend radius is never less than 6 in (152.4 mm) (Fig. 10.19).
5 After fitting the speedometer end of the cable, pull the slack cable through into the engine compartment until there is about ¾ in (19 mm) of cable between the coloured marking tape (green, white or red) and the front bulkhead (Fig. 10.20).

26 Tachometer - testing

1 The tachometer is a DC instrument which receives its signal from a transistorized circuit which counts the pulses produced by the switching action of the contact breaker points.
2 Connect a calibrated test meter to the engine and compare the readings at different engine speeds. If there is an excessive difference in reading between the test instrument and the tachometer, fit a new tachometer.

27 Fuel gauge - refitting and testing

1 When fitting the tank unit, carefully coat both sides of the gasket with a sealant to prevent any petrol leakage.
2 Carefully fit the unit ensuring that the float arm is not bent.
3 Ensure that there is a good electrical contact between the tank unit and earth.
4 The tank unit may be tested with an ohmmeter to measure the resistance between the terminal and earth, which should be as follows:

Float position	E	½	F
Resistance	95 ± 7 ohms	32.5 ± 4 ohms	3 ± 2 ohms

5 The fuel gauge is of the bimetal type and the circuit (Fig. 10.21) has a constant voltage relay built into the gauge to prevent indication errors resulting from voltage fluctuations.
6 To check the gauge, remove the wire to the tank unit and earth the tank unit terminal of the gauge. If the gauge indicates 'F' the gauge is satisfactory. If there is no indication, measure the resistance between the gauge terminals, which should be 55 ohms. A low resistance indicates a shorted coil and a high resistance (over 150 ohms) a broken coil.

28 Temperature gauge - testing

1 The temperature gauge is of the bimetal type and the circuit has a constant voltage relay supply obtained from the fuel gauge. The constant voltage supply prevents indication errors resulting from voltage fluctuations.
2 To test the gauge, disconnect the wire to the temperature sensor and connect the sensor terminal to earth through a 25 ohms resistor (Fig. 10.22). The gauge will be damaged if the terminal is connected directly to earth and not through a resistor. If the gauge is satisfactory it will indicate a temperature of about 250°F.
3 If the gauge is not satisfactory, check the resistance between the

gauge terminals, which should be 55 ohms. A low resistance indicates a shorted coil and a high resistance (over 150 ohms) a broken coil.
4 The sensor may be tested by inserting it to the prescribed depth (Fig. 10.23) in hot water and measuring the resistance between the terminal and the sensor case, when the following readings should be obtained.

Thermometer temperature	176°F (80°C)	212°F (100°C)
Standard resistance	75.4 ohms	40.9 ohms
Tolerance	± 7 ohms	± 4 ohms

29 Instrument panel - bulb renewal

1 Remove the instrument panel as described in Section 24.
2 The lamps may be removed by turning the lamp holder to unlock it and then withdrawing it (photo).
3 Insert a new bulb and refit the lamp and instrument panel.

30 Headlamp switch - removal and refitting

1 The headlamp switch is of the single-pole, double-throw type and is mounted on the instrument panel. Its 'T' contacts are rated at 11A and the 'H' contacts at 12A.
2 To change the switch, unscrew and remove the bezel ring and push the switch through to the back of the panel.
3 Withdraw the switch from beneath the instrument panel and pull off its connector.
4 When refitting, ensure that the switch is vertical and that the bezel ring is tightened so that the switch is firm, but take care not to damage the switch by overtightening.

31 Instrument panel rheostatic switch - removal and refitting

1 The rheostatic switch enables the brightness of the illumination of the instruments to be varied to reduce glare when driving at night.
2 To take out the switch, remove the knob then unscrew and remove the bezel ring.
3 Push the switch through the instrument panel and withdraw it from beneath the instrument panel, then pull off its connector.
4 Refitting is the reverse of the removal procedure. ·
5 The switch is designed for a load of five, 3.4 watt lamps and if this load is exceeded the switch will overheat and may turn out. Do not fit additional lamps, or renew the instrument lamps with any of a higher rating.

32 Stop lamp switch

1 The stop lamp switch is also the limit stop of the footbrake pedal (photo) and its adjustment is described in Chapter 9, Section 8.
2 The rating of the switch is 12.5A.

33 Oil pressure switch - testing and adjustment

1 The oil pressure switch is intended to operate at a pressure of about 5 lb/in^2.
2 Check the switch by connecting a lamp in series with a battery, or an ohmmeter between the terminal and the case to see if the switch is OFF when no pressure is applied and ON when the pressure exceeds about 5 lb/in^2.
3 To adjust the switch operating pressure, remove the contact screw, insert a small screwdriver down the central hole and turn the adjuster screw (Fig. 10.24).

34 Handbrake switch - adjustment

1 The handbrake switch is of the push-to-OFF type, mounted below the handbrake lever (photo).
2 Pull the handbrake one notch up and after loosening the switch mounting screws, slide the switch up and down until it is in the ON position when in contact with the handbrake lever.

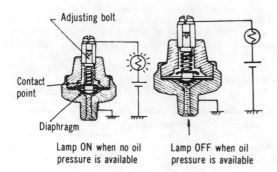

Adjusting bolt

Contact point

Diaphragm

Lamp ON when no oil pressure is available

Lamp OFF when oil pressure is available

Fig. 10.24. Oil-pressure switch

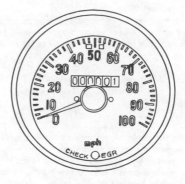

Fig. 10.25. EGR indicating lamp

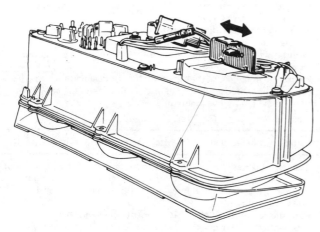

Fig. 10.26. EGR reset switch

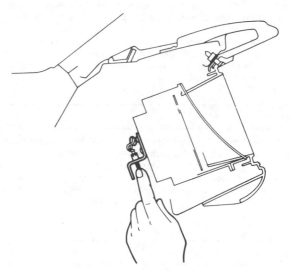

Fig. 10.27. Reset switch operation

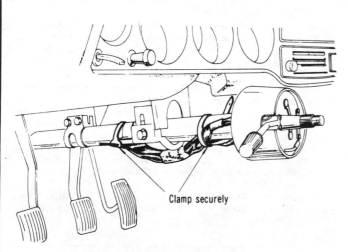

Clamp securely

Fig. 10.28. Column switch cableform cleating

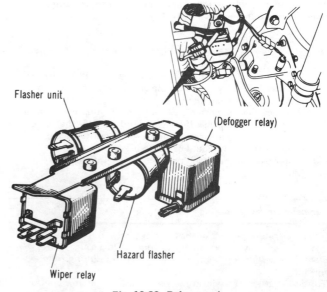

Flasher unit

(Defogger relay)

Hazard flasher

Wiper relay

Fig. 10.29. Relay panel

3   Tighten the fixing screws with the switch in this position.

35 EGR warning lamp and reset switch

1   An EGR warning lamp, when fitted, is on the speedometer dial
(Fig. 10.25) and is operated by a microswitch inside the instrument
which is switched every 15,000 miles (24,000 km).
2   When the EGR checks have been made (Chapter 3, Section 21) the
circuit must be reset by operating the slide switch on the back of the
instrument cluster (Fig. 10.26 and 27).

36 Steering column switch - removal and refitting

1   Remove the steering wheel as described in Chapter 11, Section 13.
2   Remove the steering column shroud to give access to the switch
fixings and cableforms.
3   Remove the screws securing the column switch, remove the cable
straps and separate the harness plugs and sockets then remove the
switch assembly.
4   When refitting the switch, make sure that it is concentric with the
steering column.
5   Secure the cable harnesses, taking them as close as possible to the
centre line of the column tube (Fig. 10.28).
6   Refit the steering column shroud and the steering wheel.

37 Brake failure switch

The brake failure switch, when fitted, may either be as a part of
the combination valve (Chapter 8, Section 12) (cars for USA) or may
be a separate unit located between the master cylinder and the wheel
cylinders. If either the front or rear brake pipeline pressures decrease,
the switch operates and the warning lamp will illuminate.

38 Door switches - removal and refitting

1   The door switches give warning if any door is not fully closed and
are mounted at the bottom of the door pillar.
2   To remove a switch, pull off the rubber gaiter, pull out the switch,
which is a push-fit in the hole and disconnect the wiring connector.
3   Clean the switch if necessary, or renew it if it is badly corroded.
4   Push the wiring connectors into their sockets, push the switch into
its mounting hole as far as it will go and refit the gaiter, using a new
one if the one removed was perished or damaged.

39 Relays - renewal

1   The wiper relay, demister relay, hazard flasher and direction
indicator flasher relays are mounted on a common panel beneath the
instrument panel (Fig. 10.29).
2   To renew a relay, separate its electrical connector, remove the
fixing screws and refit the relay.
3   Where a radio interference suppressor is fitted, this should be
secured with the screw that holds the demister relay.
4   Ensure that the earth wire of the front wiring harness is effectively
bonded to the panel.

40 Horn - adjustment

1   Remove the horn (photo) from the car, fix its bracket in a vise and
connect a battery of the correct voltage to the horn terminals.
2   Sound the horn and adjust its note by turning the adjuster screw
(Fig. 10.30).
3   If the horn does not sound, turn the screw UP until a weak sound
is heard, then continue turning up to a further 180 degrees to obtain
the best tone.
4   If the horn makes a harsh low sound, turn the screw UP about
half a turn to find the best tone.
5   If the horn makes a loud intermittent vibrating sound, turn the
screw DOWN, 20 to 30 degrees to find the best position.
6   Having found the best note, apply some clear lacquer to the screw
to lock it.

Fig. 10.30. Adjusting the horn

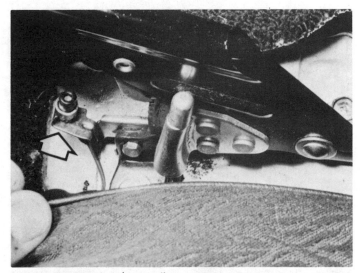

34.1 Handbrake switch (arrowed)

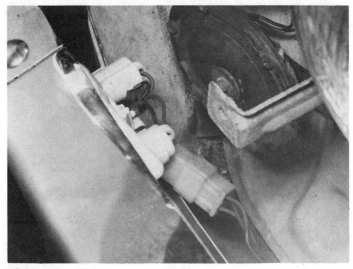

40.1 Position of horn

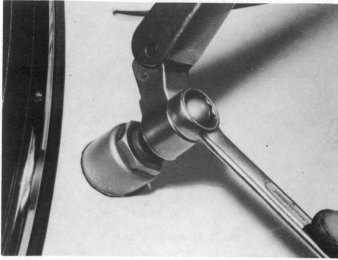

41.1 Unscrewing the windscreen wiper arm

41 Windscreen wiper arms and blades - removal and refitting

1   Unscrew and remove the cap nut from the wiper arm and pull the arm off its splines (photo).
2   To remove the blade, grip the arm and the blade and pull (photo).
3   Fit new blades if the existing ones are damaged, or do not wipe clearly.
4   Fit the arms on the splines so that in the park position the blades are about ¾ in (19 mm) above the bottom of the windscreen then refit and tighten the cap nuts.

42 Windscreen wiper motor - removal

1   Remove the windscreen wiper arms. Remove the arm shaft locknuts (photo) and push the shafts through their mounting holes.
2   Remove the cover plate from around the wiper motor (photo).
3   Remove the bolts securing the motor bracket to the body and pull the wiper motor assembly forward.
4   Hold the motor shaft firmly, with the linkage at right angles to it and separate the motor from the linkage (Fig. 10.31).
5   If required, the linkage may be removed by threading it through the hole.

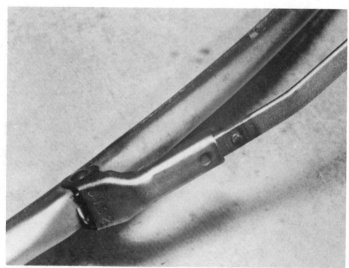

41.2 Wiper blade disengaged from arm

42.1 Wiper arm removed, showing arm shaft locknut

42.2 Wiper motor and access plate

44.1 Windscreen washer reservoir and pump

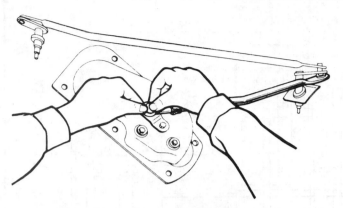

Fig. 10.31. Wiper motor linkage removal

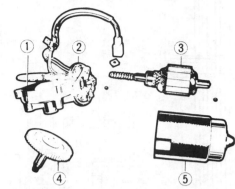

Fig. 10.32. Windscreen wiper motor components

1   Gear box
2   Brush assembly
3   Armature

4   Driven gear
5   Motor case

43 Windscreen wiper motor - dismantling and reassembly

1   Do not separate the motor and crank arm unless you have to, because they have been assembled to give the correct parking position. If it is necessary to separate them, put mating marks to ensure correct reassembly.

2   Remove the crank arm and remove the gearbox cover.

3   Remove the driven gear, take off the motor cover and remove the armature assembly, being careful not to lose the steel ball which is fitted to each end of the shaft.

4   Check the brushes for wear, the brush springs for loss of tension and also check that the brush lead is soldered securely.

5   Check the contact point for signs of bad contact or burning, check the driven gear for damage and wear and ensure that the commutator is clean and undamaged.

6   When reassembling the motor, grease the teeth of the driven gear and fix the ball to each end of the shaft with grease before refitting the armature.

7   After assembling the motor, run it under no load conditions before refitting it and check that the current is less than 3A at both low and high speed.

8   Refitting the motor is the reverse of removing it and adjust the blades to give the correct parking position.

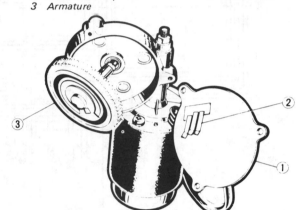

Fig. 10.33. Windscreen wiper motor gear box

1   Gear box cover
2   Contact point

3   Driven gear

44 Windscreen washer - servicing

1   Normally the windscreen washer requires no maintenance other than keeping the reservoir (photo) topped up with water to which some screen cleaning fluid has been added.

2   The nozzles should each spray an area of windscreen about 6 in by 2 in (152 by 50.8 mm) with its centre line about 12 in (304 mm) from the bottom of the screen. If the nozzles require any adjustment to achieve this, bend the nozzle bracket.

3   If the quantity of water discharged by the jets is low, check that the reservoir is full and then look for a blocked jet, or a clogged or crushed tube.

45 Fault diagnosis - electrical system

Symptom	Reason/s
Starter motor fails to turn engine No electricity at starter motor	Battery discharged. Battery defective internally. Battery terminal leads loose or earth lead not securely attached to body. Loose or broken connections in starter motor circuit Starter motor switch or solenoid faulty.
Electricity at starter motor: faulty motor	Starter motor pinion jammed in mesh with flywheel gear ring. Starter brushes badly worn, sticking, or brush wires loose. Commutator dirty, worn or burnt. Starter motor armature faulty. Field coils earthed
Starter motor turns engine very slowly Electrical defects	Battery in discharged condition. Starter brushes badly worn, sticking, or brush wires loose. Loose wires in starter motor circuit.
Starter motor operates without turning engine Mechanical damage	Pinion or flywheel gear teeth broken or worn. Battery in discharged condition.

Fault diagnosis continues on page 148

Wiring diagram for Colt Galant (UK) with non-balancer engine (Part A)

Wiring diagram for Colt Galant (UK) with non-balancer engine (Part B)

Rear Comb. Lamp R.H. (Sedan Hardtop)
Tail Turn Stop Back

Rear Comb. Lamp R.H. (Estate)
Turn Stop Tail Back

LICENSE LAMP
RH 8w
LH 8w
EARTH

Rear Comb. Lamp L.H. (Sedan Hardtop)
Back Stop Turn Tail

Rear Comb. Lamp L.H. (Estate)
Back Tail Stop Turn

BODY EARTH

FUEL GAUGE UNIT

REAR DEFOGGER

DOOR SW RR RH

DOOR SW RR LH

PARKING BRAKE SW

DOOR SW FR RH

DOOR SW FR LH

Room Lamp

Rear Room Lamp (Estate)

Rear Gate Sw. (Estate)

DEFOGGER SW

LIGHTING SW

CIGARETTE LIGHTER

ASH TRAY LAMP

BODY EARTH

PANEL LAMP

SPEAKER

RADIO

IGNITION SW

RETURN AUTOMATICALLY ON
FULL STROKE PASSING SW
DIMMER SW
COUPLED OPERATION

WASHER SW

WIPER SW

TURN SIGNAL SW
L N R

HORN SW

FUEL GAUGE

TEMPERATURE GAUGE

COMB METER LAMP 3.4w×4

UPPER BEAM INDICATOR LAMP 3.4w
TURN SIGNAL INDICATOR LAMP RH 3.4w
TURN SIGNAL INDICATOR LAMP LH 3.4w
CHARGING INDICATOR LAMP 3.4w
OIL PRESSURE INDICATOR LAMP 3.4w
PARKING BRAKE
DOOR INDICATOR LAMP

EARTH

COOLER

FUSE BLOCK

G
G
G

Wiring diagram for Colt Galant (UK) with balancer engine (Part A)

DEFOGGER SW · LIGHTING SW · CIGARETTE LIGHTER · ASH TRAY LAMP · BODY EARTH · PANEL LAMP · SPEAKER · RADIO · IGNITION SW · RETURN AUTOMATICALLY · FULL STROKE PASSING SW · DIMMER SW · COUPLED OPERATION · WASHER SW · WIPER SW · TURN SIGNAL SW · HORN SW · RHEOSTAT · FUEL GAUGE · TEMPERATURE GAUGE · COMB METER LAMP 3·4w x4 · UPPER BEAM INDICATOR LAMP 3·4w · TURN SIGNAL INDICATOR LAMP RH 3·4w · TURN SIGNAL INDICATOR LAMP LH 3·4w · CHARGING INDICATOR LAMP 3·4w · OIL PRESSURE INDICATOR LAMP 3·4w · PARKING BRAKE · DOOR INDICATOR LAMP · TACHOMETER

EARTH · COOLER · FUSE BLOCK

HEATER MOTOR · INTERMITTENT WIPER RELAY · WIPER RELAY · CONDENSER · TURN SIGNAL FLASHER UNIT · HAZARD FLASHER UNIT · STOP LAMP SW · DEFOGGER RELAY · CLOCK (CONSOLE) · PARKING BRAKE SWITCH · BACKUP LAMP SW

B · R8 · GW

WIPER MOTOR · INTERMITTENT WIPER SW. · STARTER MOTOR · STARTER MAGNETIC SW · TEMP GAUGE GAUGE UNIT · DISTRIBUTOR · ENGINE EARTH · IGNITION COIL

WASHER MOTOR · VOLTAGE REGULATOR · CONDENSER · OIL PRESSURE SW · ALTERNATOR · EARTH · FUSIBLE LINK · BATTERY

FRONT SIDE TURN 10W · FRONT SIDE TURN 10W · HORN · HORN

Headlamp RH Type 2 · Comb lamp RH · Turn · Position · Headlamp RH Type 1 · Headlamp LH Type 1 · Comb lamp LH · Position · Turn · Headlamp LH Type 2

Wiring diagram for Colt Galant (UK) with balancer engine (Part B)

Wiring diagram (typical) for Plymouth Arrow and Colt Celeste (Part A)

Wiring diagram (typical) for Plymouth Arrow and Colt Celeste (Part B)

Wiring diagram for Dodge Colt (early models) (Part A)

DEFOGGER SW
LIGHTING SW
CIGARETTE LIGHTER
ASH TRAY LAMP
BODY EARTH
PANEL LAMP
RADIO
SPEAKER
IGNITION SW (STEERING LOCK) (WARNING SW)
RETURN AUTOMATICALLY FULL STROKE PASSING
DIMMER SW COUPLED OPERATION
WASHER SW
WIPER SW
TURN SIGNAL
HORN SW
OVERHEATING INDICATING LAMP
FUEL GAUGE
TEMPERATURE GAUGE
SEAT BELT WARNING BUZZER
COMBINATION METER LAMP
MICRO SW
RESET SW
EGR INDICATING LAMP
UPPER BEAM INDICATOR LAMP
TURN SIGNAL INDICATOR LAMP R
TURN SIGNAL INDICATOR LAMP L
CHARGING INDICATOR LAMP
OIL PRESSURE INDICATOR LAMP
PARKING BRAKE, BRAKE FAILURE
SEAT BELT INDICATOR LAMP
RHEOSTAT
TACHOMETER
SPEED SENSOR (FOR CALIFORNIA)
EARTH (EXCEPT CALIFORNIA)

PANEL A
PANEL B
CONTROL UNIT
INTERLOCK RELAY
HEATER MOTOR
INHIBITER SW
INDICATOR LAMP
WIPER RELAY
CONDENSER
TURN SIGNAL FLASHER UNIT
HAZARD FLASHER UNIT
STOP LAMP SW
DEFOGGER RELAY
OVERHEATING INDICATING LAMP RELAY
BRAKE FAILURE INDICATOR SW
NEUTRAL SW
BACKUP LAMP SW

FUSE BLOCK

AT THE TYPE WITHOUT OUTSIDE FIX RESISTANCE, CIRCUIT OF ① ② JOINT TO TERMINAL ⊕ OF IGNITION COIL

WIPER MOTOR
WASHER MOTOR
VOLTAGE REGULATOR
CONDENSER
THERMO SENSOR "B"
OIL PRESSURE SW
STARTER MOTOR
STARTER MAGNETIC SW
UNDERHOOD SW
ALTERNATOR
DISTRIBUTOR
TEMP GAUGE UNIT
ENGINE EARTH
FUEL CUT SOLENOID
IGNITION COIL
FUEL CONTROL RELAY
BATTERY
FUSIBLE LINK
EARTH

AIR SHUT-OFF VALVE
FRONT SIDE MARKER RH
FRONT SIDE MARKER LH
HEADLAMP RH 50W 40W
FRONT COMB LAMP RH PARKING 8W TURN 27W (23W)
HORN
HEADLAMP LH 40W 50W
FRONT COMB LAMP LH TURN 27W (23W) PARKING 8W

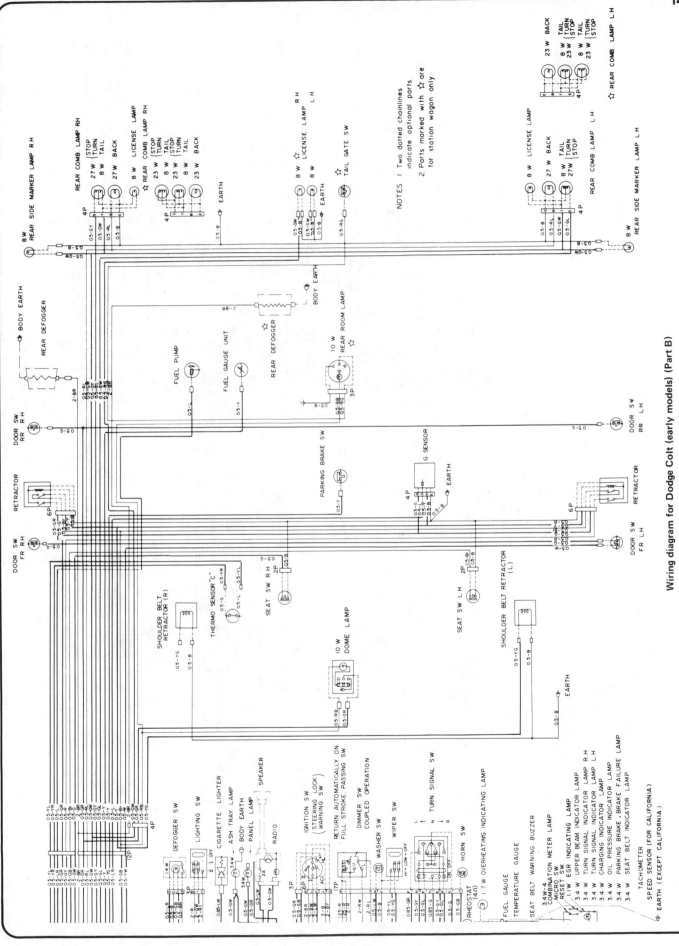

Wiring diagram for Dodge Colt (early models) (Part B)

Wiring diagram for Dodge Colt (later models) (Part A)

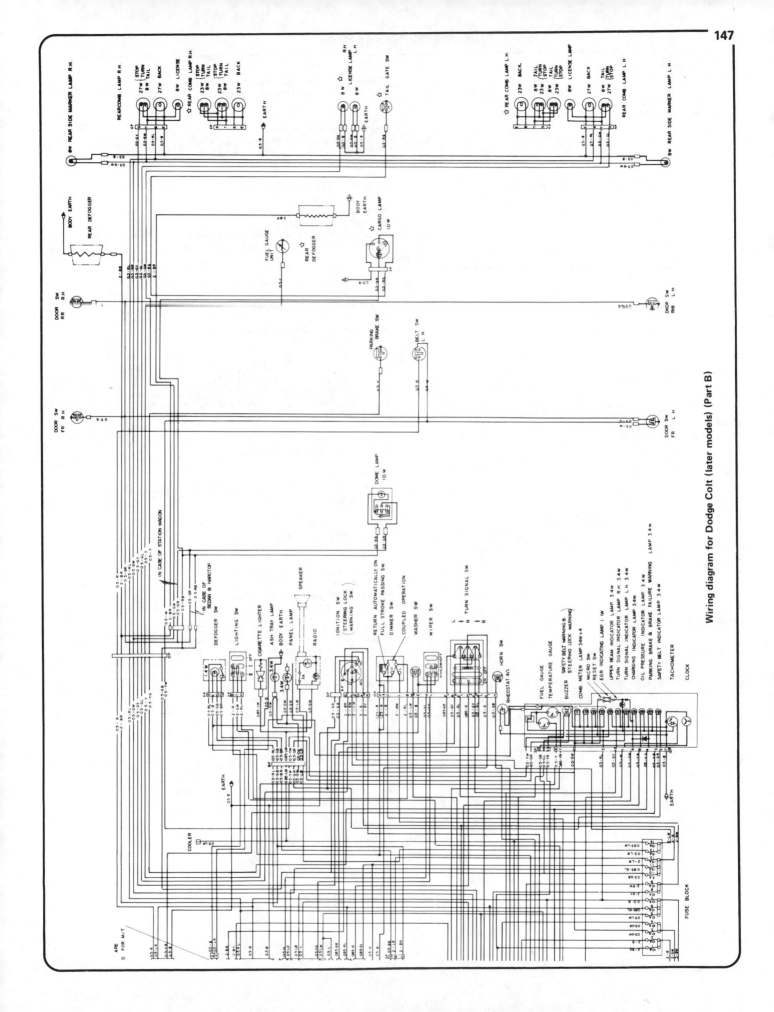

Wiring diagram for Dodge Colt (later models) (Part B)

Starter motor noisy or excessively rough engagement
Lack of attention or mechanical damage

Pinion or flywheel gear teeth broken or worn.
Starter motor retaining bolts loose.

Battery will not hold charge for more than a few days
Wear or damage

Battery defective internally.
Electrolyte level too low or electrolyte too weak due to leakage.
Plate separators no longer fully effective.
Battery plates severely sulphated.

Insufficient current flow to keep battery charged

Battery plates severely sulphated.
Drivebelt slipping.
Battery terminal connections loose or corroded.
Alternator not charging.
Short in lighting circuit causing continual battery drain.
Regulator unit not working correctly.

Ignition light fails to go out, battery runs flat in a few days
Alternator not charging

Drivebelt loose and slipping or broken.
Brushes worn, sticking, broken or dirty.
Brush springs worn or broken.
Commutator dirty, greasy, worn or burnt.
Alternator field coils burnt, open, or shorted
Commutator worn.
Pole pieces very loose.

Regulator or cut-out fails to work correctly

Regulator incorrectly set.
Cut-out incorrectly set.
Open circuit in wiring of cut-out and regulator unit.

Horn
Horn operates all the time

Horn push either earthed or stuck down.
Horn cable to horn push earthed.

Horn fails to operate

Blown fuse.
Cable or cable connection loose, broken or disconnected.
Horn has an internal fault.

Horn emits intermittent or unsatisfactory noise

Cable connections loose.
Horn incorrectly adjusted.

Lights
Lights do not come on

If engine not running, battery discharged.
Sealed beam filament burnt out or bulbs broken.
Wire connections loose, disconnected or broken.
Light switch shorting or otherwise faulty.

Lights come on but fade out

If engine not running, battery discharged.
Light bulb filament burnt out or bulbs or sealed beam units broken.
Wire connections loose, disconnected or broken.
Light switch shorting or otherwise faulty.

Lights give very poor illumination

Lamp glasses dirty.
Lamp badly out of adjustment.

Lights work erratically - flashing on and off, especially over bumps

Battery terminals or earth connection loose.
Light not earthing properly.
Contacts in light switch faulty.

Wipers
Wiper motor fails to work

Blown fuse.
Wire connection loose, disconnected, or broken.
Brushes badly worn.
Armature worn or faulty.
Field coils faulty.

Wiper motor works very slowly and takes excessive current

Commutator dirty, greasy or burnt.
Armature bearings dirty or unaligned.
Armature badly worn or faulty.

Wiper motor works slowly and takes little current

Brushes badly worn.
Commutator dirty, greasy or burnt.
Armature badly worn or faulty.

Wiper motor works but wiper blades remain static

Wiper motor gearbox parts badly worn.

Wipers do not stop when switched off or stop in wrong place

Auto-stop device faulty.

Chapter 11 Suspension and steering

For modifications, and information applicable to later models, see Supplement at end of manual

Contents

Specifications

Front suspension type

Type ... ...   MacPherson strut with telescopic dampers, co-axial coil springs and torsion bar

Coil spring free length

(1600 cc) ... ...   13.780 in (350.1 mm)
(2000 cc) ... ...   14.075 in (357.5 mm)
Spring rate ... ...   119.83 lbs/in (1.38 kg/m)

Rear suspension

Type ... ...   Semi-elliptical leaf springs with double acting dampers

Steering

Type ... ...   Recirculating ball nut

Steering geometry

Camber ... ... $5/6^o \pm \frac{1}{2}^o$
Caster ... ... $1 - \frac{1}{4}^o \pm \frac{1}{2}^o$
Toe-in ... ...   0.08 to 0.23 in (2.1 to 5.8 mm)
King pin inclination ... ... 9°

Wheels

Size ... ...   4 - ½J - 13
5J - 13 (Carousel - GT)

Tyres ... ...   6.00 - 13 - 4PR
A78 - 13 - 4PR (Carousel)
BR70 - 13

Inflation pressure
(front) ... ...   24 lb/in^2 (1.69 kg/cm^2)
(rear) ... ...   30 lb/in^2 (2.11 kg/cm^2)

Torque wrench settings

	lb f ft	kg f m
Front suspension		
Brake disc to hub	25 to 29	3.5 to 4.0
Strut to body	7 to 10	1.0 to 1.4
Strut to knuckle arm	29 to 36	4.0 to 5.0
Knuckle arm and balljoint	29 to 43	4.0 to 6.0
Crossmember to lower arm	58 to 65	8.1 to 9.1

Knuckle arm to tie rod end	...	...	...	...	...	...	...	29 to 36	4.0 to 5.0
Stabiliser bracket to chassis	...	...	...	...	...	...	...	7 to 10	1.0 to 1.4
Knuckle to brake adjuster	...	...	...	...	...	...	...	29 to 36	4.0 to 5.0
Caliper to adaptor	...	...	...	...	...	...	...	51 to 65	7.1 to 9.1

Steering

Column tube clamp	...	...	...	...	...	...	...	4 to 6	0.56 to 0.84
Steering shaft clamp	...	...	...	...	...	...	...	14.5 to 18	2.0 to 2.5
Steering wheel	...	...	...	...	...	...	...	25 to 33	3.5 to 4.6
Drop arm	...	...	...	...	...	...	...	94 to 108	13.1 to 16.2
Relay rod to drop arm	...	...	...	...	...	...	...	29 to 43	4.0 to 6.0
Tie rod ends	...	...	...	...	...	...	...	29 to 36	4.0 to 5.0
Tie rod socket to relay rod	...	...	...	...	...	...	...	29 to 36	4.0 to 5.0
Tie rod turnbuckle nuts	...	...	...	...	...	...	...	36 to 40	5.0 to 5.6
Idler arm	...	...	...	...	...	...	...	29 to 43	4.0 to 6.0
Idler arm bracket to frame	...	...	...	...	...	...	...	25 to 29	3.5 to 4.0
Relay rod to idler arm	...	...	...	...	...	...	...	29 to 43	4.0 to 6.0

Rear suspension

Spring pin assembly bracket	...	...	...	...	...	...	...	11 to 14	1.5 to 2.0
Spring U bolts	...	...	...	...	...	...	...	33 to 36	4.6 to 5.0
Shockabsorber top fixing (except estate)	...	...	...	...	...	...	47 to 58	6.6 to 8.1
(estate)	...	...	...	...	...	...	...	12 to 14	1.7 to 2.0
Shockabsorber bottom fixing	...	...	...	...	...	...	...	12 to 14	1.7 to 2.0
Spring pin and shackle pins	...	...	...	...	...	...	...	36 to 43	5.0 to 6.0

Wheel nuts	...	...	...	...	...	...	...	51 to 58	7.1 to 8.1

1 General description

The front suspension is of the MacPherson strut type, with concentric coil springs and an anti-roll bar. The single lower links are pivoted at their inner ends in rubber bushes set in the subframe assembly. The front caster angles and wheel camber are fixed and are not adjustable.

The steering system uses a recirculating ball steering box of variable ratio, a height adjustable, tilting, steering wheel and a collapsible steering tube for safety in the event of an accident. The balljoints in the steering linkage have non-metallic bearings and do not require any lubrication.

The rear suspension is conventional, with semi-elliptical leaf springs and double-acting shockabsorbers.

2 Wheel alignment

1 Camber and caster are not adjustable, but toe-in may be adjusted by screwing in or out the turnbuckle of the tie rod (Fig. 11.1).

2 The amount of toe-in of the left side front wheel may be reduced by turning the tie rod turnbuckle towards the front of the car and the amount of toe-in of the right side front wheel is reduced by the turnbuckle being turned towards the rear of the car.

3 Both turnbuckles should be adjusted by the same amount and the difference between their lengths should not exceed 0.2 in (5.1 mm).

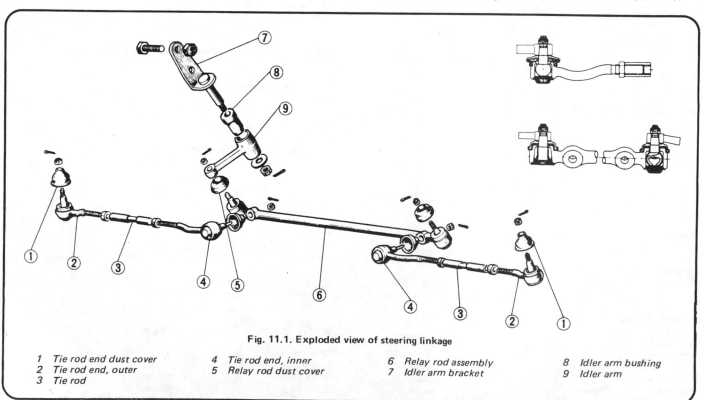

Fig. 11.1. Exploded view of steering linkage

1 Tie rod end dust cover	4 Tie rod end, inner	6 Relay rod assembly	8 Idler arm bushing
2 Tie rod end, outer	5 Relay rod dust cover	7 Idler arm bracket	9 Idler arm
3 Tie rod			

3 Front hub - dismantling and reassembly

1 Jack-up the car, support the axle on a stand and remove the wheel.
2 Remove the brake caliper assembly (Chapter 9, Section 3) and support it on the lower arm. It should not be necessary to remove the brake hose from the caliper.
3 Remove the hub cap, split pin and nut.
4 Pull off the front hub with the brake disc attached, taking care not to drop the outer bearing track and washer.
5 Remove the grease from inside the wheel hub then use a drift to drive out the outer track of the outer bearing.
6 Drive out the inner bearing outer track and oil seal.
7 Clean the stub axle and inspect it for damage and wear. Check the shockabsorber mounting area of the stub axle for cracks and if it is damaged, fit a new strut assembly.
8 Check the bearings for damage, wear and roughness and fit a new bearing if required.
9 Grease the bearings, oil seal and lip and bore of the wheel hub and pack the wheel hub cap with grease.
10 If the brake disc and hub are separated the nuts must be tightened evenly to a torque wrench setting of 25 to 29 lb f ft (3.5 to 4.0 kg f m) on reassembly and the disc should be checked for deflection (Chapter 9, Section 5).
11 Insert the inner bearing into the hub, carefully press in the oil seal with the lip inwards, until the back of the seal is flush with the end of the hub. Take great care not to distort the oil seal.
12 Fit the hub assembly onto the stub axle, taking care not to damage the oil seal.
13 Fit the outer bearing, plain washer and nut, then tighten the nut to a torque wrench setting of 14.5 lb f ft (2.0 kg f m) to bed all the assembled parts.
14 Unscrew the nut to release all the pressure and then tighten it to a torque wrench setting of 3.6 lb f ft (0.5 kg f m). Fit the lock cap and split pin, dividing and bending back the free ends of the pin. If the holes in the stub axle and lock cap cannot be aligned in any position, unscrew the nut slightly until the pin can be inserted, but do not unscrew the nut more than 15°.
15 Refit the brake caliper and tighten it to a torque wrench setting of 58 to 72 lb f ft (8.1 to 10 kg f m).

4 Front suspension strut - removal and refitting

1 Jack up the car, support it on firm stands and remove the wheel.
2 Remove the brake caliper (Chapter 9, Section 3) and wheel hub.
3 Disconnect the torsion bar from the lower arm and remove the three steering knuckle to strut attachment bolts (photo).
4 Carefully force down the lower arm and separate the strut assembly from the steering knuckle.

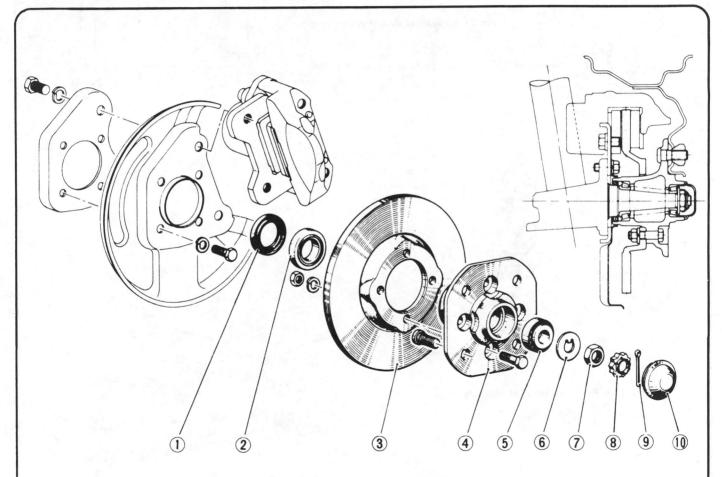

Fig. 11.2. Exploded view of front axle hub

1 Oil seal	4 Front wheel hub	7 Slotted nut	9 Split pin
2 Front wheel bearing (inner)	5 Front wheel bearing (outer)	8 Lock cap	10 Hub cap
3 Brake disc	6 Washer		

152

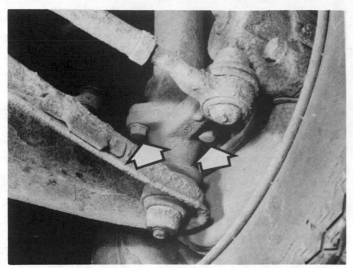

4.3 Strut to knuckle arm attachment bolts (arrowed)

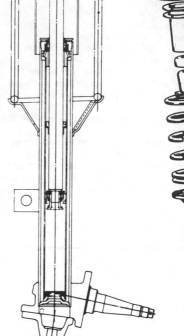

Fig. 11.3. Exploded view of strut assembly

1 Upper dust cover
2 Insulator
3 Upper spring seat
4 Dust cover
5 Dust cover plate
6 Spacer
7 Bumper rubber
8 Front spring
9 Strut sub-assembly (shock-absorber)
10 Stub axle
11 Knuckle arm

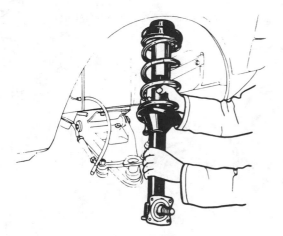

Fig. 11.4. Removing the strut assembly

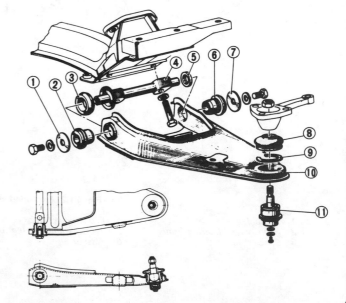

Fig. 11.5. Exploded view of lower arm

1 Washer
2 Bushing (front)
3 Stopper rubber
4 Lower arm shaft
5 Spacer
6 Bushing (rear)
7 Washer
8 Dust seal
9 Snap-ring
10 Lower arm
11 Ball joint assembly

5 Unscrew the three retaining nuts at the top of the strut and withdraw the strut assembly (Fig. 11.4).
6 When refitting the strut, first position the top of the strut and screw on the retaining nuts finger tight.
7 Apply sealer to the bottom flange and fasten the strut assembly to the steering knuckle with the three bolts.
8 Tighten the upper retaining nuts to a torque wrench setting of 7 to 10 lb f ft (1.0 to 1.4 kg f m), then tighten the knuckle arm bolts to a torque wrench setting of 30 to 36 lb f ft (4.1 to 5.0 kg f m).
9 Refit the torsion arm, the hub assembly and brake caliper.
10 Refit the road wheel and lower the car.
11 Bounce the suspension up and down a few times, then tighten the torsion arm bolt to a torque wrench setting of 7 to 10 lb f ft (1.0 to 1.4 kg f m).

5 Front suspension strut - dismantling and overhaul

The dismantling and overhaul of the struts requires special tools and facilities. If a strut is not working satisfactorily, fit an exchange unit; comprising strut and spring.

6 Front suspension strut - spring removal and refitting

1 If a coil spring compressor is available, the spring may be removed as follows, but the operation requires great care because of the large amount of energy stored in the compressed spring.
2 Clamp the lower end of the strut assembly in a soft jawed vice.
3 Fit a compressor to the spring, compress the spring and remove the dust cover, nut and insulator.
4 Slowly release the pressure on the spring and remove the spring and its seating.
5 When refitting the spring, first compress it and then fit it over the strut.
6 Extend the shockabsorber piston rod to its limit then fit the upper spring seat.
7 Fit the insulator assembly and washer, then fit and partially tighten the self-locking nut.
8 Gradually release the pressure on the spring, taking care to seat both the upper and lower ends of the spring in their retainers, then fully release and remove the spring compressor.
9 While preventing the upper spring seat from rotating, tighten the retaining nut to a torque wrench setting of 30 to 36 lb f ft (4.2 to 5.0 kg f m).

7 Front suspension - lower arm removal

1 Disconnect the strut from the steering knuckle arm as described in Section 4, paragraphs 1, 3 and 4.
2 Using a knuckle breaker, disconnect the steering knuckle arm and tie-rod balljoint (Fig. 11.6), then, using a plate puller, separate the knuckle arm and the lower arm balljoint (Fig. 11.7).
3 Remove the bolts securing the lower arm to the sub-frame and remove the lower arm assembly.

8 Lower arm balljoint - removal and refitting

1 With the lower arm removed from the car, remove the balljoint dust seal by prising it off with a screwdriver.
2 Remove the circlip and then press or drive out the balljoint.
3 Press or drive in a new joint assembly and fit a new circlip and dust cover.
4 Apply THREE BOND N0. 4 or an equivalent sealer to the inside of the dust seal metal ring after putting enough grease in the seal to half fill it.
5 Using a suitable sized piece of tube, hammer the dust seal over the circlip.

9 Front suspension - torsion bar removal and refitting

1 Jack-up the car and remove the road wheels, then support the front

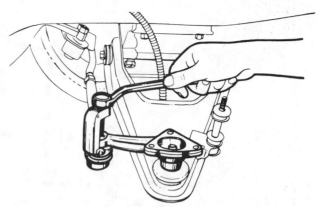
Fig. 11.6. Disconnecting the tie rod and knuckle arm

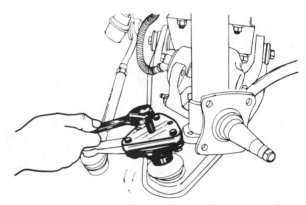
Fig. 11.7. Removing the knuckle arm

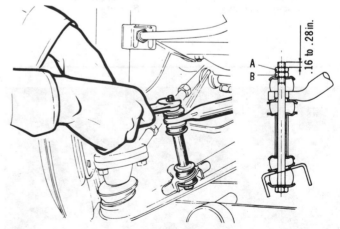
Fig. 11.8. Installing the torsion bar

of the car on two firm stands.
2 Slightly jack-up the lower arm and disconnect the torsion bar link from the lower arm.
3 Remove the torsion bar saddle fixing bolts and remove the torsion bar.
4 When refitting the torsion bar, tighten the fixing bolts to a torque wrench setting of 7 to 10 lb f ft (1.0 to 1.4 kg f m).
5 When connecting the torsion bar to the torsion bar link, set nut 'A' to the standard position (Fig. 11.8) then while holding nut 'A' in place, back nut 'B' up to it and lock the two together.

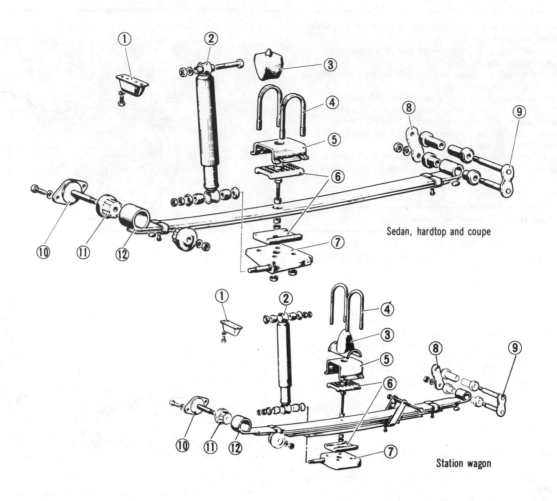

Fig. 11.9. Exploded view of rear suspension

1 Carrier bumper	4 Spring U-bolt	7 U-bolt seat	10 Spring pin assembly
2 Shockabsorber	5 Pad bracket	8 Shackle plate	11 Front eye bushing
3 Rubber cushion	6 Pad	9 Spring shackle assembly	12 Leaf spring assembly

10.3 U-bolt nuts and shockabsorber lower mounting

10.5 Front spring pin assembly fixings

10 Rear suspension - removal and refitting

1   Loosen the wheel nuts, jack the car with a jack placed under the centre of the rear axle, support the car on stands placed under the side frames, lower the jack slowly and remove the road wheels.
2   Disconnect the upper end of the shockabsorber. If the shockabsorber is to be removed, then remove the lower shockabsorber fixings from the U-bolt seat, otherwise leave the shockabsorber in place.
3   Loosen the U-bolt nuts (photo) then jack-up the rear axle until it separates from the spring seat. Remove the U-bolt nuts and take off the spring pad and spring seat.
4   Remove the two nuts from the rear shackle (Fig. 11.10), and take off the shackle plate.
5   Remove the two bolts from the front spring pin assembly (photo) and then remove the spring assembly.
6   Fit the spring to the car with the bolts of the spring pin assembly and shackle plate nuts slack.
7   Fit the upper spring pad and its bracket over the spring centre bolt and lower the axle until it is in contact with them.
8   Fit the lower spring bracket and U-bolt seat (Fig. 11.13), fit the

U-bolts through the holes in the U-bolt seat and then fit and tighten the nuts. After tightening the nuts, make sure that the pad bracket and U-bolt seat are firmly in contact with each other.
9   Refit the shockabsorber then lower the car to the ground so that the rear springs are under their normal load.
10   Tighten the spring pin bolts and shackle pin nuts to a torque wrench setting of 36 to 43 lb f ft (5.0 to 6.0 kg f m). Tighten the shockabsorber mountings to the specified torque.

11 Rear springs - dismantling, inspection and reassembly

1   Open and remove the spring leaf clamp bands and remove the centre bolts to disassemble the leaves.
2   Check each leaf for cracks and wear, looking to see whether it has acquired a permanent set.
3   Examine the rubber bushes and silencers to see if they have hardened or are distorted.
4   Clean the spring leaves with a wire brush and coat them with chassis black. Fit new silencers unless the ones which were removed are in good condition.
5   Fit the centre bolt (Fig. 11.11), with a collar at each end of it. Fit and securely tighten the nut, then centre punch the thread of the bolt to prevent the nut from rotating.
6   Fit the leaf clips and bend them over securely, then fit the front and rear eye bushings, using new ones if necessary. Smear the bushes with brake fluid to make insertion easier.
7   Press the shackle assembly in so that hwen the spring is fitted to the car, the assembly will be on the outside. Fit the shackle plate and screw on the nuts to press the bushes fully home (Fig. 11.12), then remove the nuts and plate.
8   Fit the front eye bushings with their flanges outwards then insert the spring pin assembly and tighten the nut.

12 Rear shockabsorbers - inspection and testing

1   The testing of shockabsorbers is best left to a service station having specialised equipment, but a general idea of whether or not a shockabsorber is defective can be gained by bouncing the appropriate suspension unit to see whether the movement is damped out quickly.
2   Inspect the shockabsorbers visually, looking for signs of damage, leakage of oil or deterioration of the rubber mounting bushes and fixings.

13 Steering column - removal and refitting

1   Remove the air cleaner and remove the bolt from the clamp, coupling the steering shaft to the steering box shaft. For cars fitted with air conditioning, this clamp is only accessible from beneath the car.
2   Remove the three horn pad fixing screws from the back of the steering wheel and take off the horn pad (photo).
3   Lower the steering column to its lowest position, remove the steering wheel retaining nut and use a puller to draw the steering wheel

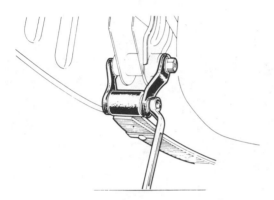

Fig. 11.10. Removing the spring shackle

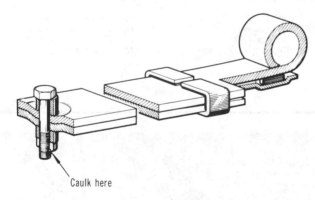

Caulk here

Fig. 11.11. Spring centre bolt and silencer

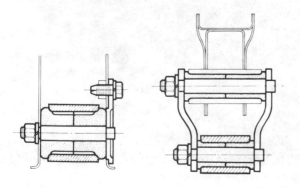

Fig. 11.12. Assembling the spring front and rear eye bushings

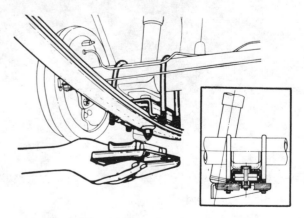

Fig. 11.13. Installing the spring pad bracket

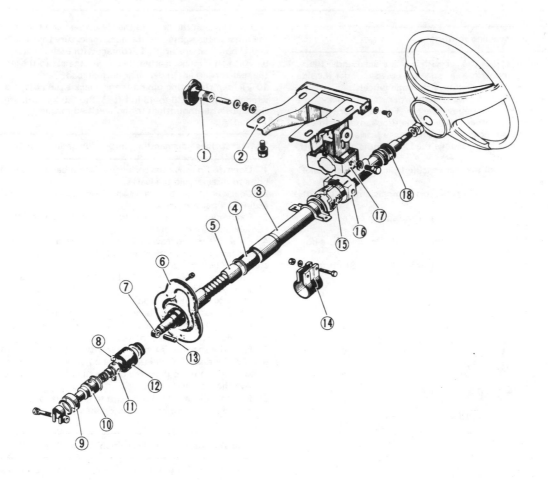

Fig. 11.14. Exploded view of steering column

1	Tilt lock knob	6	Dust cover	11	Joint bearing	15	Tilt bracket bearing
2	Tilt bracket	7	Steering shaft	12	Joint cover	16	Tilt bracket support
3	Column tube, upper	8	Joint pin (A)	13	Joint pin (B)	17	Tilt bracket holder
4	Column bushing	9	Joint pin retainer	14	Column tube clamp	18	Steering shaft bearing
5	Column tube, lower	10	Joint socket				

13.2a Removing the horn pad

13.2b Removing the steering wheel

off its shaft (photo).

4   Remove the tilt lock knob (photo) and the steering column shroud (photo). Disconnect the cable forms of the steering column switch, remove the ignition switch (photo), remove the switch assembly mounting screws and pull the switch assembly off.

5   Remove the dust cover fixing bolts and lift the cover, then remove the tilt bracket assembly fixing bolts and pull out the steering column assembly.

6   Refit the steering column assembly from inside the car, couple it to the steering box and tighten the clamp with the clamp pointing downwards when the steering is in the straight ahead position. The correct torque wrench setting for the clamp bolt is 14.5 to 18 lb f ft (2.0 to 2.5 kg f m).

7   Refit the tilt bracket, ensuring that there is a projection of 3.70 to 3.74 in from the end of the steering rod to the upper end of the steering tube.

8   Refit the steering column switch assembly and the column shroud.

9   Ensure that the steering is in the straight ahead position, then fit the steering wheel so that it is symmetrical. Fit the lock nut and tighten it to a torque wrench setting of 25 to 33 lb f ft (3.5 to 4.6 kg f m), then refit the horn pad.

14 Steering box - removal

1   Remove the clamp bolt connecting the steering column shaft and the steering box shaft.

2   Using a balljoint separator, disconnect the drop arm from the relay rod.

3   Remove the fixing bolts and detach the steering box from the chassis, then use a ball joint separator to take the drop arm off the cross shaft.

13.4a Removing the steering column shroud

13.4b Tilt lock knob

13.4c Removing the ignition switch

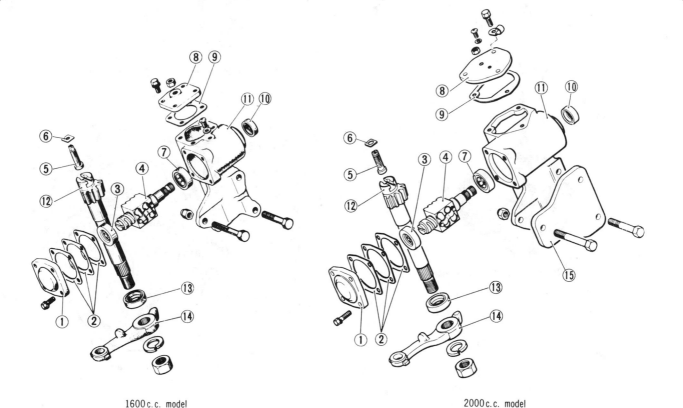

1600 c.c. model   2000 c.c. model

Fig. 11.15. Exploded view of steering gearbox

1	Gearbox end cover	5	Gear adjusting bolt	9	Packing
2	Mainshaft adjusting shims	6	Gear adjusting shim	10	Mainshaft oil seal
3	Mainshaft bearing	7	Mainshaft bearing	11	Gearbox
4	Mainshaft assembly	8	Gearbox upper cover	12	Cross shaft

13	Cross shaft oil seal
14	Drop arm
15	Plate (2000 cc model only)

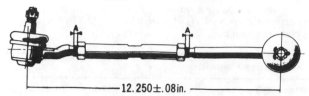

—12.250±.08 in.—

Fig. 11.16. Tie rod and tie rod ends assembled dimensions

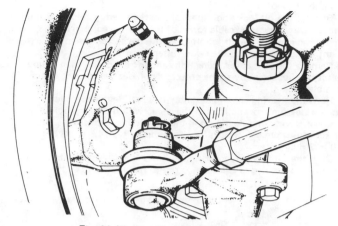

Fig. 11.17. Installing the tie rod assembly

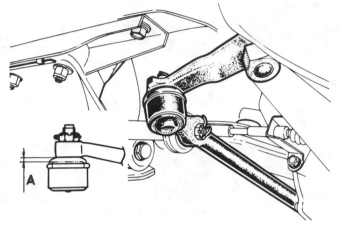

Fig. 11.18. Relay rod-to-drop arm and relay rod-to-idler arm clearance

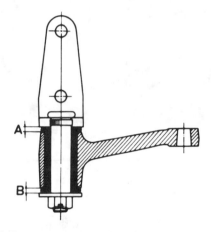

Fig. 11.19. Dimensional relationship between the bracket and arm

Fig. 11.20. Steering play adjustment

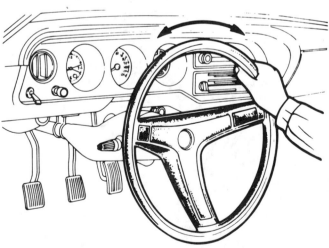

Fig. 11.21. Steering play

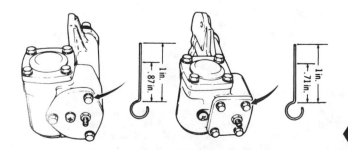

Fig. 11.22. Steering box oil level checking

15 Tie-rods - removal and refitting

1   Use a balljoint separator to disconnect the tie-rod ends. If the brake pads are worn down to near their limit, it may be difficult to fit the balljoint separator without first removing the brake pads and moving the caliper outwards.

2   Remove the tie-rod ends from the tie-rod, noting that the outer end has a left-hand thread and the inner end has a right-hand thread. The ball joints cannot be removed from the tie-rod ends.

3   Check the tie-rod ends for damage and wear and the balljoints for play and discard any unit which is defective.

4   Check the dust covers for cracks and damage and fit new ones if necessary. Fill the inside of the dust cover with grease before fitting it and apply a joint sealer to the tie-rod dust seal mounting surface.

5   Reassemble the tie-rods with a standard distance of 12.250 ± 0.08 in (311.15 ± 2.03 mm), between the ends (Fig. 11.16) making sure that dimension 'A' is the same at both ends of the rod.

6   Connect the tie-rod to the knuckle arm, tighten the nuts to a torque wrench setting of 36 to 40 lb f ft (5.0 to 5.6 kg f m), insert a split pin and bend it over as shown in Fig. 11.17.

7   Make any necessary toe-in adjustment (Section 2) then tighten the lock nuts to a torque wrench setting of 29 to 36 lb f ft (4.0 to 5.0 kg f m).

16 Relay rod - removal and refitting

1   Use a balljoint separator to disconnect the tie-rod ends and then in the same manner disconnect the drop arm and idler arm joints.

2   Remove the relay rod, examine it for damage and the joints for excessive looseness. Examine the dust covers for damage and cracks, fitting new ones if necessary.

3   Refit the relay rod, tighten the drop arm and idler arm joints to a torque wrench setting of 29 to 43 lb f ft (4.0 to 6.0 kg f m) and check that the clearance between the relay arm and the drop arm at one end and the idler arm at the other, dimension 'A' in Fig. 11.18, is 0.146 to 0.169 in (3.71 to 4.29 mm).

17 Idler arm - removal, dismantling and reassembly

1   Use a balljoint separator to disconnect the relay rod from the idler arm.

2   Remove the idler arm fixing bolts and remove the idler assembly.

3   Remove the nut and washer from the idler arm assembly, pull off the idler arm and inspect the rubber bushes for damage and wear. Renew if necessary.

4   To fit new bushes, apply soapy water to the idler arm and bushes, fit the bushes into the bore from both ends and press them in until their flanges are in contact with the idler arm.

5   Apply soapy water to the bracket shaft and use a vice to force the bracket into the bushes until the dimensions 'A' and 'B' (Fig. 11.19) are less than 0.08 in (2.03 mm) then tighten the locknut to a torque wrench setting of 29 to 43 lb f ft (4.0 to 6.0 kg f m).

6   Insert and lock the split pin.

7   Fit the idler bracket to the frame, tightening the bolts to a torque wrench setting of 25 to 29 lb f ft (3.5 to 4.0 kg f m) then reconnect the relay rod and tighten the joint to a torque wrench setting of 29 to 43 lb f ft (4.0 to 6.0 kg f m).

18 Steering play adjustment

1   Jack-up the front wheels clear of the ground and set the steering in the straight-ahead position. It is important that adjustment is only made when the steering is in the straight-ahead position, because the steering is of variable ratio type and otherwise the gear backlash would be too small, resulting in a damaged gear.

2   Loosen the locknut on the top of the steering box (Fig. 11.20), and adjust the screw to give a steering wheel play (Fig. 11.21) of not less than 1 in (25.4 mm). If the play cannot be reduced below 2 in (50.8 mm), the steering box is worn excessively and a new one should be fitted.

19 Steering box - oil level check

1   Remove the bolt at the lower inboard corner (Fig. 11.22).

2   Using a gauge, or thin screwdriver check that the oil is about 0.71 in (18 mm) from the outside surface of the top cover if the box has a square cover and 0.87 in (22 mm) if the box has a heart-shaped cover.

20 Fault diagnosis - suspension and steering

Before diagnosing faults from the following chart, check that any irregularities are not caused by:

1   *Binding brakes.*
2   *Incorrect 'mix' of radial and crossply tyres.*
3   *Incorrect tyre pressures.*
4   *Misalignment of the body frame.*

Symptom	Reason(s)
Steering wheel can be moved considerably before any sign of movement of the roadwheels is apparent	Wear in the steering linkage, gear and column coupling.
Vehicle difficult to steer in a consistent straight line - wandering	As above. Wheel alignment incorrect (indicated by excessive or uneven tyre wear). Front wheel hub bearings loose or worn. Worn ball joints.
Steering stiff and heavy	Incorrect wheel alignment (indicated by excessive or uneven tyre wear). Excessive wear or seizure in one or more of the joints in the steering linkage or suspension. Excessive wear in the steering gear unit.
Wheel wobble and vibration	Roadwheels out of balance. Roadwheels buckled. Wheel alignment incorrect. Wear in the steering linkage, suspension ball joints or track

control arm pivot.
Broken front spring.

Excessive pitching and rolling on corners and during braking   Defective shockabsorber and/or broken spring.

Chapter 12 Bodywork and fittings

For modifications, and information applicable to later models, see Supplement at end of manual

Contents

Specifications

Torque wrench settings

	lbf ft	kgf m
Front bumper stay to front frame panel	16 to 26	2.2 to 3.6
Front shockabsorber to stay	12 to 14	1.7 to 2.0
Front bumper to shockabsorber	12 to 14	1.7 to 2.0
Rear shockabsorber to body	12 to 14	1.7 to 2.0
Rear bumper to shock isolator	12 to 14	1.7 to 2.0
Front safety belt inertia reel	17 to 21	2.4 to 3.0
Front safety belt shoulder anchor	More than 17	More than 2.4
Front safety belt buckle stalk	More than 17	More than 2.4

1 General description

The body and underframe are a unitary welded construction in a 2-door and 4-door version, with different body styles. The doors are forward hinged, with anti-burst locks and flush door handles and the tailgate of the estate version is top hinged. A laminated glass windscreen is fitted as standard equipment and a heated rear window is fitted on some models.

2 Maintenance - bodywork and underframe

1 The general condition of a car's bodywork is the one thing that significantly affects its value. Maintenance is easy but needs to be regular. Neglect, particularly after minor damage can lead quickly to further deterioration and costly repair bills. It is important also to keep watch on those parts of the car not immediately visible, for instance, the underframe, inside all the wheel arches and the lower part of the engine compartment.

2 The basic maintenance routine for the bodywork is washing - preferably with a lot of water, from a hose. This will remove all the loose solids which may have stuck to the car. It is important to flush these off in such a way as to prevent grit from scratching the finish.

The wheel arches and underframe need washing in the same way to remove any accumulated mud which will retain moisture and tend to encourage rust. Paradoxically enough, the best time to clean the underframe and wheel arches is in wet weather when the mud is thoroughly wet and soft. In very wet weather the underframe is usually cleaned of large accumulations automatically and this is a good time for inspection.

3 Periodically it is a good idea to have the whole of the underframe of the car steam cleaned, engine compartment included, so that a thorough inspection can be carried out to see what minor repairs and renovations are necessary. Steam cleaning is available at many garages and is necessary for removal of the accumulation of oily grime which sometimes is allowed to cake thick in certain areas near the engine, gearbox and back axle. If steam cleaning facilities are not available, there are one or two excellent grease solvents available which can be brush applied. The dirt can then be simply hosed off.

4 After washing paintwork, wipe off with a chamois leather to give an unspotted clear finish. A coat of clear protective wax polish will give added protection against chemical pollutants in the air. If the paintwork sheen has dulled or oxidised, use a cleaner/polisher combination to restore the brilliance of the shine. This requires a little effort, but is usually caused because regular washing has been neglected. Always check that the door and ventilator opening drain holes and pipes are completely clear so that water can be drained

out. Bright work should be treated the same way as paintwork. Windscreens and windows can be kept clear of the smeary film which often appears if a little ammonia is added to the water. If they are scratched, a good rub with a proprietary metal polish will often clear them. Never use any form of wax or other body or chromium polish on glass.

3   Maintenance - upholstery and carpets

1 Mats and carpets should be brushed or vacuum cleaned regularly to keep them free of grit. If they are badly stained remove them from the car for scrubbing or sponging and make quite sure they are dry before refitting. Seats and interior trim panels can be kept clean by a wipe over with a damp cloth. If they do become stained (which can be more apparent on light coloured upholstery) use a little liquid detergent and a soft nail brush to scour the grime out of the grain of the material. Do not forget to keep the head lining clean in the same way as the upholstery. When using liquid cleaners inside the car do not over-wet the surfaces being cleaned. Excessive damp could get into the seams and padded interior causing stains, offensive odours or even rot. If the inside of the car gets wet accidentally it is worthwhile taking some trouble to dry it out properly, particularly where carpets are involved. *Do not leave oil or electric heaters inside the car for this purpose.*

4   Minor body damage - repair

The photographic sequence on pages 166 and 167, illustrate the operations detailed in the following sub-Sections.

Repair of minor scratches in the car's bodywork

If the scratch is very superficial, and does not penetrate to the metal of the bodywork, repair is very simple. Lightly rub the area of the scratch with a paintwork renovator, or a very fine cutting paste, to remove loose paint from the scratch and to clear the surrounding bodywork of wax polish. Rinse the area with clean water.

Apply touch-up paint to the scratch using a thin paint brush, continue to apply thin layers of paint until the surface of the paint in the scratch is level with the surrounding paintwork. Allow the new paint at least two weeks to harden; then, blend it into the surrounding paintwork by rubbing the paintwork, in the scratch area, with a paintwork renovator, or a very fine cutting paste. Finally, apply wax polish.

An alternative to painting over the scratch is to use a paint patch. Use the same preparation for the affected area; then simply pick a patch of a suitable size to cover the scratch completely. Hold the patch against the scratch and burnish its backing paper; the patch will adhere to the paintwork, freeing itself from the backing paper at the same time. Polish the affected area to blend the patch into the surrounding paintwork. Where the scratch has penetrated right through to the metal of the bodywork, causing the metal to rust, a different repair technique is required. Remove any loose rust from the bottom of the scratch with a penknife, then apply rust inhibiting paint to prevent the formation of rust in the future. Using a rubber or nylon applicator, fill the scratch with bodystopper paste. If required, this paste can be mixed with cellulose thinners to provide a very thin paste, which is an ideal way of filling narrow scratches. Before the stopper-paste in the scratch hardens, wrap a piece of smooth cotton rag around the top of a finger. Dip the finger in cellulose thinners and then quickly sweep it across the surface of the stopper-paste in the scratch; this will ensure that the surface of the stopper-paste is slightly hollowed. The scratch can now be painted over as described earlier in this Section.

Repair of dents in the car's bodywork

When deep denting of the car's bodywork has taken place, the first task is to pull the dent out, until the affected bodywork almost attains its original shape. There is little point in trying to restore the original shape completely, as the metal in the damaged area will have stretched on impact and cannot be reshaped fully to its original contour. It is better to bring the level of the dent up to a point which is about 1/8 in (3 mm) below the level of the surrounding bodywork. In cases where the dent is very shallow anyway, it is not worth trying to pull it out at all. If the underside of the dent is accessible, it can be hammered out gently from behind, using a mallet with a wooden or plastic head. Whilst doing this, hold a suitable block of wood firmly against the impact from the hammer blows and thus prevent a large area of the bodywork from being 'belled-out'.

Should the dent be in a section of the bodywork which has a double skin or some other factor making it inaccessible from behind, a different technique is called for. Drill several small holes through the metal inside the dent area - particularly in the deeper sections. Then screw long self-tapping screws into the holes just sufficiently for them to gain a good purchase in the metal. Now the dent can be pulled out by pulling on the protruding heads of the screws with a pair of pliers.

The next stage of the repair is the removal of the paint from the damaged area, and from an inch or so of the surrounding 'sound' bodywork. This is accomplished more easily by using a wire brush or abrasive pad on a power drill, although it can be done just as effectively by hand using sheets of abrasive paper. To complete the preparations for filling, score the surface of the bare metal with a screwdriver or the tang of a file, or alternatively, drill small holes in the affected area. This will provide a really good 'key' for the filler paste.

To complete the repair see the Section on filling and re-spraying.

Repair of rust holes or gashes in the car's bodywork

Remove all paint from the affected area and from an inch or so of the surrounding 'sound' bodywork, using an abrasive pad or a wire brush on a power drill. If these are not available a few sheets of abrasive paper will do the job just as effectively. With the paint removed you will be able to gauge the severity of the corrosion and therefore decide whether to renew the whole panel (if this is possible) or to repair the affected area. New body panels are not as expensive as most people think and it is often quicker and more satisfactory to fit a new panel than to attempt to repair large areas of corrosion.

Remove all fittings from the affected area except those which will act as a guide to the original shape of the damaged bodywork (headlamp shells etc.). Then, using tin snips or a hacksaw blade, remove all loose metal and any other metal badly affected by corrosion. Hammer the edges of the hole inwards in order to create a slight depression for the filler paste.

Wire brush the affected area to remove the powdery rust from the surface of the remaining metal. Paint the affected area with rust inhibiting paint; if the back of the rusted area is accessible treat this also.

Before filling can take place it will be necessary to block the hole in some way. This can be achieved by the use of aluminium or plastic mesh, or aluminium tape.

Aluminium or plastic mesh is probably the best material to use for a large hole. Cut a piece to the approximate size and shape of the hole to be filled, then position it in the hole so that its edges are below the level of the surrounding bodywork. It can be retained in position by several blobs of filler paste around its periphery.

Aluminium tape should be used for small or very narrow holes. Pull a piece off the roll and trim it to the approximate size and shape required, then pull off the backing paper (if used) and stick the tape over the hole; it can be overlapped if the thickness of one piece is insufficient. Burnish down the edges of the tape with the handle of a screwdriver or similar, to ensure that the tape is securely attached to the metal underneath.

Bodywork repairs - filling and re-spraying

Before using this Section, see the Sections on dent, deep scratch, rust hole, and gash repairs.

Many types of bodyfiller are available, but generally speaking those proprietary kits which contain a tin of filler paste and a tube of resin hardener are best for this type of repair. A wide, flexible, plastic or nylon applicator will be found invaluable for imparting a smooth and well contoured finish to the surface of the filler.

Mix up a little filler on a clean piece of card or board - use the hardener sparingly (follow the maker's instructions on the packet) otherwise the filler will set very rapidly.

Using the applicator, apply the filler paste to the prepared area; draw the applicator across the surface of the filler to achieve the correct contour and to level the filler surface. As soon as a contour that approximates the correct one is achieved, stop working the paste - if you carry on too long the paste will become sticky and begin to 'pick up' on the applicator. Continue to add thin layers of filler paste at twenty minute intervals until the level of the filler is just 'proud' of the surrounding bodywork.

Once the filler has hardened, excess can be removed using a metal plane or file. From then on, progressively finer grades of abrasive paper should be used, starting with a 40 grade production paper and finishing with 400 grade 'wet-or-dry' paper. Always wrap the abrasive paper around a flat rubber, cork or wooden block - otherwise the surface of the filler will not be completely flat. During the smoothing of the filler surface the 'wet-or-dry' paper should be periodically rinsed in water. This will ensure that a very smooth finish is imparted to the filler at the final stage.

At this stage the 'dent' should be surrounded by a ring of bare metal, which in turn should be encircled by the finely 'feathered' edge of the good paintwork. Rinse the repair area with clean water, until all of the dust produced by the rubbing-down operation has gone.

Spray the whole repair area with a light coat of primer - this will show up any imperfections in the surface of the filler. Repair these imperfections with fresh filler paste or bodystopper, and once more smooth the surface with abrasive paper. If bodystopper is used, it can be mixed with cellulose thinners to form a really thin paste which is ideal for filling small holes. Repeat this spray and repair procedure until you are satisfied that the surface of the filler, and the feathered edge of the paintwork are perfect. Clean the repair area with clean water and allow to dry fully.

The repair area is now ready for spraying. Paint spraying must be carried out in a warm, dry, windless and dust free atmosphere. This condition can be created artifically if you have access to a large indoor working area, but if you are forced to work in the open, you will have to pick your day very carefully. If you are working indoors, dousing the the floor in the work area with water will 'lay' the dust which would otherwise be in the atmosphere. If the repair area is confined to one body panel, mask off the surrounding panels; this will help to minimise the effects of a slight mis-match in paint colour. Bodywork fittings (eg. chrome strips, door handles etc.) will also need to be masked off. Use genuine masking tape and several thicknesses of newspaper for the masking operation.

Before commencing to spray, agitate the aerosol can thoroughly, then spray a test area (an old tin, or similar) until the technique is mastered. Cover the repair area with a thick coat of primer; the thickness should be built up using several thin layers of paint rather than one thick one. Using 400 grade 'wet-or-dry' paper, rub down the surface of the primer until it is really smooth. While doing this, the work area should be thoroughly doused with water, and the 'wet-and-dry' paper periodically rinsed in water. Allow to dry before spraying on more paint.

Spray on the top coat again building up the thickness by using several thin layers of paint. Start spraying in the centre of the repair area and then, using a circular motion, work outwards until the whole repair area and about 2 inches of the surrounding original paintwork is covered. Remove all masking material 10 to 15 minutes after spraying on the final coat of paint.

Allow the new paint at least 2 weeks to harden fully, then, using a paintwork renovator or a very fine cutting paste, blend the edges of the new paint into the existing paintwork. Finally, apply wax polish.

5 Major body damage - repair

Where serious damage has occurred or large areas need renewal due to neglect, it means certainly that completely new sections or panels will need welding in and this is best left to professionals. If the damage is due to impact it will also be necessary to completely check the alignment of the body shell structure. Due to the principle of construction the strength and shape of the whole car can be affected by damage to a part. In such instances the services of a workshop with specialist checking jigs are essential. If a body is left misaligned it is first of all dangerous as the car will not handle properly and secondly uneven stresses will be imposed on the steering, engine and transmission, causing abnormal wear or complete failure. Tyre wear may also be excessive.

6 Bumpers - general description

The bumpers of saloons and estate cars are fitted with two solid-media shock absorbers which are telescopic. Each consists of a piston rod with a metering orifice which is hermetically sealed inside a pressure cylinder filled with silicone rubber (Fig. 12.1). Under an impact load, the silicone rubber is compressed and is caused to flow through the metering orifice, the combined effect of the compression and flow being to absorb energy.

7 Bumpers - removal and refitting

Front bumper
1   Loosen the four bumper fixing bolts, disconnect the bumper from

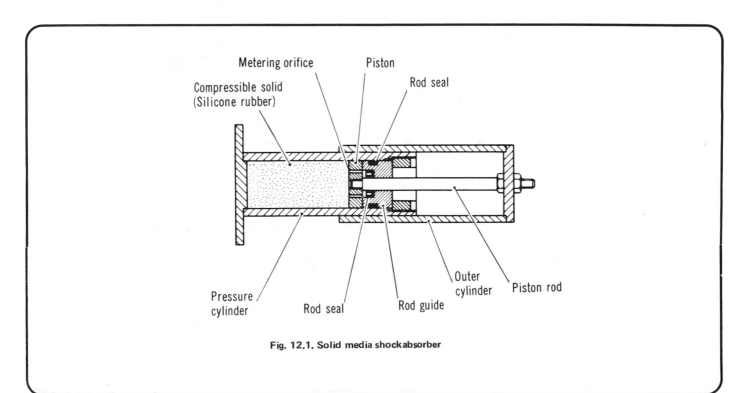

Fig. 12.1. Solid media shock absorber

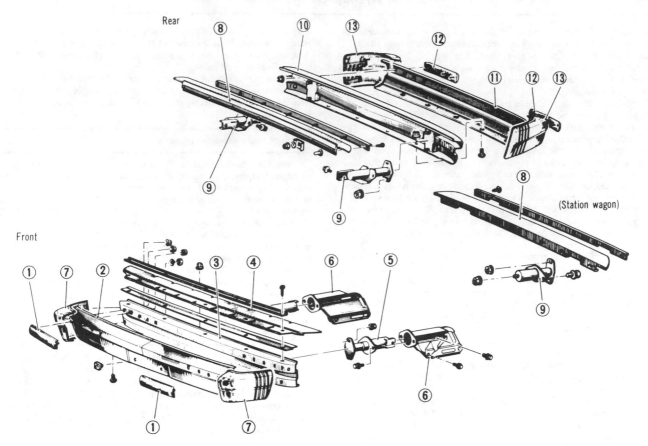

Fig. 12.2. Details of bumpers

1	Front bumper guard	5	Front shockabsorber	8	Rear filler, centre	11	Rear bumper face
2	Front bumper face	6	Front bumper stay	9	Rear shockabsorber	12	Rear bumper guard
3	Front bumper reinforcement	7	Front bumper, corner	10	Rear bumper reinforcement	13	Rear bumper, corner
4	Front filler, centre						

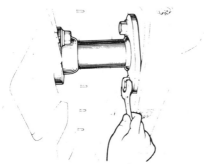

Fig. 12.3. Removing the front bumper assembly

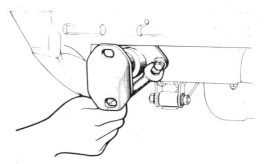

Fig. 12.4. Removing the rear shock absorber

Fig. 12.5. Removing the windscreen

Fig. 12.6. Pull cords installed in weatherstrip

the collar of the inner tube of each shockabsorber (Fig. 12.3) and remove the bumper assembly.

2 Remove the six bolts securing the shockabsorbers to the bumper stay and remove the shockabsorbers.

3 Remove the six bolts securing the bumper stay to the front frame panel, then remove the stay with the fixing bracket.

Rear bumper

4 Remove the two bolts attaching the bumper to the collar of the shockabsorber (Fig. 12.4).

5 Remove the nuts and bolts securing the centre filler, then remove the filler clip at each end.

6 Remove the bolts securing the rear sub-frame to the shockabsorber and then remove the shockabsorber.

7 When refitting the bumpers, tighten all fixings to the recommended torque. On the rear bumper, after tightening the centre filler, bend the clip to hold each end of the filler.

8 Windscreen - removal and refitting

1 Remove the windscreen wiper arms, interior mirror and sun visor.

2 From inside the car, prise out the weatherstrip, using a screwdriver (Fig. 12.5), then remove the weatherstrip from the body flange.

3 Remove the windscreen by pushing it outwards.

4 When refitting the glass, fit the weatherstrip to the glass and insert pull cords in the weatherstrip so that the ends overlap at each side of the glass, (Fig. 12.6), then fit the moulding to the weatherstrip.

5 Clean the body flange with solvent, (taking precautions proper to the handling of inflammable liquids) and rectify any damage to the flange.

6 Apply soap solution to all the car surfaces which are in contact with the weatherstrip.

7 With an assistant holding the glass in its proper position against the outside of the car, pull the cords from the inside (Fig. 12.7) while the assistant presses the glass. Pull each cord at right angles to the glass, starting at the side and working towards the centre.

8 Tap the glass until it is hard against the body flange then seal the flange to the weatherstrip and the weatherstrip to the glass, with a windscreen sealer of approved specification.

9 Refit the windscreen wiper arms, interior mirror and sun visor.

9 Rear window - removal and refitting

The rear window can be removed and fitted in exactly the same way as the front. If the glass is fitted with a demister panel, take care to insert the pull cords on top of the cable, otherwise the cable may be broken when the cord is pulled.

10 Doors - removal and refitting

1 Mark the position of the door hinges so that the door can be

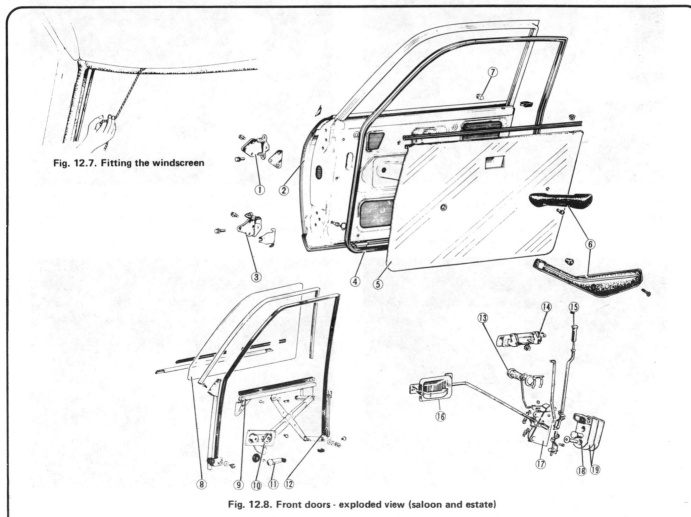

Fig. 12.7. Fitting the windscreen

Fig. 12.8. Front doors - exploded view (saloon and estate)

1 Door hinge (upper)	6 Arm rest	11 Regulator handle	16 Inside handle
2 Door body	7 Damper	12 Rear sash (lower)	17 Door lock
3 Door hinge (lower)	8 Front door glass	13 Cylinder lock	18 Door striker
4 Weatherstrip	9 Glass holder	14 Outside handle	19 Striker shim
5 Door trim	10 Regulator	15 Inside lock knob	

This sequence of photographs deals with the repair of the dent and paintwork damage shown in this photo. The procedure will be similar for the repair of a hole. It should be noted that the procedures given here are simplified — more explicit instructions will be found in the text

In the case of a dent the first job — after removing surrounding trim — is to hammer out the dent where access is possible. This will minimise filling. Here, the large dent having been hammered out, the damaged area is being made slightly concave

Now all paint must be removed from the damaged area, by rubbing with coarse abrasive paper. Alternatively, a wire brush or abrasive pad can be used in a power drill. Where the repair area meets good paintwork, the edge of the paintwork should be 'feathered', using a finer grade of abrasive paper

In the case of a hole caused by rusting, all damaged sheet-metal should be cut away before proceeding to this stage. Here, the damaged area is being treated with rust remover and inhibitor before being filled

Mix the body filler according to its manufacturer's instructions. In the case of corrosion damage, it will be necessary to block off any large holes before filling — this can be done with aluminium or plastic mesh, or aluminium tape. Make sure the area is absolutely clean before ...

... applying the filler. Filler should be applied with a flexible applicator, as shown, for best results; the wooden spatula being used for confined areas. Apply thin layers of filler at 20-minute intervals, until the surface of the filler is slightly proud of the surrounding bodywork

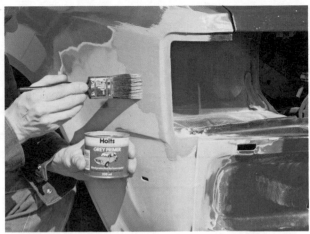

Initial shaping can be done with a Surform plane or Dreadnought file. Then, using progressively finer grades of wet-and-dry paper, wrapped around a sanding block, and copious amounts of clean water, rub down the filler until really smooth and flat. Again, feather the edges of adjoining paintwork

The whole repair area can now be sprayed or brush-painted with primer. If spraying, ensure adjoining areas are protected from over-spray. Note that at least one inch of the surrounding sound paintwork should be coated with primer. Primer has a 'thick' consistency, so will find small imperfections

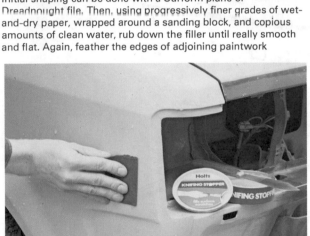

Again, using plenty of water, rub down the primer with a fine grade wet-and-dry paper (400 grade is probably best) until it is really smooth and well blended into the surrounding paintwork. Any remaining imperfections can now be filled by carefully applied knifing stopper paste

When the stopper has hardened, rub down the repair area again before applying the final coat of primer. Before rubbing down this last coat of primer, ensure the repair area is blemish-free — use more stopper if necessary. To ensure that the surface of the primer is really smooth use some finishing compound

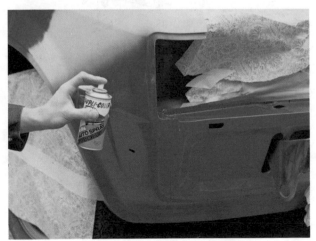

The top coat can now be applied. When working out of doors, pick a dry, warm and wind-free day. Ensure surrounding areas are protected from over-spray. Agitate the aerosol thoroughly, then spray the centre of the repair area, working outwards with a circular motion. Apply the paint as several thin coats

After a period of about two weeks, which the paint needs to harden fully, the surface of the repaired area can be 'cut' with a mild cutting compound prior to wax polishing. When carrying out bodywork repairs, remember that the quality of the finished job is proportional to the time and effort expended

refitted in the same position, then remove the wing if a front door is to be removed.

2 With an assistant holding the door, remove the bolts from the upper and lower hinges (Fig. 12.11).

3 Before refitting the door, paint primer or body sealer onto the back of the hinge and their mating surfaces on the door.

4 Tighten the hinge bolts to a torque wrench setting of 10 to 18 lbf ft (1.4 to 2.5 kgf m).

11 Doors - adjustment

1 Loosen the hinge attachment bolts on the body and then adjust

the longitudinal and vertical positions of the door to give a uniform gap between the door and the car body.

2 Alter the vertical and horizontal position by sliding the hinges up and down and obtain longitudinal adjustment by fitting shims behind the hinges.

12 Door striker - adjustment

1 Adjust the vertical and horizontal positions of the striker by loosening the attachment screws and sliding the striker plate (Fig. 12.12).

2 Adjust the longitudinal position by packing shims behind the striker plate.

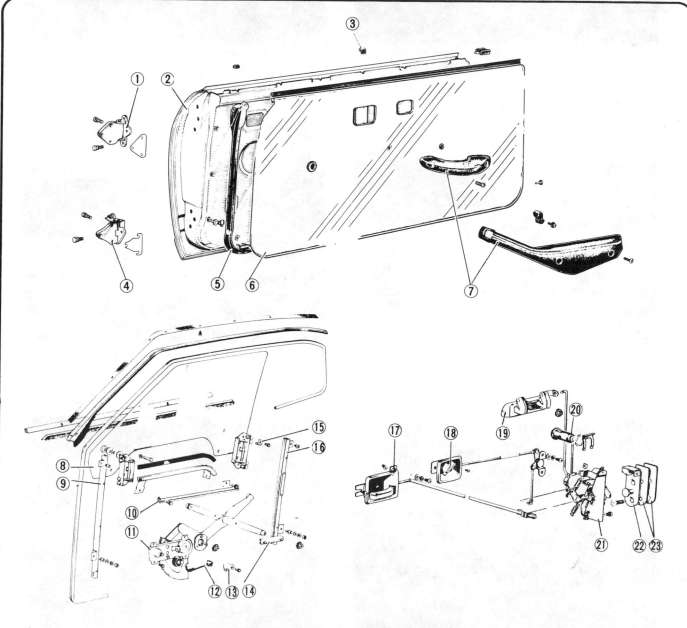

Fig. 12.9. Front doors - exploded view (hardtop and coupe)

1 Door hinge (upper)	7 Arm rest	13 Upper stopper (lower)	19 Door outside handle
2 Door body	8 Door glass	14 Sub-roller guide	20 Cylinder lock
3 Damper	9 Main roller guide (front)	15 Upper stopper	21 Door lock
4 Door hinge (lower)	10 Channel	16 Main roller guide (rear)	22 Door striker
5 Door weatherstrip	11 Regulator assembly	17 Door inside handle	23 Shim
6 Door trim	12 Regulator handle	18 Door inside lock	

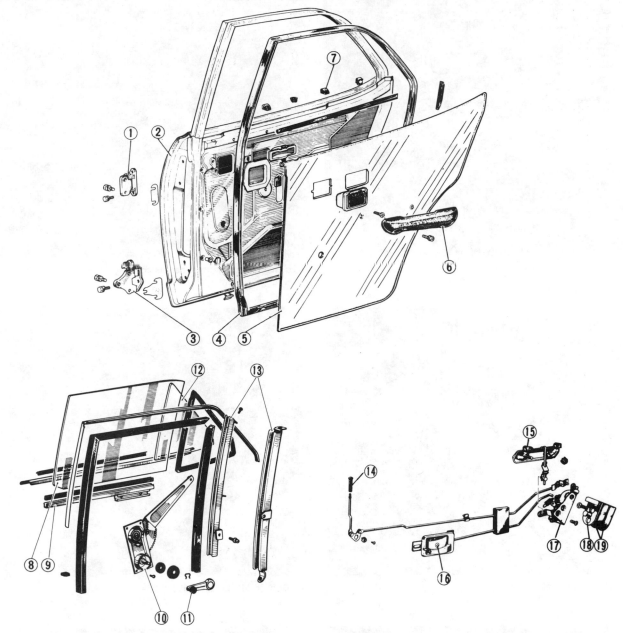

Fig. 12.10. Rear doors - exploded view

1 Door hinge (upper)	6 Arm rest	11 Regulator handle
2 Door body	7 Damper	12 Quarter glass
3 Door hinge (lower)	8 Rear door glass	13 Quarter sash
4 Weatherstrip	9 Glass holder	14 Inside lock knob
5 Door trim	10 Regulator	15 Outside handle

16 Inside handle	
17 Door lock	
18 Door striker	
19 Striker shim	

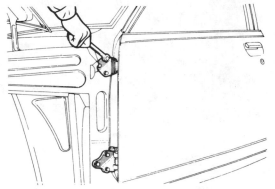

Fig. 12.11. Removing the door assembly

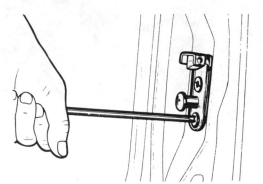

Fig. 12.12. Adjusting the door striker

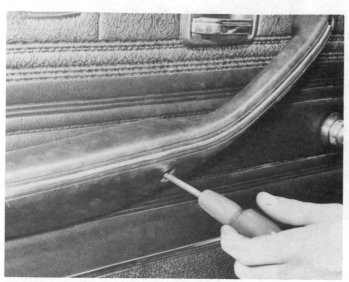
13.1a Removing the door armrest

13.1b Removing the inside handle cover

13.1c Regulator handle and fixing clip

13.4 Door inside handle rod and lock

13.6 Attachment of glass holder to regulator arm

13.7 Regulator arm roller and guide

13 Front door glass and regulator - removal and refitting

Four door models

1 Remove the arm rest and the inside handle cover (photo), then separate the door trim and the regulator handle escutcheon with a screwdriver and pull off the handle fixing clip (photo).

2 Unscrew the door inside locking knob, then insert a flat screwdriver between the door and the trim and prise off the trim.

3 Carefully peel off the weather film from the door.

4 Remove the inside handle rod from the door lock (photo), remove the fixing screws and take out the inside door handle (Fig. 12.13).

5 Remove the screws from the rear lower door sash and remove the sash by pulling it down.

6 Lower the glass to its fullest extent and remove the pin attaching the glass holder to the regulator arm (photo).

7 Hold the glass and pull the regulator arm roller out of the guide (photo), then remove the glass by lifting upwards, with the rear end of the glass tilted higher than the front (Fig. 12.14).

8 Remove the attachment screws and the regulator sub-roller guide fixing, then remove the regulator assembly (Fig. 12.15).

9 Grease the moving parts of the regulator before refitting it and refit the window and regulator in the reverse order of removal.

10 Fit the regulator handle so that when the window is fully closed, the handle is 30⁰ above horizontal and pointing forward.

Two door models

11 Carry out the operations detailed in paragraphs 1 to 4, then remove the upper and lower glass stoppers (see Fig. 12.9).

12 Lower the glass and remove the channel and anti-rattle strip from the bottom of the glass.

13 Remove the main roller guide attachment nuts and while holding the glass, remove the sub-roller guide, then pull the glass upwards to remove it from the regulator roller.

12 Remove the main roller guides.

13 Remove the fixings from both the attachments of the regulator assembly and remove the regulator assembly through the hole at the bottom of the inner door panel.

14 Before refitting, grease the moving parts of the regulator and check the door glass holder attachment bolts for looseness. If the bolts are loose, tighten them so that their positions are as shown in Fig. 12.16. Do not tighten the screws more than is necessary to stop the fixings from moving, otherwise the glass may break.

15 Insert the regulator and fix it to the hole in the inner panel, then lift up and fix the regulator body.

16 Grease the regulator arm roller, insert the sub-roller guide and fix it in position (Fig. 12.17).

17 Insert the glass from above, fit the glass roller into the main roller guide and slowly lower the glass, then with the glass in its lowest position, fit the channel and anti-rattle strip.

18 Raise the glass fully and close the door very carefully to see whether the position of the glass is correct. If so, refit the weatherstrip and door lining and set the regulator handle as described in paragraph 10. For the adjustment of the door glass see the following Section.

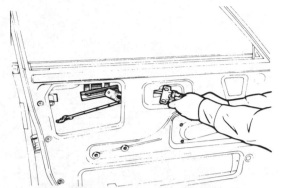

Fig. 12.13. Removing the door inside handle

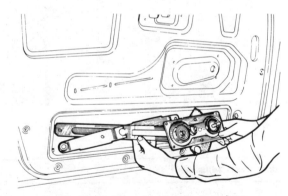

Fig. 12.14. Removing the door glass

Fig. 12.15. Removing the door regulator

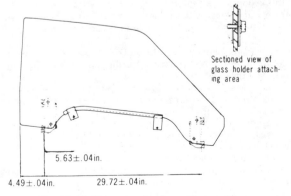

Sectioned view of glass holder attaching area

5.63±.04in.

4.49±.04in.   29.72±.04in.

Fig. 12.16. Door glass holder setting position

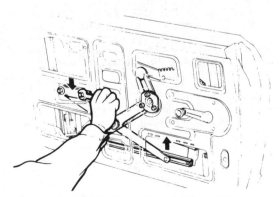

Fig. 12.17. Fixing the sub-roller guide

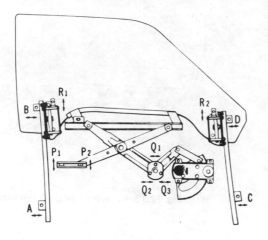

Fig. 12.18. Door glass adjustment

Adjustment points (symbol)	Direction of adjustment	Direction of glass movement
P_1, P_2	In direction of arrow	Rear of glass moves up and down
Q_1, Q_2, Q_3	In direction of arrow	Tilt of whole of glass
R_1, R_2	In direction of arrow	Setting of end of glass upward stroke
A, B, C, D	In direction of arrow	Whole of glass moves forward and backward
A	Outward	Glass moves inward. (Too tight weatherstrip contact)
B	Outward	Glass moves outward. (Too loose weatherstrip contact)
C	Outward	Glass moves inward.
D	Outward	Glass moves outward.

14 Front door glass - adjustment

See Fig. 12.18.

Tilt adjustment

1 Loosen the sub-roller guide attachment nuts and adjust it until the glass to weatherstrip clearance is equal on all sides, then tighten the nuts securely making sure that the sub-roller guide is horizontal.
2 If sufficient adjustment cannot be obtained by moving the sub-roller guide, adjust the regulator crank as well, or extend the sub-roller attachment holes.

Longitudinal adjustment

3 With the glass fully raised fully check that the front pillar weatherstrip and vertical weatherstrip overlap the glass evenly.
4 If necessary adjust by moving the main roller guide forward or backwards as required, then tighten the guide attachment points securely. The main roller guide upper nuts should be tightened with the glass raised and the lower screws tightened with the glass lowered.

Upper stopper adjustment

5 With the door closed and the door glass raised fully, set the glass so that its edge is in contact with the outer lip of the rubber moulding (Fig. 12.19).

6 Fit the upper stopper upper to the inner panel and fix it so that it is in contact with the roller in the guide, then fit the upper stopper lower in contact with the regulator quadrant.

Run out adjustment

7 With the door closed and the glass fully raised, check that the glass is uniformly in contact with the weatherstrip. Adjust the upper and lower positions of the glass, by moving the main roller guide fixing bolts.
8 To make adjustments in the GLASS DOWN position, the weather braid contact pressure is decreased by turning the upper adjusting bolt clockwise and the lower one anti-clockwise.
9 To make adjustments in the GLASS UP position, the weather braid contact pressure is decreased by turning the upper adjusting bolt clockwise and the lower one anti-clockwise as before.
10 If the front and rear roller guides are skewed, the regulator becomes stiff, so the front and rear adjusting bolts should be turned by the same amount.
11 If weatherstrip contact is too loose, rain will enter the vehicle body and if it is too tight, the glass cannot be raised fully when the door is closed. Bear this in mind when making adjustments.

15 Front door handle and lock - removal and refitting

1 Proceed with the door glass removal (Section 12), as far as

paragraph 4.

2   Remove the door inside lock rod, then disconnect the outer handle rod from the lock, remove its fixing and take out the outer handle.

3   Disconnect the cylinder lock rod from the door lock, pull off the clip and take out the cylinder lock (photo).

4   Remove the lock attachment screws and take out the door lock.

5   Grease the lock operating parts before fitting them, but do not use oil or grease on the cylinder lock. Check that each rod has been connected properly and that its fixing clip is secure (photo).

16 Rear door glass and regulator - removal

1   Remove the arm rest, regulator handle and door inside lock knob.

2   Insert a flat screwdriver between the trim and the door panel, prise off and remove the trim, then remove the weather film from the inside panel.

3   Disconnect the inside handle from the door lock and remove the inside handle.

4   Lower the window, remove the quarter sash retaining screws, take out the quarter light (Fig. 12.20) and then its sash.

5   Tilt the glass to disconnect it from the regulator arm roller, then gently push it out, rear edge first.

6   Remove the four screws securing the regulator and take the regulator out through the hole near the bottom of the panel.

7   Before refitting the quarter light, apply soap solution all over the quarter light weatherstrip and sash.

17 Hardtop quarter window and regulator - removal and refitting

1   Remove the rear seat cushion and seat back, then remove the trim cover and pull out the door opening trim.

2   Remove the regulator handle and arm rest, then take out the two screws and clips and remove the quarter trim.

3   Remove the front and rear pillar trim, remove the quarter light weatherstrip fixing screws and then remove the weatherstrip and moulding.

4   Remove the door top weatherstrip and the arm rest bracket.

5   Raise the glass and remove the bolt from the quarter light attachment bracket, using the access hole provided.

6   Lower the glass about 4 inches and pull the quarter light out upwards.

7   Remove the attachment bolts of the main roller guide, pull the regulator arm roller from its guide and then remove the main roller guide, with the quarter light bracket attached.

8   Remove the quarter light guide, then take out the regulator attachment screws and remove the regulator through its access hole.

9   Before refitting, apply grease to the moving parts of the regulator and roller.

15.3 Door handle and cylinder lock fixings

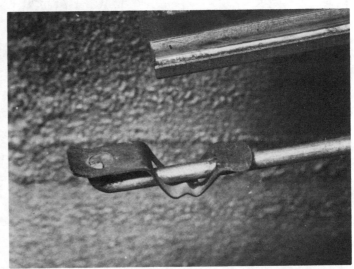

15.5 Fixing clip not fully engaged

Fig. 12.19. Adjusting the upper stopper upper

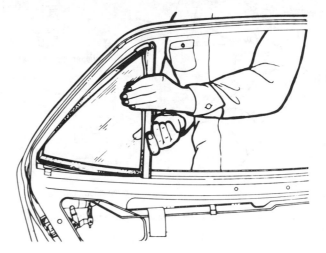

Fig. 12.20. Removing the quarter light and sash

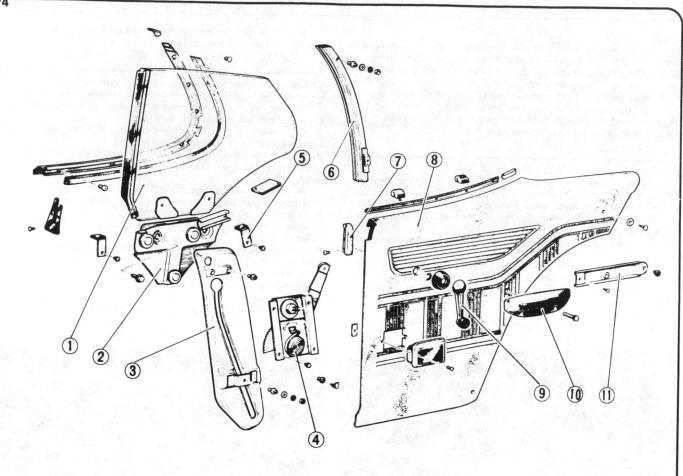

Fig. 12.21. Hardtop quarter window - exploded view

1	Quarter window glass	4	Regulator assembly
2	Quarter glass bracket	5	Upper stopper
3	Main roller guide	6	Quarter glass guide

7	Trim cover	10	Arm rest
8	Quarter trim	11	Arm rest bracket
9	Regulator handle		

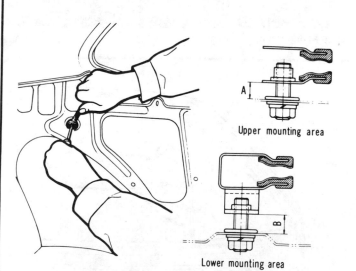

Fig. 12.22. Tightening the quarter glass guide adjusting bolt

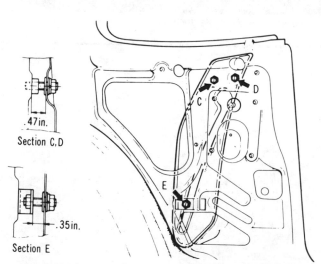

Fig. 12.23. Main roller guide adjusting bolt setting

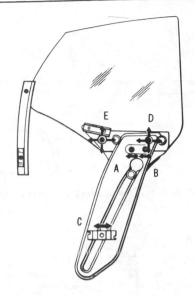

Fig. 12.24. Quarter window glass adjustment points

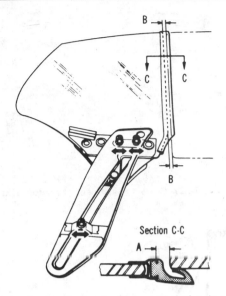

Fig. 12.25. Adjusting the longitudinal position of main roller guide

Adjustment points (symbol)	Direction of adjustment	Direction of glass movement
A, B, C, D, E	Backward and forward	Whole of glass moves backward or forward.
D, E	Upward or downward	Whole of glass moves upward or downward.
A, B	Outward	Moves outward of glass
C	Inward	

10 Set the dimension 'A' (Fig. 10.22) on the quarter light guide adjusting bolt to 0.39 in (9.9 mm) and dimension 'B' to 0.49 in (12.4 mm). Insert the guide into the panel through an access hole and temporarily tighten the bolt at the centre of the oblong hole.

11 Referring to Fig. 12.23, set the length of the main roller guide adjusting bolts to the dimensions shown. Fit the quarter light bracket roller into the main roller guide and insert the assembly into the door through the access hole.

12 After inserting the roller at the front end of the regulator arm, into the roller guide of the quarter light, temporarily tighten the main roller guide at the centre of the oblong hole in the inner panel.

13 Turn the regulator to make certain that the roller is fitted properly into the main roller guide, then turn the regulator to its mid-position and insert the glass from above.

14 Raise the regulator arm until the glass attachment area of the quarter light bracket can be seen through the access hole, then temporarily fix the glass to the bracket.

15 Adjust the lateral and longitudinal position of the glass as described in the next Section.

18 Hardtop quarter light - adjustment

1 After completing the door glass adjustment (Section 13) adjust the quarter light by reference to Fig. 12.24.

Tilt adjustment

2 Raise the glass until it touches the weatherstrip to see if it tilts and if so, proceed as follows.

3 Loosen the bolts securing the glass to the quarter light bracket and move the glass until it is parallel with the door glass. Tighten the bolts

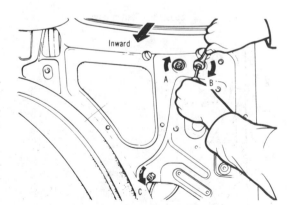

Fig. 12.26. Adjusting main roller guide run-out

and check that the glass moves up and down smoothly.

4 Loosen the main roller guide attachment nuts and adjust the longitudinal position of the guide so that the clearance between the quarter light weatherstrip and the door weatherstrip (dimension 'A' in Fig. 12.25) is 0.28 ± 0.08 in (7.1 ± 2.1 mm).

Run-out adjustment

5 Raise the glass fully, shut the door and check that all four sides of the glass are in even contact with the weatherstrip.

6 Adjust the UP and DOWN positions of the glass, using the main roller guide attachment - adjust bolts, turning the bolts (Fig. 12.26) one at a time.

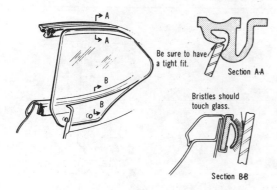

Be sure to have a tight fit.

Section A-A

Bristles should touch glass.

Section B-B

Fig. 12.27. Correct adjustment of quarter light

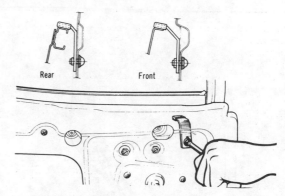

Rear   Front

Fig. 12.28. Fitting the quarter light upper stopper

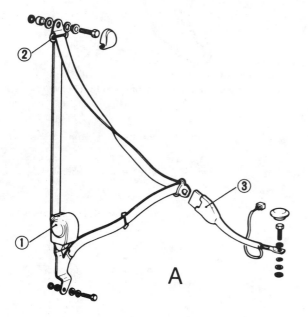

A

Sedan and Station wagon

Support the torsion bar with a pipe

Fig. 12.29. Removing the torsion bar

Fig. 12.30. Components of front safety belt

◄ 1 Inertia reel   3 Buckle stalk
  2 Shoulder anchor

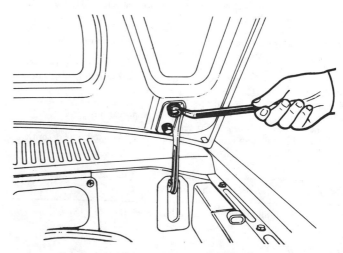

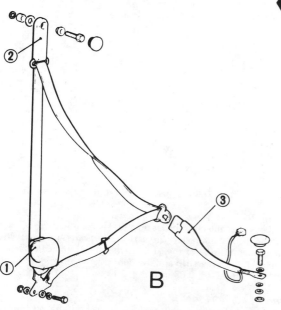

B

Hardtop and Coupe

Fig. 12.31. Removing the bonnet

7 To tilt the glass inwards turn bolts 'A' and 'B' clockwise and bolt 'C' anti-clockwise for both the UP and DOWN positions of the glass.

8 To tilt the glass outwards, turn 'A' and 'B' anti-clockwise and 'C' clockwise.

9 After adjusting the main roller guide run-out, turn the regulator handle to move the glass up and down to see that it moves smoothly and that the rear part of the glass makes proper contact with the weatherstrip (Fig. 12.27). If necessary, adjust the quarter light run-out in the same way as the main roller guide.

10 After completing the adjustments, raise the quarter light and fit the upper stopper to the quarter light bracket (Fig. 12.28).

19 Door rattles - tracing and rectification

1 The most common cause of door rattles is a misaligned, loose or worn striker plate, but other causes may be:

   a) *Loose door handles, window winder handles or door hinges*
   b) *Loose, worn or misaligned door lock components*
   c) *Loose or worn remote control mechanism*

or a combination of these.

2 If the striker catch is worn, renew and adjust, as described in Section 11.

3 Should the hinges be badly worn then it may become necessary for new ones to be fitted.

20 Tailgate and torsion bar - removal and refitting

1 Remove the hinge cover and disconnect the wiring harness.

2 Disconnect the number plate harness from the car body after attaching a string to its forward end to facilitate re-threading. Disconnect the tailgate body at the hinge and then remove it from the body.

3 To remove the torsion bar, support the bar with a pipe and remove the holder (arrowed in Fig. 12.29) to release the force in the bar. Remove the gate stop to disconnect the bar from the hinge.

4 Remove the hinge fixing bolts and remove the tailgate.

21 Seatbelts - removal and refitting

1 Remove the bolt securing the inertia reel and the bolt securing the shoulder anchor and remove the combined lap and shoulder belt.

2 Remove the bolt securing the buckle stalk to the floor and disconnect the wiring harness of the driver's belt.

3 When refitting the inertia reel must be vertical and must not foul the seat reclining adjuster for any position of the seat. Tighten the bolts to a torque wrench setting of 17 to 21 lbf ft (2.4 to 3.0 kgf m).

4 Make sure that the belt is not twisted and that the shoulder anchor is free to rotate on its mounting bolt, which should be tightened to at least 17 lbf ft (2.4 kgf m).

5 After fitting the buckle stalk and tightening its fixing bolt to 17 lbf ft (2.4 kgf m), re-connect the cable harness of the driver's belt.

22 Bonnet - removal and refitting

1 Release the bonnet lock.

2 Mark the position of the hinges so that the bonnet can be refitted in exactly the same position, remove the four fixing bolts (Fig. 12.31) while an assistant supports the bonnet and then lift it off.

23 Bonnet lock - adjustment

1 The lock can be adjusted by altering the length of the bonnet lock bolt (Fig. 12.32).

2 Set the bolt to the standard length of 2.3 in (58.4 mm) and check whether the locking is satisfactory. If locking is difficult, lengthen the bolt and if the front of the bonnet is high, shorten the bolt until the lock engages firmly.

24 Front wings - removal and refitting

1 Remove the front bumper (Section 4).

2 Remove the front grille (Chapter 10, Section 18).

3 Disconnect the side marker lamp wiring.

4 Remove the wing attachment bolts and take off the wing.

5 Fit in the reverse order, taking care to fit the seal and packing.

25 Heater unit - removal and refitting

1 Drain the radiator.

2 Remove the glove box, the instrument cluster and the console box then disconnect the heater control cables from the heater unit.

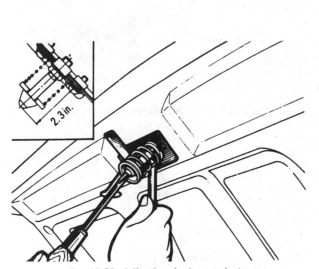

Fig. 12.32. Adjusting the bonnet lock

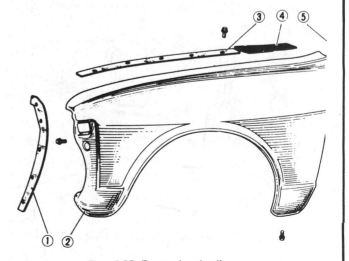

Fig. 12.33. Front wing details

1 *Front wing seal*   4 *Upper seal*
2 *Wing*   5 *Rear seal*
3 *Gasket*

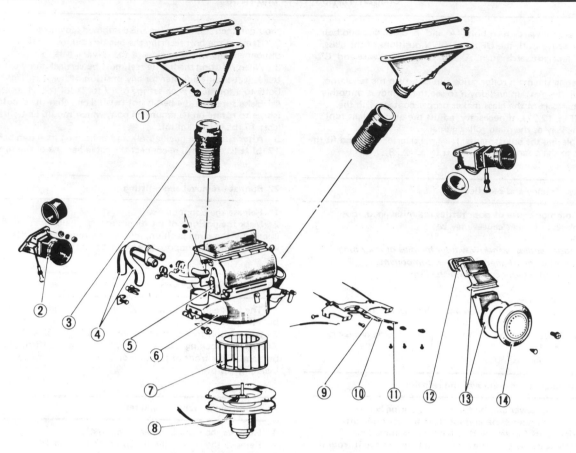

Fig. 12.34. Exploded view of heater and ventilator

1	Defroster nozzle	5	Water valve assembly	9	Heater-defroster lever	13	Duct assembly (sedan, hardtop, and coupe)
2	Ventilator duct assembly	6	Heater assembly	10	Water valve lever		
3	Air duct	7	Turbo fan	11	Air control lever	14	Ventilator garnish (sedan, hardtop, and coupe)
4	Water hose	8	Motor	12	Valve (sedan, hardtop and coupe)		

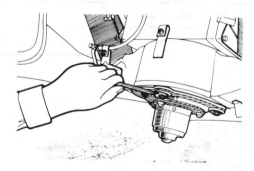

Fig. 12.36. Removing the heater fan motor

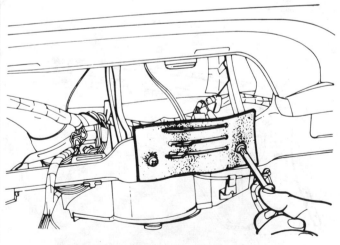

Fig. 12.35. Removing the heater control assembly

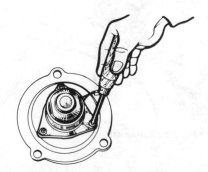

Fig. 12.37. Removing the motor armature

3   Remove the heater control assembly, (Fig 12.35) disconnect the water hoses and air ducts and remove the heater assembly, taking care not to spill any coolant remaining in it.

4   When refitting the heater, make sure that the water hoses are pushed on as far as possible and clamped securely.

5   To adjust the OUTSIDE-VENT-INSIDE control, set the control lever to INSIDE, close the outside air port of the heater, open the ports into the car and clamp the control cable.

6   To adjust the OFF-HOT control, put the control to OFF, close the water valve fully and clamp the control cable.

7   To adjust the ROOM-DEF control, put the control lever to DEF and with the heater unit butterfly closed on the car interior side, clamp the control cable.

26 Heater fan motor · removal, inspection and refitting

1   Separate the connectors of the heater motor cables (Fig. 12.36).

2   Remove the three bolts from the motor mounting flange and withdraw the motor and fan assembly. In the case of cars for Canada, the motor cannot be removed without removing the heater assembly.

3   Remove the fan locknut and take off the fan then remove the three screws from the end plate, take off the end plate and remove the armature (Fig. 12.37).

4   Examine the brushes and if they are shorter than 0.28 in (7.1 mm) fit new ones.

5   After reassembling the motor and refitting the fan, run the motor to see that the fan turns smoothly.

6   Refit the motor assembly. Refit the heater and refill the cooling system.

27 Air conditioning

Air conditioning is available on some models, but when fitted should only be removed, serviced and refitted by a competent air conditioning specialist. When it is necessary to depressurise the system, as when the engine is to be removed, this must also be entrusted to a specialist.

Chapter 13 Supplement:
Revisions and information on later models

Contents

1 Introduction

This Supplement contains information which has become available since the manual was first produced; in particular for the period from mid-1978 onwards. However, some information applies retrospectively to earlier models.

In order to use the Supplement to the best advantage, it is suggested that it is referred to before the main Chapters of the manual; this will ensure that any relevant information can be noted and incorporated within the procedures given in Chapters 1 to 12. Time and cost will therefore be saved and the particular job will be completed correctly.

2 Specifications

The Specifications below are revisions of, or supplementary to, those at the beginning of the preceding Chapters. Note that the specifications listed for GS models are also applicable to later Celeste 1600 GSR models.

Engine (4G32 with timing belt)
General
Compression ratio:
Except GS	8.5 : 1
GS	9.5 : 1

Idling speed:
Except GS	700 ± 50 rpm
GS	800 ± 50 rpm

Valve timing (GS engine)
Inlet opens	24° BTDC
Inlet closes	64° ABDC
Exhaust opens	67° BBDC
Exhaust closes	21° ATDC

Pistons and piston rings
Piston-to-cylinder clearance (GS engine)	0.0012 to 0.0020 in (0.03 to 0.05 mm)

Piston ring end gaps:
Nos 1 and 2	0.008 to 0.016 in (0.20 to 0.41 mm)
Oil ring side rail	0.008 to 0.020 in (0.20 to 0.51 mm)

Camshaft
Endfloat	0.002 to 0.006 in (0.05 to 0.15 mm)

Valve springs
Free length	1.823 in (46.3 mm)

Oil pump
Driven gear-to-body clearance	0.0039 to 0.0276 in (0.10 to 0.70 mm)
Drive gear-to-body clearance	0.0079 to 0.0276 in (0.20 to 0.70 mm)
Gear side clearance	0.0024 to 0.0047 in (0.06 to 0.12 mm)
Drive gear shaft running clearance	0.0008 to 0.0019 in (0.02 to 0.05 mm)
Oil pressure relief spring free length	1.85 in (47.0 mm)

Torque wrench settings
	lbf ft	kgf m
Camshaft bearing cap	14 to 15	1.9 to 2.1
Camshaft sprocket	44 to 57	6.1 to 7.9
Crankshaft pulley centre bolt	44 to 50	6.1 to 6.9
Crankshaft pulley to sprocket	7.5 to 8.5	1.0 to 1.2
Timing belt tensioner	16 to 21	2.2 to 3.0
Oil pump sprocket	25 to 28	3.4 to 4.0
Front case	11 to 13	1.5 to 1.8
Oil pick-up tube	13 to 18	1.8 to 2.5
Flywheel/driveplate to crankshaft	94 to 101	13.0 to 13.9

Cooling system
Capacity (1979-on models)
1597 cc engine	11.4 pints (6.5 litres)

1995 cc engine:
13.8 in (350 mm) radiator	13.2 pints (7.5 litres)
15.7 in (400 mm) radiator	14.8 pints (8.4 litres)

Torque wrench settings
	lbf ft	kgf m
Alternator mounting bolt	15 to 18	2.0 to 2.5
Alternator adjustment bolt	9 to 10	1.2 to 1.5

Fuel and exhaust systems
Idle speed
1597 cc (single carburettor)	700 ± 50 rpm
1597 cc (twin carburettors)	800 ± 50 rpm
1995 cc (pre-1979)	800 ± 50 rpm
1995 cc (1979-on)	850 ± 50 rpm

Fuel pump (mechanical)
Pressure (1597 cc engine)	3.7 to 5.1 lbf/in² (0.26 to 0.36 kgf/cm²)
Pressure (1995 cc engine)	4.6 to 6.0 lbf/in² (0.32 to 0.42 kgf/cm²)

Carburettor (Mikuni)

	Engine/model			
	4G32	*4G52*	*4G32/GS*	*4G52/GS*
Primary throttle bore – in (mm)	1.102 (28)	1.181 (30)	1.102 (28)	1.181 (30)
Secondary throttle bore – in (mm)	1.260 (32)	1.260 (32)	1.260 (32)	1.260 (32)
Primary main jet	95	102.5	95	102.5
Secondary main jet	190	200	165	150
Primary pilot jet	55	60	55	55
Secondary pilot jet	70	90	60	80
Enrichment jet	60	40	40	40
Float level – in (mm)	0.75 (19)	0.75 (19)	0.75 (19)	0.75 (19)
Idle CO%	2.0 + 0.5%			

Ignition system (1978 on)
Distributor
Contact points gap	0.018 to 0.022 in (0.45 to 0.55 mm)
Dwell angle	52° ± 3°

Ignition timing
1597 cc (except GS)	5° ± 1° BTDC at 700 rpm
1597 cc (GS)	13° ± 1° BTDC at 800 rpm
1995 cc (pre-1979)	13° ± 1° BTDC at 800 rpm
1995 cc (1979-on)	13° ± 1° BTDC at 850 rpm

Pick-up coil (electronic ignition, 1979-on)
Resistance	1050 ± 50 ohms

Spark plugs
Type:	
1597 cc (except GS)	Champion RN11YC
1597 cc (GS)	Champion RN9YC
1995 cc	Champion RN9YC
Gap	0.028 in (0.7 mm)

Clutch
Pedal setting dimensions
Pedal height:	
1977/1978 models	6.5 to 6.7 in (165 to 170 mm)
1979-on models	6.4 in (163 mm)
Pedal stroke:	
1977/1978 models	5.1 in (130 mm)
1979-on models	5.5 in (140 mm)

Manual gearbox (KM 119)
Ratios
First	3.215 : 1
Second	2.000 : 1
Third	1.316 : 1
Fourth	1.000 : 1
Fifth	0.853 : 1
Reverse	3.667 : 1

Oil capacity
	3.5 pints (2.0 litres)

Propeller shaft
General
Type (1979-on)	Two-piece, tubular

Torque wrench settings
	lbf ft	kgf m
Centre yoke to front section	120 to 160	16 to 22
Flange coupling bolts	18 to 22	2.4 to 3.0
Centre bearing to underbody	25 to 29	3.0 to 4.0

Rear axle
Ratio (1979-on)
1597 cc 4-speed manual	3.909 : 1
1597 cc 5-speed manual	4.222 : 1
1995 cc 5-speed manual	3.909 : 1
1995 cc 3-speed automatic	3.545 : 1

Braking system (1979-on models only)
Brake pedal height
Manual transmission models	6.4 in (163.0 mm)
Automatic transmission models	6.5 ± 0.1 in (165.0 ± 3.0 mm)

Electrical system
Voltage regulator
Regulated voltage .... 14.1 to 14.7 V at 20°C (68°F)

Alternator
Minimum brush length:
    Mitsubishi .... 0.315 in (8.0 mm)
    Nippon Denso .... 0.394 in (10.0 mm)

Fuses (1979-on models)

No	Rating (amps)		Circuits protected
1	10	....	Radio and cigarette lighter
2	15	....	Wipers and washers
3	15	....	Stop-lamps and horn
4	10	....	Hazard warning lamps
5	5	....	Interior lamp and instrument panel
6	10	....	Tail lamps, parking lights, number plate lights, instrument panel lights
7	10	....	Headlamp relay
8	15	....	Heated rear window
9	10	....	Direction indicators, reversing light and voltage regulator
10	15	....	Heater and instrument panel lights

Bulbs (later models)
	Wattage
Side repeater	10
Front direction indicator	21
Front parking lamp	10
Headlamp:	
Inner	37.5
Outer	37.5/50
Tail lamps	10
Rear direction indicator	21
Stop-lamp	21
Reversing lamp	21
Number plate lamp	10
Stop/tail lamp	21/5
Interior lamp	10
Luggage compartment lamp (Galant Estate)	10

Suspension and steering
Steering geometry (1979-on)
Camber .... 1° ± 30'
Castor .... 1° 45' ± 30'

Wheels and tyres
Roadwheel size (1979-on) .... 5J x 13
Tyre size:
    1597 cc 4-speed models .... 165/80 SR 13
    Except 1597 cc 4-speed models .... 175/70 HR 13
Tyre pressures (front and rear) .... 24 lbf/in² (1.7 kgf/cm²)

Torque wrench settings (1979-on)
	lbf ft	kgf m
Front suspension		
Lower arm pivot nut	43 to 51	6.0 to 7.0
Lower arm pivot shaft to crossmember	6 to 9	0.8 to 1.2
Rear suspension		
Shock absorber mountings (upper and lower)	12 to 14	1.6 to 2.0

General dimensions, weights and capcities
Dimensions – Galant models
Overall length .... 165.9 in (4215 mm)
Overall width .... 62.2 in (1580 mm)
Overall height .... 54.3 in (1380 mm)
Track:
    Front .... 51.4 in (1305 mm)
    Rear .... 51.2 in (1300 mm)

Dimensions – Celeste models
Overall length .... 162.0 in (4115 mm)
Overall width .... 63.4 in (1610 mm)
Overall height .... 52.4 in (1330 mm)
Track:
    Front .... 52.2 in (1325 mm)
    Rear .... 51.0 in (1295 mm)

Weights – Galant models
1597 cc Saloon/Hardtop	2072 lb (940 kg)
1597 cc Estate	2205 lb (1000 kg)
1995 cc Saloon/Hardtop	2216 lb (1005 kg)

Weights – Celeste models
1597 cc (except GS)	2083 lb (945 kg)
1597 cc (GS)	2116 lb (960 kg)
1995 cc	2205 lb (1000 kg)

Capacities – all models
Engine oil (including oil filter):	
1597 cc	7.0 pints (4.0 litres)
1995 cc	7.6 pints (4.3 litres)
Cooling system – see Chapters 2 and 13	
Fuel tank:	
Celeste	9.9 gallons (45.0 litres)
Galant:	
Saloon	11.2 gallons (51.0 litres)
Estate	9.2 gallons (42.0 litres)
Manual gearbox:	
3-speed	2.6 pints (1.5 litres)
4-speed	3.0 pints (17 litres)
5-speed (KM132)	4.0 pints (2.3 litres)
5-speed (KM119)	3.5 pints (2.0 litres)
Automatic transmission:	
Borg Warner	9.3 pints (5.3 litres)
Torqueflite	11.3 pints (6.4 litres)
Rear axle	1.9 pints (1.1 litres)

3 Routine maintenance

1 On all models, maintenance intervals are based on a nominal annual mileage of 10 000 miles or more. Vehicles covering less than this mileage in a year should have the 5000 or 6000-mile maintenance tasks performed every six months, the 10 000 or 12 000-mile tasks performed annually, and so on.

2 Older vehicles, and those used under adverse conditions, will benefit from more frequent maintenance. 'Adverse conditions' include extremes of climate, full-time trailer towing, taxi work and driving on unmade roads.

3 The maintenance schedule for 1979 and later models is summarized below.

Weekly, every 250 miles (400 km) or before a long journey
    Check engine oil level
    Check coolant level
    Check brake fluid level
    Top up screen washer reservoir
    Check tyre pressures
    Check operation of lights, direction indicators etc
    Check tightness of wheel nuts

Every 6000 miles (10 000 km nominal) or six months, whichever comes first
    Change engine oil
    Inspect spark plugs; clean and regap, or renew
    Inspect air cleaner element; clean or renew
    Inspect contact breaker points (when applicable); regap or renew
    Check fan belt tension and condition
    Inspect brake disc pads for wear, check calipers for leaks
    Inspect brake and fuel system pipes and hoses
    Check for leakage of fuel, coolant, or oils
    Check brake pedal free play
    Lubricate hinges, latches, cables etc
    Check dwell angle (when applicable) and ignition timing
    Check operation of brakes
    Check automatic transmission fluid level
    Check handbrake adjustment
    Check idle speed and mixture

Every 12 000 miles (20 000 km) or annually (additional work)
    Change engine oil filter
    Check tightness of cylinder head and manifold fastenings

    Lubricate distributor
    Inspect fuel strainer; renew if necessary
    Check manual gearbox oil level
    Check rear axle oil level
    Check tightness of front suspension, rear spring and propeller shaft flange bolts
    Check condition of suspension components
    Check condition of propeller shaft joints
    Inspect rear brake shoes for wear, check wheel cylinders for leaks and inspect drums
    Check steering linkage for smooth operation and free play
    Check engine valve clearances
    Check front wheel alignment
    Renew brake fluid by bleeding

Every 24 000 miles (40 000 km) or two years (additional work)
    Check oil level in steering box
    Change rear axle oil
    Inspect front wheel bearings, repack with grease and adjust
    Renew coolant

Every 30 000 miles (50 000 km) or 30 months (additional work)
    Change manual gearbox oil or automatic transmission fluid

Every 36 000 miles (60 000 km) or three years (additional work)
    Renew all braking system rubber seals and flexible hoses
    Renew timing belt and balancer shaft drivebelt, when applicable (recommended as a precautionary measure)

4 Engine

1597 cc engine with timing belt – description

1 From late 1977, the 1597 cc engine (code 4G32) is fitted with a timing belt instead of the previous timing chain. The main timing belt also drives the gear-type oil pump which is located in the front case to the left of the crankshaft.

2 The UK version of this engine is fitted with balancer shafts located in the upper right and lower left of the cylinder block. The right shaft is driven by a small toothed belt from the front of the crankshaft and thus rotates in the same direction as the crankshaft. The left shaft is keyed to the oil pump driven gear and thus rotates in an opposite direction to the crankshaft.

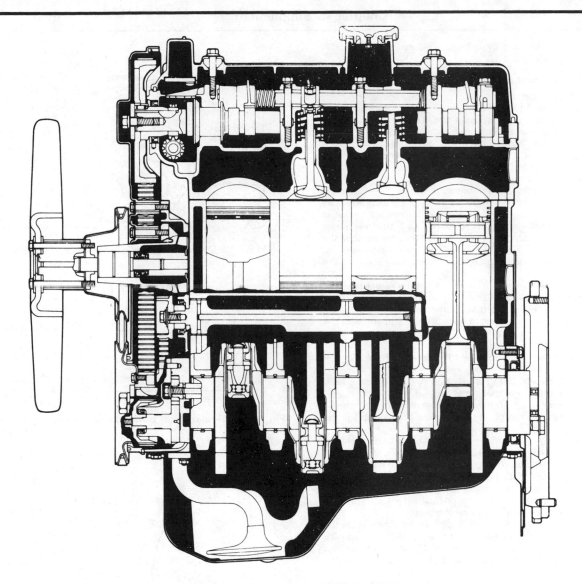

Fig. 13.1 Longitudinal section of 1597 cc engine with timing belt (Sec 4)

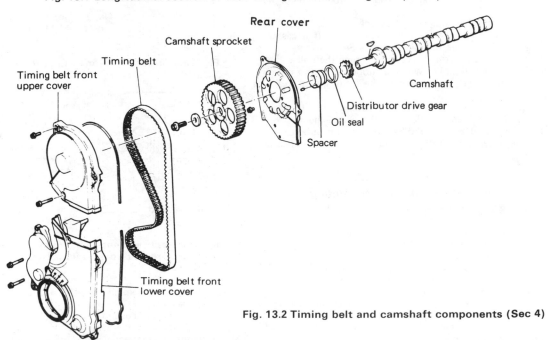

Fig. 13.2 Timing belt and camshaft components (Sec 4)

3 The following sub-sections describe procedures which are different to those given in Chapter 1.

Cylinder head – removal and refitting

4 Drain the cooling system as described in Chapter 2.
5 Disconnect the radiator top hose.
6 Disconnect the vacuum advance hose and HT leads, then remove the distributor with reference to Section 7 of this Supplement.
7 Disconnect the coolant hoses from the cylinder head.
8 Remove the air cleaner, fuel pump, exhaust manifold, and inlet manifold together with the carburettor with reference to Chapter 3, and Section 6 of this Supplement.
9 Unbolt the timing belt front upper cover.
10 Using a socket on the crankshaft pulley bolt, turn the engine in its normal direction until the timing mark on the camshaft sprocket is aligned with the mark on the sprocket rear cover. No 1 piston will now be at TDC on the compression stroke. Check also that the notch in the crankshaft pulley is aligned with the 'T' mark on the timing plate.
11 Make a mark on the timing belt in line with the timing marks on the sprocket and cover.
12 Unscrew the camshaft sprocket bolt, then lever the sprocket off the camshaft and rest it on the support provided on the front lower cover, leaving the timing belt still engaged with the sprocket. If necessary, insert packing beneath the sprocket to keep it in alignment with the camshaft.
13 Unbolt the sprocket rear cover.
14 Unbolt the rocker cover and remove the gasket and the rear half round rubber plug.
15 Using a 5/16 in Allen key, progressively unscrew the cylinder head bolts in the reverse sequence to that shown in Fig. 13.4.
16 With all the bolts removed, lift the cylinder head vertically from the cylinder block and remove the gasket. Take care not to damage the location dowels.
17 Clean the surfaces of the cylinder head and block and locate the new gasket on the dowels.
18 Lower the cylinder head onto the block and insert the bolts loosely.
19 Tighten the bolts to 25 lbf ft (3.5 kgf m) using the sequence shown in Fig. 13.4 then, using the same sequence, tighten them to the final torque wrench setting given in Specifications, Chapter 1.
20 Fit the sprocket rear cover and tighten the bolts.
21 Lift the camshaft sprocket from the support and locate it on the camshaft. If the dowel pin on the spacer is not accurately aligned with the hole in the sprocket, small movements of the camshaft may be made by tapping the projections behind No 2 exhaust cam lobe with a screwdriver.
22 Insert the sprocket bolt and tighten it to the specified torque while holding the sprocket stationary with a bar inserted through one of the holes.
23 Check that the crankshaft pulley and sprocket marks are still in alignment together with the mark on the timing belt. If necessary retension the timing belt as described later in this Section.
24 Refit the timing belt front upper cover and tighten the bolts.
25 Refit the rocker cover together wth the rubber plug and a new gasket, but first apply sealing compound to the areas shown in Fig. 13.6. Fit and tighten the bolts.
26 Refit the inlet and exhaust manifolds, fuel pump and air cleaner with reference to Chapter 3 and Section 6 of this Supplement.
27 Refit the distributor wth reference to Section 7 of this Supplement.
28 Reconnect the hoses and fill the cooling system as described in Chapter 2.

Camshaft and rocker shafts – removal and refitting

29 Remove the air cleaner (Chapter 3) and disconnect the breather hoses.
30 Remove the distributor and fuel pump as described in Sections 7 and 6 of this Supplement respectively.
31 Unbolt the timing belt front upper cover.
32 Remove the camshaft sprocket and locate it on the support by following the procedure given in paragraphs 10 to 13.
33 Lever the spacer from the front of the camshaft.
34 Unbolt the rocker cover and remove the gasket and the rear half-round rubber plug.
35 Progressively unscrew the camshaft bearing cap bolts, then lift off the rocker shafts, arms and caps as an assembly.
36 If necessary dismantle the rocker shaft components by removing

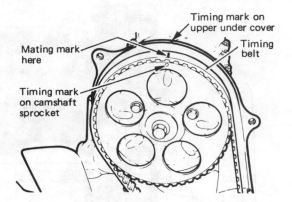

Fig. 13.3 Camshaft sprocket timing marks (Sec 4)

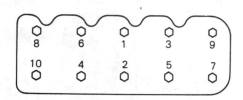

Fig. 13.4 Cylinder head bolt tightening sequence (Sec 4)

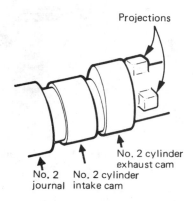

Fig. 13.5 Projections for turning the camshaft (Sec 4)

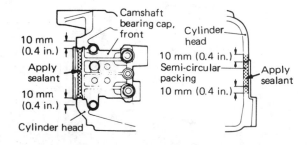

Fig. 13.6 Apply sealant as indicated before refitting the rocker cover and gasket (Sec 4)

the bolts, but keep them all in their correct order of removal to ensure correct reassembly.
37 Withdraw the oil seal and distributor drivegear from the front of the camshaft, then lift out the camshaft.
38 Clean the components, including the bearing surfaces and cap locations on the head.

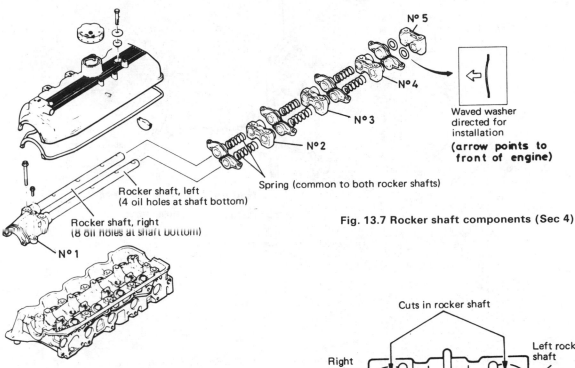

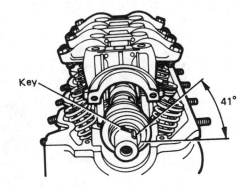

Rocker shaft, left
(4 oil holes at shaft bottom)

Spring (common to both rocker shafts)

Rocker shaft, right
(8 oil holes at shaft bottom)

Nº 1

Nº 2

Nº 3

Nº 4

Nº 5

Waved washer
directed for
installation

**(arrow points to
front of engine)**

Fig. 13.7 Rocker shaft components (Sec 4)

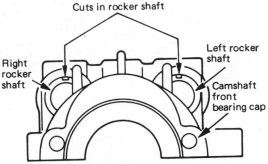

Cuts in rocker shaft

Right
rocker
shaft

Left rocker
shaft

Camshaft
front
bearing cap

**Fig. 13.8 Correct assembly of rocker shafts in the camshaft
front bearing cap (Sec 4)**

39 Oil the camshaft journals and lobes, and locate the camshaft on the cylinder head.

40 Slide the distributor drivegear on the front of the camshaft over the Woodruff key.

41 Re-assemble the rocker shaft assembly, making sure that the slots at the front of the shafts are uppermost in the front cap.

42 Set the camshaft in the No 1 TDC position as shown in Fig. 13.9, then fit the rocker shaft assembly and tighten the cap bolts in two stages, first to half the specified torque, and then to the full specified torque, in the following sequence: No 3 (centre), No 2, No 4, No 1 (front), No 5 (rear).

43 Press the new oil seal into position squarely using a metal tube, or if available, Mitsubishi tool MD 998287. The latter tool has a half-round shoulder which contacts the distributor drivegear to ensure correct positioning of the oil seal, but if this is not available, position the oil seal flush with the front face of the cap.

44 Smear the oil seal lips with oil, then slide the spacer onto the camshaft and check that the oil seal locates on it correctly.

45 Refit the camshaft sprocket by following the procedure given in paragraphs 20 to 24.

46 Adjust the valve clearances as described in Chapter 1, Section 28.

47 Refit the rocker cover as described in paragraph 25.

48 Refit the distributor and fuel pump as described in Sections 7 and 6 of this Supplement respectively.

49 Reconnect the breather hoses and refit the air cleaner (Chapter 3).

Timing belt and crankshaft sprockets – removal and refitting

50 Remove the fan belt (Chapter 2).

51 Unbolt the timing belt front upper cover.

52 Follow the procedure given in paragraphs 10 and 11 to set the crankshaft at TDC, No 1 piston firing.

53 If the crankshaft sprockets are to be removed, engage top gear or lock the flywheel ring gear with a screwdriver through the starter aperture, then unscrew and remove the crankshaft pulley centre bolt.

54 Unbolt the pulley from the crankshaft sprocket. Note the location dowel.

55 Unbolt the timing belt front lower cover.

56 Loosen the timing belt tensioner nut and bolt, pull the tensioner against the spring tension to the end of the slot, then tighten the nut to retain the tensioner.

57 Remove the timing belt from the crankshaft, oil pump, and

Key

41°

Fig. 13.9 Camshaft set at No 1 TDC position (Sec 4)

**Fig. 13.10 Tool MD 99287 for fitting camshaft front oil seal
(Sec 4)**

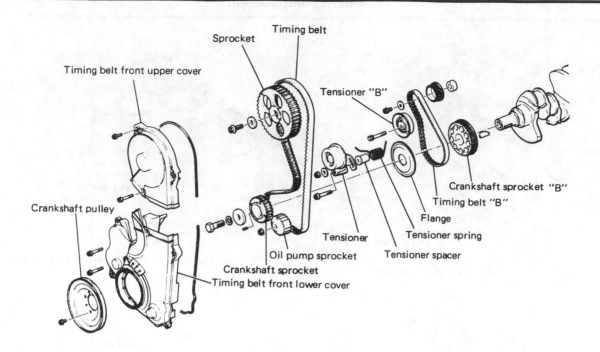

Fig. 13.11 Timing belt components (Sec 4)

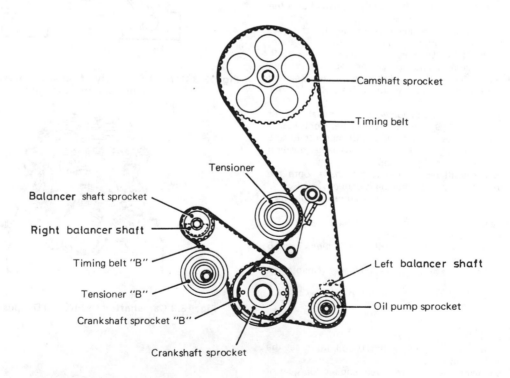

Fig. 13.12 Timing belt configuration (Sec 4)

camshaft sprockets. If the belt is to be refitted, mark its normal direction of rotation to ensure correct refitting.

58 If necessary remove the crankshaft sprocket, using a puller if it is tight. The tensioner may also be removed if required.

59 Check the timing belt thoroughly for signs of deterioration and cracking. If it has completed 40 000 miles (65 000 km) it should be renewed as a matter of course. If any oil is found on the belt, check and renew if necessary the camshaft, crankshaft and balancer shaft front oil seals.

60 If the timing belt is being renewed it is wise to also renew the right-hand balancer shaft drivebelt. To do this, unscrew the tensioner bolt to release the tension then slip the belt from the sprockets. Slide the front flange and the large sprocket from the crankshaft.

61 Check the tensioners for smooth running and renew them if necessary.

62 Locate the large sprocket on the crankshaft and fit the drivebelt over the right-hand balancer shaft sprocket. Check that the alignment marks are as shown in Fig. 13.13 and fully engage the belt. Fit the front flange.

63 Turn the tensioner eccentric clockwise until the top run of the belt is taut, then tighten the bolt.

64 Refit the main timing belt tensioner and the crankshaft sprocket.

65 Check that the camshaft, crankshaft and oil pump sprocket timing marks are correctly aligned, then fit the timing belt and release the tensioner.

66 Check that the oil pump is correctly aligned by removing the plug from the cylinder block and inserting a 0.315 in (8.0 mm) diameter metal rod or screwdriver. It should be possible to insert the rod by at least 2.36 in (60.0 mm) but if it can only be inserted 1.0 in (25.4 mm) the alignment is incorrect. Remove the metal rod and refit the plug after the check.

67 Flex the timing belt slightly to ensure the tensioner is free, then release it and tighten the tensioner nut followed by the bolt, in that order.

68 Temporarily refit the crankshaft pulley and (if removed) the bolt, then turn the engine one complete revolution in a clockwise direction without stopping. Remove the pulley.

69 Loosen the tensioner nut and bolt, then retighten the nut followed by the bolt. Check the final tension by holding the belt as shown in Fig. 13.16 and make sure all the timing marks align correctly.

70 Refit the front lower cover and the crankshaft pulley, followed by the front upper cover and the fan belt (Chapter 2). If the pulley centre bolt was slackened, remember to tighten it to the specified torque.

Front case and oil pump – removal and refitting

71 Apply the handbrake, then jack up the front of the car and support on axle stands.

72 Drain the engine oil, then unbolt and remove the sump. Remove the gasket.

73 Unscrew the nuts and remove the oil pick-up pipe (oil screen) from the bottom of the front case. Remove the gasket.

74 Remove the timing belts and crankshaft sprockets as described in paragraphs 50 to 60.

75 Unscrew the nut and pull the sprocket from the oil pump

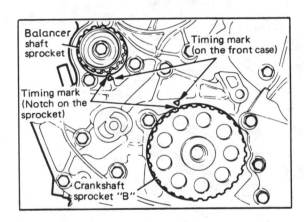

Fig. 13.13 Alignment marks on the crankshaft sprocket and right-hand balancer shaft sprocket (Sec 4)

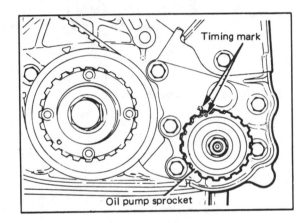

Fig. 13.14 Oil pump sprocket alignment marks (Sec 4)

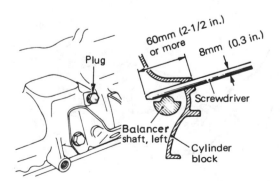

Fig. 13.15 Method of checking the left-hand balancer shaft and oil pump sprocket alignment (Sec 4)

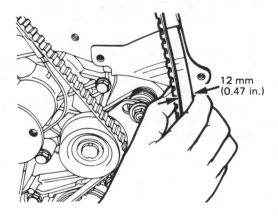

Fig. 13.16 Checking the timing belt tension (Sec 4)

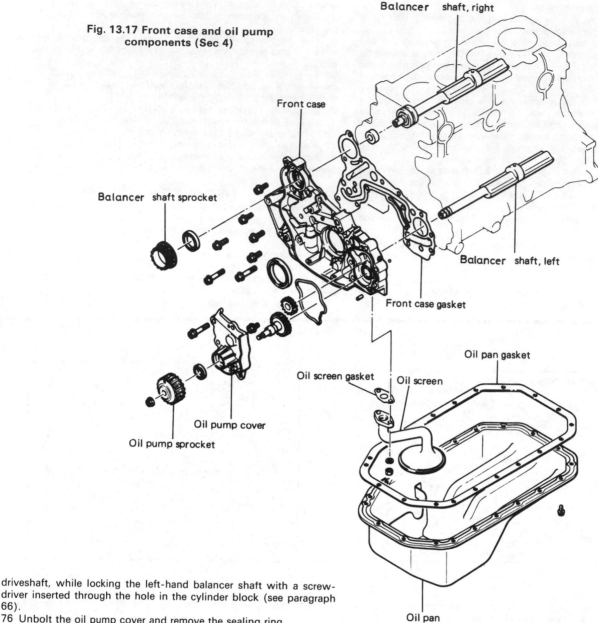

Fig. 13.17 Front case and oil pump components (Sec 4)

driveshaft, while locking the left-hand balancer shaft with a screwdriver inserted through the hole in the cylinder block (see paragraph 66).

76 Unbolt the oil pump cover and remove the sealing ring.

77 Loosen the nut on the front of the left-hand balancer shaft (ie on the oil pump driven gear). Remove the screwdriver from the cylinder block.

78 Unscrew the bolt from the front of the right-hand balancer shaft and pull off the sprocket. Remove the spacer.

79 Unscrew the front case mounting bolts and remove the front case from the cylinder block. If it is stuck tight, lever it off with a screwdriver inserted in the special groove (Fig. 13.18). If the engine is removed from the car withdraw the case together with the left-hand balancer shaft, otherwise remove the oil pump driven gear first.

80 Remove the front case gasket.

81 If necessary withdraw the right-hand balancer shaft from the cylinder block.

82 Clean all the components and check them for damage and wear. Prise the oil seals from the front case and oil pump cover, clean the seatings, and press in new oil seals until flush.

83 Using a feeler gauge, check that the oil pump gear clearances are as given in Specifications.

84 Unscrew the plug and remove the oil pressure relief spring and plunger from the front case. Clean the spring, plunger and seating, and check that the spring free length is as given in Specifications.

85 Commence reassembly by dipping the plunger in oil and inserting it in the front case. Fit the spring and tighten the plug.

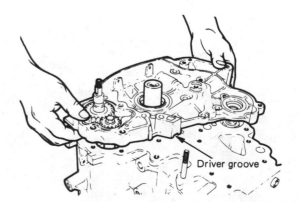

Fig. 13.18 Removing the front case (Sec 4)

Note the groove for levering off case

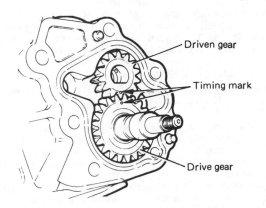

Fig. 13.19 Oil pump gear alignment marks (Sec 4)

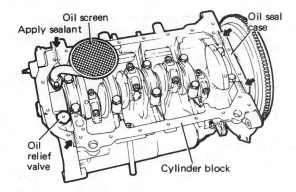

Fig. 13.20 Sealant application areas (arrowed) before refitting the sump and gasket (Sec 4)

86 Oil the balancer shaft journals, then insert the shafts in the cylinder block.
87 Oil the oil pump gears, then locate them in the front case with the timing marks aligned (Fig. 13.19).
88 Smear the lips of the oil seals with oil.
89 Locate a new gasket on the cylinder block and retain with a little grease.
90 Refit the front case, making sure that the oil seal locates correctly on the front of the crankshaft. Insert and tighten the bolts.
91 Fit the spacer, chamfered edge first, onto the right-hand balancer shaft followed by the sprocket. Fit the bolt finger tight.
92 Fit the nut on the left-hand balancer shaft. Insert a screwdriver through the special hole in the cylinder block and fully tighten the nut. special hole in the cylinder block and fully tighten the nut.
93 Refit the oil pump cover together with a new sealing ring. Insert and tighten the bolts.
94 Refit the sprocket to the oil pump driveshaft and tighten the nut.
95 Refit the timing bolts as described in paragraphs 61 to 70, and also tighten the right-hand balancer shaft bolt.

96 Refit the oil pick-up pipe together with a new gasket and tighten the nuts.
97 Wipe clean the gasket face on the cylinder block, then apply sealant to the areas indicated in Fig. 13.20.
98 Refit the sump together with a new gasket and tighten the bolts.
99 Lower the car to the ground and refill the engine wth oil.

5 Cooling system

Thermostat – fitting direction
1 When fitting the thermostat in its location on the inlet manifold, the jiggle pin should be facing rearwards as shown in Fig. 13.21.

Water pump (1597 cc engine with timing belt) – removal and refitting
2 Disconnect the battery negative lead.
3 Drain the cooling system and remove the fan belt as described in Chapter 2.
4 Unbolt the fan shroud from the radiator.
5 Disconnect the bottom hose from the water pump.
6 Unscrew the bolts and remove the cooling fan, spacer, and pulley from the water pump drive flange.
7 Remove the timing belt, camshaft sprocket, and timing belt tensioner as described in Section 4 of this Supplement.

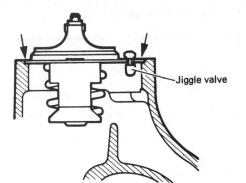

Fig. 13.21 Thermostat location showing jiggle valve (Sec 5)

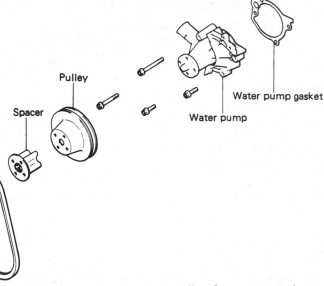

Fig. 13.22 Water pump and cooling fan components – 1597 cc engine with timing belt (Sec 5)

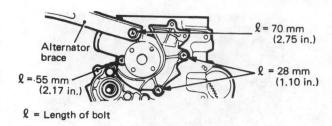

Fig. 13.23 Water pump mounting bolt lengths – 1597 cc engine with timing belt (Sec 5)

8 Unscrew the four water pump mounting bolts, noting that the alternator adjusting link is located on the upper bolt.
9 Remove the water pump from the front of the cylinder block and clean all traces of gasket from both mating surfaces.
10 It is no longer possible to overhaul the water pump, so if it is in any way damaged or if it is leaking, it should be renewed complete.
11 Refitting is a reversal of removal, but fit a new gasket and tighten all bolts to the specified torque. Refer to Section 4 and Chapter 2 as required. Note the different lengths of the water pump mounting bolts shown in Fig. 13.23.

6 Fuel and exhaust systems

Automatic air intake temperature control
1 Celeste models from 1979 onwards may be fitted with an air cleaner incorporating an automatic air intake temperature control. A vacuum controlled flap is located in the air cleaner intake, and is supplied with vacuum from the inlet manifold via a bi-metal temperature sensor in the air cleaner body.
2 With the engine cold, the warm air duct from the exhaust manifold is open, however, as the optimum air temperature is reached the flap valve gradually opens the cold air duct, at the same time closing the warm air duct. The air temperature is then controlled within specific limits in order to achieve good engine performance and economy.

Mechanical fuel pump – general
3 A sealed-type mechanical fuel pump is fitted to later 1597 cc engines (Fig. 13.25), however, the removal and refitting procedure is as given in Chapter 3, Section 5. Bring the engine to TDC, No 2 piston firing, before refitting the fuel pump.

Carburettor (Mikuni) – general description
4 Celeste models from 1979 onwards are fitted with the Mikuni dual barrel downdraught carburettor. On GS models, twin carburettors are fitted.
5 The carburettor has a bypass idling system and a fuel cut-off solenoid, and operation of the secondary throttle valve is by a vacuum diaphragm chamber. A conventional accelerator pump is provided, and in addition an enrichment diaphragm and jet ensures extra fuel for high load operation.
6 The automatic choke is operated by a thermo-wax element in the cooling system. Immediately, on starting the engine, a vacuum-controlled choke breaker partially opens the choke, and for full throttle operation when cold, a link rod from the throttle manually opens the choke.
7 A manual choke system is employed on GS models.

Float level (Mikuni) – adjustment
8 The procedure is as described in Chapter 3, Section 14.

Carburettor (Mikuni) – removal and refitting
9 The procedure is as described in Chapter 3, Section 18, but in addition the wiring must be disconnected from the fuel cut-off solenoid. Make sure that the new gasket is fitted the correct way round.

Carburettor (Mikuni) – dismantling, cleaning and reassembly
10 Clean the exterior surface of the carburettor.
11 Disconnect the return springs from the throttle and intermediate lever.
12 Prise out the C-clip and disconnect the link from the choke unloader lever.
13 Disconnect the vacuum hose, then unscrew the diaphragm chamber screws and disconnect the link.
14 Unscrew the float chamber screws and lift the float chamber from the main body. Remove the gasket. Do not invert the main body at this

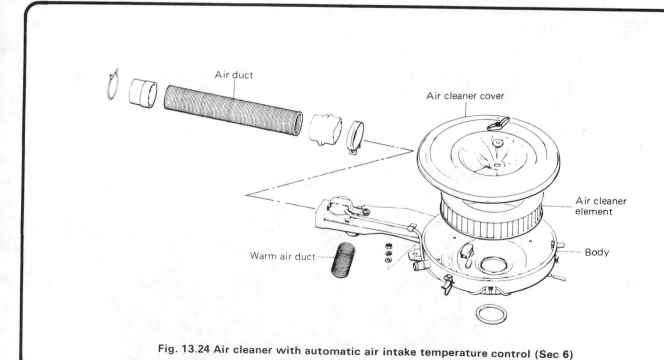

Fig. 13.24 Air cleaner with automatic air intake temperature control (Sec 6)

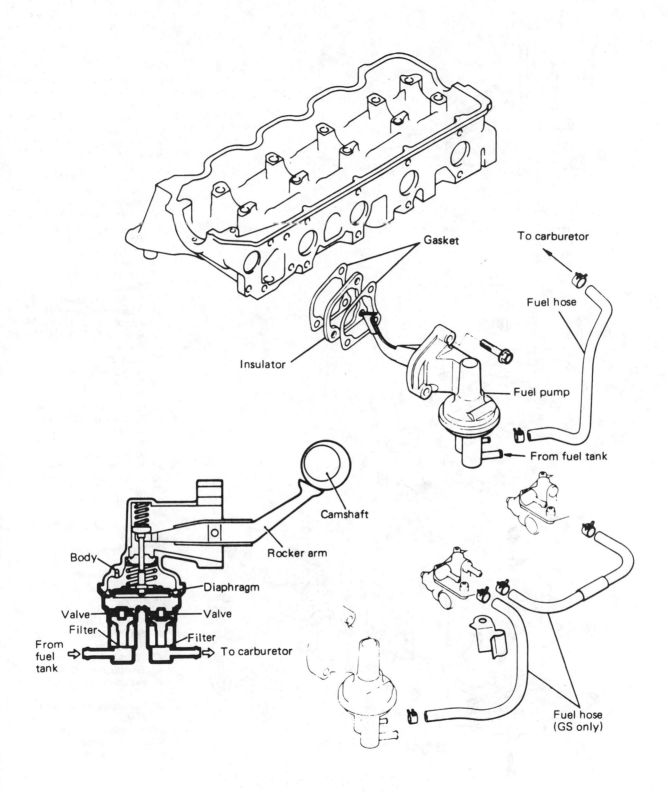

Fig. 13.25 Detail of sealed-type mechanical fuel pump fitted to later 1597 cc engines (Sec 6)

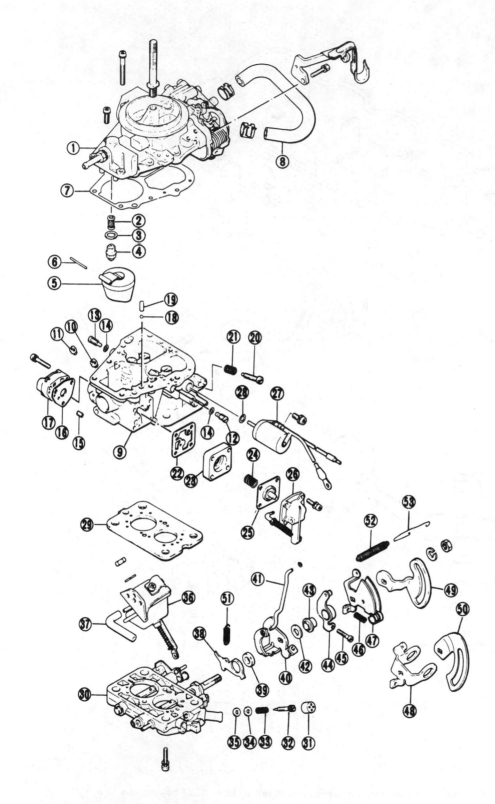

1 Cover
2 Filter
3 Washer
4 Needle valve
5 Float
6 Pivot pin
7 Gasket
8 Hose
9 Main body
10 Primary main jet
11 Secondary main jet
12 Primary pilot jet
13 Secondary pilot jet
14 O-ring
15 Enrichment jet
16 Gasket
17 Enrichment cover
18 Accelerator pump ball
19 Accelerator pump weight
20 Idling speed adjusting screw
21 Spring
22 Gasket
23 Accelerator pump body
24 Return spring
25 Diaphragm
26 Accelerator pump cover
27 Fuel cut-off solenoid
28 O-ring
29 Insulator
30 Throttle body
31 Idle limiter
32 Mixture adjusting screw
33 Spring
34 Washer
35 Seal
36 Vacuum chamber
37 Hose
38 Intermediate lever
39 Ring
40 Abutment lever
41 Link
42 Ring
43 Collar
44 Fast idle lever
45 Fast idle adjusting screw
46 Spring
47 Throttle lever (RHD)
48 Throttle lever (LHD)
49 Automatic transmission (RHD)
50 Automatic transmission (LHD)
51 Throttle return spring
52 Return spring
53 Damper spring

Fig. 13.26 Exploded view of the Mikuni carburettor with automatic choke (Sec 6)

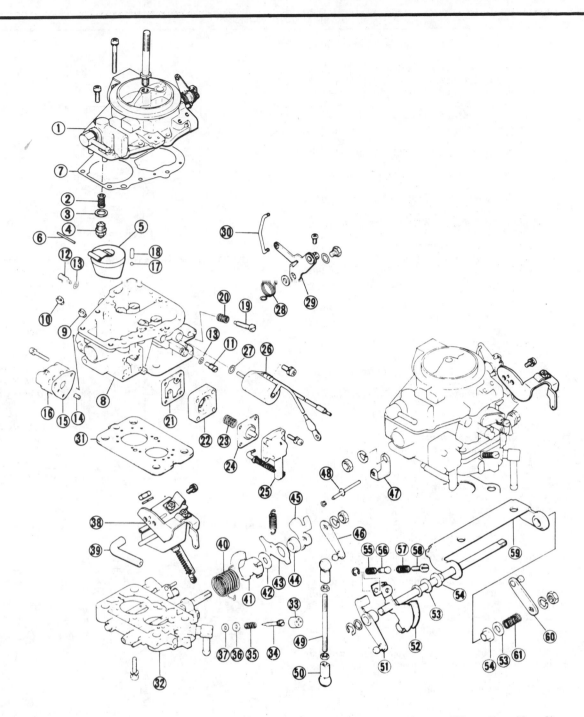

Fig. 13.27 Exploded view of the Mikuni carburettor for twin installation on GS engines (Sec 6)

1 Cover	17 Accelerator pump ball	32 Throttle body	47 Lever
2 Filter	18 Accelerator pump weight	33 Idle limiter	48 Rod
3 Washer	19 Idling speed adjusting screw	34 Mixture adjusting screw	49 Adjusting rod
4 Needle valve	20 Spring	35 Spring	50 Socket
5 Float	21 Gasket	36 Washer	51 Front lever
6 Pivot pin	22 Accelerator pump body	37 Seal	52 Throttle lever shaft
7 Gasket	23 Return spring	38 Vacuum chamber	53 Washer
8 Main body	24 Diaphragm	39 Hose	54 Collar
9 Primary main jet	25 Accelerator pump cover	40 Throttle return spring	55 Spring
10 Secondary main jet	26 Fuel cut-off solenoid	41 Abutment lever	56 Pushrod
11 Primary pilot jet	27 O-ring	42 Washer	57 Spring
12 Secondary pilot jet	28 Choke return spring	43 Intermediate lever	58 Throttle balance adjusting
13 O-ring	29 Choke operating lever	44 Collar	screw
14 Enrichment jet	30 Link	45 Lever	59 Bracket
15 Gasket	31 Insulator	46 Throttle lever	60 Rear lever
16 Enrichment cover			61 Spring

stage otherwise the accelerator pump check ball and weight will fall out.

15 Push out the float pivot pin and remove the float.

16 Unscrew the needle valve and remove the washer and filter.

17 Carefully invert the main body, pour out the remaining fuel, and remove the accelerator pump check ball and weight.

18 Unscrew and remove the fuel cut-off solenoid.

19 Unscrew and remove the jets shown in Fig. 13.28 keeping them identified for location.

20 Do not remove the bypass adjusting screw, as this is preset at the factory and is sealed with white paint.

21 Remove the screws and dismantle both the enrichment and accelerator pump devices.

22 Remove the screws and separate the throttle body from the main body. Remove the gasket.

23 Unscrew the idle speed adjusting screw and remove the spring, washer, and packing.

24 Clean all the components and check them for wear and damage with reference to Chapter 3, Section 19, paragraphs 11 to 14.

25 Check the diaphragm chamber by fully pressing the lever against the spring, then placing a finger over the connector. If the lever moves out, the diaphragm is faulty and the unit must be renewed.

26 Check the fuel cut-off solenoid by connecting a 12 volt supply to the terminals. The needle should move inwards and then move out again when the supply is disconnected.

27 Reassembly is a reversal of dismantling, but fit new gaskets and observe the following points:

(a) *Set the mixture adjusting screw $1^1/2$ turns out from its seated position*

(b) *Lightly lubricate the throttle and choke levers and spindles with engine oil*

Twin carburettors – idling adjustment

28 Run the engine to normal operating temperature.

29 Remove the air cleaner.

30 Disconnect the throttle rod from either the front or rear carburettor so that adjustment of each carburettor may be made independently.

31 Using a flowmeter, adjust the speed adjustment screws on each carburettor so that the flow of air through each is equal. It is possible to use a length of plastic tube to make the adjustment, by comparing the 'hiss' at the carburettor inlets. However, the flowmeter method is more accurate.

32 With the engine stopped, set both mixture adjusting screws $1^1/2$ turns out from their seated positions.

33 Using an exhaust gas analyser, turn the mixture adjusting screws by equal amounts until the idling CO% is correct. If an analyser is not available, a less accurate method is to adjust the screws until the engine runs smoothly at the highest speed.

34 Adjust the speed adjustment screws by equal amounts to regain the correct idling speed if necessary.

35 Reconnect the throttle rod, but if necessary adjust the link screw so that the throttle positions are not altered in relation to each other. Check this by using the flowmeter again.

36 Refit the air cleaner and recheck all settings.

Accelerator cable – adjustment

37 Fully release the manual choke control. On models fitted with the Mikuni carburettor with automatic choke, run the engine to normal temperature to ensure the choke lever is clear of the throttle lever.

38 Working in the engine compartment, turn the ferrule on the bulkhead until the cable free play is between 0 and 0.04 in (0 and 1.0 mm). Lock the ferrule with the locknut.

Accelerator cable – removal and refitting

39 Remove the air cleaner.

40 Loosen the clamp and disconnect the outer cable at the carburettor, then unhook the inner cable from the throttle lever.

41 Disconnect the outer cable from the clamp on the cylinder head.

42 Unhook the inner cable from the pedal.

43 Loosen the locknut and withdraw the cable from within the engine compartment.

44 Refitting is a reversal of removal, but adjust the cable as described in paragraphs 37 and 38.

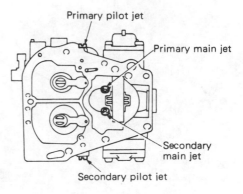

Fig. 13.28 Jet locations on the Mikuni carburettor (Sec 6)

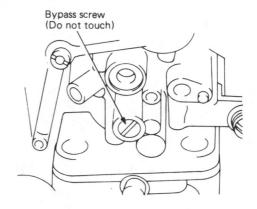

Fig. 13.29 Do not attempt to adjust the bypass screw (Sec 6)

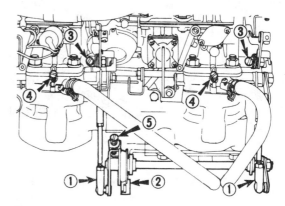

Fig. 13.30 Adjustment screw locations on the twin Mikuni carburettor installation (Sec 6)

1 *Rods*	4 *Mixture adjusting screws*
2 *Throttle lever*	5 *Throttle link adjusting screw*
3 *Idling speed adjusting screws*	

Choke cable – removal and refitting

45 Remove the air cleaner.

46 Disconnect the inner cable at the carburettor and the outer cable clamps.

47 Working inside the car, unscrew the nut behind the facia and withdraw the choke cable through the grommet in the bulkhead.

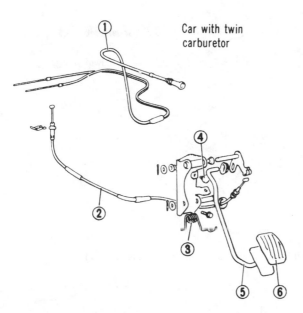

Car with twin carburetor

Fig. 13.31 Accelerator and choke cables (Sec 6)

1 Choke cable (twin carburettor version)   4 Stop
2 Accelerator cable   5 Accelerator pedal
3 Return spring   6 Rubber pad

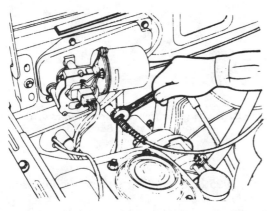

Fig. 13.32 Adjusting the accelerator cable (Sec 6)

48 Refitting is a reversal of removal, but before tightening the inner cable fitting, fully push in the control knob and check that the choke valves are fully open. On some models the sliding resistance of the cable may be set by turning the adjustment beneath the knob.

Exhaust system (1979-on)
49 The exhaust system fitted to Celeste models from 1979 onwards is shown in Fig. 13.34. The removal and refitting procedure is the same as described in Chapter 3, Section 25.

Fuel system adjustments – caution
50 Depending on model and year, various carburettor adjusting screws may be 'tamperproofed' by plugs, caps or seals. The purpose of tamperproofing is to discourage, and to detect, adjustment by unqualified persons. In some countries (though not yet in the UK) it is an offence to use a vehicle with tamperproof seals missing. Satisfy yourself that you are not breaking any local or national laws by removing tamperproof devices. Fit a new device when adjustment is complete, where this is required by law.
51 Adjustment of the idle mixture screw on later models may be made without disturbing the tamperproof cap, using a special screwdriver with two small prongs instead of a plain blade.

7 Ignition system

Distributor (1597 cc engine with timing belt) – removal and refitting
1 The distributor is driven by a gear located near the front of the camshaft, and is retained on the cylinder head by a stud and nut.

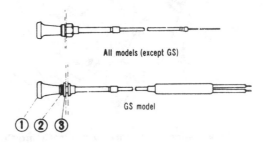

All models (except GS)

GS model

Fig. 13.33 Choke cable details (Sec 6)

1 Knob   3 Locknut
2 Resistance adjustment

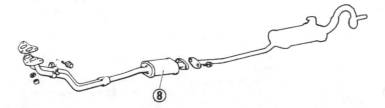

Fig. 13.34 Exhaust system fitted to 1979-on Celeste models (Sec 6)

1 Front pipe (single)
2 Clamp
3 Main silencer assembly
4 Hanger
5 Bracket
6 Heat deflector
7 Tail pipe
8 Front pipe (twin)

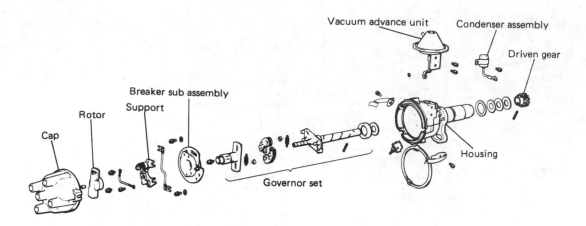

Fig. 13.35 Exploded view of the contact-type distributor fitted to 1979-on models (Sec 7)

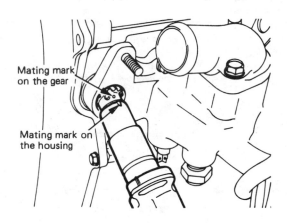

Fig. 13.36 Gear alignment marks when refitting the distributor (Sec 7)

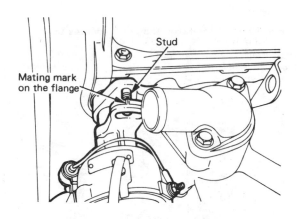

Fig. 13.37 Distributor flange mark aligned with the mounting stud (Sec 7)

2   The removal and refitting procedure is basically as described in Chapter 4, Sections 2 and 3, however, the oil pump references should be ignored.

3   When refitting the distributor, first align the gear marks (Fig. 13.36) then insert the distributor so that the flange slot is slightly clockwise from the stud. As the gear teeth engage, rotate the distributor anti-clockwise until the mark on the flange is aligned with the stud.

Ignition timing (later models)

4   On all later models the ignition timing is adjusted by loosening the flange nut and turning the distributor in the required direction. Adjustment using a cross-head screwdriver is no longer possible.

5   Where electronic ignition is fitted, an approximate **static** setting may be made by aligning the reluctor tips with the stator posts, but this must always be followed by the dynamic method with a timing light.

Electronic ignition – description

6   All 1995 cc engines from 1979 onwards and also 1995 cc GS engines prior to this date are fitted with electronic ignition. Instead of contact points within the distributor, a reluctor and pick-up coil system is fitted. This sends electrical pulses to a transistorized control unit, which then switches the ignition coil primary windings on and off in order to induce the secondary HT current.

7   The HT voltages produced in the electronic ignition system are substantially higher than on conventional systems, and extreme care must therefore be taken not to touch the associated wiring when the ignition is switched on.

Distributor (1995 cc engine with electronic ignition) – removal and refitting

8   The procedure is as described in Chapter 4, Sections 2 and 3, but the low tension leads must be disconnected from the control unit on the side of the distributor.

Distributor (1995 cc engine with electronic ignition) – dismantling and reasssembly

9   Remove the two screws and pull the control unit outwards from the distributor body (if applicable). Do not wipe away the silicone grease, as this acts as a heat transfer medium.

10 Remove the distributor cap by pressing and turning the hooks with a cross-head screwdriver.

11 Extract the screws and withdraw the rotor assembly.

12 Remove the screw and lift off the centrifugal advance assembly together with the reluctor.

13 Extract the screws and remove the pick-up coil.

14 Unscrew the vacuum unit screws, extract the clip, then release the arm from the stator and withdraw the vacuum unit.

15 Remove the stator.

16 If necessary drive out the pin and remove the gear from the bottom of the shaft.

17 Remove the screws and withdraw the shaft together with the bearing and retaining plate.

18 Prise out the oil seal.

19 Clean all the components and check them for wear and damage. If

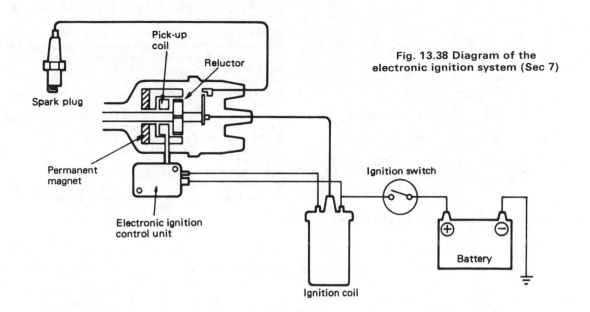

Fig. 13.38 Diagram of the electronic ignition system (Sec 7)

Fig. 13.39 Exploded view of the electronic ignition distributor (Sec 7)

1   Cap
2   Carbon contact
3   Rotor assembly
4   Spring
5   Centrifugal advance plate
6   Centrifugal advance weight
7   Baseplate
8   Reluctor
9   Pick-up coil
10 Stator
11 Retaining plate
12 Vacuum unit
13 Clip
14 Washer
15 Shaft
16 Ball bearing
17 Oil seal
18 Distributor body
19 Control unit
20 O-ring
21 Gear
22 Pin

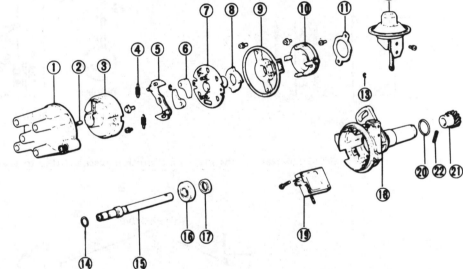

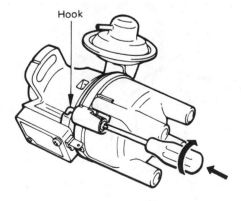

Fig. 13.40 Method of releasing the spring tensioned hooks on the distributor cap (Sec 7)

the bearing is worn excessively obtain a new one. Obtain a new oil seal.

20 Using an ohmmeter, check that the resistance of the pick-up coil is 1050 ± 50 ohms for 1979-on models, or 500 to 700 ohms on earlier models.

21 Note that on pre-1979 models, the control unit may be located away from the distributor (see Fig. 13.42).

22 Reassembly of the distributor is a reversal of dismantling.

Electronic ignition (1979-on) – testing

23 Remove the distributor cap and rotor assembly as described previously.

24 Disconnect the coil HT lead from the centre of the distributor cap and hold it with insulated pliers 0.2 to 0.24 in (5.0 to 6.0 mm) from the cylinder head.

25 Switch on the ignition, then insert a small insulated screwdriver between the reluctor and stator as shown in Fig. 13.43. If there is no HT spark, a fault is indicated in the control unit, pick-up coil, ignition coil, or HT lead.

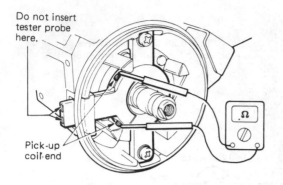

Fig. 13.41 Checking the resistance of the pick-up coil
(Sec 7)

Dwell angle (all models with contact breaker ignition) – adjustment

26 Dwell angle is defined as the angle through which the distributor cam turns between the instants of closure and opening of the contact breaker points. It is a more accurate means of adjusting the points than using feeler blades, because it is done dynamically and so takes distributor wear into account.

27 To measure dwell angle, a dwell meter must be used as instructed by the maker. Typically a dwell meter is connected across the coil terminals (or sometimes in place of the coil) and a reading is taken with the engine idling or being cranked on the starter motor.

28 The desired dwell angle is given in the Specifications. If the measured angle is too small, reduce the points gap; if it is too large, adjust the gap.

29 If the specified dwell angle cannot be obtained in conjunction with the specified points gap, the distributor is excessively worn.

30 Check the ignition timing after adjusting the dwell angle.

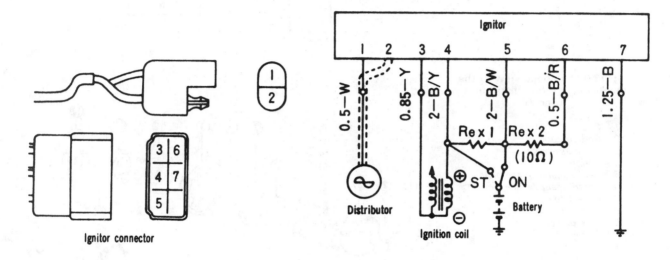

Fig. 13.42 Diagram of the electronic ignition system fitted to pre-1979 models (Sec 7)

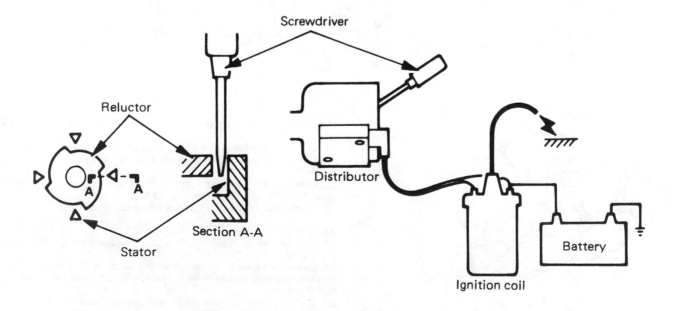

Fig. 13.43 Method of testing the electronic ignition for 1979-on models (Sec 7)

8 Clutch

Clutch pedal and cable – adjustment

1 The clutch pedal height and stroke dimensions are different on later models. Refer to the Specifications for details.

9 Manual gearbox

Five-speed gearbox (with 1597 cc engine)

1 The five-speed gearbox described in Chapter 6 is fitted to the 1995 cc engine and has the code number KM 132. For the 1597 cc engine the five-speed gearbox has the code number KM 119 and it differs in the following respects. The 1st/2nd speed selector rod is shorter, the reverse idler gear is longer, the reverse idler shaft locates in the housing without any bolts, and a spring-tensioned sub-gear is located on the front of the countershaft. The sub-gear effectively eliminates endplay between the gears and reduces 'chatter' when idling in neutral.

2 Although the dismantling and reassembly procedure is basically as given in Chapter 6, the information given in the following paragraphs should be noted.

3 When removing the extension housing move the selector fully towards the reverse/5th position.

4 The mainshaft rear bearing may be removed before withdrawing the mainshaft from the gearbox provided that a bearing puller is available (Fig. 13.46). If this method is used, care must be taken not to damage the 3rd/4th synchronizer unit, and it is recommended that stop-plates are used to hold the unit in place. These should be made with reference to Figs. 13.47 and 13.48 using metal plate 0.24 in (6.0 mm) and 0.37 in (9.5 mm) thick.

5 To assemble the sub-gear to the front of the countershaft first insert the spring long extension in the hole in the countershaft.

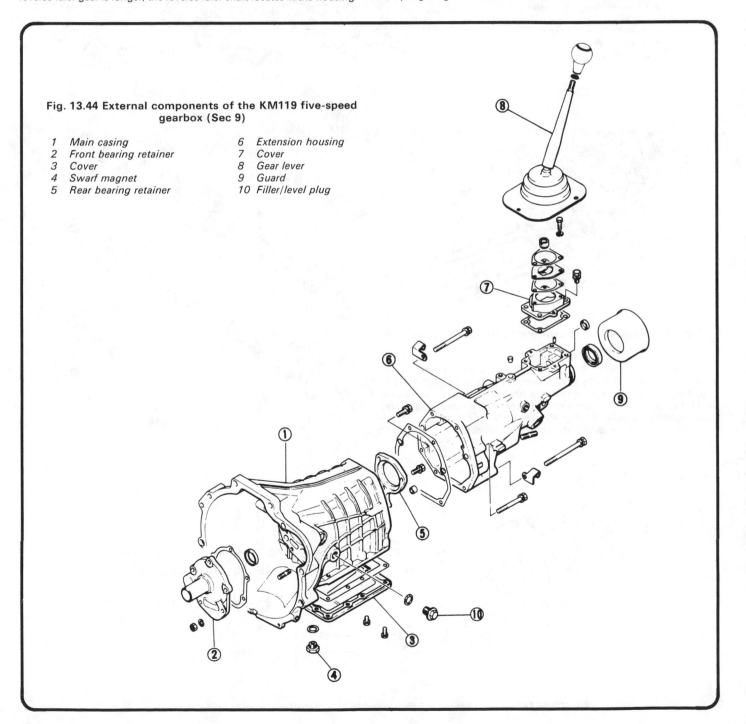

Fig. 13.44 External components of the KM119 five-speed gearbox (Sec 9)

1 Main casing
2 Front bearing retainer
3 Cover
4 Swarf magnet
5 Rear bearing retainer
6 Extension housing
7 Cover
8 Gear lever
9 Guard
10 Filler/level plug

Fig. 13.45 Internal components of the KM119 five-speed gearbox (Sec 9)

1   3rd/4th selector shaft
2   5th/Reverse selector shaft
3   1st/2nd selector shaft
4   Reverse lamp switch
5   Neutral return plunger
6   Main drive pinion
7   3rd speed gear
8   Mainshaft
9   2nd speed gear
10 1st speed gear
11 5th speed gear
12 Speedometer driven gear
13 Countershaft gear cluster
14 5th drive gear
15 Reverse idler gear shaft
16 Reverse idler gear
17 Selector control shaft

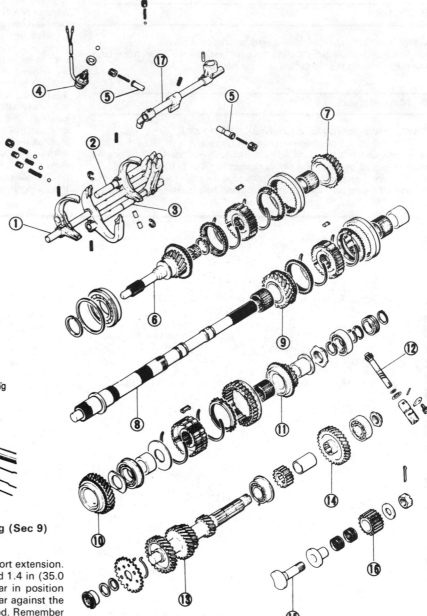

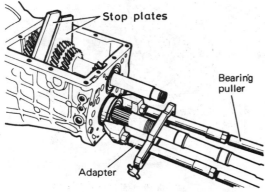

Fig. 13.46 Removing the mainshaft rear bearing (Sec 9)

6   Locate the sub-gear on the spring and engage the short extension.
7   A metal dowel rod 0.315 in (8.0 mm) in diameter and 1.4 in (35.0 mm) long is now required in order to hold the sub-gear in position while the countershaft is being refitted. Turn the sub-gear against the spring until the holes are aligned, then insert the dowel rod. Remember to remove the dowel rod after the countershaft is fitted.

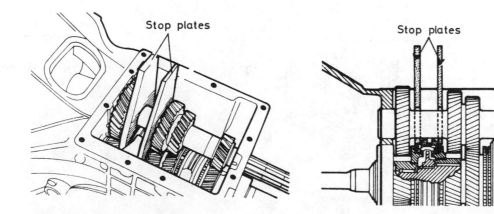

Fig. 13.47 Using stop plates when removing the mainshaft rear bearing (Sec 9)

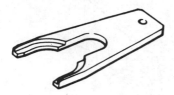

Fig. 13.48 Stop plate showing recess for synchro sleeve
(Sec 9)

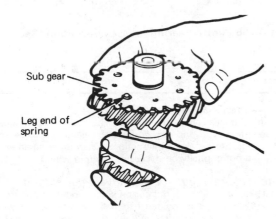

Fig. 13.50 Engage the sub-gear with the spring (Sec 9)

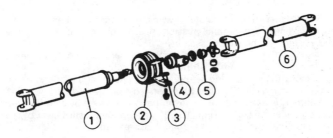

Fig. 13.52 Two-piece propeller shaft components (Sec 10)

1 Front section	4 Centre yoke
2 Centre bearing assembly	5 Nut
3 Spacer	6 Rear section

10 Propeller shaft

Two-piece propeller shaft – removal and refitting
1 Some later models are fitted with a two-piece propeller shaft supported by a centre bearing.
2 The removal and refitting procedure is as given in Chapter 7, but additionally the centre bearing mounting bolts must be removed. Note the location of the spacers between the centre bearing and the underbody, and make sure they are refitted in the same position.
3 When fitted, the rear propeller shaft must be inclined 1°30' to 3°10' downwards from the front shaft. To check this accurately, a special gauge will be required, or alternatively, a template may be made out of card. If the angle is incorrect, spacers must be inserted at the centre bearing mounting bolts. Spacers are available in a variety of thicknesses, and for guidance purposes the insertion of a 1.2 mm (0.047 in) spacer will reduce the angle of inclination by approximately 0°15'.

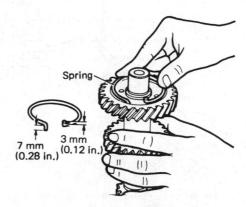

Fig. 13.49 Locate the spring on the countershaft (Sec 9)

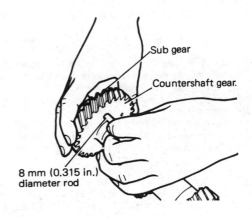

Fig. 13.51 Insert the metal rod (Sec 9)

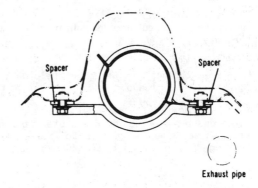

Fig. 13.53 Spacer location on the centre bearing bracket
(Sec 10)

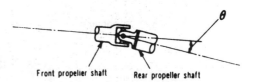

Fig. 13.54 Two-piece propeller shaft inclination angle (θ)
(Sec 10)

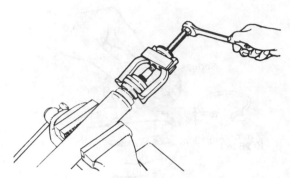

Fig. 13.55 Removing the centre bearing from the front section (Sec 10)

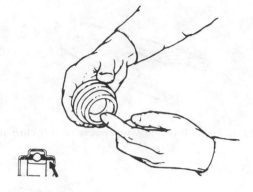

Fig. 13.56 Centre bearing grease application (Sec 10)

Centre bearing – renewal
4   With the propeller shaft removed, lightly clamp the front section in a vice.
5   Mark the front and rear sections and the yoke in relation to each other.
6   Unscrew the nut and separate the two sections. If access to the nut proves difficult, dismantle the centre universal joint with reference to Chapter 7, Section 3, then use a normal socket.
7   Prise the rubber support from the bearing groove and remove it together with the bracket.
8   Using a puller remove the centre bearing from the front section.
9   Clean the components and check them for wear and damage. Check the rubber support for deterioration. Renew the items as required.
10 Fill the new centre bearing with multi-purpose grease with reference to Fig. 13.56, then re-assemble using a reversal of the dismantling procedure. Observe the alignment marks (paragraph 5) when reassembling in order to preserve the original balance of the shafts.

11 Braking system

Rear brake shoes – spring identification
1   Note that on later models the colour of the right-hand latch spring may be light blue, grey, or black and grey.

Brake pedal – adjustment
2   On later models the distance from the top of the pedal to the toeboard is as given in the Specifications.

Brake pad and shoe renewal (all models)
3   When new pads or shoes have been fitted, avoid harsh braking as far as possible for the first few hundred miles to allow the new linings to bed in. Full braking efficiency will not be available until bedding-in has occurred.

Fig. 13.57 Exploded view of alternator with external voltage regulator (Sec 12)

12 Electrical system

Battery maintenance (all models)
1   Modern batteries are generally of the 'low-maintenance' or 'maintenance-free' type, and rarely require the electrolyte to be topped up. Follow the battery maker's instructions. Charging from an external source should not normally be necessary, even in winter.

Alternator voltage regulator – removal and refitting
2   From 1979, the voltage regulator on some models is integral with the alternator. Where it is located externally, it may be removed by extracting the two screws then withdrawing the cover followed by the regulator. Where it is located internally follow the procedure in the following paragraphs.
3   With the alternator removed, unscrew the three through-bolts. Prise the front housing from the stator and remove it together with the rotor.
4   Note the location of the stator wires, then unsolder them from the rectifier using the minimum possible heat to prevent damage to the diodes. Remove the stator assembly.
5   Unscrew the nut and remove the condenser from the 'B' terminal.
6   Unsolder the 'B' and 'L' strips from the rectifier.
7   Remove the screws and withdraw the voltage regulator and brush holder. Note that they cannot be separated from each other.
8   Refitting is a reversal of removal, but use a piece of wire inserted through the end housing (Fig. 13.59) to keep the brushes clear of the slip rings while the housings are being assembled.

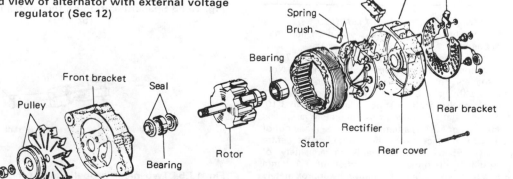

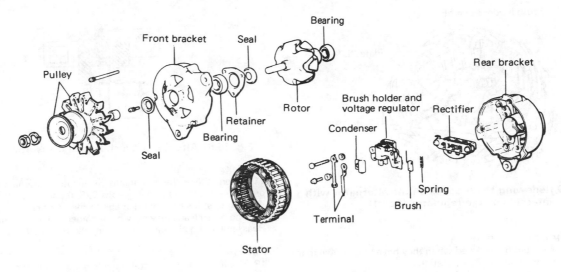

Fig. 13.58 Exploded view of alternator with internal voltage regulator (Sec 12)

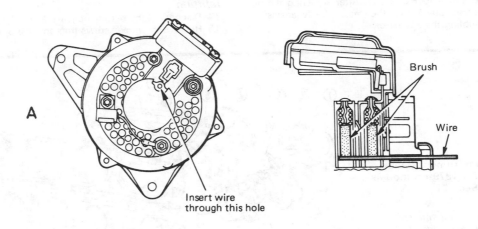

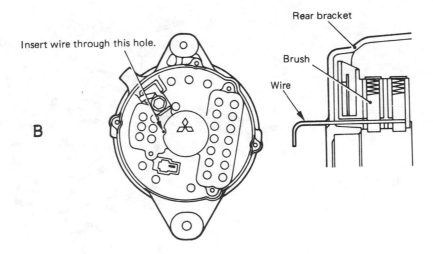

Fig. 13.59 Method of retaining brushes when reassembling the alternator (Sec 12)

A External voltage regulator type   *B Internal voltage regulator type*

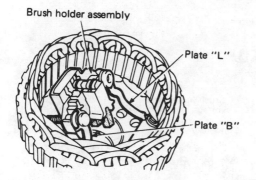

Fig. 13.60 Renewing the brushes on the alternator with internal voltage regulator (Sec 12)

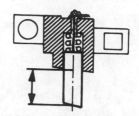

Fig. 13.61 Alternator brush length measurement (Sec 12)

Alternator brushes – renewal

9 The brushes should be renewed when they have worn down to the minimum length given in the Specifications.

10 Where the voltage regulator is located externally on the alternator, remove the regulator as described in paragraph 1 then fully dismantle the alternator with reference to Fig. 13.57. After soldering the new brush leads into position, check that they move freely against the springs before reassembling the alternator.

11 Where the voltage regulator is located internally carry out the procedure described in paragraphs 2, 3, 5 and 7, carefully bending the 'B' and 'L' strips to avoid damage to the rectifier.

12 The brush leads may now be unsoldered and the brushes renewed. Reassemble the alternator as previously described.

Fuses

13 The fuse ratings for later models are given in the Specifications.

Instrument panel (1979-on models) – removal and refitting

14 Disconnect the battery negative lead.

15 Remove the three screws from the top of the instrument panel.

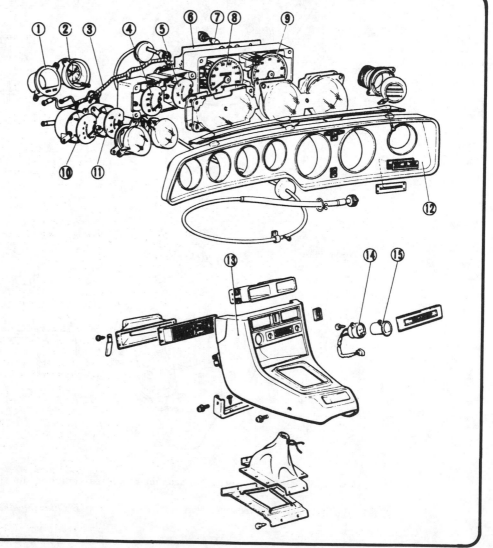

Fig. 13.62 Instrument panel components for 1979-on models (Sec 12)

1 Coin box (certain models)
2 Clock (certain models)
3 Wiring harness
4 Water temperature gauge
5 Fuel gauge
6 Printed circuit board
7 Warning lamp bulb
8 Speedometer
9 Tachometer
10 Oil pressure gauge (not all models)
11 Ammeter (not all models)
12 Instrument panel
13 Centre console
14 Clock (certain models)
15 Coin box (certain models)

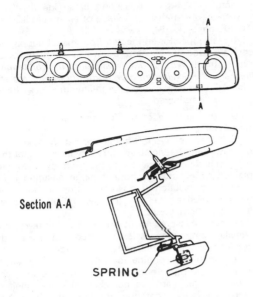

Section A-A

SPRING

Fig. 13.63 Instrument panel removal for 1979-on models (Sec 12)

16 Withdraw the panel and release it from the lower springs, then disconnect the wiring plugs and speedometer cable.
17 When refitting the instrument panel, make sure that the wiring is not trapped.

Speedometer cable length
18 The speedometer cables fitted to later models are several inches longer than those described in Chapter 10, Section 25.

Fuel gauge tank unit – testing
19 On models manufactured from 1979, the tank unit winding resistances are as follows:

Empty float position: 120 ± 6.5 ohms
Full float position: 17 ± 2.1 ohms

The resistance of the gauge used with this tank unit is 120 ohms.

Temperature gauge – testing
20 On models manufactured from 1979, the temperature gauge should be tested as described in Chapter 10, Section 28, but using a 75 ohm resistor. The gauge should indicate a temperature of approximately 80°C (180°F).

Radio (pre-1979) – removal and refitting
21 Disconnect the battery negative lead.
22 Remove the glovebox. This is secured by seven screws; the top four must be removed, but the bottom three need only be slackened.
23 Pull off the knobs and unscrew the two nuts.
24 Disconnect the aerial, speaker and supply leads from the rear of the radio.
25 Remove the bracket and withdraw the radio.
26 Refitting is a reversal of removal.

Radio (1979-on) – removal and refitting
27 Disconnect the battery negative lead.
28 Release the centre console by extracting the four cross-head screws.
29 Remove the screw and disconnect the earth wire from the parcel tray bracket.
30 Disconnect the aerial, speaker and supply leads from the rear of the radio.
31 Pull off the knobs and unscrew the two nuts, also unscrew the bracket side bolts.
32 Withdraw the radio from its location.
33 Refitting is a reversal of removal.

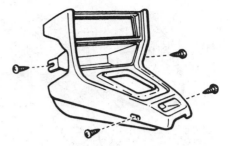

Fig. 13.64 Centre console removal for 1979-on models (Sec 12)

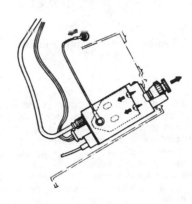

Fig. 13.65 Radio removal for 1979-on models (Sec 12)

Radio interference
In general, when electric current changes abruptly, unwanted electrical noise is produced. The motor vehicle is filled with electrical devices which change electric current rapidly, the most obvious being the contact breaker.

When the spark plugs operate, the sudden pulse of spark current causes the associated wiring to radiate. Since early radio transmitters used sparks as a basis of operation, it is not surprising that the car radio will pick up ignition spark noise unless steps are taken to reduce it to acceptable levels.

Interference reaches the car radio in two ways:

(a) by conduction through the wiring.
(b) by radiation to the receiving aerial.

Initial checks presuppose that the bonnet is down and fastened, the radio unit has a good earth connection (not through the aerial download outer), no fluorescent tubes are working near the car, the aerial trimmer has been adjusted, and the vehicle is in a position to receive radio signals, ie not in a metal-clad building.

Switch on the radio and tune it to the middle of the medium wave (MW) band off-station with the volume (gain) control set fairly high. Switch on the ignition (but do not start the engine) and wait to see if irregular clicks or hash noise occurs. Tapping the facia panel may also produce these effects. If so, this will be due to the voltage stabiliser, which is an on-off thermal switch to control instrument voltage. It is located usually on the back of the instrument panel, often attached to the speedometer. Correction is by attachment of a capacitor and, if still troublesome, chokes in the supply wires.

Switch on the engine and listen for interference on the MW band. Depending on the type of interference, the indications are as follows.

A harsh crackle that drops out abruptly at low engine speed or when the headlights are switched on is probably due to a voltage regulator.

A whine varying with engine speed is due to the alternator. Try temporarily taking off the fan belt – if the noise goes this is confirmation.

Regular ticking or crackle that varies in rate with the engine speed is

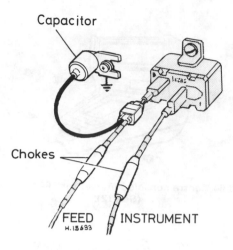

Fig. 13.66 Voltage stabiliser interference suppression (Sec 12)

due to the ignition system. With this trouble in particular and others in general, check to see if the noise is entering the receiver from the wiring or by radiation. To do this, pull out the aerial plug (preferably shorting out the input socket or connecting a 62 pF capacitor across it). If the noise disappears it is coming in through the aerial and is *radiation noise*. If the noise persists it is reaching the receiver through the wiring and is said to be *line-borne*.

Interference from wipers, washers, heater blowers, turn-indicators, stop lamps, etc is usually taken to the receiver by wiring, and simple treatment using capacitors and possibly chokes will solve the problem. Switch on each one in turn (wet the screen first for running wipers!) and listen for possible interference with the aerial plug in place and again when removed.

Electric petrol pumps are now finding application again and give rise to an irregular clicking, often giving a burst of clicks when the ignition is on but the engine has not yet been started. It is also possible to receive whining or crackling from the pump.

Note that if most of the vehicle accessories are found to be creating interference all together, the probability is that poor aerial earthing is to blame.

Suppression methods – ignition

Suppressed HT cables are supplied as original equipment by manufacturers and will meet regulations as far as interference to neighbouring equipment is concerned. It is illegal to remove such suppression unless an alternative is provided, and this may take the form of resistive spark plug caps in conjunction with plain copper HT cable. For VHF purposes, these and 'in-line' resistors may not be

effective, and resistive HT cable is preferred. Check that suppressed cables are actually fitted by observing cable identity lettering, or measuring with an ohmmeter – the value of each plug lead should be 5000 to 10 000 ohms.

A 1 microfarad capacitor connected from the LT supply side of the ignition coil to a good nearby earth point will complete basic ignition interference treatment. *NEVER fit a capacitor to the coil terminal to the contact breaker – the result would be burnt out points in a short time.*

If ignition noise persists despite the treatment above, the following sequence should be followed:

(a) Check the earthing of the ignition coil; remove paint from fixing clamp.

(b) If this does not work, lift the bonnet. Should there be no change in interference level, this may indicate that the bonnet is not electrically connected to the car body. Use a proprietary braided strap across a bonnet hinge ensuring a first class electrical connection. If, however, lifting the bonnet increases the interference, then fit resistive HT cables of a higher ohms-per-metre value.

(c) If all these measures fail, it is probable that re-radiation from metallic components is taking place. Using a braided strap between metallic points, go round the vehicle systematically – try the following: engine to body, exhaust system to body, front suspension to engine and to body, steering column to body, Bowden cable to body, metal parcel shelf to body. When an offending component is located it should be bonded with the strap permanently.

(d) As a next step, the fitting of distributor suppressors to each lead at the distributor end may help.

(e) Beyond this point is involved the possible screening of the distributor and fitting resistive spark plugs, but such advanced treatment is not usually required for vehicles with entertainment equipment.

Electronic ignition systems have built-in suppression components, but this does not relieve the need for using suppressed HT leads. In some cases it is permitted to connect a capacitor on the low tension supply side of the ignition coil, but not in every case. Makers' instructions should be followed carefully, otherwise damage to the ignition semiconductors may result.

Suppression methods – general components

Wiper motors – Connect the wiper body to earth with a bonding strap. For all motors use a 7 ampere choke assembly inserted in the leads to the motor.

Heater motors – Fit 7 ampere line chokes in both leads, assisted if necessary by a 1 microfarad capacitor to earth from both leads.

Horn – A capacitor and choke combination is effective if the horn is directly connected to the 12 volt supply. The use of a relay is an alternative remedy, as this will reduce the length of the interference-carrying leads.

Electrostatic noise – Characteristics are erratic crackling at the receiver, with disappearance of symptoms in wet weather. Often

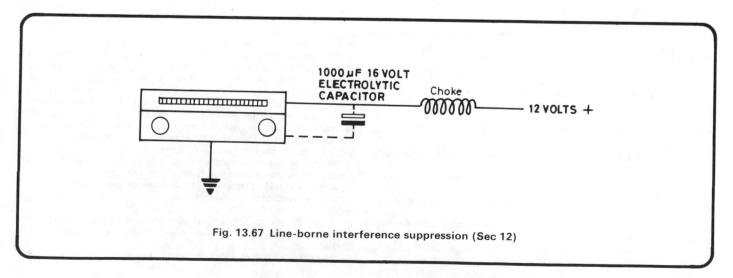

Fig. 13.67 Line-borne interference suppression (Sec 12)

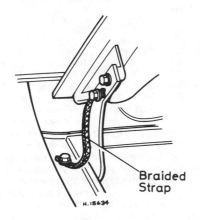

Fig. 13.68 Braided earth strap between bonnet and body (Sec 12)

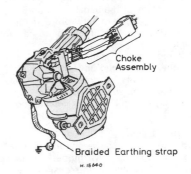

Fig. 13.69 Wiper motor suppression (Sec 12)

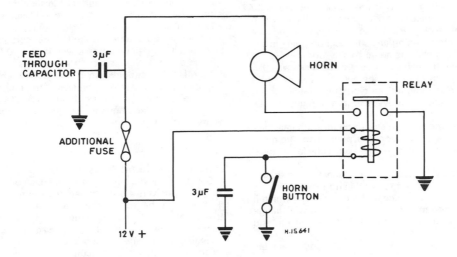

Fig. 13.70 Use of relay to reduce horn interference (Sec 12)

shocks may be given when touching bodywork. Part of the problem is the build-up of static electricity in non-driven wheels and the acquisition of charge on the body shell. It is possible to fit spring-loaded contacts at the wheels to give good conduction between the rotary wheel parts and the vehicle frame. Changing a tyre sometimes helps – because of tyres' varying resistances. In difficult cases a trailing flex which touches the ground will cure the problem. If this is not acceptable it is worth trying conductive paint on the tyre walls.

Fluorescent tubes – Vehicles used for camping/caravanning frequently have fluorescent tube lighting. These tubes require a relatively high voltage for operation and this is provided by an inverter (a form of oscillator) which steps up the vehicle supply voltage. This can give rise to serious interference to radio reception, and the tubes themselves can contribute to this interference by the pulsating nature of the lamp discharge. In such situations it is important to mount the aerial as far away from a fluorescent tube as possible. The interference problem may be alleviated by screening the tube with fine wire turns spaced an inch (25 mm) apart and earthed to the chassis. Suitable chokes should be fitted in both supply wires close to the inverter.

VHF/FM broadcasts

Reception of VHF/FM in an automobile is more prone to problems than the medium and long wavebands. Medium/long wave transmitters are capable of covering considerable distances, but VHF transmitters are restricted to line of sight, meaning ranges of 10 to 50

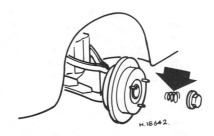

Fig. 13.71 Use of spring contacts at wheels (Sec 12)

miles, depending upon the terrain, the effects of buildings and the transmitter power.

Because of the limited range it is necessary to retune on a long journey, and it may be better for those habitually travelling long distances or living in areas of poor provision of transmitters to use an AM radio working on medium/long wavebands.

When conditions are poor, interference can arise, and some of the suppression devices described previously fall off in performance at very high frequencies unless specifically designed for the VHF band. Available suppression devices include reactive HT cable, resistive distributor caps, screened plug caps, screened leads and resistive spark plugs.

For VHF/FM receiver installation the following points should be particularly noted:

(a) Earthing of the receiver chassis and the aerial mounting is important. Use a separate earthing wire at the radio, and scrape paint away at the aerial mounting.

(b) If possible, use a good quality roof aerial to obtain maximum height and distance from interference generating devices on the vehicle.

(c) Use of a high quality aerial downlead is important, since losses in cheap cable can be significant.

(d) The polarisation of FM transmissions may be horizontal, vertical, circular or slanted. Because of this the optimum mounting angle is at 45° to the vehicle roof.

Citizens' Band radio (CB)

In the UK, CB transmitter/receivers work within the 27 MHz and 934 MHz bands, using the FM mode. At present interest is concentrated on 27 MHz where the design and manufacture of equipment is less difficult. Maximum transmitted power is 4 watts, and 40 channels spaced 10 kHz apart within the range 27.60125 to 27.99125 MHz are available.

Aerials are the key to effective transmission and reception. Regulations limit the aerial length to 1.65 metres including the loading coil and any associated circuitry, so tuning the aerial is necessary to obtain optimum results. The choice of a CB aerial is dependent on whether it is to be permanently installed or removable, and the performance will hinge on correct tuning and the location point on the vehicle. Common practice is to clip the aerial to the roof gutter or to employ wing mounting where the aerial can be rapidly unscrewed. An alternative is to use the boot rim to render the aerial theftproof, but a popular solution is to use the 'magmount' – a type of mounting having a strong magnetic base clamping to the vehicle at any point, usually the roof.

Aerial location determines the signal distribution for both transmission and reception, but it is wise to choose a point away from the engine compartment to minimise interference from vehicle electrical equipment.

The aerial is subject to considerable wind and acceleration forces. Cheaper units will whip backwards and forwards and in so doing will alter the relationship with the metal surface of the vehicle with which it forms a ground plane aerial system. The radiation pattern will change correspondingly, giving rise to break-up of both incoming and outgoing signals.

Interference problems on the vehicle carrying CB equipment fall into two categories:

(a) Interference to nearby TV and radio receivers when transmitting.

(b) Interference to CB set reception due to electrical equipment on the vehicle.

Problems of break-through to TV and radio are not frequent, but can be difficult to solve. Mostly trouble is not detected or reported because the vehicle is moving and the symptoms rapidly disappear at the TV/radio receiver, but when the CB set is used as a base station any trouble with nearby receivers will soon result in a complaint.

It must not be assumed by the CB operator that his equipment is faultless, for much depends upon the design. Harmonics (that is, multiples) of 27 MHz may be transmitted unknowingly and these can fall into other users' bands. Where trouble of this nature occurs, low pass filters in the aerial or supply leads can help, and should be fitted in base station aerials as a matter of course. In stubborn cases it may be necessary to call for assistance from the licensing authority, or, if possible, to have the equipment checked by the manufacturers.

Interference received on the CB set from the vehicle equipment is, fortunately, not usually a severe problem. The precautions outlined previously for radio/cassette units apply, but there are some extra points worth noting.

It is common practice to use a slide-mount on CB equipment enabling the set to be easily removed for use as a base station, for example. Care must be taken that the slide mount fittings are properly earthed and that first class connection occurs between the set and slide-mount.

Vehicle manufacturers in the UK are required to provide suppression of electrical equipment to cover 40 to 250 MHz to protect TV and VHF radio bands. Such suppression appears to be adequately effective at 27 MHz, but suppression of individual items such as alternators, clocks, stabilisers, flashers, wiper motors, etc, may still be necessary. The suppression capacitors and chokes available from auto-electrical suppliers for entertainment receivers will usually give the required results with CB equipment.

Other vehicle radio transmitters

Besides CB radio already mentioned, a considerable increase in the use of transceivers (ie combined transmitter and receiver units) has taken place in the last decade. Previously this type of equipment was fitted mainly to military, fire, ambulance and police vehicles, but a large business radio and radio telephone usage has developed.

Generally the suppression techniques described previously will suffice, with only a few difficult cases arising. Suppression is carried out to satisfy the 'receive mode', but care must be taken to use heavy duty chokes in the equipment supply cables since the loading on 'transmit' is relatively high.

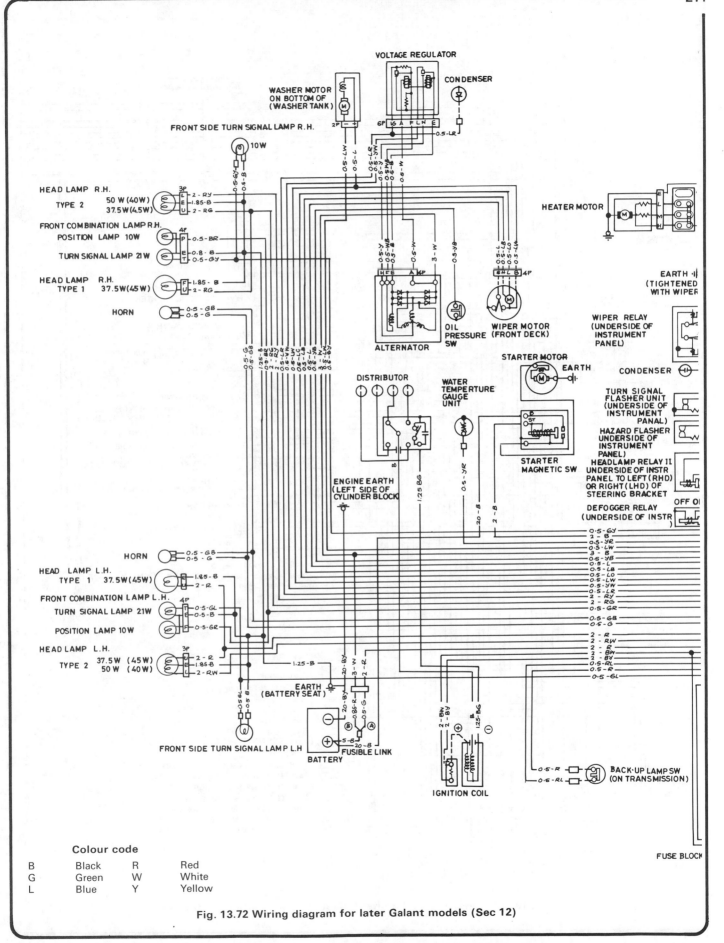

Fig. 13.72 Wiring diagram for later Galant models (Sec 12)

Colour code

B	Black	R	Red
G	Green	W	White
L	Blue	Y	Yellow

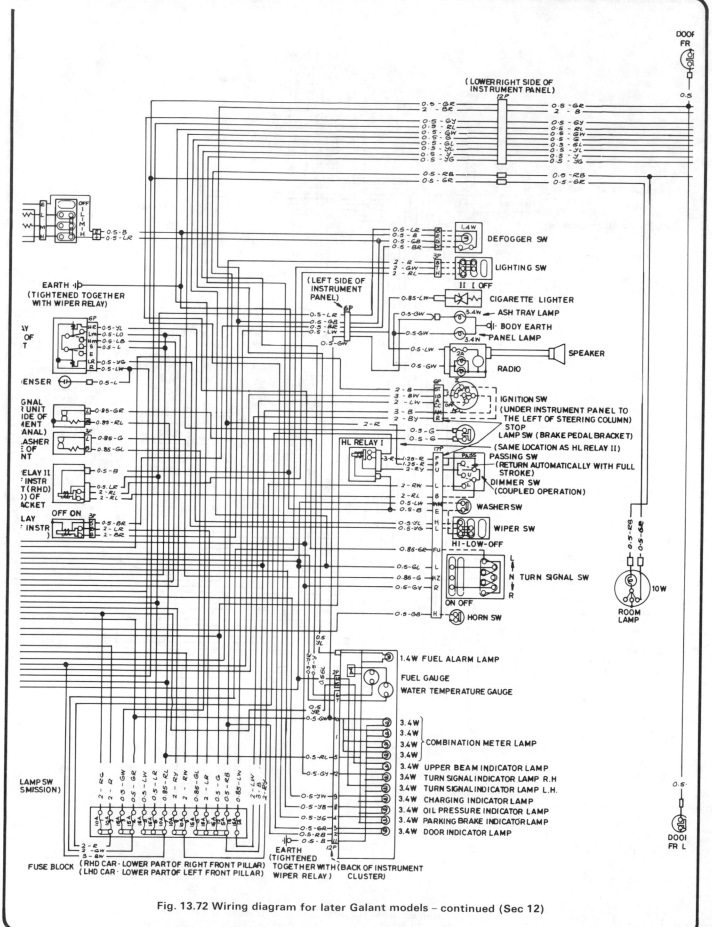

Fig. 13.72 Wiring diagram for later Galant models – continued (Sec 12)

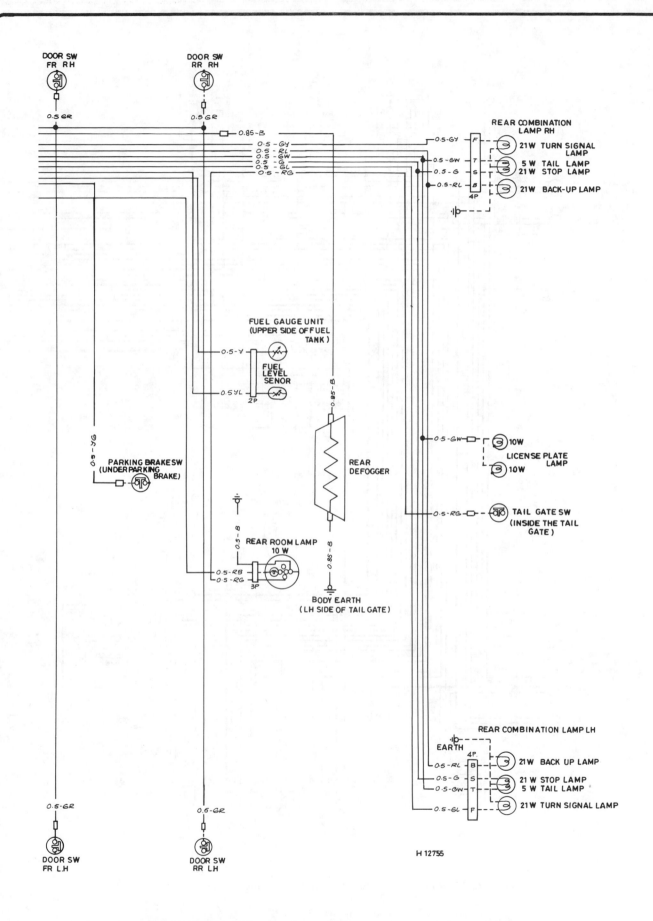

Fig. 13.72 Wiring diagram for later Galant models – continued (Sec 12)

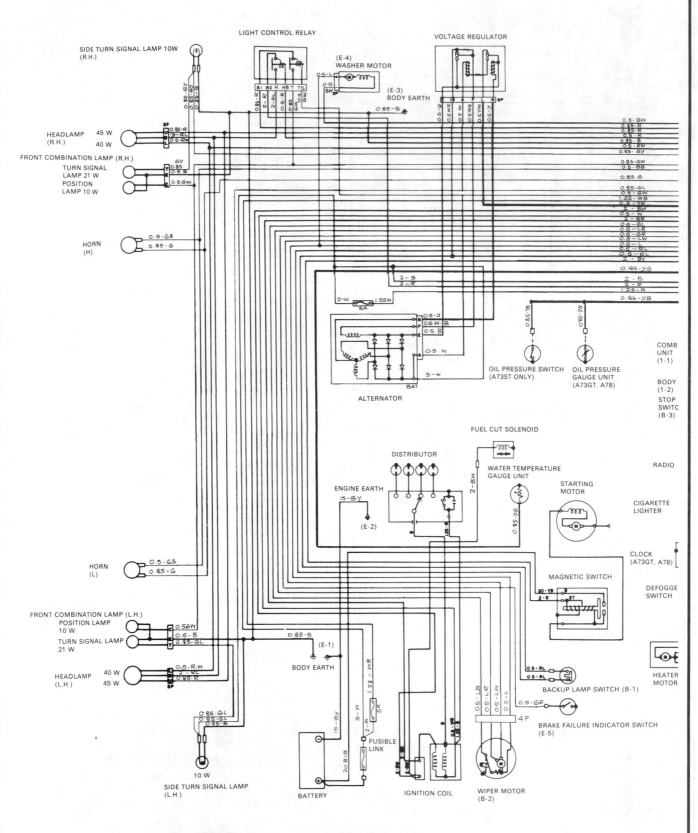

Fig. 13.73 Wiring diagram for 1979-on Celeste models (Sec 12)

For colour code, see Fig. 13.72

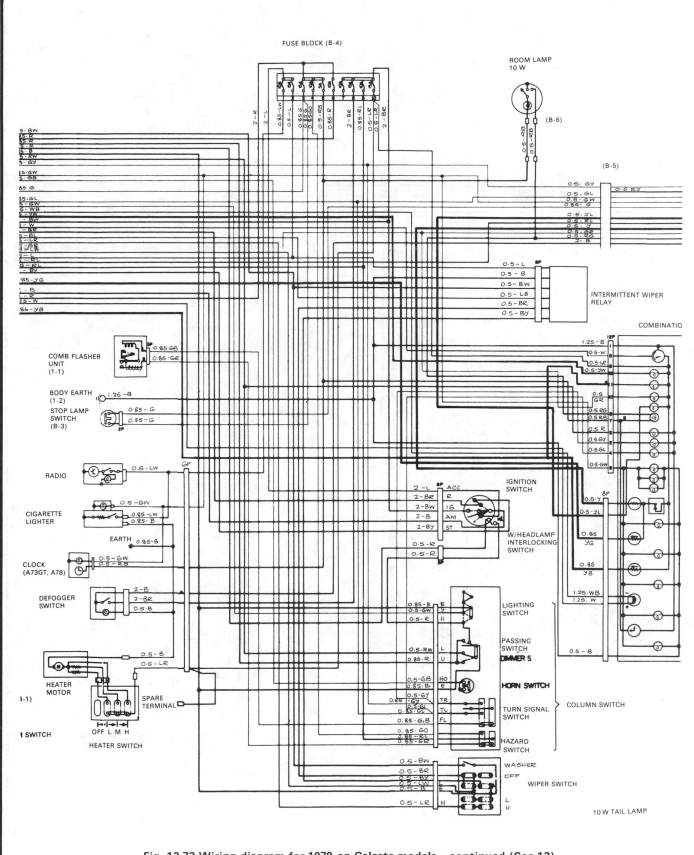

Fig. 13.73 Wiring diagram for 1979-on Celeste models – continued (Sec 12)

For colour code, see Fig. 13.72

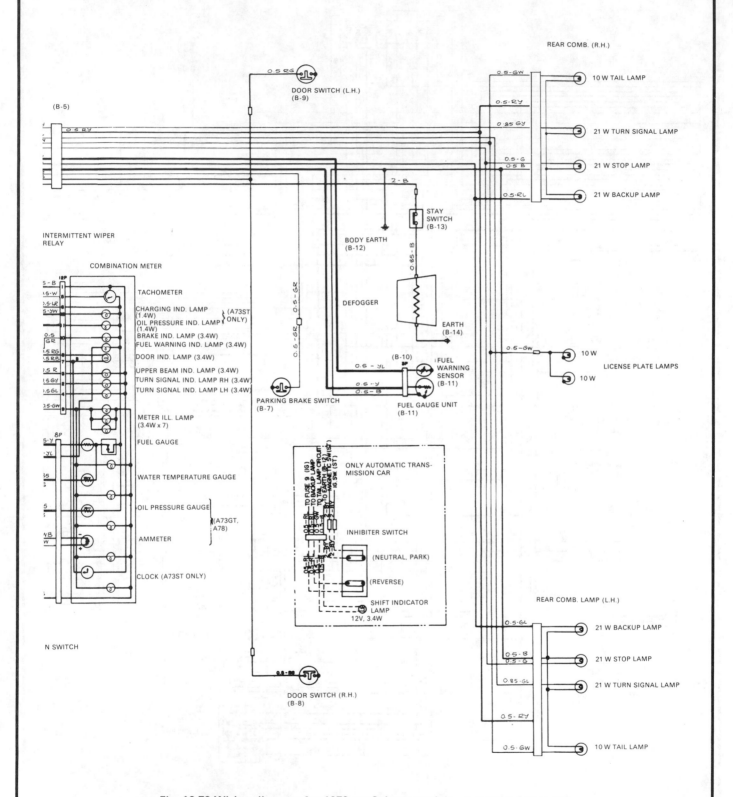

Fig. 13.73 Wiring diagram for 1979-on Celeste models – continued (Sec 12)

For colour code, see Fig. 13.72

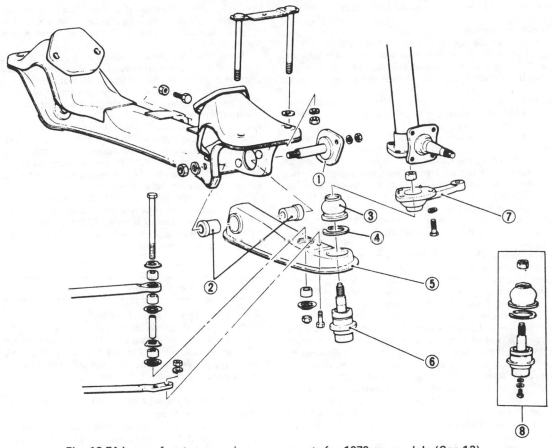

Fig. 13.74 Lower front suspension components for 1979-on models (Sec 13)

1 Inner pivot shaft	3 Dust seal	5 Lower arm	7 Steering arm
2 Bushes	4 Clip	6 Balljoint	8 Balljoint kit

13 Suspension and steering

Front suspension lower arm (1979-on models)
1 The front suspension lower arm inner pivot shaft on 1979-on models is as shown in Fig. 13.74, however, the removal and refitting procedure remains as described in Chapter 11. Do not fully tighten the pivot shaft nut until the weight of the car is on the suspension.

Rear shock absorbers (1979-on models)
2 As from 1979 the rear shock absorbers are of the gas filled type instead of the previous hydraulic type. Removal and refitting procedures remain as given in Chapter 11, Section 10, paragraphs 1, 2, 9 and 10. Refer to the Specifications for torque wrench settings.

Rear spring bump stop (1979-on models)
3 Effective from June 1978 the rear spring bump stop is larger, and a curved plate is fitted beneath it.

Steering linkage (1979-on models)
4 Instead of the balljoints being fitted at each end of the relay rod, they are now located on the ends of the steering box drop arm and idler arm.

Wheels and tyres – general care and maintenance
Wheels and tyres should give no real problems in use provided that a close eye is kept on them with regard to excessive wear or damage. To this end, the following points should be noted.

Ensure that tyre pressures are checked regularly and maintained correctly. Checking should be carried out with the tyres cold and not immediately after the vehicle has been in use. If the pressures are checked with the tyres hot, an apparently high reading will be obtained

Fig. 13.75 Curved plate fitted beneath the rear spring bump stop from June 1978 (Sec 13)

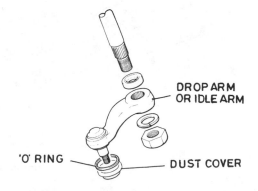

Fig. 13.76 Steering drop arm/idler arm fitted from 1979 (Sec 13)

owing to heat expansion. Under no circumstances should an attempt be made to reduce the pressures to the quoted cold reading in this instance, or effective underinflation will result.

Underinflation will cause overheating of the tyre owing to excessive flexing of the casing, and the tread will not sit correctly on the road surface. This will cause a consequent loss of adhesion and excessive wear, not to mention the danger of sudden tyre failure due to heat build-up.

Overinflation will cause rapid wear of the centre part of the tyre tread coupled with reduced adhesion, harsher ride, and the danger of shock damage occurring in the tyre casing.

Regularly check the tyres for damage in the form of cuts or bulges, especially in the sidewalls. Remove any nails or stones embedded in the tread before they penetrate the tyre to cause deflation. If removal of a nail *does* reveal that the tyre has been punctured, refit the nail so that its point of penetration is marked. Then immediately change the wheel and have the tyre repaired by a tyre dealer. Do *not* drive on a tyre in such a condition. In many cases a puncture can be simply repaired by the use of an inner tube of the correct size and type. If in any doubt as to the possible consequences of any damage found, consult your local tyre dealer for advice.

Periodically remove the wheels and clean any dirt or mud from the inside and outside surfaces. Examine the wheel rims for signs of rusting, corrosion or other damage. Light alloy wheels are easily damaged by 'kerbing' whilst parking, and similarly steel wheels may become dented or buckled. Renewal of the wheel is very often the only course of remedial action possible.

The balance of each wheel and tyre assembly should be maintained to avoid excessive wear, not only to the tyres but also to the steering and suspension components. Wheel imbalance is normally signified by vibration through the vehicle's bodyshell, although in many cases it is particularly noticeable through the steering wheel. Conversely, it should be noted that wear or damage in suspension or steering components may cause excessive tyre wear. Out-of-round or out-of-true tyres, damaged wheels and wheel bearing wear/maladjustment also fall into this category. Balancing will not usually cure vibration caused by such wear.

Wheel balancing may be carried out with the wheel either on or off the vehicle. If balanced on the vehicle, ensure that the wheel-to-hub relationship is marked in some way prior to subsequent wheel removal so that it may be refitted in its original position.

General tyre wear is influenced to a large degree by driving style – harsh braking and acceleration or fast cornering will all produce more rapid tyre wear. Interchanging of tyres may result in more even wear, but this should only be carried out where there is no mix of tyre types on the vehicle. However, it is worth bearing in mind that if this is completely effective, the added expense of replacing a complete set of tyres simultaneously is incurred, which may prove financially restrictive for many owners.

Front tyres may wear unevenly as a result of wheel misalignment. The front wheels should always be correctly aligned according to the settings specified by the vehicle manufacturer.

Legal restrictions apply to the mixing of tyre types on a vehicle. Basically this means that a vehicle must not have tyres of differing construction on the same axle. Although it is not recommended to mix tyre types between front axle and rear axle, the only legally permissible combination is crossply at the front and radial at the rear. When mixing radial ply tyres, textile braced radials must always go on the front axle, with steel braced radials at the rear. An obvious disadvantage of such mixing is the necessity to carry two spare tyres to avoid contravening the law in the event of a puncture.

In the UK, the Motor Vehicles Construction and Use Regulations apply to many aspects of tyre fitting and usage. It is suggested that a copy of these regulations is obtained from your local police if in doubt as to the current legal requirements with regard to tyre condition, minimum tread depth, etc.

14 Bodywork and fittings

Bumpers – removal and refitting
1   The shock absorbers described in Chapter 12, Section 7 are not fitted to UK models. Removal and refitting procedures are straightforward with reference to Fig. 13.77 for 1979-on models. Note that where applicable the front side/indicator lamp must be disconnected before removing the front bumper.

Windscreen, side and rear window glass (1979-on) – removal and refitting
2   From 1979 the windscreen, side and rear window glass is bonded to the body and therefore removal and refitting should be entrusted to a specialist.

Rear quarter window (Celeste) – removal and refitting
3   Unscrew the seat belt anchor bolt.
4   Pull the door weatherstrip from the centre pillar trim then remove the trim.
5   Support the quarter glass then remove the hinge and latch screws and withdraw the glass.

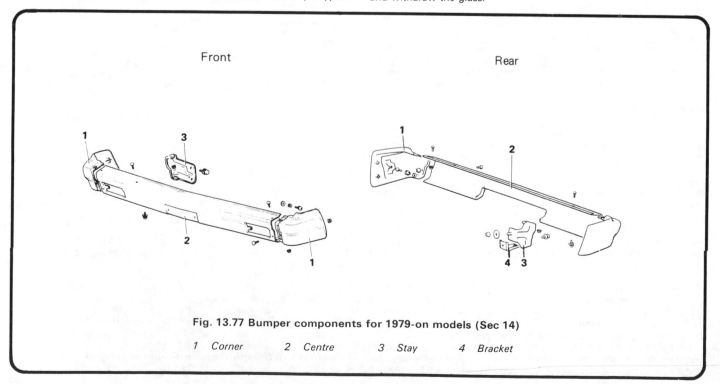

Fig. 13.77 Bumper components for 1979-on models (Sec 14)

1   Corner   2   Centre   3   Stay   4   Bracket

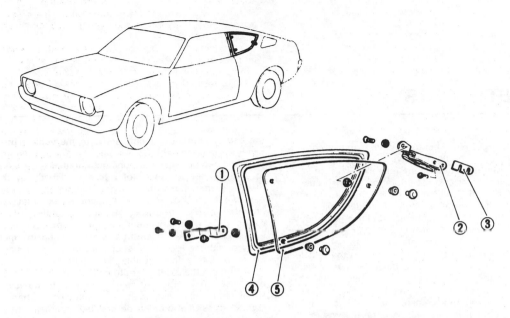

Fig. 13.78 Rear quarter window components (Sec 14)

1 Hinge	3 Shim	5 Glass
2 Latch	4 Weatherstrip	

6   Remove the hinges and bracket from the glass then pull off the weatherstrip.
7   Refitting is a reversal of removal, but if necessary adjust the pressure of the window on the body by increasing or decreasing the shims beneath the latch.

Heater motor (1979-on) – removal and refitting
8   Remove the glovebox, ashtray, centre console and instrument panel.
9   Separate the wiring connector at the heater motor.
10 Unbolt the motor and withdraw it.
11 Refitting is a reversal of removal.

Fault diagnosis

Introduction

The vehicle owner who does his or her own maintenance according to the recommended schedules should not have to use this section of the manual very often. Modern component reliability is such that, provided those items subject to wear or deterioration are inspected or renewed at the specified intervals, sudden failure is comparatively rare. Faults do not usually just happen as a result of sudden failure, but develop over a period of time. Major mechanical failures in particular are usually preceded by characteristic symptoms over hundreds or even thousands of miles. Those components which do occasionally fail without warning are often small and easily carried in the vehicle.

With any fault finding, the first step is to decide where to begin investigations. Sometimes this is obvious, but on other occasions a little detective work will be necessary. The owner who makes half a dozen haphazard adjustments or replacements may be successful in curing a fault (or its symptoms), but he will be none the wiser if the fault recurs and he may well have spent more time and money than was necessary. A calm and logical approach will be found to be more satisfactory in the long run. Always take into account any warning signs or abnormalities that may have been noticed in the period preceding the fault – power loss, high or low gauge readings, unusual noises or smells, etc – and remember that failure of components such as fuses or spark plugs may only be pointers to some underlying fault.

The pages which follow here are intended to help in cases of failure to start or breakdown on the road. There is also a Fault Diagnosis Section at the end of each Chapter which should be consulted if the preliminary checks prove unfruitful. Whatever the fault, certain basic principles apply. These are as follows:

Verify the fault. This is simply a matter of being sure that you know what the symptoms are before starting work. This is particularly important if you are investigating a fault for someone else who may not have described it very accurately.

Don't overlook the obvious. For example, if the vehicle won't start, is there petrol in the tank? (Don't take anyone else's word on this particular point, and don't trust the fuel gauge either!) If an electrical fault is indicated, look for loose or broken wires before digging out the test gear.

Cure the disease, not the symptom. Substituting a flat battery with a fully charged one will get you off the hard shoulder, but if the underlying cause is not attended to, the new battery will go the same way. Similarly, changing oil-fouled spark plugs for a new set will get you moving again, but remember that the reason for the fouling (if it wasn't simply an incorrect grade of plug) will have to be established and corrected.

Don't take anything for granted. Particularly, don't forget that a 'new' component may itself be defective (especially if it's been rattling round in the boot for months), and don't leave components out of a fault diagnosis sequence just because they are new or recently fitted. When you do finally diagnose a difficult fault, you'll probably realise that all the evidence was there from the start.

Electrical faults

Electrical faults can be more puzzling than straightforward mechanical failures, but they are no less susceptible to logical analysis if the basic principles of operation are understood. Vehicle electrical wiring exists in extremely unfavourable conditions – heat, vibration and chemical attack – and the first things to look for are loose or corroded connections and broken or chafed wires, especially where the wires pass through holes in the bodywork or are subject to vibration.

All metal-bodied vehicles in current production have one pole of the battery 'earthed', ie connected to the vehicle bodywork, and in nearly all modern vehicles it is the negative (–) terminal. The various electrical components – motors, bulb holders etc – are also connected to earth, either by means of a lead or directly by their mountings. Electric current flows through the component and then back to the battery via the bodywork. If the component mounting is loose or corroded, or if a good path back to the battery is not available, the circuit will be incomplete and malfunction will result. The engine and/or gearbox are also earthed by means of flexible metal straps to the body or subframe; if these straps are loose or missing, starter motor, generator and ignition trouble may result.

Assuming the earth return to be satisfactory, electrical faults will be due either to component malfunction or to defects in the current supply. Individual components are dealt with in Chapters 10 and 13. If supply wires are broken or cracked internally this results in an open-circuit, and the easiest way to check for this is to bypass the suspect wire temporarily with a length of wire having a crocodile clip or suitable connector at each end. Alternatively, a 12V test lamp can be used to verify the presence of supply voltage at various points along the wire and the break can be thus isolated.

If a bare portion of a live wire touches the bodywork or other earthed metal part, the electricity will take the low-resistance path thus formed back to the battery: this is known as a short-circuit. Hopefully a short-circuit will blow a fuse, but otherwise it may cause burning of the insulation (and possibly further short-circuits) or even a fire. This is why it is inadvisable to bypass persistently blowing fuses with silver foil or wire.

Spares and tool kit

Most vehicles are supplied only with sufficient tools for wheel changing; the *Maintenance and minor repair* tool kit detailed in *Tools and working facilities,* with the addition of a hammer, is probably sufficient for those repairs that most motorists would consider attempting at the roadside. In addition a few items which can be fitted without too much trouble in the event of a breakdown should be carried. Experience and available space will modify the list below, but the following may save having to call on professional assistance:

Spark plugs, clean and correctly gapped
HT lead and plug cap – long enough to reach the plug furthest from the distributor
Distributor rotor, condenser and contact breaker points (where applicable)
Drivebelt(s) – emergency type may suffice
Spare fuses
Set of principal light bulbs
Tin of radiator sealer and hose bandage
Exhaust bandage
Roll of insulating tape
Length of soft iron wire
Length of electrical flex
Torch or inspection lamp (can double as test lamp)
Battery jump leads
Tow-rope
Ignition waterproofing aerosol
Litre of engine oil
Sealed can of hydraulic fluid
Emergency windscreen
'Jubilee' clips
Tube of filler paste

If spare fuel is carried, a can designed for the purpose should be used to minimise risks of leakage and collision damage. A first aid kit and a warning triangle, whilst not at present compulsory in the UK, are obviously sensible items to carry in addition to the above.

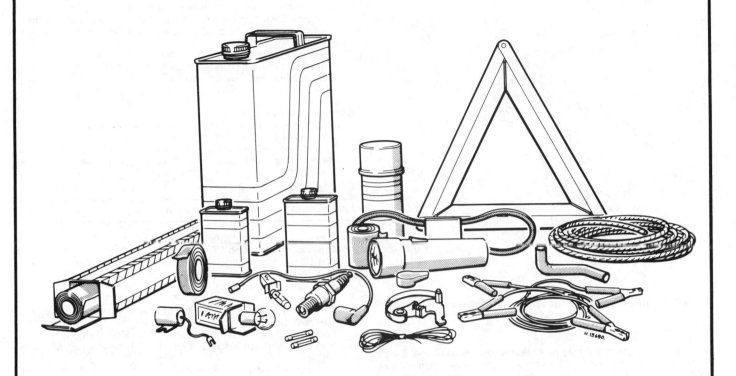

Carrying a few spares can save you a long walk!

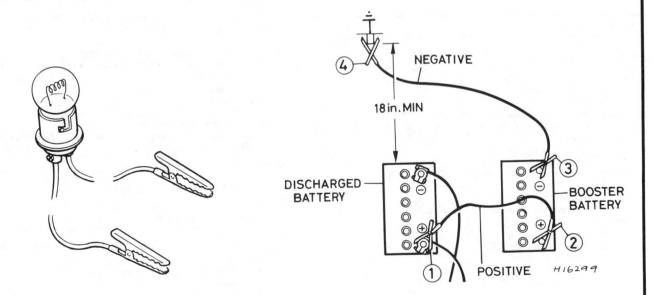

A simple test lamp is useful for tracing electrical faults

Jump start lead connections for negative earth vehicles –
connect leads in order shown

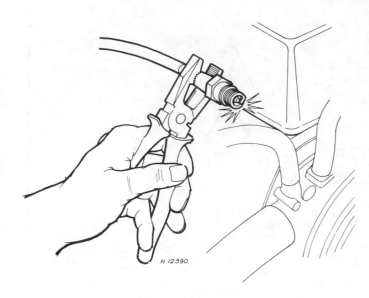

Crank engine and check for spark. Note use of insulated tool

When touring abroad it may be advisable to carry additional spares which, even if you cannot fit them yourself, could save having to wait while parts are obtained. The items below may be worth considering:

Clutch and throttle cables
Cylinder head gasket
Alternator brushes
Fuel pump repair kit
Tyre valve core

One of the motoring organisations will be able to advise on availability of fuel etc in foreign countries.

Engine will not start

Engine fails to turn when starter operated
Flat battery (recharge, use jump leads, or push start)
Battery terminals loose or corroded
Battery earth to body defective
Engine earth strap loose or broken
Starter motor (or solenoid) wiring loose or broken
Automatic transmission selector in wrong position, or inhibitor switch faulty
Ignition/starter switch faulty
Major mechanical failure (seizure)
Starter or solenoid internal fault (see Chapter 10)

Starter motor turns engine slowly
Partially discharged battery (recharge, use jump leads, or push start)
Battery terminals loose or corroded
Battery earth to body defective
Engine earth strap loose
Starter motor (or solenoid) wiring loose
Starter motor internal fault (see Chapter 10)

Starter motor spins without turning engine
Flat battery
Starter motor pinion sticking on sleeve
Flywheel gear teeth damaged or worn
Starter motor mounting bolts loose

Engine turns normally but fails to start
Damp or dirty HT leads and distributor cap (crank engine and check for spark)
Dirty or incorrectly gapped distributor points (if applicable)

No fuel in tank (check for delivery at carburettor)
Excessive choke (hot engine) or insufficient choke (cold engine)
Fouled or incorrectly gapped spark plugs (remove, clean and regap)
Other ignition system fault (see Chapters 4 and 13)
Other fuel system fault (see Chapters 3 and 13)
Poor compression (see Chapter 1)
Major mechanical failure (eg camshaft drive)

Engine fires but will not run
Insufficient choke (cold engine)
Air leaks at carburettor or inlet manifold
Fuel starvation (see Chapters 3 and 13)
Ballast resistor defective, or other ignition fault (see Chapters 4 and 13)

Engine cuts out and will not restart

Engine cuts out suddenly – ignition fault
Loose or disconnected LT wires
Wet HT leads or distributor cap (after traversing water splash)
Coil or condenser failure (check for spark)
Other ignition fault (see Chapters 4 and 13)

Engine misfires before cutting out – fuel fault
Fuel tank empty
Fuel pump defective or filter blocked (check for delivery)
Fuel tank filler vent blocked (suction will be evident on releasing cap)
Carburettor needle valve sticking
Carburettor jets blocked (fuel contaminated)
Other fuel system fault (see Chapters 3 and 13)

Engine cuts out – other causes
Serious overheating
Major mechanical failure (eg camshaft drive)

Engine overheats

Ignition (no-charge) warning light illuminated
Slack or broken drivebelt – retension or renew (Chapter 2)

Ignition warning light not illuminated
Coolant loss due to internal or external leakage (see Chapter 2)
Thermostat defective
Low oil level
Brakes binding
Radiator clogged externally or internally
Engine waterways clogged
Ignition timing incorrect or automatic advance malfunctioning
Mixture too weak

Note: *Do not add cold water to an overheated engine or damage may result*

Low engine oil pressure

Gauge reads low or warning light illuminated with engine running
Oil level low or incorrect grade
Defective gauge or sender unit
Wire to sender unit earthed
Engine overheating
Oil filter clogged or bypass valve defective
Oil pressure relief valve defective
Oil pick-up strainer clogged
Oil pump worn or mountings loose
Worn main or big-end bearings

Note: *Low oil pressure in a high-mileage engine at tickover is not necessarily a cause for concern. Sudden pressure loss at speed is far more significant. In any event, check the gauge or warning light sender before condemning the engine.*

Engine noises

Pre-ignition (pinking) on acceleration
    Incorrect grade of fuel
    Ignition timing incorrect
    Distributor faulty or worn
    Worn or maladjusted carburettor
    Excessive carbon build-up in engine

Whistling or wheezing noises
    Leaking vacuum hose
    Leaking carburettor or manifold gasket
    Blowing head gasket

Tapping or rattling
    Incorrect valve clearances
    Worn valve gear
    Worn timing chain or belt
    Broken piston ring (ticking noise)

Knocking or thumping
    Unintentional mechanical contact (eg fan blades)
    Worn drivebelt
    Peripheral component fault (alternator, water pump etc)
    Worn big-end bearings (regular heavy knocking, perhaps less under load)
    Worn main bearings (rumbling and knocking, perhaps worsening under load)
    Piston slap (most noticeable when cold)

General repair procedures

Whenever servicing, repair or overhaul work is carried out on the car or its components, it is necessary to observe the following procedures and instructions. This will assist in carrying out the operation efficiently and to a professional standard of workmanship.

Joint mating faces and gaskets

Where a gasket is used between the mating faces of two components, ensure that it is renewed on reassembly, and fit it dry unless otherwise stated in the repair procedure. Make sure that the mating faces are clean and dry with all traces of old gasket removed. When cleaning a joint face, use a tool which is not likely to score or damage the face, and remove any burrs or nicks with an oilstone or fine file.

Make sure that tapped holes are cleaned with a pipe cleaner, and keep them free of jointing compound if this is being used unless specifically instructed otherwise.

Ensure that all orifices, channels or pipes are clear and blow through them, preferably using compressed air.

Oil seals

Whenever an oil seal is removed from its working location, either individually or as part of an assembly, it should be renewed.

The very fine sealing lip of the seal is easily damaged and will not seal if the surface it contacts is not completely clean and free from scratches, nicks or grooves. If the original sealing surface of the component cannot be restored, the component should be renewed.

Protect the lips of the seal from any surface which may damage them in the course of fitting. Use tape or a conical sleeve where possible. Lubricate the seal lips with oil before fitting and, on dual lipped seals, fill the space between the lips with grease.

Unless otherwise stated, oil seals must be fitted with their sealing lips toward the lubricant to be sealed.

Use a tubular drift or block of wood of the appropriate size to install the seal and, if the seal housing is shouldered, drive the seal down to the shoulder. If the seal housing is unshouldered, the seal should be fitted with its face flush with the housing top face.

Screw threads and fastenings

Always ensure that a blind tapped hole is completely free from oil, grease, water or other fluid before installing the bolt or stud. Failure to do this could cause the housing to crack due to the hydraulic action of the bolt or stud as it is screwed in.

When tightening a castellated nut to accept a split pin, tighten the nut to the specified torque, where applicable, and then tighten further to the next split pin hole. Never slacken the nut to align a split pin hole unless stated in the repair procedure.

When checking or retightening a nut or bolt to a specified torque setting, slacken the nut or bolt by a quarter of a turn, and then retighten to the specified setting.

Locknuts, locktabs and washers

Any fastening which will rotate against a component or housing in the course of tightening should always have a washer between it and the relevant component or housing.

Spring or split washers should always be renewed when they are used to lock a critical component such as a big-end bearing retaining nut or bolt.

Locktabs which are folded over to retain a nut or bolt should always be renewed.

Self-locking nuts can be reused in non-critical areas, providing resistance can be felt when the locking portion passes over the bolt or stud thread.

Split pins must always be replaced with new ones of the correct size for the hole.

Special tools

Some repair procedures in this manual entail the use of special tools such as a press, two or three-legged pullers, spring compressors etc. Wherever possible, suitable readily available alternatives to the manufacturer's special tools are described, and are shown in use. In some instances, where no alternative is possible, it has been necessary to resort to the use of a manufacturer's tool and this has been done for reasons of safety as well as the efficient completion of the repair operation. Unless you are highly skilled and have a thorough understanding of the procedure described, never attempt to bypass the use of any special tool when the procedure described specifies its use. Not only is there a very great risk of personal injury, but expensive damage could be caused to the components involved.

Conversion factors

Length (distance)

Inches (in)	X	25.4	= Millimetres (mm)	X 0.0394	= Inches (in)
Feet (ft)	X	0.305	= Metres (m)	X 3.281	= Feet (ft)
Miles	X	1.609	= Kilometres (km)	X 0.621	= Miles

Volume (capacity)

Cubic inches (cu in; in³)	X	16.387	= Cubic centimetres (cc; cm³)	X 0.061	= Cubic inches (cu in; in³)
Imperial pints (Imp pt)	X	0.568	= Litres (l)	X 1.76	= Imperial pints (Imp pt)
Imperial quarts (Imp qt)	X	1.137	= Litres (l)	X 0.88	= Imperial quarts (Imp qt)
Imperial quarts (Imp qt)	X	1.201	= US quarts (US qt)	X 0.833	= Imperial quarts (Imp qt)
US quarts (US qt)	X	0.946	= Litres (l)	X 1.057	= US quarts (US qt)
Imperial gallons (Imp gal)	X	4.546	= Litres (l)	X 0.22	= Imperial gallons (Imp gal)
Imperial gallons (Imp gal)	X	1.201	= US gallons (US gal)	X 0.833	= Imperial gallons (Imp gal)
US gallons (US gal)	X	3.785	= Litres (l)	X 0.264	= US gallons (US gal)

Mass (weight)

Ounces (oz)	X	28.35	= Grams (g)	X 0.035	= Ounces (oz)
Pounds (lb)	X	0.454	= Kilograms (kg)	X 2.205	= Pounds (lb)

Force

Ounces-force (ozf; oz)	X	0.278	= Newtons (N)	X 3.6	= Ounces-force (ozf; oz)
Pounds-force (lbf; lb)	X	4.448	= Newtons (N)	X 0.225	= Pounds-force (lbf; lb)
Newtons (N)	X	0.1	= Kilograms-force (kgf; kg)	X 9.81	= Newtons (N)

Pressure

Pounds-force per square inch (psi; lbf/in²; lb/in²)	X	0.070	= Kilograms-force per square centimetre (kgf/cm²; kg/cm²)	X 14.223	= Pounds-force per square inch (psi; lbf/in²; lb/in²)
Pounds-force per square inch (psi; lbf/in²; lb/in²)	X	0.068	= Atmospheres (atm)	X 14.696	= Pounds-force per square inch (psi; lbf/in²; lb/in²)
Pounds-force per square inch (psi; lbf/in²; lb/in²)	X	0.069	= Bars	X 14.5	= Pounds-force per square inch (psi; lbf/in²; lb/in²)
Pounds-force per square inch (psi; lbf/in²; lb/in²)	X	6.895	= Kilopascals (kPa)	X 0.145	= Pounds-force per square inch (psi; lbf/in²; lb/in²)
Kilopascals (kPa)	X	0.01	= Kilograms-force per square centimetre (kgf/cm²; kg/cm²)	X 98.1	= Kilopascals (kPa)
Millibar (mbar)	X	100	= Pascals (Pa)	X 0.01	= Millibar (mbar)
Millibar (mbar)	X	0.0145	= Pounds-force per square inch (psi; lbf/in², lb/in²)	X 68.947	= Millibar (mbar)
Millibar (mbar)	X	0.75	= Millimetres of mercury (mmHg)	X 1.333	= Millibar (mbar)
Millibar (mbar)	X	1.40	= Inches of water (inH₂O)	X 0.714	= Millibar (mbar)
Millimetres of mercury (mmHg)	X	1.868	= Inches of water (inH₂O)	X 0.535	= Millimetres of mercury (mmHg)
Inches of water (inH₂O)	X	27.68	= Pounds-force per square inch (psi, lbf/in², lb/in²)	X 0.036	= Inches of water (inH₂O)

Torque (moment of force)

Pounds-force inches (lbf in; lb in)	X	1.152	= Kilograms-force centimetre (kgf cm; kg cm)	X 0.868	= Pounds-force inches (lbf in; lb in)
Pounds-force inches (lbf in; lb in)	X	0.113	= Newton metres (Nm)	X 8.85	= Pounds-force inches (lbf in; lb in)
Pounds-force inches (lbf in; lb in)	X	0.083	= Pounds-force feet (lbf ft; lb ft)	X 12	= Pounds-force inches (lbf in; lb in)
Pounds-force feet (lbf ft; lb ft)	X	0.138	= Kilograms-force metres (kgf m; kg m)	X 7.233	= Pounds-force feet (lbf ft; lb ft)
Pounds-force feet (lbf ft; lb ft)	X	1.356	= Newton metres (Nm)	X 0.738	= Pounds-force feet (lbf ft; lb ft)
Newton metres (Nm)	X	0.102	= Kilograms-force metres (kgf m; kg m)	X 9.804	= Newton metres (Nm)

Power

Horsepower (hp)	X	745.7	= Watts (W)	X 0.0013	= Horsepower (hp)

Velocity (speed)

Miles per hour (miles/hr; mph)	X	1.609	= Kilometres per hour (km/hr; kph)	X 0.621	= Miles per hour (miles/hr; mph)

Fuel consumption*

Miles per gallon, Imperial (mpg)	X	0.354	= Kilometres per litre (km/l)	X 2.825	= Miles per gallon, Imperial (mpg)
Miles per gallon, US (mpg)	X	0.425	= Kilometres per litre (km/l)	X 2.352	= Miles per gallon, US (mpg)

Temperature

Degrees Fahrenheit = (°C x 1.8) + 32   Degrees Celsius (Degrees Centigrade; °C) = (°F - 32) x 0.56

*It is common practice to convert from miles per gallon (mpg) to litres/100 kilometres (l/100km), where mpg (Imperial) x l/100 km = 282 and mpg (US) x l/100 km = 235

Index

Printed by
J H Haynes & Co Ltd
Sparkford Nr Yeovil
Somerset BA22 7JJ England